SIMPLE DECENCY & COMMON SENSE

BLACKS IN THE DIASPORA
Darlene Clark Hine, John McCluskey, Jr., and David Barry Gaspar, General Editors

SIMPLE DECENCY & COMMON SENSE

The Southern Conference Movement, 1938–1963

LINDA REED

INDIANA UNIVERSITY PRESS

Bloomington and Indianapolis

The paper used in this publication meets the minimum requirements of American
National Standard for Information Sciences—Permanence of Paper for Printed
Library Materials, ANSI Z39.48-1984.

Manufactured in the United States of America

Library of Congress Cataloging-in-Publication Data

Reed, Linda, date.
    Simple decency and common sense : the southern conference
movement, 1938–1963 / Linda Reed.
        p.   cm.—(Blacks in the diaspora)
    Includes bibliographical references and index.
    ISBN 0-253-34895-1 (cloth)
    1. Southern States—Race relations.   2. Afro-Americans—Civil
rights—Southern States.   3. Liberalism—Southern States—
History—20th century.   4. Southern Conference for Human Welfare—
History.   5. Southern Conference Educational Fund—History.
I. Title.   II. Series.
E185.61.R306   1991
305.8′00975—dc20   91-7803

1 2 3 4 5   95 94 93 92 91

For my mother, Mary E. Felton, whose love and sacrifice I have come to cherish unconditionally, and for mentors William H. Harris and Nell Irvin Painter, whose encouragement and generosity saw me through the best and worst of times and helped to make this book a reality.

CONTENTS

CHRONOLOGY

1938   The Southern Conference for Human Welfare founded in Birmingham, Alabama.
        SCHW forms its Civil Rights Committee, which in turn establishes the National Committee to Abolish the Poll Tax.

1940   SCHW's Second Biennial meeting, Chattanooga, Tennessee.
        James A. Dombrowski selected as SCHW's executive secretary.

1941   Many moderates leave SCHW because of its liberal views on race relations.

1942   SCHW's Third Biennial meeting, Nashville, Tennessee.
        SCHW begins its monthly, the *Southern Patriot*.

1943   SCHW publicly condemns the numerous 1943 race riots and runs its own Double Victory Campaign.

1944   Skips Biennial meeting because of World War II shortages.
        Editors' Conference; Voters' Rights; Advocates permanent Fair Employment Practice Commission.

1945   Campaigns to oust Mississippi Senator Theodore Bilbo as the South's Number One Enemy, a slogan Bilbo had applied to SCHW.

1946   Mary McLeod Bethune tours South for SCHW fundraiser/membership drive.
        SCHW creates Southern Conference Educational Fund.
        SCHW's Fourth Biennial meeting, New Orleans.
        Clark Foreman and James Dombrowski conflict develops.

1947   House Un-American Activities Committee reports on SCHW's alleged communism; Dombrowski begins to run SCEF; Aubrey Williams becomes SCEF's president and starts American Family Homes, Inc., to reduce housing discrimination against Alabama blacks.

1948   SCHW disbands. SCEF adheres to single-issue advocacy, integration.
        SCEF surveys reveal that a large number of southern and border state higher education faculty favors integration.

1949   SCEF publicizes integrated use of library in Louisville, Richmond, and Chattanooga while calling for the entire region to follow the three examples.

1950   Southwide Conference on Discrimination in Higher Education at Atlanta.
        SCEF files an *amicus curiae* brief to the U.S. Supreme Court in the Herman Marion *Sweatt* case.

1951   SCEF sponsors southern tour of widely acclaimed photographic exhibit, "Children in America." An effective shot from the exhibit shows three unsmiling children "playing" in a filthy alley within eyeshot of the capitol.

1952   SCEF's president, Aubrey Williams, appears before the platform committee of the Democratic party at its Chicago convention and advocates an uncompromising civil rights plank.

1954   Anne and Carl Braden integrate a Louisville neighborhood, which creates chaos for them and the black family involved.
James O. Eastland hearings, New Orleans.

1955   Death of faithful SCHW-SCEF member, Mary McLeod Bethune.
Rosa Parks attends Highlander Folk School.
Montgomery Bus Boycott.

1956   Autherine Lucy integrates University of Alabama.

1957   SCEF supports Daisy and L. C. Bates in the Little Rock school-integration crises.

1958   Voter Registration campaign.

1960   SCEF highly active in Civil Rights Movement.

PREFACE

"The country needs, and unless I mistake its temper, the country demands bold,
persistent experimentation. It is common
sense to take a method and try it: If it
fails, admit it frankly and try another. But
above all, try something."

Franklin Delano Roosevelt, at Oglethorpe
University, May 22, 1932

President Franklin Delano Roosevelt's leadership and approach to America's desperation in the 1930s provided an example for many southerners
who witnessed firsthand the many problems that plagued the South. As
Roosevelt advised, they wanted to try "persistent experimentation," and
they accepted wholeheartedly his bold approach presented in the New
Deal. Although many southerners continued to dream of a New South of
economic prosperity, the Great Depression brought only more nightmares
of economic disaster. In the late 1930s many southerners identified the
Southern Conference for Human Welfare as the experimentation that
would lead to economic solutions. Indeed, many came to understand that
the principle of equality allowed in the concept of the New Deal was exactly what the South needed to rectify so much that continued to go
wrong there. These southerners came to see that the South's poor economic standing remained so partly because not all southerners were allowed to share equally in its development. As they devised their
experiment, they hoped to address economic woes along with equal economic opportunity. Moreover, they invited underrepresented groups,
most notably organized labor, the working class, and African Americans
from all ranks, to share in the experiment.

The participants in the SCHW (or the southern conference movement,
as I call it) set out on a mission to change the South. This small group of
white and black southerners believed that segregation and discrimination
interfered with the South's ability to build a sound economy. It made
sense, common sense, that wages played a role in the South's backwardness. During the Great Depression when there was so much talk about
bountiful goods when people had little money to buy them, it only added
to the logic that a better economic situation would come if more people
had money to make purchases. And more people would have a greater
amount of money if all workers made equal wages regardless of race.

The southern conference movement operated on high idealism and
wanted for the South what most southerners were not willing to allow—
equal opportunity without the handicap of racial bias perpetuated by
segregation. Such idealism fueled a movement that sought to convert

segregationists by focusing media attention on the specific situations that resulted from segregation and discrimination. It is significant that SCHW operated for ten years against major opposition from segregationists, but it is equally important that SCHW's Southern Conference Educational Fund carried forth the former's mission of creating a New South even beyond the Civil Rights Act of 1964 and Voting Rights Act of 1965. This book covers the southern conference movement through 1963, but it is important to note that SCEF existed until the early 1970s.

Every generation faces limitations and boundaries from the era in which it lives. SCHW/SCEF relied on tradition in the extensive use of conferences, literature campaigns, speaking engagements, and legislative lobbying. These were measures most familiar to movement leaders in the 1930s and 1940s. The groups broke with tradition when they repeatedly called for a just and equitable society. Because they stepped ahead of most southerners with their concept of equality, their idealism must not be forgotten. Many Americans agreed with the high road taken by the southern conference movement before 1954, but an even larger number joined in that idealism in the late 1950s and 1960s. A different generation, however, chose a new method of focusing attention on the inequities that leaders of the southern conference movement had addressed. Although they disagreed on strategy, participants in the direct-action campaigns of the 1950s and 1960s accepted support from the southern conference movement. In this sense the movement served as a bridge across generational lines. The clearest example is the longtime friendship of two staunch supporters from each group—Virginia Foster Durr of the southern conference movement and Martha P. Norman of the Student Nonviolent Coordinating Committee. Members of each group came to understand fully the times and boundaries in which they operated. The common element, however, remains that groups represented by both Durr and Norman reached beyond the limitations and boundaries of their times.

Roosevelt's words in 1932 so appropriately convey how a small group of southerners reacted to the Great Depression. Common sense dictated that something had to be done. The 1932 message also imparts how another group of Americans reacted to years of oppression linked to segregation and discrimination, and having seen where the method of the earlier movement did not bring the wanted results, a different generation tried a new approach.

The twenty-five-year history of the southern conference movement in this book is but a small piece of the larger story told by other historians. Included are works by John A. Salmond on Aubrey Williams and Lucy Randolph Mason, John Kneebone on southern liberal journalists, Sarah Shouse on Herman Clarence Nixon, Virginia Hamiliton on Hugo Black, John Glen on Highlander Folk School and Myles Horton—to name a few. We could learn more through studies about the various SCHW state committees and the efforts of many other individuals whose lives fit into the large network of folks and organizations active in the southern conference movement. In the meantime we await studies on the New Dealers and Henry Wallace's 1948 presidential bid from Patricia Sullivan, assistant director of the Civil Rights Center at the University of Virginia; on Osceola McKaine from Miles Richards, a graduate student at the University of South Carolina; and on Modjeska Simkins from Barbara Woods, research fellow at the Center for Research on Women at Duke University and the University of North Carolina. These studies help us to learn more about the phenomenon of southern liberalism. Franklin Roosevelt, after all, did advise in an address at Temple University in February 1936 that "the truth is found when [we] are free to pursue it."

ACKNOWLEDGMENTS

In recent times we have heard a lot about giving back to people and places part of that which was given to us. The concept probably works most appropriately when applied to the environment and the need to return to the earth that which the earth can return to us. We call it recycling, but we cannot recycle people. We can share with others the generosity and kindness that our role models (another one of those terms we have heard repeatedly) provided for us. In my application of the recycling concept to people, I want to begin by thanking a large number of persons whose lives and spirit of giving represent the sorts of things that I hope to put back through what is presented in *Simple Decency and Common Sense*. Second, I shall strive to be as caring and sensitive toward undergraduate and graduate students with whom I shall work as these individuals were toward me and my work.

I sincerely thank William H. Harris, eminent historian and president of Texas Southern University. As professor of history at Indiana University when my work on the southern conference movement began, William Harris helped me choose and refine the topic, served as dissertation director even after he had become president of Paine College, and read through other drafts once I began revisions for the book. I realized long years of work on this project when I recalled that Harris's children, Cynthia and William, Jr., were not even teenagers when I started; they are now college students (and Cynthia will have graduated when the book actually appears). This is just one reminder that getting a Ph.D. takes time and so does making a book. I also want to thank Wanda Harris for the many times that she and the Harris family made me welcome and listened to long conversations about SCHW and SCEF.

Other kind souls and brilliant scholars started with me in the early stage of my work with the southern conference movement. George Juergens, John Bodnar, and Stephen Stein also served on my dissertation committee, and several of the questions left unresolved in the early phase I hope to have worked out in the book. I acknowledge their input and hope to be putting back for them as well.

None of the people with whom I worked at Indiana University deserted me along the way, but as I continued to grow as a scholar and refine my ideas about the southern conference movement, another eminent historian, Nell Irvin Painter, played a major role in helping me formulate ideas for the book. Probably only two people have read *Simple Decency and Common Sense* more times than I have, and they are William Harris and Nell Painter. A mere thank you seems so small for what I deem a huge gift of time and effort on their part. It is in this spirit that I dedicate the book to three key people in my life: my mother, Mary E.

Felton, William Harris, and Nell Painter. Each of them indeed gave me a starting place.

Research undertakings are cooperative in nature, but they are also expensive. Financial support came from several sources. Between 1982 and 1985, an Indiana University History Department Scholarship, a Doctoral Student Grant from the Graduate School, a small grant from the Indiana University Foundation, and a two-year research fellowship at the Carter G. Woodson Institute for Afro-American and African Studies at the University of Virginia, Charlottesville, provided time and money for the bulk of the archival research and writing of the dissertation.

The Institute also brought me in touch with several persons who were interested in my work and provided forums through which I could frequently discuss it. I thank Armstead Robinson, director of the Woodson Institute; William E. Jackson, associate director of research at the Institute; Paul M. Gaston and William A. Elwood, Institute affiliates, and William Abbott, editor of the George Washington Papers. I have incorporated ideas from conversations we had over lunch or just in passing as I made my way around the "grounds." Friends and Woodson Institute staff members, Mary Rose, Gail Shirley, and Mary Farrer, assisted with printing different copies of the manuscript and have remained my friends over the years. I am indeed grateful for such wonderful support.

In the final stage of work on the book, I had the opportunity of time and financial support provided by the Carolina Minority Post-Doctoral Fellowship, University of North Carolina, Chapel Hill. My tenure at UNC put me in touch with Nell Painter, who was on the faculty there at the time, and Robin Kelley. Robin's work, *Hammer and Hoe: Alabama Communists during the Great Depression* (1990), led us to long discussions about twentieth-century social movements. I especially thank him for our conversation that helped me to see SCHW/SCEF as a southern conference movement. A special thanks to Robin and Diedra Harris-Kelley, his wife, for the countless meals that we shared in Chapel Hill. Not only is Robin a great historian, he is a great chef.

Several other close friends and scholars read and commented on parts or all of the manuscript, saving me from a number of errors. For believing in me and my project and for taking time and care with the manuscript, I thank Wilma King, Julius Scott III, Lynda Morgan, Jacquelyn Dowd Hall, Robert Korstad, Walter Jackson, Gail O'Brien, Patricia Sullivan, and Barbara Woods. I owe special thanks to friends and colleagues at the University of Houston, most especially Cheryl Cody, Sarah Fishman, John Hart, Joseph Glatthaar, Joseph Pratt, and James Jones. I thank Dean James Pickering for granting that my affiliation with UH would begin with the first year on leave so that I could complete book revisions and the second year of my postdoctoral fellowship at UNC.

Daniel T. Williams, the archivist at Tuskegee University; Minnie Clayton and Wilson N. Flemister, archivists at Atlanta University Center's

Woodruff Library; Harold L. Miller at the State Historical Society of Wisconsin (SHSW), and Miriam Jones, now retired, at the Alabama State Archives made long hours of work at these facilities comfortable and productive. When I notified Jones of my scheduled time for work in Montgomery, she voluntarily arranged a lunch for my first meeting with Virginia Foster Durr and later transported me to Durr's home for an interview. Indeed this book would have been impossible without the assistance of archivists, but Williams, Clayton, Miller, and Jones went above and beyond the call of duty with my work on SCHW and SCEF. Flemister, Clayton, and staff at SHSW helped again when I searched for photographs for the book. Acknowledging them here is a pleasure. I would also like to thank the staff at the Birmingham Public Library and the Southern Historical Collection at the University of North Carolina.

SCHW/SCEF participants proved to be invaluable in their generosity with time for oral-history interviews. Many thanks to Virginia Durr, Anne Braden, Fred Shuttlesworth, Amelia Platts Boynton Robinson, and now deceased Palmer Weber. Their stories added to the richness of my study, and just as important, of my life. I had the wonderful opportunity to meet Joseph Gelders's daughter, Marge Frantz, at the 1990 Berkshire Conference in New Jersey and was heartened that she agrees with my interpretation of the inner tensions of the SCHW. I thank her and Anne Braden, too, for special permission to use photographs in the book.

My acquaintance with Southern Conference leaders reminded me of my connection with my maternal grandparents, Edna and William Reed. Many people disagree with me that wisdom can be taught, but I feel all the wiser simply because I grew to know and understand Durr, Braden, Shuttlesworth, Weber, Myles Horton, Modjeska Simkins, and Edna and William Reed. My grandparents, now deceased, reared me in Five Points, Alabama, and instilled in me a constant drive for organization, excellence, and the sacrifices that go along with reaching accomplishments. Their love and support was always unfailing.

My mother, Mary Felton, gave me a start in life; this is obvious. But she also, because she had little choice in the matter as a single mother, allowed the best possible situation when she and my grandparents agreed that I would live in Alabama and she would migrate to work in the urban center of Atlanta where I would see her only during summers and holidays. As a child I did not always understand or even appreciate my mother's decision, but now I fully comprehend her dilemma. She gave doubly. For the windfall of devoted grandparents to me that was such a sacrifice for her, I shall always be more than grateful. All these things make this book, I hope, all the more significant for her.

Last, but not least, many other family members and friends have supported my effort over the years by taking various reprieves and by feeding me and giving me a place to stay on research trips. It is a pleasure to thank my father, Benjamin Paige, and his sister, Aunt Mozelle Gipson, and all his brothers, especially Uncle Vernice and his wife, Aunt Mary. My mother's brothers and sisters gave just as much, especially Uncles Raymond and Robert Reed and Aunt Katherine Hellems and her family (who seem like siblings since I grew up with them in my grandparents' household). I thank them and all seven of my siblings, but especially Robert and Rickey Felton for the many rides to and from the Atlanta airport and to the library. Several friends are just like family and have probably heard more stories about SCHW/SCEF than they have cared to. But what are friends for? Sincere thanks go to Martha Norman, Jandava Cattron, Natalie Rivers, Jessie Riley, and Ann Harris. Jandava's relative, Elizabeth Richardson, welcomed me for several long stays for archival work in Tuskegee simply because Jandava told her I was "good people." Richardson's kindness deserves my attempt to give back three times over.

Another group deserves special recognition, and they are the editors of this series. Darlene Clark Hine and Barry Gaspar have always been excited about this study since they first heard of it, and we have talked in detail about it at many of the historians' meetings. Darlene read the entire manuscript and decided that it merited inclusion in the series. John McCluskey's interest in my career takes me full circle in that he served for a few years as director of CIC—the Committee on Institutional Cooperation (the Big Ten universities plus the University of Chicago), and it was a CIC Graduate Fellowship that brought me to Indiana University, put me in touch with William H. Harris (who served as CIC's first director), and got me through the Ph.D. program in the first place. I thank Darlene, Barry, and John for prolonged enthusiasm and interest.

Graduate assistants Bradley Raley and Ime Ukpanah assisted with the index.

I hope that the book is deserving of all the tremendous cooperation and financial support that sustained me through the research and writing. Whatever shortcomings are mine alone to bear.

INTRODUCTION

During the 1870s and 1880s, as southerners struggled to compete with the North's rapidly growing economy, progressive southerners coined the term *New South* to draw attention to the region's industrial growth. The South proved hospitable to a variety of industries—textiles, tobacco, steel and iron, railroads. Southern industries, in one way or another, enjoyed the advantages of proximity to raw material, low transportation costs, and cheap labor. With industry concentrated in large cities such as Richmond, Louisville, Birmingham, and Atlanta, the New South eventually came to represent the South of cities, factories, and blast furnaces as opposed to the rural South.

By the 1930s and 1940s, however, the South remained in many ways the same as the South of the 1880s and 1890s, despite the claim of some southerners that after the turn of the century the region could be labeled a New South. In 1938 a small group of mostly white, southern liberals gave the term a new meaning. Southern liberals of the twentieth century did not dissociate the New South totally from its original intended use. In addition to New South denoting industrial development, the term was used by southern liberals to suggest that southerners finally dismantle Old South values in regard to racial equality. In assessing southern economic problems of the late 1930s, southern liberals, unlike most white southerners, figured inequities and discrimination against African Americans as major drawbacks for the fullest development of the southern economy.

Although the region had gone far in its industrial growth, southern liberals argued that racial inequities slowed economic progress and the realization of the New South. Blacks, still treated as inferior, continued to be disfranchised, to face violence at the hands of racist whites, to be denied well-paying jobs, to experience injustice in the judicial system, and to be forced to live in narrowly circumscribed and substandard housing. Simply put, blacks in the South during the twentieth century, like those of the late nineteenth century, continuously faced conditions of economic, political, and social oppression. Numerous black people sought refuge in the North. Indeed, between 1920 and 1930, over a million blacks left the region hoping to find a better life in the North. Yet the South held the majority of the black population. Liberal southern whites eventually allied themselves with those educated blacks who stayed in the American South in their struggle for justice, initially addressing the economic gap between the races and later the political and social unfairnesses.

The federal government helped southern liberals associate industrialism with southern values. However productive the South had been at the turn of the century, by 1938 the New South prosperity had become precarious. That same year, the National Emergency Council (NEC), a group that President Franklin D. Roosevelt set up to study economic conditions in the South, described the region as "the Nation's No. 1 economic problem—the nation's problem, not merely the South's." Although the South was the poorest region in the country, the NEC's *Report on the Economic Conditions of the South* argued, it had the potential for becoming the richest. The *Report* contended that institutional deficiencies kept the South from realizing its potential. In discussions on economic resources, education, health, housing, and labor, the NEC addressed the same issues that southern liberals tackled to create a just society. The NEC concluded that the South's white population suffered because of the region's poor economy, and the situation was worse for blacks. The Roosevelt administration and the NEC linked southern poverty and racism in an unprecedented way, but having presented a negative comment on the South, left southerners to search for their own solutions.

Southerners, in general, agreed with the findings of the NEC *Report* but refused to support it because of anti-Roosevelt and anti-New Deal sentiment. At the same time, southern liberals in particular accepted that the region's economic problems were tied to its resistance to end racial discrimination. In direct response to the NEC report a group of southern black and white liberals founded the Southern Conference for Human Welfare (SCHW) in Birmingham in the fall of 1938. SCHW and the Southern Conference Educational Fund (SCEF), the group SCHW set up in 1946 for tax-exempt purposes and to further its work in race relations, sought to create a democratic South, an effort that faced numerous and difficult obstacles. Indeed, the importance of maintaining white supremacy, especially the economic dominance of whites over blacks, was so paramount in the minds of many southern whites that they were willing to see the entire region languish in order to maintain their way of life.

Most southern whites considered economic dominance central to the maintenance of white supremacy and remained committed to maintaining racial segregation. Even at the height of the Civil Rights Movement of the 1960s, most white southerners resisted efforts to end racial discrimination.

Yet, not all whites were segregationists, as the activities of the interracial SCHW and SCEF made clear. Organized in the fall of 1938, largely through the efforts of Louise O. Charlton, a southern white woman and United States Commissioner in Birmingham, SCHW sought to help southern whites to understand that to remove limitations on its black citizens was to ensure the region greater prosperity. The southern-led SCHW, for its time, became the progressive movement, a movement that would respond to the NEC *Report* with specific prescriptions to cure the ills the *Report* described.

SCHW's recommendations challenged President Roosevelt, the Congress, and especially southern citizens to improve the region. SCHW singled out, for instance, the unequal facilities for white and black school children, unequal salaries of black and white teachers, and unequal incomes of black and white tenant farmers as examples of the inequity and wastefulness of a racially segregated society. Races that could not reap equal benefits for their labor could not live together harmoniously.

SCHW became involved in many issues even though its origins grew out of a determination to improve the South economically. From 1938 to 1948, SCHW's major goal was the repeal of the poll tax. Its Civil Rights Committee instituted a National Committee to Abolish the Poll Tax (NCAPT), thus demonstrating the national dimensions of that problem. NCAPT led a major ten-year campaign to rid the South of this one instance of voter restriction. The Southern Conference addressed issues of health problems, education, child labor, farm tenancy, civil rights, and constitutional rights in an attempt to rectify the South's wrongs. Its Board of Representatives in Richmond, Virginia, voted on November 21, 1948, to suspend the operation of the SCHW. Adopting a resolution to that effect, the board pointed out the ten years of SCHW's intensive educational work, and announced that the SCEF would carry on the public awareness campaign to convert the heretofore unconvinced white supremacists. Since its inception in 1946, the Southern Conference Educational Fund had specifically addressed integration in education so that the SCHW could devote more time in the political arena. Thus, during the 1950s and 1960s the SCEF took an active part in school integration, especially in higher education, as well as in other aspects of the Civil Rights Movement, including the preeminently important voter-registration drive.

Although SCHW was disbanded in 1948, its leaders made its importance felt beyond that time. James Anderson Dombrowski, the major link between SCHW and SCEF, remained a staunch advocate of integration after 1948. His personal appeal and personality drew others like Virginia Durr and Mary McLeod Bethune close to SCEF when they considered being less active after 1950. The continuity of southern liberalism is made evident with an analysis of both the SCHW and SCEF. Indeed, to study one without the other does injustice to the decades of a sustained southern conference movement.

SCHW and SCEF offered a program, then, of "simple decency and common sense" to rectify the region's imbalances. This rectification called for identifying the poor economic status of black people as a southern problem and including their input when seeking solutions. Neither SCHW nor SCEF formally termed the effort of transforming the South as simple decency, but several individuals linked with the southern conference movement often spoke of a simple decency and common sense approach for bringing about reforms. SCEF President Aubrey Williams wrote in 1950 that "we need to take some chances in behalf of decency. . . . We need to believe a little more in the decency of the common man." In October 1955 the southern conference movement's monthly publication, the *Southern Patriot*, headlined "New Orleans Integration Petition Proves Decency's Strength." Black leaders said it best when they protested Senate Un-American hearings in 1954. They collectively demanded of Mississippi Senator James Eastland "that as an act of simple decency and common sense, you make appropriate apologies to those individuals whose names have been sullied in the press." In 1958 one supporter said, "I certainly want to support the cause of decency in the South."[1]

This book addresses numerous unanswered questions about SCHW and SCEF. In the realm of black leadership and black interaction in the two organizations, largely well-educated blacks became involved. Founder and president of North Carolina's Palmer Memorial Institute, Charlotte Hawkins Brown, and founder and president of Florida's Bethune-Cookman College, Mary McLeod Bethune, served on the executive boards of SCHW and SCEF for more than a decade. Other black community leaders active in SCHW and SCEF included: Tuskegee Institute President Frederick Patterson; Osceola McKaine, SCHW's first black field representative in the 1940s; John P. Davis of the National Negro Congress; Charles S. Johnson, noted sociologist and Fisk University president; Roscoe Dunjee, editor of the *Black Dispatch* of Oklahoma City; A. Philip Randolph, president of the Brotherhood of Sleeping Car Porters; Benjamin E. Mays, president of Morehouse College; and many others, including Martin Luther King, Sr. and Jr. In the 1950s blacks numbered increasingly among SCEF officers, and the organization had a series of black presidents in the 1960s, particularly Fred Shuttlesworth, who had established his own record in civil rights activity by 1960 in Birmingham and worked closely with Martin Luther King, Jr., upon his arrival there.

In the general efforts of blacks to help themselves, the work of SCHW and SCEF fit into the ongoing interracialism evident in the National Association for the Advancement of Colored People (NAACP), the Congress of Racial Equality, and, by 1960, the Student Nonviolent Coordinating Committee (SNCC). The creation of new civil rights organizations did not displace the ones already established but allowed for various methods and approaches for transforming society.[2] The issue of class explains in part why fewer of the masses of African Americans became involved in the groups. SCHW was a middle-class organization of educated people, and no doubt the masses of either race felt out of place in the organization. Still a larger part of the black masses more willingly trusted the efforts of the NAACP and the later direct-action organizations than the largely white SCHW and SCEF. By pursuing these issues, I have attempted to assess the effectiveness of SCHW and SCEF in addressing civil rights issues and to examine how SCHW and SCEF strategies compared with those of the NAACP, the SNCC, and various other civil rights groups. This book illustrates the interrelatedness of two southern interracial organizations in the ongoing civil rights struggle and, like Robert J. Norrell's *Reaping the Whirlwind*, takes into account a particular component of the larger movement.[3] Indeed, SCEF must be viewed as a continuation of the SCHW's liberalism, especially considering the longevity of influential leaders like James Anderson Dombrowski, Eleanor Roosevelt, and Virginia Durr.

As was true of the NAACP, SNCC, or any of the civil rights advocate groups, opponents (largely segregationists) accused SCHW and SCEF of being Communist-front organizations. For segregationists any amenities to African Americans became synonymous with communism. If SCHW and SCEF tolerated a few Communists, it was because they too were considered outsiders to most white southerners. The alleged Communist affiliation played a more limited role in SCHW's decline in the 1940s than internal dissension or finances. Evidence in the records reveals that Communist charges hurt SCHW and SCEF in two ways: in the loss of some financial support and in the time each had to spend defending itself when the effort could have been better expended elsewhere. SCHW disbanded, however, at the point when President Harry S Truman's guidance gave attention to the very issues it had addressed between 1938 and 1948. It did not seem likely that liberals would divide their efforts when the issues they had been addressing reached the level of national prominence, but they did. In 1948 when the NAACP was just as red-baited as SCHW, SCHW faltered while the NAACP did not. Perhaps SCHW would have folded anyway. In SCEF's time the Senate joined the House Un-American Activities Committee, which in 1948 had targeted SCHW as Communist inspired and infiltrated. Even the SCHW-instituted SCEF carried on in the height of Cold War hysteria.

Since almost all white leaders had worked diligently to create the Jim Crow system that limited black participation on all levels, a fundamental question remains: What allowed a group of white southerners to go against the status quo of southern society? Only a few lonely voices had pointed out the inequities as Americans had set them into motion in earlier times—the 1896 minority dissent of Supreme Court Justice John Marshall Harlan of Kentucky, the Committee on Interracial Cooperation, the Southern Women for the Prevention of Lynching, and the Southern Tenant Farmers Union.[4]

According to William H. Harris, in celebrated causes where blacks stood to benefit through the assistance of whites, the whites' role and their racial identity warrant explanation. This book attempts to explain the importance of a large group of white southerners to the Civil Rights Movement.[5]

What, then, was the background of the white founders and significant white leaders of SCHW and SCEF? Who were the founders, and what were they doing before 1938? What were their roles in the two organizations? What in their backgrounds brought them to SCHW in 1938 and SCEF in 1946? Various members of the NEC such as Frank Graham, president of the University of North Carolina; Barry Bingham, owner and publisher of the *Louisville Courier-Journal*; Arkansas Governor Carl Bailey;

Lucy Randolph Mason, a direct descendant of the author of the Virginia Declaration of Rights; H. L. Mitchell, an executive of the Southern Tenan? Farmers Union; and a number of other prominent white southerners became members and influential leaders of SCHW and SCEF. James Dombrowski is an example of how SCHW truly passed the torch to the SCEF; he had become executive secretary for SCHW in 1942, served in that position until the group disbanded and became executive director of SCEF, holding both positions even while the two groups coexisted. Having worked in liberal causes before 1938, steering SCHW to address racial inequities in 1938 did not present for some of them any major drawback.[6] Undoubtedly, the despair of the Great Depression also helped many of SCHW's founders transcend race. In some ways this study of SCHW and SCEF is as much a collective biography of individuals as it is organizational history.

Generally small in number, southerners who belonged to SCHW and SCEF tended to be cosmopolitan, well-traveled, well-educated, and religious. Presbyterians made up a great number of southerners who worked in the southern conference movement. This profile, however, does not fully explain their work in liberal causes. As one of SCHW's field secretaries observed in the 1940s, the same profile fit many segregationists. A look at SCHW and SCEF work does help us to see that post-1940 liberalism became more aggressive for racial equality.

White activism did not always exist through organizational support.[7] An episode about a white Kentucky couple, Anne and Carl Braden, during the 1950s offers a unique observation in this regard and also helps to explain why some white southerners joined with blacks in a struggle for justice. In October 1954 the Bradens were indicted in Louisville, Kentucky, under a state sedition law by the Jefferson Country Grand Jury after the house they had purchased for a black family (Andrew and Charlotte Wade) was bombed. The charges against Anne Braden and five other people were dropped, but Carl was held under a $40,000 bail, tried, and found guilty of sedition. He was fined $5,000 and sentenced to fifteen years in prison. Anne campaigned for his release; and after he had served eight months of his term, the Kentucky Court of Appeals reversed his conviction. As a result of their experiences in the Wade Case, Anne Braden wrote *The Wall Between* (1958), explaining that she and Carl had acted because it was the right thing to do.[8] As a result of the Wade Case and economic reprisals, the Bradens could not maintain present employment or find new jobs. Eventually, SCEF heard of their plight and offered to help by first hiring them as field secretaries and continuing to seek an end to segregation and discrimination, the factors that initially led to the Braden's unfortunate circumstances. The Bradens, of their own accord and largely alone, had taken on a major effort for racial justice by attempting to integrate housing in Louisville while other whites in SCHW and SCEF seemed to need the comfort of a group. The Bradens' radicalism added significantly to the roles of whites who chose to participate in the Civil Rights Movement. Their radical approach comes closer to the direct-action demonstrations of the 1960s than the paper campaigns of SCHW and SCEF.

In addition to their positions as field secretaries for SCEF in the 1950s, the Bradens became executive directors of the SCEF in the 1960s. During that period, they moved SCEF's central office from New Orleans to Louisville, and endorsed a stand against the war in Vietnam, another radical effort.

Recognizing that opposition to SCHW and SCEF would probably exist beyond their lifetime, SCHW and SCEF leader James Dombrowski took the initiative in placing both organizations' records at what was then Tuskegee Institute because he and others of the two groups' leaders saw the importance in years to come of scholars working at an historically black institution and communicating the work of a unique group of white southerners in the fight for a just society. Dombrowski understood that white scholars at that time had access to African-American institutions and libraries when blacks might not experience the same access to white institutions and their facilities.[9]

In a history that touches on four decades, the SCHW and SCEF in cooperation with the NAACP and other civil rights organizations sought to solve major problems of the southern region. SCHW and SCEF leaders wanted to remain respectable while they also wanted to bring about fundamental economic, social, and political change in the South. The Civil Rights Movement showed that basic reform requires unseemly acts by masses of people—boycotts, demonstrations, jailings—which SCHW and SCEF had neither the numbers nor the courage to undertake.

For the most part, white liberals failed to see that southern white conservatives had to have an incentive other than being told that they were wrong and that the South suffered for its inequities. Most southern whites understood this well, having assured the arrangement in the first place and having lived with this knowledge for years as part of southern tradition.

The number of southern whites who worked earnestly with blacks to change their region's racial views became all the more important. The southern liberals had great ideals for the South, the most significant and controversial of which became integration. By 1963, when the Civil Rights Movement was reaching a culmination, southern white leaders from SCHW and SCEF who had sought changes when most white southerners did everything possible to maintain white dominance over blacks, deserve a place in history for their role in demanding the fundamental changes that the federal government inevitably addressed.

By 1963, however, because the outstanding leaders of SCHW and SCEF had put forth their ideas in paper campaigns, much like the muckrakers of the Progressive era, while the Civil Rights Movement took to the streets with demonstrations and other direct-action tactics, they could claim little credit for the changes ushered in during the 1960s. Yet, the attempt by SCHW and SCEF to create a different society during crucial years when the majority of white southerners refused to consider racial equality deserves a prominent place in American and southern history because it illustrates the weaknesses of organizations who refuse to take direct action in situations that call for revolutionary means. Lest both organizations be treated in the historical sense that we see the Abolitionists, the Populists, and even the muckrakers of the Progressive era, we fail to appreciate the major significance of their efforts. The Abolitionists, the Populists, and the muckrakers represent different time periods far removed from the time in which the SCHW and SCEF operated, but each group, like the southern liberals, foresaw and anticipated resolutions to grave societal problems that the federal government eventually addressed. The Abolitionists continuously pressed for an end to slavery. The Populists called for the direct election of senators and a more participatory democracy. The muckrakers wrote extensively about many of the same shortfalls the Populists outlined and federal regulation of consumer goods.

The idealism so prevalent in SCEF had existed in earlier groups that marked significant historical periods. One hundred years had marked the time since Abolitionists, after decades of insisting that slavery was morally wrong, observed America confront a division over controversy surrounding the peculiar institution. During the Reconstruction period that followed, however, the Congress and the states, not the Abolitionists, ended slavery. Radical Republicans, inspired by their own philosophy on equality and the idealism of Abolitionists, succeeded in their efforts to guarantee civil rights for the freedmen. But enforcement of the Reconstruction Amendments would come only during SCEF's lifetime. In the 1890s Populists outlined reform measures that would enable Americans to share more fully in the democratic process. Populists faced failure while progressives of the early twentieth century adopted almost all the measures Populists had proposed. Two groups, the muckrakers and suffragists, eventually accomplished their objectives. Various political, social, and economic reforms adopted during the Progressive era were linked to issues the muckrakers addressed, and the Nineteenth Amendment ended the suffragists' long battle for voting rights. Abolitionists, the Radical Republicans, the Populists, the muckrakers, and the suffragists envisioned an America that would offer equal footing to all its citizens. Like these groups, SCEF relied on idealism and trusted the strategy of moral consciousness raising that had worked well for its reform-oriented predecessors. And also like them, individuals with the southern conference movement, though it had come quicker because of direct-action activity, had predicted a South transformed.

One gets a clearer understanding of the obstacles liberals or radicals sought to overcome by viewing *Our Land* and *Eyes on the Prize*, films that depict the struggles of the Southern Tenant Farmers Union and farm laborers and civil rights organizations and activists, respectively, for the decades between the 1930s and the 1970s.[10] It becomes apparent that even though we may not see so many of the goals of SCHW and SCEF reached, it does not mean that the individuals in the struggles lacked enthusiasm and dedication to the success that came. Almost all the members and leaders worked for at least forty years to see that their examples would make a difference. People in the southern conference movement held up the right examples, the right ideals, but their opposition proved too formidable.

The chapters that follow are organized topically. Chapter one places southerners' hope for an improved economic South in the historical context and provides the backdrop against which liberals founded SCHW. Chapter two details the southern conference movement's administration, personnel, finances, membership, and a brief comment on its literature. Ambivalence and red-baiting within liberalism are discussed in chapter three, and chapter four addresses the specific topic of the poll tax and SCHW's fight against it. World War II provided a rich opportunity for liberals to make clearer their opposition to segregation and discrimination, and chapter five treats this subject. Chapter six analyzes the internal dissensions of SCHW and its end in 1948. SCEF carries forth the mission that SCHW set out, and chapter seven treats the subject of SCEF as a SCHW legacy. Chapters eight and nine show SCEF specifically addressing integration and the hope for a just society and its cooperation with other civil rights organizations. Proceeding from chapter one, the chapters follow a chronological layout.

SIMPLE DECENCY & COMMON SENSE

1

A New Answer to the Old Questions of Southern Poverty and Backwardness

The ideas and ideals underlying the creation of the Southern Conference for Human Welfare (SCHW) have a history stretching back to the New South era of the 1880s. During the 1880s, a number of prominent white southerners coined the term *New South* in a concerted effort to incite actions for southern economic growth, but as it became more widely used certain of its advocates brought another connotation to the term. New South eventually became equated with white supremacy because so many of its proponents openly expressed a belief that black people were forever to remain subservient to whites. As such, the term New South remained in use to denote southern economic improvement and a strong belief in the racial superiority of whites. At least half a century passed before a small group of mostly white-liberal southerners would challenge the unstated assumptions that undergirded the phrase New South, both the economic and racial underpinnings of its concept.[1]

Despite what proponents of the New South doctrine hoped for, the South did not develop, remaining one of the poorest parts of the nation. Even as the nineteenth century gave way to the twentieth, the southern economy lagged far behind that of the rest of the nation. In 1900, when the overall estimated per capita wealth of the United States was $1,165, that of the South was less than half of the national average at $509.[2]

However dismal the situation for the southern states, they had begun to develop industrially by the turn of the century. The South possessed many advantages. It had abundant machinery, cheap labor, low taxes, close proximity to raw materials, cheap water power, and a mild climate. All these whetted the interest of northern investors. Accordingly, northern investors had ventured south, placing hope and money in the railway and other industries. They built and financed new factories, especially textile mills, in more and more cities, while simultaneously the tobacco industry had begun to flourish. The South in 1938 was indeed emerging as the New South.[3]

The generation of southerners in the two decades preceding 1938 sought to solve the South's major problems, especially that of race, by adhering to the advice and optimism of the New South spokesmen. Henry W. Grady and Richard H. Edmonds, perhaps the most notable of this group, were inspired by their own optimism. They believed that the South "was to be the richest country upon the globe." Ever mindful of the southern defeat during the Civil War, these men of the New South creed believed all scars of that defeat would be healed and that their region would reign victorious over the North through economic domination.[4] According to these seers, the South would exercise dominance because of the significant marriage between southern agriculture and new southern industrialism taking place in the region.

The New South spokesmen had much to say about social and political matters, too. Part of the appeal for some of the northern investors in industrial endeavors had been the illusion that racial harmony existed in the South because blacks liked the inequality that existed there. One of the longest-lived myths of American history was the belief among southern whites that black people accepted their status and would never demand equal justice and economic well-being. A few northern investors, upon learning differently, had serious worries on this question. But the southerners held to their position. When the Boston Merchants' Association asked Henry Grady to discuss the racial problem, Grady scolded the northerners for meddling in what he considered a solely southern affair. Such confrontations disturbed Grady and others of the New South leadership for fear northerners would withhold needed capital if they grew too suspicious of southern ways, especially when those ways might result in property damage in the event of violent racial unrest.[5]

Grady, however, did not bother to keep his feelings about race hidden, not even from northerners. In 1890 he wrote:

> But the supremacy of the white race of the South must be maintained forever, and the domination of the negro race resisted at all points and at all hazards—because the white race is the superior race. This is the declaration of no new truth. It has abided forever in the marrow of our bones, and shall run forever with the blood that feeds Anglo-Saxon hearts.[6]

Grady was determined that whites should always remain unmistakably in control of public affairs. He even reasoned that whites were "entitled" to such control. After all, all property had been obtained through their "intelligence" and "responsibility." And such control should extend to politics. About black voters Grady expressed fear . . . that this vast swarm of ignorant, purchasable, and credulous voters will be compacted and controlled by desperate and unscrupulous white men, and made to hold the balance of power wherever the whites are divided. This fear has kept, and will keep the intelligence and responsibility of any community, North or South, solid.[7]

Leaving no room for doubt about his stand on social equality of the races, Grady insisted "that the whites and blacks must walk in separate paths in the South."[8] Industrial educator and president of Tuskegee Institute, Booker T. Washington reinforced Grady's and other white spokesmen's accommodationism with his famous Atlanta Exposition speech in 1895.

The Southern Society for the Promotion of the Study of Race Conditions in the South (SSPSRC) meeting in Montgomery, Alabama, in 1900 epitomized the views of Grady and others for whom he spoke on the concept of white supremacy. This lily-white gathering set out to solve the southern racial problem, beginning with placing the blame on black people for the backwardness of the southern economy.[9] The conferees failed to produce a single responsible proposal by which to resolve their grave problem because they defined the South and southerners as white and refused to see black people as an integral part of the southern economy. This analysis contained a serious contradiction, as the SSPSRC blamed blacks for the region's economic troubles. Indeed, if the economic situation of whites improved and that of blacks remained dismal all would be well. The social dominance of whites and absolute degradation of black people remained their most important goal. Black Americans must be kept wholly within the limits of Jim Crow, at all cost.[10]

Little relief for blacks came even as white liberal southerners invited their participation in an organization that moved toward the concept of equality. The Commission on Interracial Cooperation (CIC), formed in Atlanta in 1919 in the aftermath of racial strife, sought to restore harmony between the races, with the understanding that white southerners might gradually accept equality as long as segregation was maintained. Commission members believed that segregation could exist without black people being discriminated against, not realizing that segregation served as a form of discrimination. The premise was that blacks could hope to improve their status in southern society if they adhered to the rules of Jim Crow and did not interfere with the well-guarded folkway of separate but equal. If CIC could decrease violence and lessen tension between the races, it deemed its work successful. CIC's highest mark, therefore, was evident when it sponsored internationally acclaimed black singer Roland Hayes in concert in Atlanta in 1925. Instead of blacks being confined solely to the poorer balcony seats of the city auditorium, they were allowed seats from the top to bottom of an entire side as long as whites had the other side. The vertical segregation arrangement represented for Will Alexander, CIC's executive director, a symbol that segregation had been dealt a small blow. This was as far as the CIC could go.

Blacks acquiesced in continued segregation as a matter of survival, but CIC's existence indicated two significant changes in the South. Along with white liberals, blacks were participating in the formulation of goals on their behalf. White liberals did not blame them for the economic stagnation of the South. Southerners in CIC, however, created a problem within its work toward racial harmony; they made segregation compatible with liberalism. In years ahead many white liberals could seek economic and political equality while being unable to accept integration as a matter of principle. Advocacy of economic and political equality for all helped several of the white liberals avoid addressing the issue of segregation.[11]

For more than four decades following the meeting of the Southern Society the views expressed in that initial conference dominated white southern thought. The hopeful promise of New South publicists, which was formulated to lead the region out of poverty, had helped only to convert thousands to the confidence that a South of abundance was a certainty in the near future. Yet, the region's leaders made little progress in solving either its economic or social problems. The dream of abundance remained unfulfilled, and the South continued to be the poorest and least economically progressive section of the country.[12]

The Great Depression, of course, only made matters worse. The terrible conditions of that era should have convinced southerners and other white Americans of the futility of their views and made them willing to relinquish racial discrimination in hope of the betterment of all. But most white southerners clung steadfastly to white supremacy and objected loudly when voices from outside the region attempted to propose a different approach. They were especially suspicious of New Dealers even when they were from the South.[13]

President Franklin D. Roosevelt, an adopted son of the South with a home at Warm Springs, Georgia, knew well the dire poverty of that region and wanted to do something to end it. As always, he had political motives as well. If he could help to ease the harshness of the South's poverty, he could gain ground in his efforts to purge Congress of several conservative southern Democrats who sought to obstruct the New Deal. Thus, in the summer of 1938 he requested Clark Foreman of the Public Works Administration (PWA) Power Division, under the direction of Secretary of Interior Harold Ickes and Lowell Mellett, executive director of the National Emergency Council (NEC), to have the NEC "undertak[e] to bring together certain information relating to economic conditions in the South."[14]

In response to the president's request, and in the tradition of the time, Mellett and Foreman asked for the advice of several distinguished white southerners who could give "special knowledge of and interest in the needs and problems of their region." Mellett invited Frank Porter Graham, president of the University of North Carolina to chair this group, which Roosevelt called the Conference on Economic Conditions of the

South. The conference convened for its first meeting on July 5, 1938.[15] The group included several liberals the South would hear about in the next couple of decades as their life experiences brought them together in other causes for the improvement of the South. Among its many prominent white southerners, the group included representatives of several phases of the region's economy: Graham; Barry Bingham, publisher of the *Louisville Courier-Journal;* Lucy Randolph Mason of Atlanta, fieldworker for the Congress of Industrial Organizations (CIO); H. L. Mitchell, secretary-treasurer of the Southern Tenant Farmers Union, Memphis; and Paul Poynter, publisher of the *St. Petersburg* (Fla.) *Times.*[16]

The advisory group decided what subjects the report would include and the conclusions to be drawn from data collected, and Foreman became editor of the *Report on Economic Conditions of the South.* Many white southerners sent unsolicited observations to Graham, who in turn shared the information with Foreman. Foreman received it too late for its inclusion in the report, but he assured fellow white southerners that the NEC would not have the final word on the South, that the future would offer other such opportunities.[17]

When the government published the *Report* in early August 1938, it praised the South for all its contributions to the nation, but it cited numerous problems that remained to be resolved. It showed the South to be as poor as the NEC suspected. The South needed a massive injection of marketable goods, especially food and clothing, but did not have the money to purchase them.

The *Report* noted that the South led the world in the production of cotton, tobacco, naval stores' products, and paper, and yet had relatively little to show for the bounty. The *Report* echoed old voices (Grady's) on the southern paradox: the South, while rich in natural resources, was poor. Unless the region could develop other industries, NEC argued, it would be forced to continue as a colonial economy.[18]

Some of the more damaging conclusions included the revelation that the South's population constituted one of the region's greatest assets, but large numbers of skilled workers migrated annually to other sections of the country in search of better opportunity. Blacks accounted for a smaller portion of the skilled laborers in the South because whites forced them to take menial jobs, but as unemployment remained at a high level in 1937 whites took many of the jobs they had previously allocated to blacks, causing harder times for blacks already at the bottom of the economic ladder. The *Report*, however, does not elaborate on the poor condition of blacks.

In 1937 the average per capita income in the South was $314, while in the rest of the United States it was $604, almost twice as much. Southern laborers in twenty important industries received $.16 an hour less than laborers in other sections received for the same type of work. Poorer citizens were prevented from political participation by the poll tax in eight southern states. The South had to educate one-third of the nation's

children with one-sixth of the nation's school revenues. And higher education fared no better since the total endowments of southern colleges
and universities amounted to less than the combined endowments of Yale
and Harvard. Labor organizers had made slow and difficult progress
among low-paid workers. The southern states had the largest proportion
of women and children in gainful work, but only one southern state
maintained an eight-hour day for women in any industry. More than half
of the nation's farmers lived in the South, but it raised less than a third of
the nation's livestock. The South's public utilities—railroad systems, elec-
tric holding-company systems, and others—were almost completely controlled by outside interests. In sum, "ever since the War between the
States the South has been the poorest section of the Nation."[19] Roosevelt
summed up: "the South presents right now the Nation's No. 1 economic
problem—the Nation's problem, not merely the South's." He so informed
members of the southern advisory committee in a letter of July 5, 1938,
before the committee sifted through its findings.[20]

It mattered little that prominent southerners could witness for themselves the terrible state of their region, especially during the nationwide
suffering of the Great Depression. Many of them refused to accept the
findings outlined in the *Report* and complained vehemently about exter-
nal meddling in southern affairs.[21] Others objected to the whole notion of
the NEC's *Report* because they were anti-New Dealers, and again many
southerners equated white supremacy with economic dominance. They
sensed that even though President Roosevelt chose not to create problems
for himself by directly challenging the southern tradition of white supremacy, his New Deal did imply equality for *all*.[22]

Southerners had learned of President Roosevelt's request and the
NEC's mission largely through local newspapers.[23] Apprehension and
suspicion set in well before the *Report* appeared. One example of such
misgivings surfaced in the *Textile Bulletin* in an article entitled "Roosevelt
Appoints a Slumming Commission." White southerners charged that
since the Civil War, northerners had given themselves the task of regulat-
ing the affairs of "benighted" southern citizens. Most white southerners
generally did not accept willingly criticism from the North because they
still adhered strongly to the principle that southerners were capable of
handling their own problems. When President Roosevelt, the native New
Yorker, asked for the NEC investigation, many southerners viewed him as
just another northerner trying to dictate to them. If he wanted to appoint
a slumming commission, let him begin with New York City. Besides, the
belief was that Graham and Mason, though they were southerners, had
already drawn their conclusion and that no evidence given at the advisory committee meeting would make any difference to them; they were
interested only in criticizing southern industries. Mason's work with the
CIO and Graham's support for a group of strikers at a hosiery mill made
clear their motives.[24]

Nor did southern newspapers respond positively to the committee's negative findings. Southern publishers and politicians were defensive about criticism of the South, even if it came from fellow southerners. As Bingham stated to Graham, "Of course some of the publishers, . . . are only too glad to find a new subject for criticism of President Roosevelt."[25] Newspapers took such a position despite the fact that when the Citizens Fact Finding Movement of Georgia distributed authoritative statements each month on the same kinds of matters covered in the *Report*, southerners accepted their findings for the simple reason that the sponsorship had been southern.[26]

Eventually, white southern businessmen argued that statistics in the *Report* were inaccurate or distorted and that the Roosevelt administration had done "the South a very grave injustice." They reasoned that northern investors who had been helping the region's development might now calculate the risk as too great for future investment after reading the *Report*.

Opponents of the *Report* mixed economic issues with the race issue. As among many white southerners previously, the argument continued in 1938 that the terrible state of the southern economy was the fault of blacks. Without offering answers, the 1938 argument moved one step further than what most white southerners expected when a few raised the question, "Why does not the South do something about raising the standards for the Negroes?"[27]

The NEC took some of the criticisms seriously, as one member put it, "those that [were] not simply hysterical diatribes." It agreed with its critics that there was hope for the South but only if the people of that section of the country used the NEC *Report* as a guideline to formulate solutions to the long list of inequities. On industrialization, it repeated examples that Birmingham shipped steel north for the manufacture of finished products that the North then reshipped south for sale; that the North manufactured locomotives for southern railroads; that the North even manufactured the plow with which the southern farmer tilled the soil. In regard to blacks lowering regional standards, the NEC admitted that blacks faced depressed living standards wherever they lived in the United States and that the largest number of blacks lived in the South. But the agency insisted that one race could not be totally responsible for the region's economic ills. The NEC followed the policy of the Roosevelt administration with its hands-off approach to addressing outright equality for blacks. It completely ignored the question raised about improving the status of blacks, a question that would be picked up later and explored further by a few southern white liberals. They began to recognize that blacks were not to blame for all regional ills, and that the South would be slow to grow as long as most whites insisted that their lives existed totally separate from those of blacks.[28]

The *Report* otherwise stimulated a large number of positive responses. Southerners who had only heard about it and wanted to read it for themselves requested copies; such a large number of requests came to Graham that his secretary referred a long list of names to Mellett in Washington. Southerners who thought highly of Graham appreciated him even more for contributing to the work done by the NEC, requesting him to write articles or to do presentations on the southern economy. Graham, already with many obligations as president of the University of North Carolina, declined such engagements and graciously thanked all who extended invitations.[29]

Because of the NEC's *Report*, 1938 became the year of meetings and conferences on the southern economy, and the SCHW surpassed all in outlining objectives and goals for the region. It offered no solutions beyond calling for a national effort of some sort to enhance the region's purchasing power. Discussion groups sprang up in various communities, and civic clubs, religious and educational gatherings, colleges and high schools held public forums to address the situation. So popular had southern economics become that Duke University in Durham, North Carolina, included in its centennial celebration a symposium on the topic. Its program participants, including Secretary of Agriculture Henry A. Wallace, discussed topics such as "Toward a Balanced Regional and National Economy" and "Factors Producing Change in the Domestic and Foreign Demand for the Staple Products of the South." The stimulus provided by the *Report* made its publication one of the most significant events of recent times for white southerners. It defined the crisis in which they found themselves, especially after continuously being convinced that the New South of industrial prosperity was finally being realized.[30]

The NEC's *Report*, therefore, had provided a focus for meetings on the broad issues of the economy. It gave every indication that the South had undergone little economic change since 1900. Although the *Report* had not addressed racial attitudes, those southerners who reacted negatively to it because of the racial implications showed that many still supported the premises of the 1900 Montgomery meeting. The rise of a new organization willing to get past vertical segregation on its understanding of the race issue, inclusive of black people's involvement, as part of a broader survey of southern society, however, evidenced that a significant change had occurred.

The NEC's *Report* brought together a number of southerners from various backgrounds who would remain dedicated to the efforts of the SCHW, some for only a few years but several for the greater portion of their lives. Three—Frank Graham, Clark Foreman, and Lucy Randolph Mason—had worked directly with the NEC in its formulation of the *Report*. They and others who had not already known one another earlier came together for the first time during the period of SCHW's founding.[31] All had shown outstanding leadership ability in their local communities, many on the national level. The most significant characteristic of the persons in the following discussion is that they and all the others who became members of the SCHW represented everything that the New South creed stood strongly against.

Before his presidency of the University of North Carolina (UNC), Graham, a North Carolinian, had been selected to serve on the board of the Southern Summer School for Workers in Industry, a group dedicated to strengthening organized labor in the South. He continued on the board after 1930. Graham had reluctantly become the president of UNC in June 1930 after Harry W. Chase resigned to serve as president of the University of Illinois. He had served as UNC dean of students in 1919 but loved teaching more; so he gave up the post to return to full-time teaching. He preferred to continue teaching history at UNC, his alma mater, a job he had enjoyed and at which he had excelled for ten years, but UNC's trustees wanted him for president. Graham's responsibilities at the university demanded much of his time, but this did not prevent him contributing whatever he could to the quest for social and economic justice.

Graham's work with the NEC in 1938 had not been his first experience with the Roosevelt administration. Roosevelt had appointed him in 1933 as vice-chairman of the Consumers Advisory Board, where Graham developed ambitious plans for nationwide organizations of local consumers' councils that would rival in power the trade associations and labor organizations. As chairman of the National Advisory Council on Social Security, Graham had worked with Secretary of Labor Frances Perkins in advocating a strong social-security program. Graham embraced Roosevelt's ideas for the New Deal, prompting some southerners to be as much against him as they were against the president.

Graham's activities with the New Deal president did not create as much public controversy for him as did his standing bond for a former UNC student who had been arrested while involved in the same strike for which the *Textile Bulletin* had lashed out at Graham. The strikers' demands for recognition of their union and a thirty-hour work week without reduced pay was galling enough for southern manufacturers. But when they learned that Alton Lawrence, the student involved, was the secretary of the Socialist party in North Carolina, Graham became a figure of notoriety. In this incident four years before the establishment of the SCHW, Graham experienced firsthand the abuse associated with being identified with organized labor and leftist politics in the South.[32]

Lucy Randolph Mason came to her union convictions early in life. She had been a member of the Union Label League in Richmond, Virginia, and in New York was a member of the International Ladies Garment Workers Union Label Committee. She believed that union members were the better-paid workers, and was aware that they had an eight-hour workday and only worked a half day on Saturdays. Thus, her attraction to organized labor, she said, "seemed natural." In her memoirs she told how employers worked to spread the rumor that to belong to a union was "communism" and that all organizers were "foreigners," even though most people knew that the labor leaders in question were born in the South.

Mason became the general secretary of the National Consumers League when Florence Kelley died in 1932, and through this organization Mason met and began to do related work with Eleanor Roosevelt. Eleanor Roosevelt was both a vice-president of the National Consumers League and a member of the women's division of the Democratic National Committee, in which Mason was also active. In 1937 Mason met John L. Lewis, head of the CIO, at a dinner in her brother-in-law's home in honor of Frances Perkins. The two arranged to get together shortly afterward for a chat, as a result of which Mason became public relations representative for the CIO in the South.[33]

Clark Foreman also believed that organized labor would ultimately improve conditions in the South, but his commitment was to black Americans, who were only just now being admitted to labor unions associated with the CIO. He first became vividly aware of the South's race problem after witnessing a lynching during his undergraduate days at the University of Georgia. Foreman was only seventeen years old at the time, and a good friend of his commented that the incident "burned a hole in his head." Since that day Foreman was said to have done crazy things for the sake of racial equality. Even when confronted by a racist sheriff with a shotgun aimed at his face, Foreman allegedly yelled at the sheriff to "go to hell."[34]

Foreman did not act on his impulse for racial concerns until after he completed his undergraduate degree and attended Harvard for a year. He also studied at the London School of Economics, where a teacher assigned *Christianity and the Race Problem* by G. H. Oldham. The book described the work of the CIC, a group Foreman had never heard about, though its first meeting was in Atlanta, his hometown. Foreman returned from Europe, sought membership in CIC, and eventually became secretary for the Georgia chapter.

Foreman completed his doctor of philosophy degree in political science at Columbia University in 1932, and subsequently became an assistant to the director for the Phelps-Stokes Fund, director of studies for the Julius Rosenwald Fund, and advisor on the economic status of blacks and special counsel to Secretary of the Interior Harold L. Ickes. While director of studies for the Julius Rosenwald Fund, Foreman published his dissertation, "Environmental Factors in Negro Elementary Education" (1932), and coauthored with Joan Raushenbush *Total Defense* (1940).[35]

In November 1933 Foreman hired Robert C. Weaver, a young black man with a Ph.D. degree in economics from Harvard University, as his chief assistant. Foreman took great pride in having a black assistant at a time when Washington was segregated. Perhaps aware of the administration's policy of status quo on racial segregation and the fact that Washington was a southern city, Foreman decided that this was something he should do on his own. Perhaps he understood also that such action placed him in opposition to the tradition of his region. If he wanted to keep any kind of regional respectability and accomplish certain progressive goals, the racial issue was to be dealt with "cautiously."[36] Caution, however, did not interfere with his sense of justice and equality.

When Graham and Foreman first met in 1938, Foreman was director of the Power Division of the Public Works Administration. At first Graham knew so little of Foreman that he often misspelled his name "Forman," but within one month of their meeting Graham spoke highly of him.[37]

For Graham, Mason, and Foreman the call for them to do something about the South's welfare came much sooner than expected. In fact, another group pondered the idea of a regional effort almost at the same time that the NEC and advisory group met in Washington. Just one month after the *Report* was made public, the SCHW had been organized.

Southern white liberals began groundwork for a group such as the SCHW in early July 1938. Fifteen people, including U.S. Commissioner of the northern Alabama district, Judge Louise O. Charlton, and Joseph Gelders, a former assistant professor of physics at the University of Alabama, met in Birmingham and discussed problems affecting the southern states, pointing to shortcomings in educational opportunities, the plight of southern farmers, labor problems, and several other inequities that the NEC would bring out in its August report. Realizing that the South had grown so accustomed to the situation that any attempt to change it would probably be taken as an attack, the small group worried whether it could recruit enough persons to mount a regional campaign. By mid-August, and after a second Birmingham meeting, however, it numbered at least forty-five people and organized to be the SCHW with Judge Charlton general chair for a regional conference set for fall 1938.

SCHW's organizing strategy involved writing to key persons in all the southern states, telling them about its plan in order to recruit additional sponsors and committee workers for the fall conference. A major part of the SCHW's support came from the Southern Policy Committee (SPC), an organization founded in 1935 by southern whites with the broad objectives of reducing poverty, raising the general standard of living, and creating a land policy to end tenancy. Members of SPC comprised the first list of names used in the mailing, and the response proved encouraging. Not only did SPC members agree to work with SCHW, but they supplied the names of others they thought would show an interest. By August the number of persons who had responded favorably was large enough to assure a successful conference.[38] Support from SPC brought inherent problems; with the exception of Charles S. Johnson, it was lily-white with a large number of conservatives. If SCHW was to be progressive and reach a wider range of southerners, it had to seek out liberals like Graham, Mason, and Foreman and recruit as many blacks as possible.

On September 6, 1938, about one hundred representatives of seven of the thirteen southern states met again in Birmingham to discuss the social conditions and the economic realities that the NEC had articulated so well. At this meeting the organization elected temporary officers (expected to serve only until November), drafted a program for the regional conference in November, and selected various committees to be responsible for different aspects of the November program, such as publicity and finance committees.[39]

The question of whether any particular person took sole responsibility for the various activities between July and November has been a difficult puzzle for historians to unravel. Influential Tulane University historian H. C. Nixon, Louise Charlton, and Joseph Gelders played large roles. Each added a different dimension to what issues the SCHW would focus on.

Gelders's function in founding SCHW is evident by his proposal to Lucy Randolph Mason in early 1938 that they convene a conference on civil liberties. Mason arranged for Gelders to meet and present his ideas to Eleanor Roosevelt, who suggested that any such conference should address all the South's major problems. Eleanor Roosevelt, in turn, arranged a meeting for Gelders with Franklin Roosevelt. The president endorsed his wife's ideas, but emphasized that a conference such as the one Gelders had in mind should also seek to abolish the poll tax. The president had long been interested in expanding the southern electorate and saw the poll tax as an obstacle to that goal.

Gelders later approached H. C. Nixon, chairman of the SPC and organizer of the Alabama Policy Committee (APC), a state branch of the SPC. The APC numbered among its members prominent industrialists, publicists, labor leaders, civil servants, and professional people, individuals whom Gelders and Charlton would invite to participate in the SCHW. Nixon, growing weary of the moderation of the SPC, responded promptly to Gelders's proposed southern conference work. Gelders's and Nixon's efforts clearly indicate that no one person can be credited with the founding of the SCHW. The founders of the Southern Conference included all those persons who met in July and September.[40]

Having worked to help organize SCHW, Gelders served on the publicity committee, and his name also appears on the first letterhead the group used that included the officers, a long list of sponsors from the southern states, and the various committees and committee members. Gelders also met with Graham at least twice at the University of North Carolina before the November conference, when Charlton or Nixon had been unable to go there.[41]

While the *Report* provoked a few southerners to discuss and seek solutions to economic problems, Gelders and Nixon seized the opportunity to draw attention to civil liberties. Related incidents played an equally important role in heightening concern about civil liberties for all. One such incident involved the ultra-right-wing Louisiana Coalition of Patriotic Societies (LCPS), which had mounted an unsuccessful campaign in 1936 to have Nixon and other Tulane University faculty members fired for bringing the intellectual elite together in the SPC. Nixon's ideas that the South needed an organization more militant than the SPC and more closely connected with organized labor especially infuriated LCPS.[42]

Most white southerners equated advocates of civil rights, civil liberties, and organized labor with communism. Gelders had represented the National Committee for the Defense of Political Prisoners (NCDPP), and he was also attempting to organize workers around the Birmingham area. The same year that LCPS harassed Nixon at Tulane for his work with the SPC and support for organized labor, Joseph Gelders was targeted for physical abuse and abducted as he returned home from a meeting in Birmingham, beaten until he lost consciousness, and left to die on a back road near Clanton, Alabama. When he regained consciousness, Gelders, with great pain and difficulty, eventually reached the hospital in Clanton where he received treatment for his injuries, from which he eventually recovered. Although Gelders and others came forth with ample evidence to identify the assailants, they were never convicted.[43] Indeed people like Nixon and Gelders knew firsthand the importance of forming the SCHW.

Gelders had joined the NCDPP in 1935, and in 1936 he became its southern representative. By 1938 the group had changed its name to the National Committee for People's Rights, and included among the more than eighty-five names on its letterhead those of Sherwood Anderson, Hamilton Basso, Erskine Caldwell, Malcolm Cowley, Countee Cullen, Langston Hughes, Upton Sinclair, and, especially, Virginia Foster Durr and H. C. Nixon, who became particularly committed to the SCHW. Thus, Gelders was intimately involved with a large pool of influential intellectuals, all of whom southerners looked on with suspicion.[44]

Charlton, too, cared about civil liberties but directed attention to the overall aspects of the southern economy as presented in the NEC *Report*. Plans went smoothly for the regional meeting in November after the September 6 SCHW meeting in Birmingham, aiding the general conference chair's efforts to publicize it. The public learned in the *New Republic* that the SCHW would address social and economic issues and that liberal southerners representing every phase of the region's life sponsored the Conference. Readers got some idea of who some of these southern liberals were since the article included a few of the Conference's sponsors. The Conference represented a progressive surge, and, if its findings could be put into effective action, the SCHW could make a positive, lasting impact on the South.[45] From the Conference's headquarters, the Hotel Tutwiler in Birmingham, Charlton and others circulated forms listing possible subjects in an attempt to gauge issues more pressing for delegates to the November meeting. A few individuals and organizations that sympathized with the interests of the SCHW made contributions. Radio stations generously offered time to speakers in some of the larger southern cities while newspapers devoted space to advertise the conference, and by late October many people knew of the November meeting. The CIO and the United Mine Workers contributed much of the money for the SCHW, enabling delegates to register at the nominal fee of one dollar.[46]

SCHW had decided at its September 6 meeting to present an annual award to the person representing the "Southern statesman who [had been] most active in promoting the ideals of human welfare and justice embodied in the philosophy of Thomas Jefferson." The award committee chose Supreme Court Justice Hugo L. Black as the first recipient. Black's selection became the only issue that caused problems before the November meeting. Controversy arose immediately after Graham, who served on the committee, notified Black that he had been chosen unanimously.[47]

Liberal whites and blacks did not like the idea of Black getting an award because of his Ku Klux Klan ties. Among the many letters that were sent in protest to Graham, one person in response to a *New York Times* article declared that Jefferson's life and philosophy contrasted to that of Black's. The protester did not think that Jefferson would have accepted support from any group as anti-American as the Klan and that Jefferson certainly would not have remained silent if Americans questioned his actions. "The South and the Human Welfare," the disappointed Virginia Democrat wrote, "are certainly discredited in such an ignoble undertaking and my deepest sympathy goes out to our great philosopher." One southerner voiced the sentiments of many others who did not want Black as a Supreme Court Justice or to receive the Thomas Jefferson Award because of his alleged background.[48]

Blacks had been particularly apprehensive about Senator Black's appointment to the Supreme Court in 1937. The National Association for the Advancement of Colored People (NAACP), the leading organization for racial equality, feared that if Black had in fact been a Klan member, he certainly would not do anything to improve the conditions of blacks. The NAACP sent telegrams to both President Roosevelt and Senator Black requesting that Black break the silence on his alleged life membership in the Klan, but when the Senate confirmed Black's appointment, leading spokesmen of the NAACP sent letters of congratulations, leaving an open door for a cordial relationship with the justice.[49] Some NAACP members, however, remained as skeptical of Black's credentials in 1938 as they had been the previous year. Mary McLeod Bethune, director of the Division of Negro Affairs in the Roosevelt administration, hesitated when John P. Davis, secretary of the National Negro Congress, asked if she would serve on a committee at the Southern Conference for Human Welfare. Bethune finally agreed to participate at the November conference in spite of the award to Justice Black and in spite of his Klan connection, stating that her commitment to racial uplift was more important and that others, like Eleanor Roosevelt, F. D. Patterson, and Charles S. Johnson, who shared her commitment would be participating as well.[50]

When the meeting actually occurred, SCHW put to rest the doubts that Bethune and others harbored. Palmer Weber, a friend of SCHW founders and later conference supporter, identified the liberals who gathered between November 20 and 23, 1938, as radicals, a term too strong for what actually transpired. Although those who attended the SCHW convention did not think of themselves as radicals, before they adjourned they had drawn up the blueprint to create a democratic South, one totally different from that of years past.[51]

On November 20 between 1,200 and 1,500 delegates of various labor locals, clubs, churches, politicians, and educators registered for the SCHW at the city auditorium in Birmingham. Only southern delegates could vote on decisions of the organization, however; all others were simply visitors. White delegates were housed at the Tutwiler, Birmingham's major hotel; black delegates had to find accommodations through churches and other local organizations. Sessions took place at various locations—general sessions at the auditorium, smaller sessions at the Tutwiler or local churches.[52]

With an estimated one million people represented, the Southern Conference represented a cross section of every possible special-interest group of the region. It attempted to accommodate all interests represented by adopting a large number of resolutions addressing various causes.[53] With the NEC's *Report* as its yardstick, SCHW raised many of the same questions that concerned organized labor, farmers, and disfranchised voters, three groups to whose problems the SCHW would continue to pay special attention over the next several years. The heterogeneity of the groups, an asset in 1938 that attracted a large constituency for SCHW's beginning, increased the likelihood of future conflicts.

Conference delegates made a who's who of southern liberals, and the same was true of the organizations represented. SCHW founders—Charlton, Gelders, Nixon, Graham, Foreman, Mason, and many others—topped the list. They were joined by Donald Comer, industrialist and owner of Avondale Mills, Inc., of Birmingham; William Mitch, president of the Alabama Industrial Union Council, a part of CIO; Myles Horton and James A. Dombrowski of the Highlander Folk School of Monteagle, Tennessee; H. L. Mitchell, of the Southern Tenant Farmers Union; and delegates from the AFL. Clergymen, journalists, politicians, lawyers, teachers, professors, youth, Socialists and Communists (including Hosea Hudson, a Communist from Birmingham and labor union organizer) flocked to the Conference. Other well-known participants included Governor Bibb Graves of Alabama; Congressmen Luther Patrick and Brooks Hays; Florida Senator Claude Pepper; historians C. Vann Woodward and Arthur Raper; sociologist Charles S. Johnson of Fisk University; such college presidents as Mary McLeod Bethune of Bethune-Cookman College, F. D. Patterson of Tuskegee Institute, and J. B. Watson of Arkansas State College; Bishop J. A. Bragg; Jesse O. Thomas, regional director of the

National Urban League; John P. Davis, Secretary of the National Negro Congress; and Horace Mann Bond.[54]

President Roosevelt sent greetings to the Southern Conference and expressed his sincere desire to see the endeavor succeed. He acknowledged awareness of the ongoing efforts of a few southerners to promote "human welfare" in that region and emphasized the importance of seeking solutions "in a united front." He hoped that the SCHW would be able to make a difference in the quality of life among southern people, writing: "I believe you will find it impossible in many instances to separate human from economic problems. But it you steer a true course and keep everlasting at it, the South will long be thankful."[55]

Appearing in person, Eleanor Roosevelt offered more than words of encouragement. She showed up to participate in the program and even addressed the group on November 22. The First Lady argued strongly for universal education as the "real basis of democracy," and stressed the need to incorporate liberal values in the schools, especially the idea of equality for all, a radical and insidious thought among white southerners.[56]

A longtime advocate of social justice, especially as it applied to the rights of blacks, Eleanor Roosevelt had received immense abuse at the hands of many southern whites. But unlike her husband, Eleanor Roosevelt did not compromise her views. She won great acclaim in the black community, speaking more often and more clearly on the demands of racial justice in a democracy than any other public white figure during the New Deal era.[57]

When local racial mores intruded at the SCHW, Eleanor Roosevelt responded defiantly. Although whites and blacks had separate accommodations and ate separately, they sat wherever they desired at the opening session on November 20 and even until late afternoon on the 21st. None of the participants had complained, and Virginia Durr has described the integrated sessions as "just a love feast, you'd never seen anything like it in your life." But when the police department learned of the integrated seating, an order came to the SCHW from City Commissioner Theophilus Eugene Connor (the same infamous "Bull" Connor who would become noted for ordering the use of fire hoses and police dogs on civil rights marchers, largely children, in the streets of Birmingham in the 1960s) that the audience had to segregate—whites on one side of the aisle and blacks on the other—or the group would not have further use of the auditorium. If the SCHW continued to use the auditorium and the audience remained mixed, the commissioner threatened to arrest members of the audience on the charge of violating Birmingham's city ordinance on segregation.[58]

Doubting that any local official would dare arrest the First Lady, Eleanor Roosevelt sat with the blacks, until the police requested that she move. But even then she did so restively and continued to make her point by placing a folding chair in the aisle, just beyond the center, and she sat there during all of the sessions she attended. For the remainder of the conference police came to enforce the ordinance, sometimes creating such anxiety that some participants would not even cross the aisle to speak to a friend of the other race for fear of being arrested.[59]

Probably the only intent of Birmingham's police department had been to harass the Southern Conference for daring to disregard Jim Crow practices. A more far-reaching objective would have sought to destroy the SCHW's hope for social equality in the South, but until Connor interfered, SCHW had formulated no plan for dismantling segregation. The success of the police department's harassment, however, helped SCHW realize Roosevelt's prophecy, the impossibility of separating human-welfare needs from economic needs. At a conference convened to address regional economic woes, liberal southerners grew more determined to address racial justice as a result of the episode with the police department. The SCHW adopted a resolution against segregation, one of many such resolutions it would pass during its history. In 1938 SCHW:

> Resolved: That the action of Birmingham City officials in enforcing existing segregation ordinances, as affecting sessions of this conference, demonstrates a situation that we condemn, and be it further Resolved: that this Conference instructs its officers in arranging future meetings to avoid a similar situation, if at all possible, by selecting a locality in which the practices of the past few days would not be applied.[60]

Many of the CIC members were present, but even they welcomed SCHW's public display against vertical segregation. For future meetings the organization chose cities on the basis of whether integration would be allowed.

Frank Graham and Hugo Black in the opening and closing addresses, respectively, added to the radicalism Eleanor Roosevelt brought to SCHW. Graham's opening remarks supported SCHW's resolution on segregation before the police department acted to halt integration. Graham spoke uncharacteristic words for a southern white man in 1938:

> Repression, whether it be of the Negro, Catholic, Jew or laborer, is the way of frightened power; freedom is the enlightened way. With all the black marks that have been placed against us in the South, let us prove at this Southern Conference for Human Welfare that we stand for the more helpless minorities and the underprivileged.[61]

Without directly addressing the matter of segregation, Graham's words revealed a new approach toward racial issues in 1938. The mere fact that he spoke at a gathering inclusive of blacks and whites to discuss regional issues, even racial issues, marked a positive distinction from the 1900 lily-white Montgomery meeting where whites set an agenda that blacks were expected to blindly follow at their detriment.

In 1938 Graham and a few other white southerners broke from defining the South as exclusively white, accepting the fact that blacks were an integral part of the southern economy. If the region were ever to build a New South of industrial development and national economic participation, all southerners had to share equally in its making.

Presenting Justice Black with the Thomas Jefferson Award, John Temple Graves II, columnist for the *Birmingham Age-Herald,* spoke briefly about Black's work as a progressive before his appointment to the Supreme Court. He summed up Black's life as the "small town boy [who] made good" and related how Black, when president of Alabama's Prison Reform Association, had played an instrumental part in preventing convicts from working in coal mines; how Black had believed in a philosophy of justice for all, as evident in his career as legislator and jurist; and how Black had sponsored a bill limiting hours of work before Congress passed the National Recovery Act.

Black, in the closing session, pursued the theme that Graham had hinted at as the conference opened. He relied on Jefferson's philosophy and the problems reviewed in the NEC *Report,* raising yet more questions about how the South should resolve them, questions that had been discussed at various sessions during the Conference. Black offered the approach that he thought Jefferson would have taken: The Conference should stress the importance of owning land and the importance of all people sharing equally in the distribution of wealth. He contended that this view should form the centerpiece of SCHW philosophy.[62]

The idealism of which Graham, Eleanor Roosevelt, and Justice Black spoke became evident in various Conference resolutions that addressed problems identified in the NEC *Report*—farm tenancy, constitutional rights, education, labor relations and unemployment, prison reform, housing, suffrage, race relations, child labor, women wage earners, freight rate differentials, and health. Civil liberties, major concerns of Joseph Gelders and H. C. Nixon, became the focus of resolutions that dealt with the Dies Committee and the Scottsboro cases. The Dies Committee, a congressional committee established earlier in 1938 and headed by the Texas Democrat Martin Dies, investigated federal employees suspected of subversive activities or disloyalty to the government. It launched one of its first attacks against Roosevelt and his administration. The Scottsboro cases involved nine black youths who were convicted of raping two white women in northern Alabama in 1931. Since they were hastily and unjustly tried and convicted in Scottsboro, Alabama, their cases gained national attention. In the 1930s only four of the youths saw freedom.

The SCHW protested the procedures of the Dies Committee, resolving that it condemned its obvious use of congressional investigatory power to discredit the Roosevelt administration. In regard to the Scottsboro cases the Southern Conference asked Alabama Governor Bibb Graves to exercise the power of executive clemency to free the remaining five Scottsboro prisoners.[63] Governor Graves ignored the plea, but eventually all of the "Scottsboro boys" were released.

At the general session on November 23 the director of the University of North Carolina Press, W. T. Couch, chairman of the committee for a permanent organization, presented the group with a plan to establish the Southern Conference for Human Welfare as a permanent southern institution. In adopting the committee's proposal by Couch, SCHW established six major objectives, stated that the Conference would meet annually, designated the general officers, and set as the governing bodies the southern council and executive board.[64]

Having established a new organization, the group elected officers. The general officers included honorary president, Louise Charlton; president, Frank Graham; secretary, Mollie Dowd, board member of the Women's Trade Union League, Birmingham; executive secretary, H. C. Nixon; and treasurer, Clark Foreman. General officers also included fifteen vice-chairs, one from each southern state and two from the South at large; one hundred twenty members made up the southern council, which consisted of the twenty general officers and one hundred representatives. Within this group seven members came from each southern state and nine members from the South at large.[65]

The SCHW proved once again that southerners still wanted to handle their own problems, but in 1938 this group of liberals suggested that a fundamental change in attitude had occurred. People in SCHW were willing to accept criticism from outside sources such as the NEC and to challenge the status quo concerning the status of blacks. Indeed, the SCHW based its reason for being on the principle of equality for *all*. Its members advocated abolishing racial discrimination, going so far as to adopt a resolution endorsing the first Congress of Mexican and Spanish-American Peoples of the United States scheduled for March 24–26, 1939, in Albuquerque, New Mexico.[66] When the SCHW spoke of a New South, it was not in reference to the old term embracing white supremacy that had been thrown around since the nineteenth century; this *New* South meant a racially and politically democratic South.

In 1938 the South witnessed the origin of an unprecedented and determined effort by its own inhabitants to rectify wrongs for which they held the myth of the New South responsible. So uncharacteristic for its time were its makeup and its attitudes that this group of southerners brought national attention to its effort to improve the American South. When participants in the Southern Conference for Human Welfare used the term New South in 1938, for them it meant a southern society free of racial discrimination as instrumental to the solution of southern economic, political, and social problems.

2

How the Southern Conference Movement Operated

Administration, Finances, Membership, and Literature

Delegates to the 1938 conference influenced SCHW's liberal path. They included: Louise O. Charlton, Joseph Gelders, H. C. Nixon, Frank Porter Graham, Clark Foreman, Lucy Randolph Mason, Virginia Durr, Mark Ethridge, Barry Bingham, William Mitch, president of the Alabama Industrial Union Council, a part of the Congress of Industrial Organizations (CIO); Myles Horton and James A. Dombrowski of the Highlander Folk School of Monteagle, Tennessee; and H. L. Mitchell of the Southern Tenant Farmers Union. They became the administrators, supporters, or even opponents as the organization launched its program to transform the South.

Shortly after the November 1938 conference, Mark Ethridge and Barry Bingham called for a small group of SCHW members to meet in late December to propose a program on which Congress would introduce legislation in answer to several of the issues identified in the NEC *Report* on which SCHW was founded. Ethridge reasoned that such legislation would have a greater chance of passage if initiated by southerners. The proposal never materialized because so many of the persons Ethridge and Bingham had in mind for the meeting were members of numerous organizations and had too many other responsibilities to attend a special session.[1] In many instances SCHW members' active participation in other organizations proved beneficial in that SCHW could know firsthand how other groups responded to certain issues, but frequently SCHW work went neglected owing to the limited time of highly active members.

Addressing a large array of southern problems and failing to decide about future meetings added to SCHW's unattended work. Leaders overlooked almost no segment of the southern population; they even included a place for a youth council. At the November 1938 conference Howard Lee, Helen Fuller, a lawyer in Alabama, Myles Horton, and Eleanor Roosevelt were the main speakers for the session on youth problems. This section submitted a resolution for the formation of an SCHW youth council and summarized programs and principles that it endorsed. SCHW's youth service administration would resemble the National Youth Administration and Civilian Conservation Corps that the New Deal had provided. The youth panel concerned itself with the needs of rural and urban youth for vocational and technical training in schools and colleges, which would offset unemployment. The Council of Young Southerners (CYS), organized in December 1938 with Howard Lee as executive secretary, helped to coordinate youth meetings in various southern states and laid the groundwork for the formation of youth councils and cooperating youth organizations in the South. The group favored student cooperatives and long-term loans at low interest rates for farm youth.[2]

Initially, SCHW decided on annual membership meetings, and Clark Foreman reminded Graham in July 1939 that plans should begin for the

The Council of Young Southerners later became the League of Young Southerners. Top row, left to right: unidentified person, Mike Ross, unidentified person, James Dombrowski; bottom row: unidentified person, Junius Scales, Malcolm "Tex" Dobbs, James E. Jackson. Courtesy of Marge Frantz, Joseph Gelders's daughter.

meeting that year. Foreman suggested that the organization could be more successful if it focused the scope of its work more narrowly. He considered voting and political control of paramount importance and "Democracy in the South" as the theme. Annoyed and overwhelmed by the several small meetings under SCHW auspices in Birmingham, Foreman sought to limit the time in which state groups would present information on various problematic conditions. Such a well-organized meeting would still allow ample time for a few small groups to discuss other issues. Considering the negative press reaction to the 1938 conference, he also suggested having the next membership meeting in Chattanooga, New Orleans, or Louisville, cities where journalists might be more sympathetic to SCHW causes.[3] The support of liberal newspaper editors could prove favorable for SCHW's future.

While Foreman focused on the theme and meeting format for a second conference, George Stoney in mid-September discussed coordination with Birmingham members including Judges Louise O. Charlton and Virginia Henry Mayfield, and Mollie Dowd. The women agreed to handle arrangements as they had in 1938 despite the fact of SCHW's negative press since the Birmingham meeting. Charlton wanted Birmingham as the headquarters again, but in the end the executive council hired Howard Lee as coordinator. In October 1939 the executive council also chose Chattanooga as the site for the meeting, hoping that much of the negative reaction about interracial cooperation and the inclusion of known Communists would not surround it. The 1938 meeting gained some negative reactions in regard to integrated seating. George C. Stoney reported that "even *Earl Browder* [secretary of Communist party USA] spoke there without protest!"[4]

A leadership vacancy gave the executive council yet another task. Since H. C. Nixon had returned to full-time teaching during the summer of 1939, the council agreed with an SCHW committee headed by Graham to replace Nixon with Howard Lee. The Conference's financial status dictated special interest in a person who would work well at fund raising. Eleanor Roosevelt had shown great interest in the Council of Young Southerners and thereby had introduced Lee to numerous wealthy people who had contributed money to the CYS. Lee accepted SCHW's offer but worried about what Eleanor Roosevelt and Helen Fuller would think since he had not resigned as CYS's executive secretary. With wider responsibility for seeking financial contributions, Lee feared approaching some of the same people twice, thereby decreasing his chances in many instances for getting contributions for both groups.[5]

As it turned out, financial shortcomings forced SCHW to forgo its planned 1939 membership meeting. It announced, however, that its second conference would take place in April 1940, which established a lasting pattern of biennial gatherings.

As SCHW developed into a more recognizable organization, alleged Communist charges mounted, dating back to 1938. Charges singled out individuals who held official positions in the organization; conservative opponents identified Joseph Gelders and Howard Lee as Communists or fellow travelers. Present-day scholars reveal that Gelders and Lee indeed belonged to the Communist party USA, but in 1938 SCHW officials did not take the charges very seriously, hoping that by its 1940 meeting the accusations would have subsided. When the 1940 conference was just a few months away, they worried about what impact these charges might have. The charges could lead to the SCHW being denied use of the city auditorium in Chattanooga, or stir up antagonisms for conservative patri- otic groups. The greatest harm might come by driving off interested per- sons, the very people the organization had been trying to reach with its numerous resolutions directed at the various groups that had attended its first meeting.

The possible damage of one local paper concerned SCHW officers as they worried about the chance that false reports might spread nationally, and thus cause great harm. Alarmed about "this unwarranted and ill founded" red-baiting, Barry Bingham advised:

> There is no use for the Southern Conference to continue to operate merely to influence its own little group of people already convinced on its liberal prin- ciples. If we are to be effective at all we must touch the minds of many other Southerners who do not class themselves as liberals, conservatives or any- thing else. I am afraid that all this red baiting by the [*Chattanooga*] *Free Press* may serve to close many minds against us, so that it will be impossible for us to get our message over to the general public.[6]

Bingham grew apprehensive enough about the bad publicity the *Free Press* might give SCHW's scheduled April 1940 meeting that he suggested "barring reporters" from attending. Liberalism reigned over hypocrisy, though, as the protectors of democracy decided that anyone who paid the one-dollar registration fee could attend.[7]

If the purpose of the attacks had been to force SCHW to consider changing its plan for its second meeting in Chattanooga, the scheme worked as such suggestions came from some of the officers. Mason sug- gested moving the conference to Louisville; Bingham suggested Nash- ville. Still others interpreted the attacks as perhaps coming from such persons as "Francis Miller's element, which is somewhere to the right of center," who wished that SCHW would disappear from the scene alto- gether so that "there can be a Southwide 'Southern Policy Association.' " Thus, SCHW had to contend with rival forces within its own organization and vie for power and money with other groups. Possibly the opposition wanted to "smear" Eleanor Roosevelt, who had given symbolic support to SCHW's interracial effort.[8]

In late 1940 some SCHW leaders still detected trouble in the organiza- tion. Barry Bingham wrote Virginia Durr, "I certainly agree with you that the Conference seems to be dying on the vine. I was afraid this would happen as soon as Frank Graham stepped out as chairman, but of course he could not keep up the job forever." Graham's responsibilities as president of the University of North Carolina demanded his full attention, but the red-baiting of SCHW had helped him no doubt in deciding not to be SCHW's major leader. Bingham thought SCHW too important and hoped to talk with Graham for ways to keep it alive, for Graham did not sever completely his ties with the South's leading liberal organization. Bingham shared his views with Durr, saying "there were certainly some useful elements in the Conference, and it seems a shame to allow them to be swallowed up by the special interests that have taken over control of the organization."[9] While Bingham referred to the alleged Communist infiltrators, SCHW's financial status also caused enthusiasm to wane among members. Red-baiting and financial constraints did not necessarily go hand in hand; many supporters who could work around the charges of communism could never accept SCHW's racial policy.

SCHW could not expect to dispel allegations of Communist influence as long as it continued to hold integrated meetings. In an effort to prevent a repeat of the Birmingham segregation incident, Howard Lee had an attorney check the laws of Tennessee concerning local segregation ordinances. The attorney did not turn up any ordinances, but he did find a code that would allow local agencies, the auditorium commission in Chattanooga, for example, to rule on separate seating arrangements. Lee, therefore, met with the auditorium manager and chairman of the auditorium board to get their permission for SCHW's integrated meeting. In writing to Eleanor Roosevelt to request that she attend and take part in the 1940 conference, Graham thanked her for supporting SCHW "personally, financially, and spiritually," assuring her that all precautions were being taken against "any untoward happenings."[10]

SCHW held its second membership meeting in Chattanooga, April 14–16, 1940, using as its general theme "Democracy in the South." The second meeting, with over a thousand delegates, showed few signs of bad publicity negatively affecting SCHW or that most liberal southerners doubted SCHW's faith in accomplishing its goals. Convinced in the two-year period since 1938 that many regional problems had only intensified, the group identified the same major problems as the 1938 conference with special sessions on the southern youth, meaning of religion in democracy, southern rural life, southern industrial life, and citizenship. Southern economic improvement remained the overall concern, however, as SCHW saw an interconnection among all the issues that prevented it from singling out one to attack. It pointed to the overlaps, saying

Wage and freight differentials still work to prevent the South from assuming its rightful place in the nation's economy. Poverty is widespread and millions are landless. Two-thirds of the Southern people do not vote. The poll tax works to disfranchise the poor in eight Southern states. Almost a whole generation of youth is growing up lacking proper education and without knowing steady work. Mob rule and lynch law still exist. Everywhere we stand in need of better health facilities.

SCHW only made its work more difficult by not being more narrowly focused.

The makeup of the 1940 conference resembled the first. Organized labor constituted a large part of representation with William Green, president of the American Federation of Labor (AFL), endorsing SCHW and making it easier for AFL union members to participate. Farmers came from the Southern Tenant Farmers Union; blacks were represented by leaders from the National Association for the Advancement of Colored People (NAACP), the National Urban League (NUL), and other groups.[11]

The program listed over one hundred sponsors, not all of whom contributed money or necessarily attended the 1940 meeting.[12] To attract as many people as possible, SCHW showed off several prominent members as sponsors including William Green; Roscoe Dunjee, editor, *Oklahoma City Black Dispatch*; John L. Lewis, president of CIO; Arthur Howe, president of Hampton Institute, Virginia; Charles S. Johnson, noted black sociologist, Fisk University; Howard Kester, Fellowship of Southern Christians, Black Mountain, North Carolina; David E. Lilienthal, director of the Tennessee Valley Authority, Knoxville; Ralph McGill, executive editor, *Atlanta Constitution*; John P. Davis of the National Negro Congress; and A. Philip Randolph, president of the Brotherhood of Sleeping Car Porters.[13]

The $1 registration fee continued, but the youth paid its $1 to the Council of Young Southerners, reducing funds that would normally have gone directly into SCHW's treasury. Conference sessions took place at the city auditorium, and the Hotel Patten served as headquarters. Eleanor Roosevelt addressed the "Children in the South" session on April 15, emphasizing children and education as she had in 1938. The conference closed with the presentation of the Thomas Jefferson Award to Will W. Alexander, whom several SCHW members had met through the Southern Policy Committee and various other liberal causes.[14]

Alexander, a former Methodist minister, led an active life promoting the ideals of human welfare and justice for his region. Like many other leaders in SCHW, he had been a prominent figure in the public sphere. When the aftermath of World War I had brought interracial tensions, Alexander, other white leaders, and blacks had created the Commission on Interracial Cooperation (CIC) in Atlanta. Conservative whites, however, soon convinced CIC's founders that the key to their organization's acceptance in the South depended on a deliberate avoidance of attempts to end segregation. Within this limitation, Alexander, who served as CIC executive director for twenty-five years, sought in daily experiences (succeeding in isolated instances) to break through barriers established by white supremacists.

Clark Foreman's work with CIC as secretary of the Georgia chapter brought him and Alexander together for the first time; their mutual concern for racial problems tied them to eventual lifelong efforts. In 1931 Alexander, while still executive director of CIC, helped in the initial stages of the founding of Dillard University, which opened its doors in 1935, by acting as its president. He served as trustee of the Julius Rosenwald Fund between 1930 and 1948, combining that role with that of vice-president from 1940 to 1948, an endeavor that allowed him closer contact with his close friend, Charles S. Johnson, its director of race relations from 1943 to 1947.

Alexander combined efforts in race relations with his concern for underprivileged groups. He brought attention to the plight of southern tenant farmers by writing with Charles S. Johnson and the Rosenwald Fund's president, Edwin Embree, *The Collapse of Cotton Tenancy* (1935) in which the authors criticized the Washington bureaucracy for neglecting displaced farmers in the national recovery programs. Partly because of that criticism, Rexford Tugwell, undersecretary of agriculture and head of the Resettlement Administration, summoned Alexander to Washington as his assistant. Alexander accepted the position in 1935 and succeeded Tugwell when he resigned in 1936 as head of the New Deal agency, which had been renamed the Farm Security Administration.[15] By awarding Alexander its Thomas Jefferson Award, SCHW had taken advantage of an opportunity to applaud a statesman well known for his efforts in southern race relations.

Alexander's selection for the Thomas Jefferson Award at the 1940 conference made clear which issues SCHW deemed more important. It centered attention on education, voter registration, and eliminating the poll tax and adopted virtually the same resolutions in 1940 as it had in 1938. The one exception, an antiwar resolution, opposed the appropriation of money for armaments to any belligerent of World War II, at the expense of funds deemed necessary for the solution of domestic problems. In this regard SCHW placed itself in the isolationist camp, wanting to maintain American neutrality, though within the next several months France would fall to Hitler's Nazism. SCHW stepped in tune with many Americans who opposed the United States becoming involved in the war until after the Japanese attack on Pearl Harbor in 1941.[16]

Southern liberals remained outspoken in the field of organized labor and social legislation in the various states and before the Congress. SCHW remained committed to the belief that workers had a right to bargain collectively and maintained its stand that southern wage standards ought to equal those of the North. All workers deserved equal pay, regardless of race. SCHW proposed that its members and delegates take the responsibility for widespread use of union-made products in their respective communities. Deeming unemployment to be the number one national problem, SCHW hoped that the Works Progress Administration

Will W. Alexander receiving the Thomas Jefferson Award of the SCHW from Frank Porter Graham. Others in the picture are Judge Louise O. Charlton and Representative Maury Maverick of Texas. Courtesy of Archives and Special Collections of the Robert W. Woodruff Library, Atlanta University Center, Atlanta, Georgia.

could carry on its operation for relief to the unemployed and tried to persuade President Roosevelt to call a conference of representatives of industry, labor, and workers for a permanent solution.[17]

SCHW sought relief for farmers, too, who, accordingly, deserved the same protection of the right to organize for improved economic conditions as other workers. It wanted an expansion of the Farm Security Administration program for meeting the needs of a larger number of indigent farmers. The organization, moreover, wanted farmers included in the social-security legislation and called for special provisions for migratory workers within the social-security cases.

The rights for African Americans underscored all the provisions SCHW sought, but it addressed racial issues with a section called "Negro Rights," where the agency advocated passage of antilynching legislation pending in Congress. When most other organizations no longer mentioned the youths in the Scottsboro cases, SCHW, with faith that the youths were innocent, requested the Alabama Board of Pardons to grant freedom to the defendants who, by 1940, had spent nine years in prison. The conference resolved that it was

> cognizant of the special limitations of life imposed upon the Negro people through race discrimination, limited job opportunities, inadequate and unequal school and recreational facilities, [and] call[ed] upon the Southern people to work toward the general equalization of opportunity in all spheres, and toward the development of the friendliest of relations between our two racial groups.

In its resolution on education, SCHW called upon southern states to equalize expenditures for *all* educational facilities. It deferred an outright demand that the South end segregation, choosing instead to condemn all southern organizations and individuals who sought to maintain or attain power and privileges by exploiting racial prejudices. Along the same lines SCHW called for increased tax revenues to go toward improving southern education and the right of teachers to organize. Education, the group believed, was necessary for the solution of its many economic and social problems.[18]

SCHW did not hesitate in 1941, however, to embrace the new direction in race relations as illustrated by the Roosevelt administration, an administration that most SCHW members praised. The organization could find inspiration that its efforts were not futile. Noticing that the Roosevelt administration had reluctantly changed its attitude toward racial discrimination, John P. Davis asked that SCHW commend Roosevelt for Executive Order 8802, which sought to curb employment discrimination in government and industry. SCHW endorsed as well H.R. 3994, another measure against discrimination. And, focusing on poor health care in the region, SCHW called on Congress to enact a bill that recommended provisions for adequate medical and health facilities in the South. It even recommended "Birth Spacing Clinical Service" in public health programs.[19]

SCHW urged all its members and delegates to participate in political affairs of their respective localities and to encourage neighbors, fellow workers, and friends to do the same. It pointed up the poll tax, the payment for voting, as an "undemocratic restriction on the franchise" and encouraged its Civil Rights Committee, set up in 1938, in its efforts against that egregious affront to democracy.[20]

Eventually, SCHW followed its 1938 pattern of the separate CRC in an effort to abolish the poll tax, neglecting the problem of registration for African Americans, the exclusive white primaries, and increased police brutality against blacks. The literary figure and outspoken, southern white liberal Lillian Smith, editor of the *North Georgia Review* and a newly elected SCHW board member in 1942, recommended that SCHW maintain at least twelve committees that functioned throughout the year. Smith believed that a total of 120 to 150 southerners on these committees could "make the conference one of the most significant folk movements active in the world today."[21] SCHW leaders discussed her ideas of instituting various committees, each representative of an issue of importance to the Conference. For example, it established a committee to fight against racial discrimination, one to fight against lynching, and even one to address the question of academic freedom. In actuality SCHW gave priority to the national anti-poll-tax committee, the civil liberties committee, and the committee on discrimination in voter registration, electing Atlanta University President Rufus Clement as its chair. It left the other new committees' development for a later time.[22]

Smith had suggested various topics that SCHW had addressed since 1938. Her ideas for a publications committee eventually would be instituted, though not as a committee, but in the creation of *Southern Patriot* by the executive board in the fall of 1942. This booklet would be a process of educating the southern masses on labor, agriculture, and child welfare. She called, too, for creative acts in the South, a committee to promote general interest in music, painting, sculpture, writing, and drama, primarily works that would stress folk art. Admittedly, Smith viewed this committee and the one on publications as her "two pets," tremendous fun to work with. SCHW, however, never adopted the recommendations on southern creativity.[23]

If SCHW found it difficult to focus on a single issue or to maintain the committees to focus attention, it was just as unsettled on its central office location. In 1940 its board thought the headquarters should remain in Birmingham despite objections from a few SCHW members because of the adverse response to integrated seating there in 1938. Those few recommended that any southern city would probably be better than Birmingham. Reacting in part to such sentiments, the board chose Chattanooga until the report of 1940 biennial proceedings could be organized and published. Yet, the 1940 meeting had its share of adverse reaction as Dorothy Stafford resigned her position on the executive committee solely because of the ridicule she suffered as a result of Knoxville newspapers linking her name with labor and African-American representation on the committee.[24]

At an October 1941 meeting the SCHW board decided that the 1942 biennial conference should be held in Nashville and authorized that Nashville would become the location of the SCHW's central office. Such a move set the pattern that wherever the membership met so followed the central office—Birmingham in 1938, Chattanooga in 1940, and Nashville in 1942. Nashville, however, remained the location of the central office until 1946, since the biennial meeting in 1944 would be skipped because of shortages created by World War II. The 1946 meeting was in New Orleans, and SCHW transferred headquarters there.[25]

In 1941 SCHW's administration underwent several changes, changes that a young organization might seek to avoid. The mounting opposition to its basic program called for at least a steady leadership. Upon Graham's resignation, John Thompson served a short interim as president just before Foreman's election. Alton Lawrence replaced Howard Lee as executive secretary for a short time as well. John P. Davis, who had been elected one of the Southern Council's members at large in 1938, now won election along with William Mitch and Virginia Durr as one of the vice-chairpersons during Thompson's interim as president. Under Foreman's presidency Roscoe Dunjee served as vice-chair along with Durr, Mitch, George Googe, Paul B. Kern, and Hollis V. Reid.[26]

Organized labor had always constituted one of the strongest segments of support for the Southern Conference. Its relationship with SCHW could have gone in a new direction, however, when Alton Lawrence returned to union work in 1941. He had taken a leave from the CIO in 1940 to replace Howard Lee as SCHW executive secretary. When Lawrence became an organizer for the International Union of Mine, Mill, and Smelter Workers, the Conference board asked Helen Fuller to take his place. Fuller declined, leaving only James Dombrowski, whom Lawrence had recommended as a candidate. At the time, Dombrowski was a member of the American Federation of Teachers, an affiliation that would continue the Conference's alliance with organized labor.[27] Better yet, he promised to dedicate substantial time and energy to the crucial job of fund raising.

Several board members, including Virginia Durr, knew Dombrowski from his previous associations with SCHW and the Highlander Folk School at Monteagle, Tennessee. They especially liked his deep concern for the interests of organized labor.[28] Durr had met Dombrowski during a visit to Highlander while he was chair. One of his major responsibilities at Highlander involved attending meetings and reporting on labor relations around Tennessee, a capacity that brought him into contact with several members of the Southern Conference.[29]

Though SCHW was not a religious organization, many of its leaders had strong religious convictions. They expressed the need to get more southern church members actively involved in SCHW's program. Dombrowski reinforced religion as a foundation of the SCHW's social reform. A native of Tampa, Florida, he had graduated in 1923 from Atlanta's Emory University. In 1926–27 he had served as chaplain at the University of California at Berkeley. In 1935 he received a D.D. degree from the Union Theological Seminary at Harvard, where he worked as an assistant in the Department of Christian Ethics; he earned a Ph.D. in philosophy from Columbia University in 1936. During his first year at Highlander, Columbia University Press published his dissertation, *The Early Days of Socialism in America*, in which Dombrowski describes nineteenth-century religious leaders who were active social reformers and whose examples illuminated twentieth-century phenomena.[30]

The Highlander Folk School, which like the Southern Conference included many religious leaders, had provided an outlet for Dombrowski's combined interest in religion and social reform. Founded in 1932 by Myles Horton of Tennessee and Don West of Georgia, the school became a regional center for worker education, holding workshops and weekend conferences on subjects ranging from politics to organizing unions. One of the few southern places that practiced racial integration during the 1930s, Highlander became a haven for southern liberals and counted Conference supporters such as Eleanor Roosevelt and Frank Graham among its sponsors. Eleanor Roosevelt visited Highlander occasionally and used her influence to attract other prominent figures there. Highlander's liberal influence continued through the 1960s.[31]

Although a majority of the Conference board favored Dombrowski's appointment, Clark Foreman revealed later that Dombrowski's Polish name initially caused him misgivings. Foreman overcame this fear when he realized that Dombrowski had Eleanor Roosevelt's support and that no better candidate would accept such a difficult job for which payment was uncertain. By the 1942 biennial Foreman praised Dombrowski because he said, "I am sure that his money-raising ability has tided us over a serious juncture."[32] Dombrowski even reported a favorable financial picture since his joining the Conference.[33]

With Dombrowski's hiring, plans for the 1942 meeting set for late spring in Nashville became more definite. The organization's Washington Committee contacted Eleanor Roosevelt, a favorite sponsor, to assure that the Roosevelt administration would continue its support with at least another encouraging letter from FDR. The First Lady promised again to take part in discussions and even to present the Thomas Jefferson Award. She, moreover, encouraged persons from her husband's administration to join her at the meeting. Organizational leaders figured that the greater the attendance from Washington and the Northeast the better its efforts would be at fund raising.

During Dombrowski's first month as secretary his activities consisted of work on the 1942 conference, getting speakers, arranging the program, and raising funds. He reserved April 19–21, the only available dates for Nashville's War Memorial Auditorium, as the dates for the meeting. Early on Dombrowski reported having received $1600 and expected other funds, and he sent board members a tentative program and call, asking for suggestions and criticisms.[34] Since the board had decided to move its central office from Chattanooga to Nashville, Dombrowski had, in addition to making arrangements for the conference, the responsibility of transferring office files and materials.[35]

At the Nashville gathering which took place according to Dombrowski's schedule, the Conference elected officers at the business session on the last day. These officials included honorary chairs Louise O. Charlton and Frank Graham, and Homer P. Rainey as the new president;

Left to right: Jacob Potofsky, Ruth Field (wife of Marshall Field), Homer Rainey, Mary Warburg (wife of Edward M. M. Warburg), Clark Foreman, and R. J. Thomas attend a Conference on Fair Employment Practices at the Hotel Commodore in New York City, September 23, 1945, under the auspices of SCHW. Courtesy of Archives and Special Collections, Robert W. Woodruff Library, Atlanta University Center, Atlanta, Georgia.

Roscoe Dunjee, Virginia Durr, Clark Foreman, Bishop Paul B. Kern, William Mitch, and Hollis V. Reid as the vice-chairs; Alva W. Taylor became the new secretary/treasurer, and Dombrowski remained the executive secretary. The executive board numbered eighteen persons and, like the membership, African Americans constituted one-third. By April 1943 SCHW increased its board to thirty-six, counting twelve African-American members. Charlotte Hawkins Brown, president of Palmer Institute in Sedalia, North Carolina, became a member of the board in 1943. Brown, John P. Davis, Mary McLeod Bethune, Charles S. Johnson, Rufus Clement, F. D. Patterson, and Ira DeA. Reid represented the strongest of black supporters.[36]

In other matters of business in Nashville the Southern Conference adopted a new set of bylaws that declared the organization nonprofit, established the board as the policy body of the group instead of the southern council, which had been created in 1938, and declared that, with the exception of the executive secretary, board members would continue to serve without compensation. These new bylaws reaffirmed that any person could become a member of SCHW "EXCEPT THAT no person who either advocates the overthrow of the government of the United States by force or violence or who is a member of an organization which advocates the overthrow of the government of the United States, shall be eligible for membership." This exclusionary measure aimed at dismissing red-baiting from SCHW's opposition, but by excluding only one group it left open the way for Klansmen, for example, to join. This seemed highly unlikely, however, when even moderates who earlier had actively participated in the Conference had backed off from it by 1941. The executive board, upon notice from any SCHW member, could determine if a person should be denied membership, or be expelled if already a member, but no such expulsion ever occurred. Another change in the bylaws raised annual membership dues from $1 to $2. To help finances, the *Proceedings* were sold for 25 cents each.[37]

Between 1946 and 1948 SCHW made a dramatic transition, establishing the Southern Conference Educational Fund as its nonprofit unit to allow for SCHW's political activism.[38] A single-issue organization, SCEF differed from SCHW by focusing its attention on integration. It viewed the poll tax and poor education as direct consequences of segregation and campaigned against the former and for the latter in the *Southern Patriot*. Red-baiters forced SCEF's attention on communism as they had with SCHW so that in the 1950s the Senate Subcommittee on Internal Security became to SCEF what the Dies Committee or HUAC had been to SCHW.

During the 1950s SCEF continued to build on its Southern Conference for Human Welfare foundation. The function of SCEF's advisory committee, which the group established in 1957, became an example. The committee included more than sixty people, all prominent community leaders, all of whom strongly believed in an integrated society and were willing to devote time and energy to make it a reality. SCHW had limited its voting membership to southerners yet realized that it needed to "function as a part of the general progressive movement in the country." Its advisory associates had been, it said, "extremely important . . . as a bridge between our work and the progressive movement generally." Advisory associates for the Educational Fund kept that organization in touch with the broader Civil Rights Movement and its leaders and involved a larger number of people in its daily activities.[39]

SCEF's advisory committee consisted of leading educators, attorneys, physicians, and other professionals. In 1958 the committee grew to more than ninety prominent individuals from southern and border states with a few individuals from as far west as New Mexico, which made the organization appear more national. By this time SCEF's board of directors had grown to more than seventy-five people, and it also had a special Medical

Advisory Committee, which consisted exclusively of physicians, a few of whom resided as far west as Arizona. The advisory committee did not meet officially as did the SCEF board; it simply permitted prominent persons to show their moral support for the Fund. Some members of the advisory committee served on the SCEF board; the board urged others to take part in routine organizational business.[40]

SCEF gained new supporters, but it lost old-guard soldiers like *Black Dispatch* editor Roscoe Dunjee, who resigned from the board because of a serious heart condition in 1958. Another staunch Fund supporter, Charlotte Hawkins Brown, only a year younger than Dunjee and who also had health problems, also had been forced to give up various organizational activities. But the Fund kept its former supporters informed of its work and even ran a story on Brown, which prompted the new Palmer Memorial Institute President, Wilhelmina Crosson, to tell SCEF officers that the story brought "such delight to a noble woman." SCEF's monthly publication, the *Southern Patriot*, carried the article on Brown, and coincidentally Crosson read it to her only a few days before her death.[41]

In 1958 SCEF's officers still included Williams as president and Dombrowski as executive director; both had served in these positions since the organization's founding. Noticeably, in the late 1950s, for the first time in SCEF's history, blacks held a larger share of administrative positions. All of the organization's vice-presidents were African Americans: Herman H. Long, Bishop Edgar A. Love, and Modjeska M. Simkins. The organization had a new secretary, James L. Hupp; an assistant secretary, Mrs. Fred Zenzel; and treasurer, Herman L. Mildo. But not all were black: The Fund had hired Anne and Carl Braden in 1957 as field directors because the two white liberals could not find employment after the ordeal that followed their purchasing a house for a black couple to integrate an area in Louisville in 1954.[42]

Despite these developments, some thought that changes were in order, that aging officials stood in the way of much-needed younger supporters. Williams believed in 1958 that one person should not hold the position for such a long time and affirmed that it was time for someone else to serve as president. SCEF, he was convinced, would be strengthened by change. He offered to resign as president, preferring to serve on the board, which would keep him in close association with Dombrowski. But that was not to be at the time. Williams continued to serve as SCEF's president until 1961, despite the fact that he was diagnosed as a cancer patient in 1959.[43] SCEF eventually got new officers in the 1960s. After Williams's resignation in 1961, SCEF's presidents included black leaders. Bishop Edgar A. Love, the first black president, served only one year because of medical problems and his obligations to other groups. After his 1961–1962 term, Fred Shuttlesworth succeeded him for one year.[44]

With the periodic persistence of conservative criticism, SCHW had the same problem with finances, only the latter problem plagued the Conference more often and hampered operations during times when there were no attacks. Occasionally, SCHW subgroups, such as the Council of Young Southerners, attempted to absorb some of the financial difficulties.[45]

SCHW's precarious finances left its leaders with a formidable task. Clark Foreman, its first treasurer, reported at an October 1939 council meeting that between December 1938 and August 1939 donations had come to less than $1,000. The largest contributor, Robert Marshall, gave $500, with the remainder coming from a few other individuals; Robert F. Hall's buying 200 copies of the 1938 SCHW proceedings; and the *Virginia Quarterly Review*'s purchase of SCHW's mailing list. After paying H. C. Nixon, former Conference executive secretary, and George C. Stoney for expenses incurred during his tour of the South in August 1939, the organization's balance was a mere $28.05.[46] Early in 1940 Lucy Randolph Mason compiled a list of contributors inclusive of Foreman's October 1939 report; her list totaled $2,250. The Amalgamated Clothing Workers of America, second largest contributor to Robert Marshall, gave $300, which Mason called "glorious news." Taking this contribution to imply that more would be forthcoming from organized labor, she said "that will mean everything to the textile union men in the South. I think we are beginning to move." Eleven persons gave $100, including Eleanor Roosevelt, Barry Bingham, and Lowell Mellett.[47]

Since SCHW had difficulties obtaining contributions, Howard Lee began procedures in January 1940 to have the organization incorporated in the state of Tennessee. His actions began the first steps to gain for SCHW tax-exempt status from the U.S. Department of the Treasury. SCHW leaders reasoned that wealthy individuals and foundations might be inclined to give more if they could get tax deductions for contributions, and letters from the public wishing SCHW success further convinced them of this line of thinking.[48]

SCHW funds were still close to nothing after the 1940 meeting. The Conference owed more than $500, not including the salary of Howard Lee. To raise a little money, Lee suggested that Conference members and delegates pay 10 cents each for the printed report of the meeting, convinced that they would not mind if the organization explained that it needed the money to pay for the printing of the pamphlet.[49] In other matters of finances, SCHW's executive board placed the financial responsibility of the Civil Rights Committee on SCHW's treasurer, Clark Foreman, and specified that separate accounts would be set up for the two (CRC and SCHW). The SCHW treasurer, the president, or the CRC chairman, Maury Maverick, would approve cash disbursements. Funding interfered with the CRC work as it did for SCHW. Maverick agreed to raise as much money for CRC as he could, and Joseph Gelders spent a lot of time asking for contributions.[50]

In mid-1940 SCHW and CRC had only $200 on hand while liabilities were at $550, the largest part of which amounted to salaries owed

Howard Lee and Joseph Gelders. Failure to keep separate treasuries for SCHW and CRC created confusion. CRC owed over $350 to SCHW's general funds. Between August and December 1940 SCHW took in over $1,200, but by February 1941 had to borrow more than $100 to pay off obligations.[51] Later in 1941 financial difficulty warranted that the central office in Chattanooga operate without a phone. For the remainder of that year SCHW operated at a deficit.[52]

Problems of finance created interruptions in officers fulfilling their obligations. Howard Lee took a temporary leave of absence in June 1941, but when Alton Lawrence (the same person for whom Graham stood bond to free from jail in 1934 during the textile strike in North Carolina) questioned Clark Foreman, Frank Graham's successor as president, as to whether the names of Lee and Gelders should be left on the organization's stationery, Foreman advised Lawrence to leave the names off. Lawrence did not feel justified in dropping Lee's name because as he understood it, Lee was executive secretary on leave until he resigned or the executive board fired him. Lee had sacrificed for SCHW in that he was not eating properly and got little exercise, oftentimes working until midnight. Perhaps his inattention to himself resulted from a lack of funds, which was caused by SCHW's inability to pay him. Foreman blamed Lee and Gelders for Conference shortcomings, and his removal of their names from the stationery did not help matters. As of August 2, 1941 SCHW owed Lee $221.36 for back salaries and Gelders $1,470, while the organization had only $1,032.90 on hand. Lee resigned at the August 1941 board meeting.[53] In September 1941 SCHW had not settled its debt to Gelders. Having lost his job at the University of Alabama for alleged Communist affiliation, Gelders was compelled to ask for his pay because creditors were demanding payments. He was not paid since SCHW still operated at a deficit.[54]

SCHW had developed no systematic method of keeping track of addresses and names of financial supporters, which was illogical since it survived largely on contributions. Mason claimed in 1940 that SCHW had 7,000 members, but funds did not bear this out.[55]

By 1941 SCHW had begun to recognize the need for better organization. Rufus Clement, in particular, observed that its general work and its committees should be continued under a more direct control by the board. Aware that one of SCHW's major problems had been finances, Clement suggested that contributions and other money solicited and received through the central office and treasurer be spent only after authorization from the board in accordance with an adopted budget.[56]

Partly to raise funds for the organization, but mainly to stimulate actions on a smaller scale and to get more accomplished, SCHW outlined plans for state affiliates. It was hoped that state affiliates would attract new members, and that individuals who might be unable to attend biennial conferences could participate within respective states. To set up a state affiliate a temporary chair, preferably a prominent progressive leader, would solicit key people to attend an initial meeting at which temporary organizing officers would be elected to serve until a sufficient number had been reached and permanent officers for the state could be elected. State affiliates, also called committees, were to pay particular attention to broad geographical state representation, especially from rural areas and, to provide for effective work, state committees were urged to have a fulltime executive. SCHW advised state committees on how to raise funds and recommended that a minimum budget of $10,000 per year would suffice to run a state office. The parent organization urged affiliates to begin with a volunteer staff if sufficient funds could not be raised.[57]

The first two state committees, Georgia and Virginia (Georgia established in 1941 and Virginia in 1942), addressed the same issues as the parent organization.[58] During the course of the SCHW's history, affiliates would include all thirteen southern states, plus a Washington, D.C., committee and a New York committee. Each committee usually took on a special project, though they all helped the parent organization carry out its functions. New York, for instance, was established specifically to raise funds, and the Washington committee became a central part of efforts to abolish the poll tax.[59]

State committees may have improved SCHW's outreach to southerners, but the central organization had to carry its own financial burden. Between 1942 and 1945, its finances would improve as a direct result of the thrifty management of a new executive secretary, James Anderson Dombrowski, and larger contributions from organized labor, particularly the CIO.

To raise money Dombrowski sent out letters that used the theme, in keeping with SCHW's ultimate aim, "The South's Part in Winning the War for Democracy," in his appeal to foundations to provide funds for the 1942 conference. In a typical letter, like the one to Gardner Jackson of the Robert Marshall Fund, Dombrowski placed special emphasis on SCHW's efforts at bringing organized labor and other liberal groups together in the South. He linked SCHW to American involvement in World War II, saying, "No doubt you will agree that there is nothing more important from the standpoint of winning the war than to secure the whole hearted support of labor." An enclosed memorandum outlined SCHW plans and purposes, identified its outstanding leaders, showed its support from the Roosevelt administration and local spokesmen, and emphasized its interracial makeup.[60] And, explaining that a few foundations had agreed to match $2,500 contributions from other foundations, Dombrowski requested $2,500 from the Rosenwald Fund. Since 1941 had ended with SCHW in a serious financial strait, Dombrowski used this scheme to assure getting the full $2,500.[61]

Securing support was not an easy undertaking since SCHW had not yet obtained tax-exempt status from the federal government and still had difficulty persuading foundations and individuals to contribute. The

Marshall Field Foundation, one of the first foundations Dombrowski had appealed to for funds for the March 1942 Conference, particularly liked the organization's special interest in race relations. But money from the Field Foundation could be granted only to tax-exempt organizations. Having ties with Myles Horton and the Highlander Folk School, which presumably had tax-exempt status, Dombrowski had approached Horton about his receiving SCHW funds and later releasing the money to the Southern Conference. When Horton did not agree to this plan, Dombrowski correctly acknowledged that "it is doubtful if that arrangement would satisfy the legal stipulations involved." Dombrowski, perhaps growing weary of working so hard to get so little in way of funds for SCHW, had been willing to take extreme measures to obtain the Field grant but wanted no sign of his suggested underhandedness historically recorded. He added a note to Foreman at the end of his March 25 letter in which he discussed the intended arrangement with Horton, instructing Foreman to destroy the letter. Foreman disagreed with his suggestion and replied that

> We should have our records clear. . . . In this connection, I did not destroy the letter which you wrote about the Highlander Folk School, as I do not think that we can afford to destroy our files. As a public organization, incorporated as an educational institution, we should have everything open and above board at all times, and ready for any investigation that anybody wants to make. This is also another reason for keeping our financial accounts scrupulously straight so that they can never be successfully challenged.[62]

Dombrowski followed Foreman's advice about SCHW records, and no signs of tampering with them appeared at later dates.

Dombrowski and Louis Weiss from the Field Foundation found a solution for SCHW to receive the grant when they agreed to treat it as a loan, pending acquisition of tax-exempt status, at which time the loan obligation would be canceled. The Conference acted in March 1942 on the procedure for tax exemption by filing application for its charter of incorporation in Tennessee, specifically naming Nashville as the site of its central office, but the ruling from the Treasury Department granting tax exemption did not come until October.[63]

At the end of 1942 the four-year-old SCHW had more to show in terms of achievement for that year alone than for the previous three years combined. The executive secretary outlined those outstanding accomplishments in applying to the Marshall Fund for $8,000. In his request, Dombrowski emphasized the interracial makeup of the Conference and the importance of the support it received from organized labor, without which one of the more important elements for developing a mass base for the spread of civil liberties would be lost.[64]

The financial situation of SCHW was in good standing according to the financial report at the August 30, 1942, board meeting. Until then the

Southern Conference had received over $11,000 and spent just over $8,000, leaving the organization with the largest amount of cash on hand since its founding. At the end of 1942 the Conference still had surplus money. It had received $10,000 in funds from foundations, and individual contributions and membership came to over $4,500. It allocated the largest portion of the funds for the year to special campaigns on civil liberties and win-the-war meetings, and the smallest sum went toward the biennial Jefferson Awards.[65]

SCHW had advanced considerably by having Dombrowski to better manage finances, and the organization was to be commended for the number and scope of projects attempted with such meager funds. The organization took on tasks of greater scope than any southern group had ever attempted.

In 1943 the Conference continued the strategy that had brought it accomplishments and status. This momentum was maintained largely through correspondence since wartime difficulties prevented a full board meeting that spring.[66] The 1943 agenda included adding an administrative assistant to the Nashville staff and an office secretary. Because this enlargement of office staff would require an increase in the budget, additional money would need to be raised. By increasing the central office staff, SCHW hoped that Dombrowski would spend more time planning local meetings and contacting more people to enlarge the membership. Thus the Conference proposed $16,810 for its 1943 budget, and Dombrowski's salary would be set at $3,200. The organization authorized the additional personnel to work in greater detail in its development of applications of support from foundations. If SCHW could show definite accomplishments, it would be more successful in obtaining grants. Moreover, foundations required detailed reports in an attempt to assess the charge that Communists controlled SCHW. Although World War II had diminished much concern for communism, many Americans remained uneasy even while Communist Russia fought as an ally.[67]

Having reached financial security, SCHW decided in 1942 to publicize its work through a monthly publication, the *Southern Patriot*.[68] The original mailing list consisted of all the people who had attended its three biennial conferences. Aware of its past financial shortcomings, the board authorized initiation of the publication only if funds could be found to support it.[69]

Dombrowski, who worked out all the preliminaries of the mailing list, which numbered between 12,000 and 15,000 names, annual subscriptions, selecting the printer, and costs, determined that the first issue would go to all SCHW contacts, inclusive of those who registered at Nashville and made other contributions, but that subsequent issues would go only to paid subscribers. Low cost would increase the likelihood of widespread distribution. Thus, annual subscriptions would be $1, and bundle orders of twenty or more mailed to the same address would cost 25 cents per bundle per year. Single issues of the *Southern Patriot* would cost 10 cents.[70] Sometimes interested persons wanted information that the *Southern Patriot* provided but had no funds with which to subscribe to the magazine or to join SCHW. Or persons would send $1 for the *Southern Patriot* and say that the $1 for membership would come later: "If I can I will send you my membership fee." In a few instances members sent the names of others to contact for distribution of the *Southern Patriot* but requested that SCHW not mention their names when contacting these potential subscribers.

The promotional letter went out, and the first *Southern Patriot* appeared in December 1942. The front page headlined: "Its a People's War," emphasizing FDR's speech before the nation after the Japanese bombing of Pearl Harbor.[71] Generally, Conference members collected the information for the *Patriot*, but in some cases others brought missed or overlooked incidents to SCHW's attention.

During its entire existence SCHW had had to struggle for financial security, and the condition hardly improved under the early years of Dombrowski's administration. Yet the administrative and programmatic changes that he implemented lay the groundwork for the development of a sound fiscal condition for the organization. In May 1943 Dombrowski reported that with only $200 in the bank the Conference's treasury was nearly depleted. He nevertheless had plans to stage a conference on the food situation and the small farmer in an effort to make the public aware of the still-much-needed Farm Security Administration. Dombrowski asked for money from the Marshall Fund for the new project and to replenish SCHW's treasury.[72] Dombrowski's enthusiastic approach to SCHW projects and, most important, the nature of the proposed undertakings, convinced various foundations that the Conference deserved their financial support. His persuasiveness with the foundations and the development of much racial strife during summer 1943, a major concern all the contributing foundations shared with SCHW, helped temporarily to eliminate the Conference's financial troubles. By the end of 1944 SCHW could again report a favorable financial status. From the total amount received for that year, $18,936.47, the organization had $4,118.39 available in cash.[73]

The Conference showed its greatest monetary gain in 1945 when total receipts amounted to over $86,000. Individual contributions alone, from at least 5,727 people, totaled over $34,000; unions contributed $28,395 and foundations came forward with more than $17,000. Sales from the *Southern Patriot* grossed $1,082.47, and other literature brought in $918.54. These funds made it possible to raise Dombrowski's salary to $4,999.91.

The major financial increase could be attributed to donations, but state committees and major literature campaigns depleted the treasury almost as fast as funds came in. State committees were taking out more than they were contributing, and the organization had finally been able to pay expenses for board members to travel to meetings, another drain on financial resources. When all expenses were paid, SCHW still found it had only a small amount of available cash.[74]

In 1946 while planning the move of the central office to New Orleans, SCHW leaders also studied efforts to launch a major capital campaign to rid SCHW of its repeated money worries. Branson Price, a former U.S. Labor Department employee and sister of SCHW stalwart Mary Price, headed a new drive in New York City dubbed the "Lend a Hand for Dixieland" campaign planned for September 19–21, 1946. Price organized 3,000 New York volunteers to raise funds on street corners in the city. As the words of the song "Lend a Hand for Dixieland" hinted, the campaign advocated an end to voter restrictions and lynching in the South, and leaders succeeded in getting the messages of the speakers broadcast over radio. As usual, the SCHW leadership faithfully counted on the presence of outstanding public figures to boost its campaign. This time heavyweight boxing champion Joe Louis and actor Orson Welles cochaired the campaign committee. An estimated crowd of 3,000 turned out on September 20 to hear Joe Louis, who sold his necktie and handkerchief for around $500. Louis's gathering alone raised over $1,000.[75]

Despite the New York fund-raising effort, SCHW's finances worsened rather than improved. The board, disregarding Dombrowski's objection, approved the employment of Frank Bancroft in 1946 as Dombrowski's assistant at a salary of $6,000 per year. In October, Field Secretaries Osceola McKaine and Witherspoon Dodge severed relations with the Southern Conference because SCHW still owed their travel expenses for June, July, and August 1946. Nor could state committees make salary payments to respective employees.[76] Not anticipating such shortcomings, SCHW had agreed to take full responsibility of the National Committee to Abolish the Poll Tax (NCAPT) in May 1946 even though NCAPT was already in arrears. SCHW envisioned potential financial gains from the NCAPT's mailing list of about 27,000 names, a list that the Conference failed to consider had not been good for alleviating NCAPT's debt. Since SCHW had not paid NCAPT's staff's salaries since it became a SCHW "stepchild," Foreman reasoned that the NCAPT would have been better off to continue operating on its own. In December 1946 the SCHW board decided that the NCAPT would not be continued under the auspices of SCHW because the Conference did not have the money. If finances improved tremendously, the Southern Conference would take NCAPT again in the future. When SCHW terminated its support of the poll-tax group, NCAPT chairman Jennings Perry advised SCHW not to mention the federal anti-poll-tax campaign in its appeal for funds. NCAPT struggled along on its own until 1949.[77]

SCHW owed over $25,000 by the end of October 1946, and that month the organization paid neither Foreman, Dombrowski, nor Bancroft. SCHW's major problem was one of cash flow. With an unstable income, it

SCHW sponsors a Joe Louis dinner. Clark Foreman is shaking hands with Louis while Frank Sinatra and Carole Landis look on. Courtesy of Archives and Special Collections, Robert W. Woodruff Library, Atlanta University Center, Atlanta, Georgia.

might receive $25,000 one month and much less the next. But Dombrowski and Foreman remained confident that funds would arrive. Sometimes they were right; by the end of 1946, SCHW's total income was nearly $150,000, a figure that far exceeded the projected goal of $100,000.[78] Such a major increase resulted largely from funds coming in to support SCHW's cooperative efforts on the racial unrest in Columbia,

Tennessee. Circumstances surrounding the injustice in Columbia boosted SCHW's treasury since it received money that organizations such as the NAACP aided in raising. Moreover, in 1946 SCHW benefited from creating SCEF as its tax-exempt, educational arm.

The Educational Fund gained much from examining SCHW's miscalculations in regard to finances. Unlike the Southern Conference for Human Welfare, SCEF did not disillusion itself with the hope of attracting and keeping a sizable membership. It maintained the *Southern Patriot* as its major publication and utilized the subscription list that SCHW had developed. But the funds from contributors did not constitute membership. When individuals made donations, which accounted for the major source of SCEF's income, they automatically became part of the mailing list to receive the magazine. Dombrowski published and edited the *Southern Patriot* after late 1947 as the magazine of the Educational Fund, not SCHW, because SCHW had been unable to pay its debts to the printer for the past several issues.[79]

Under Dombrowski's management the Educational Fund had begun to balance its budget with a small surplus even before SCHW would disband in 1948. All the Fund's debts had been paid in full except for a balance of $550 still owed on an SCHW account, a debt that had been reduced from $2,700 for that organization's publication "Look Him in the Eye." In 1947 one of the most noticed changes was that funds from unions, which had been one of the largest contributors to SCHW, represented the smallest revenues for the Educational Fund. Another significant change was that SCEF had begun to operate on less than one-tenth of the last largest annual income for SCHW. SCEF did not find it easier to raise money, but unlike its predecessor did not make commitments or launch projects unless it had the money on hand. The propensity toward deficit financing had been one of the causes of SCHW's financial difficulties. Whenever SCEF's expenses exceeded income for any given year, the organization paid these expenses from the first of the subsequent year's contributions. SCEF's work against segregation and discrimination, however, continued in the SCHW vein (that is, it was too political) so that it lost its tax-exempt status in 1949 and never regained it.[80]

SCEF raised large sums of money at private parties. In 1950 Dombrowski asked Mary Bethune if she would invite Ambassador Vijaya Lakshmi Pandit from India to be an honored guest along with her at a fund raising party in New York. Bethune extended the invitation to Pandit and to Eleanor Roosevelt, and they both attended this gathering at the Ritz-Carlton Hotel. Dombrowski reported raising $10,000 from the party.[81] By 1955 the group had perfected its system of fund raising based largely on a direct-mail appeal. From a list of about 3,000 contributors about two-thirds contributed each year and the other third sometimes skipped a year. Since names were filed according to the month individuals last contributed, the organization sent an annual letter to them on the

Finances for SCEF, 1947–1956

	Total Revenues	Total Expenses	Cash at Year's End
1947	$ 9,931.90	$ 8,549.56	$ 1,382.34
1948	23,850.72	19,489.02	4,361.70
1949	28,170.92	19,348.02	8,822.90
1950	15,904.72	20,775.37	-4,870.65
1951	25,105.72	18,800.77	6,304.95
1952	23,922.58	27,254.57	-3,331.99
1953	22,025.05	18,504.34	3,520.71
1954	28,682.89	26,312.70	2,370.19
1955	24,172.42	21,925.40	2,247.02
1956	23,094.25	22,181.26	912.99

Sources: "Southern Conference Educational Fund, Inc. Summary, Auditor's Report, 1947," folder 2, box 22, Braden Papers; SCEF Statement of Revenues and Expenses, 1948, ibid.; ibid., 1949, ibid.; Financial Statements as of December 31, 1950, in *Southern Patriot*, 9 (February 1951); ibid. as of December 31, 1951, in ibid. 10 (February 1952); Statement of Income and Expenses, December 31, 1953, December 31, 1954, and December 31, 1955, folder 3, box 22, Braden Papers; Treasurer's Report for the Year Ending December 31, 1956, ibid. The SCEF maintained a savings account with the cash overflow from various years so that in the years that SCEF suffered deficits the amount needed came from the unappropriated funds. By 1956 this sum had grown to over $20,000.

anniversary of their gift and made an appeal for funds. This method paid off in large sums. In 1951 at least five persons donated sums at $1,000 and above to SCEF. Fannie Mayer Kohn gave at least a $1,000; Ethel Clyde, Bettine F. Goodall, and Mrs. M. S. Ingalls, each contributed over $2,500 while Loula D. Lasker donated $5,000.[82]

Ethel Clyde provided support for the Educational Fund in other ways. In 1954 she paid for hotel accommodations for the persons who were to appear before the Senate Internal Security Committee hearings in Louisiana. She even went to the hearings. An octogenarian in the 1950s, Ethel Clyde was a close friend of Dombrowski and Myles Horton of the Highlander Folk School. Her husband owned the Clyde Steamship Company, and Virginia Durr described her as "just rich as all get-out." Thus she had money that she could donate to projects like the Educational Fund.[83]

In 1956 the SCEF raised a substantial amount of money, more than $1,000, for the Inter-Civic Council of Tallahassee, Florida, in support of a bus boycott. The organization could not have done so if it did not have its own financial house in order.[84]

Whether in good financial times or bad, the Southern Conference movement maintained consistency in its message to southerners. The Southern Conference had established the *Southern Patriot* to make its message widespread, and other pamphlets served the same purpose. Many times SCHW received requests from individuals who wanted information on race relations for community distribution or school activities in an effort to improve local conditions.[85] Initially, SCHW did not have its own pamphlets but sent information with references to CIO material. By 1945 SCHW had created at least two pamphlets for major distribution. In one for support of organized labor, a major Conference sponsor, "For Your Children, Too," the message read: "Labor Unions are people, millions of people, working together to improve living conditions for themselves and their children, and *for your children, too."* SCHW dedicated its other pamphlet to black soldiers, focusing attention on the contribution African-American soldiers had made to World War II and how it was now time to give black soldiers and their people at home the freedom they had been fighting for abroad. SCHW challenged the American public to "Look Him in the Eye" and tell him these rights would not be forthcoming. For these pamphlets and the *Southern Patriot,* the group received letters of praise.[86]

3

Alienation, Fear, and Red-baiting

After the sizable turnout for the November meeting and as 1938 drew to a close, SCHW leaders applauded themselves for the new organization. However, the more radical element of liberals had committed one of the gravest sins that a white southerner could commit. By adopting a resolution in support of integrated SCHW meetings, even moderate liberals experienced alienation. Although SCHW had not urged Eleanor Roosevelt to place her seat midway between the separate seating for blacks and whites, symbolically protesting segregation, it had shown its own support for her action with the integration resolution.

The 1938 conference established SCHW's mixed elements of moderates and extreme liberals (even a few ultraconservatives and extreme radicals, i.e., Communists); such representation was impossible to contain. Race became the group's single most divisive issue. SCHW's radical attitude and approach toward this one issue set it apart from the philosophy of the New South of the late nineteenth and early twentieth centuries. The new departure on racial matters also sent the organization in the same direction as the popular-front efforts of the 1930s and 1940s.

The Southern Conference for Human Welfare, an organization that broke with southern tradition on the ideology of white supremacy, and a group with great promise of new direction for democracy, found in its first few years that its principles would be tested as opponents used every chance, even false rumors, to turn people against it. Although SCHW for the most part ignored such accusations, and though no substantial amount of evidence supports them, the accusations and attacks caused a drop in membership and fewer people showed interest in its activities. Moreover, the accusations caused a decline in finances because SCHW depended on voluntary contributions. Internal disagreements also caused problems for the organization. The Southern Conference exemplified the dilemma of southern liberals who had established a determined path but who showed great uncertainty on how far to go.

The pull of southern racist tradition confounded SCHW during the first several months of its existence as forces aligned to oppose its liberal approach to solutions for the South's many problems. In challenging the status quo, SCHW expected opposition from the majority of white southerners, but it did not expect the protest from whites who appeared to support its founding, indeed people who were SCHW delegates in 1938. Perhaps SCHW had been too ambitious when it brought together as many southern progressive and liberal organizations as possible in its efforts to form an umbrella group for liberals. Before 1938 the National Association for the Advancement of Colored People (NAACP), Commission on Interracial Cooperation, Southern Tenant Farmers Union (STFU), and other groups, now constituents in SCHW, had addressed issues that SCHW confronted, but SCHW's founders hoped for a more forceful stance than that taken by many members of these earlier groups. The South's long list of problems presented individuals and organizations of SCHW with numerous alternatives when any particular issue proved too adverse. The loudest protests, if not the most hurtful, came from conservative southerners who did not belong to the Southern Conference. One SCHW founder, Louise Charlton, observed that most white southerners condemned entirely the resolutions SCHW adopted at its November 1938 meeting, even its attempt to strengthen the New Deal, southern freight rate parity, and organized labor. These would only improve southern economic conditions.

SCHW leaders waited for the flurry of reactionary criticism that immediately followed November 1938 to blow over, which it did for a while. As early as March 1939 the *Emancipator*, a southern labor bulletin, invited SCHW to use its facilities to alert southerners of SCHW goals and ideas. The *Emancipator* publicized its "hearty accord with all the principles of the Conference and with the numerous and comprehensive resolutions adopted."[1]

During the course of its history SCHW would often be attacked. Regardless of the Southern Conference's action, these attacks continued and usually came from the same sources. Yet, SCHW leaders carried on the regular order of business, sometimes more determined because of conservative opposition. Frank Graham, reluctant to serve at first, agreed to give his support and remain as president because he believed in the democratic principles advocated by SCHW. Moreover, negative conservative reactions heightened national attention to the new organization. Although it is doubtful that communications were as good in 1939, Palmer Weber's statement on public awareness, that all radicals or liberals had heard of the SCHW, held some merit. As a result of the conservative criticism it could very well be said that by early 1939 most southerners, liberal or conservative, and a large number of northerners, had heard about SCHW.[2]

When SCHW addressed the racial issue, however indirectly at first, individuals who had given support were frightened, and opponents now had the one weapon around which to wrap various accusations against the group. Of the thirty-six resolutions adopted in 1938, at least eight directly concerned racial equality. Beyond denouncing Birmingham's segregation ordinance and the injustices involved in the Scottsboro cases, SCHW maintained that the whole Scottsboro incident had occurred largely as a direct consequence of the lack of employment or other constructive activities for black youth. SCHW called special attention to inadequate recreational facilities in the South generally and recommended that the federal government include funds in the housing and slum–clearance projects to provide for adequate playground and recreational facilities in Birmingham in particular. Such facilities would deter juvenile delinquency and crime, and help to eradicate human misery. SCHW placed special emphasis on Birmingham under the premise that even though all its resolutions pointed out ills throughout the South, specified areas would eventually lead the way to improvement for the entire region. SCHW also recommended that African-American physicians be allowed to render professional service to black patients in all public health institutions, not just the smaller number of segregated facilities.[3]

It is significant that SCHW made the plight of black people part of all its major concerns. When the Panel on Interracial Groups reported at the 1938 meeting, its resolutions included the same major concerns that African-American improvement organizations expressed as their major goals.[4]

SCHW's call for equal funding for African-American graduate education in state-supported institutions may be interpreted as an adherence to the "separate but equal" principles established by the Supreme Court decision in *Plessy* v. *Ferguson* in 1896 and therefore too weak on integration. The major concern at this point in southern history, however, was that the majority of white southerners remained convinced that blacks needed little or no education, let alone access to graduate work. This white majority believed that in the long run to raise the level of education for black people only guaranteed a nourished and strengthened mass of black protestors, the last thing most white southerners wanted to encourage.[5]

Southern history was such that southern liberalism held only a small number within its ranks, a definite political minority. SCHW had swelled the numbered few and added organizational stamina. Historian/sociologist Gunnar Myrdal, who attended the 1938 conference, strongly praised its creation. He

> had a feeling that the real importance of this meeting was that here for the first time in the history of the region, since the era of the American Revolu-

tion, the lonely Southern liberals met in great numbers, actually more than twelve hundred—coming from all states and joined by their colleagues in Washington; and that they, in this new and unique adventure, experienced a foretaste of the freedom and power which large-scale political organization and concerted action give.[6]

The attitudes of local whites forced southern liberals to act conservatively on certain issues. Where the race issue was involved, their approach to bring improvement had to be an indirect or back-door strategy. The New Deal reforms of President Franklin D. Roosevelt, however, caused these liberals to grow accustomed to a more rapid pace of changes, even when it meant opposing local prejudices.[7]

SCHW founders took precautions with liberalism even before November 1938. Louise O. Charlton was confident that the Scottsboro incident would "be consummated and finally disposed of before the conference date" and wanted SCHW to avoid "controversial" racial relations questions. She unrealistically assured at least one would-be participant that no resolutions would be forthcoming on the Scottsboro matter.[8] The group proved Charlton wrong, of course, and passed a resolution on the Scottsboro cases and other controversial subjects.

Charlton had grounds for being cautious on racial matters. Although some white southerners could be committed to a resolution on constitutional rights or civil liberties, they did not welcome civil rights for blacks. Disgruntled whites did not fail to express their disapproval, and protest did not always come from SCHW's opponents. Pointing to all-white juries, one of the most significant symbols of injustice to blacks in the South, W. C. Henson had attended the 1938 conference and approved the resolutions, but later wrote:

> Frankly I am not in favor of going as far to the left as the resolution indicated. I would not at all agree to have negroes on juries in Bartow County [Georgia] where I live and practice [law] for I think it would be bad for the whites and negroes both, and worse for the negroes, things like this have come slowly as people are fitted for them. Whites have been growing into the institutions they have for thousands of years . . . the whites are not secure enough themselves and if you mix the negroes, well, you just can't do it.[9]

White southerners repeated the strong opposition to the SCHW's boldness in race relations just as so many had done when they learned of the NEC's *Report* in July and August 1938. The conferees, however indirect in their approach, could not convince white southerners to accept the notion that white supremacy would eventually become a fact of the past. Most white southerners, even some SCHW supporters, wanted assurances that racial segregation in the South would continue indefinitely.[10]

As demonstrated by Birmingham police officials when they forced conferees to discontinue integrated seating, white segregationists made SCHW, despite its weaker liberals, all the more determined to include racial equality in its work. Similar actions played a role in Frank Graham's willingness to serve as SCHW's president. Graham, who attended only the first two days of the conference, hesitated to serve because he was already committed to so many other organizations in addition to his presidency of the University of North Carolina. He so informed the nominating committee before he left Birmingham, but it chose him anyway. Among the many letters of opposition to Graham's new post, physician and University of North Carolina alumnus L. A. Crowell, Jr., told Graham: "I continued to have . . . high regard for you until I read recent press dispatches about the social welfare conference in Birmingham, and the exceptions that body made to the segregation of negroes and whites. I read that you were made president of that body." Realizing Graham's strong adherence to liberal concepts, Crowell said he could not go that far, that if he had to favor social equality for blacks in order to be liberal and democratic, "then I have no hesitation in renouncing liberality and democracy." Crowell vowed to fight and risk his life in battle for white supremacy if he had to and, furthermore, he would from that day forward stand against Graham "with all the power of my being." Such letters convinced Graham to accept the post.[11] As president, Graham headed an organization that linked economic equality with social equality, and since most white southerners refused either to blacks in order to maintain their way of life, he and SCHW remained the target of conservatives.[12]

Graham defended SCHW's liberalism. He understood that several of its resolutions resembled what the Conference for Social Service in North Carolina had long stood for, namely equality and justice for all. He had also observed that interracial meetings had taken place in North Carolina with integrated seating before 1938 without incident. Graham believed that SCHW, by promising to have only its meetings integrated, had not specifically stated that it planned to abolish racial segregation in the entire southern region. Segregationists, therefore, had no need to raise a fuss.[13]

Had the SCHW and its members decided to meet only once, voice their liberal views, and not be heard from in the future, the white southern majority would have taken little notice. The fact that the Conference made itself a permanent institution to address southern reform made it that much more threatening to segregationists. Even though the Southern Conference did not have the power to enforce the resolutions it adopted, the attendance and support of various state and national politicians gave the appearance to the majority of white southerners that these people would support legislation that would end segregation.

Graham, however, received support and praise from the white liberal minority and blacks that balanced the negative responses to the Southern

Conference. Letters came immediately after the conference that expressed hope that he would accept the presidency because he was the "logical" and "the best choice of the South to head this very significant and history-making Conference." Several persons welcomed the news that the SCHW planned to continue as a permanent institution in the South, but no one expressed this view as well as Earl Long of the Society for Extension of Free Medical Care and Public Assistance in Charleston, South Carolina. Long used a regional metaphor to describe his expectation of the SCHW's future.

> The mule has been hitched to the plow and made to till the soil. Our conditions indeed should be fertile soil for the work of the members of the Conference; and I trust that the field will be well plowed and harrowed to destroy the old systems, and may the seeds of true social justice and economic freedom be planted to grow into a glorious crop of healthy, satisfied, contented, noble citizens bound together with brotherly love and respect for each other.[14]

The noted American socialist Norman Thomas sent a congratulatory letter to Graham for his acceptance of SCHW's presidency, and so did Margaret Sanger of the Birth Control Clinical Research Bureau of New York City. Sanger, who learned of the resolutions through a mutual friend of hers and Graham who had attended the conference, thanked Graham and the group for adopting a resolution recommending the need for "birth spacing clinical" service in the public health agencies in the South.[15]

The National Council of Negro Women (NCNW), of which Mary McLeod Bethune was founder and president, endorsed Graham's attitude toward African Americans as he had expressed it in his opening statement to the conference. The NCNW urged Graham to continue to take the opportunity to influence public opinion in regard to race relations as leader of SCHW. Calling Graham "fearless" and "uncompromising," the NCNW stated that African Americans needed "a friend like you."[16]

With so many represented interests, the Southern Conference founders envisioned that their group would become an umbrella organization for all others that shared similar goals. One of the first to propose this kind of effort was Howard W. Odum, the noted sociologist at the University of North Carolina.[17] Odum, having proposed a Council on Southern Regional Development (CSRD) early in 1938, had regional improvement plans for the South along the same lines as the Conference. Odum's procedure for improvement of the South, however, differed from that of the Southern Conference. The former expected to work through an academic setting, and the latter more closely resembled a mass movement or involvement of the masses. Odum had followed the plans for the SCHW through several of its founders, especially H. C. Nixon and Frank Graham, but he harbored ill will toward the Southern Conference because its structure and goals closely resembled his own for the CSRD.[18] Odum stayed away from the SCHW in November, but on November 21 he contacted Graham, saying that he had been unable to talk with him before the Birmingham Conference and asked if he would discuss the program and prospects of the CSRD with Mark Ethridge, vice-president and manager of the *Louisville Courier-Journal*, the person designated to represent CSRD at the SCHW. Odum suggested that it "would seem good for joint committees to attain unity in [a] southern program."[19]

Ethridge had a chance to talk with Graham at the conference, but later wrote Graham that he and Barry Bingham, president of the *Louisville Courier-Journal*, "feel that the Conference . . . inevitably must be one phase of Southern activity, and that the ultimate solution is the regional council originally proposed by Dr. Odum." Ethridge and Bingham proposed that Francis Miller, executive secretary of Virginia's Southern Policy Committee, convene a committee of twenty-five to discuss the formation of "the council." Plans advanced to the point of Miller sending Bingham and Ethridge a list of twenty-five names. The proposed merger never occurred because of the difference in approach of Graham's and Odum's groups and Odum's unwillingness to support SCHW. Moreover, Odum shunned a direct confrontation with the white southern majority on the race issue. Odum and Will W. Alexander, for example, both supported the Commission on Interracial Cooperation (CIC), an organization that avoided a direct attack on racial segregation for many years, but Alexander's record as an individual in race relations and his support for SCHW showed him in a light different from Odum. In 1944 when the Southern Regional Council (SRC), the successor of Odum's CSRD, evolved with Odum as its first president, the Southern Conference would not align with it because of SRC's moderate stand on equality for blacks.[20]

Just as opposition to the Southern Conference used the race question to discredit all the good the liberal alliance wanted to bring about in the South, the accusations, both during and after the first meeting, that Communists dominated the SCHW served the same purpose. The scholar and educator Arthur F. Raper, professor of sociology at Agnes Scott College (Decatur, Georgia), who attended the conference, defended SCHW officials as "no Reds" only a few days after the conference adjourned. In defense of Frank Graham, Louise Charlton, Mark Ethridge, and H. C. Nixon, Raper speculated that perpetrators of the Communist rumor were persons who disliked the "prominence" of the Conference and "the number of New Dealers present." "Certain elements" might have been annoyed also, Raper pointed out, by the discussion of the problems of organized labor and tenant farmers.[21]

Southerners reasoned as well that SCHW must have had Communist affiliation because organized labor made up part of its constituents. The South violently resisted unions, whether the American Federation of Labor (AFL) or the Congress of Industrial Organizations (CIO). Employers often used the label of communism to turn the public against unions and accused organizers of being "foreigners." And in state after state, legislatures thwarted organized labor through "right to work laws."[22]

Any concern for the equality of blacks usually led to accusations of communism and other abuses from the southern white majority. Indeed the 1930s witnessed the whole notion of interracialism becoming synonymous with communism.[23] The immediate accusation of communism in the SCHW proved no different. Hubert Baugh, editor of *Alabama*, a conservative news magazine of the South whose office was in Birmingham, believed strongly "that the International Labor Defense Committee and persons who may fairly be called career radicals in Birmingham had been particularly active in promoting discontent among the negroes." Baugh claimed to have proof that Communists contributed large sums of funds to the Conference and helped actively to organize it. As it turned out he had based his accusation on statements from a few disgruntled participants who grew disturbed because the proceedings took on "a radical or controversial trend." In search of answers Baugh wrote to Frank Graham demanding an explanation for the Conference's founding, delegate selection, the extent of governmental agencies' involvement, and who paid expenses.[24]

George Londa, a former reporter for the *Birmingham Age-Herald*, summed up the various reasons for the attack on the SCHW. In a letter to the *New Republic* requesting that the periodical allow him to write an article on the attacks against the Southern Conference, Londa concluded that a few persons acted solely out of personal vindictiveness. For example, J. D. Brown, a publicity agent for the Republican party in Alabama, had attempted to get the same job with the Conference but had not succeeded. Brown, according to Londa, then informed Eugene Connor about the integrated seating, knowing what Connor's reaction would be. Brown hoped to make it appear that the Southern Conference had ordered the segregated seating. If he could show the negative reaction of southern Democrats to racial equality, Brown anticipated that blacks would be alienated, especially northern blacks who exercised more political freedom, from the Democratic party and would return to the Republican fold in the next election. Several members of the Conference would notice this same tactic in the 1944 election. Brown even paid youth one dollar each to hiss whenever Franklin Roosevelt appeared in newsreels at theaters in Birmingham. Brown later tried to sell a story to the *Chicago Tribune* that the Conference was Communist inspired. The *Tribune's* correspondent in Birmingham investigated and found Brown's allegation false. Failing at that attempt, Brown finally resolved to spread the charges himself against the "Communist Conference."[25]

Brown's rumors and those of others carried some influence. The Alabama Council of Women's Democratic Clubs, even though it had no official ties with the Democratic National Committee, requested that Louise

Charlton resign from the Alabama Democratic Executive Committee because of her work with the Conference. Charlton, of course, did not resign nor did she believe that Birmingham took the "smear very seriously."[26] Because of alleged Communist connections, the SCHW also received more attention as various groups demanded the Dies Committee to investigate.[27]

By the end of 1938 several prominent individuals who were either convinced that the alleged Communist attack was true or who opposed the Conference's new direction in race relations parted association with it. Persons such as Senator John Bankhead found that the SCHW had made "expressions . . . in favor of social race equality and in favor of the sectional Wagner [anti-] lynching bill," which "demonstrate[s] that a majority of those participating do not understand fundamental Southern conditions." The Conference had elected Francis P. Miller as one of its vice-presidents, but Miller refused to serve. Miller, a Virginia delegate to the Conference, based his refusal on the grounds that the SCHW allowed members of the Communist party to serve as officers. He referred specifically to Donald Burke, also a delegate from Virginia, and John P. Davis, whom the Conference had elected as one of its vice-presidents-at-large for the South. Davis served as executive secretary of the National Negro Congress (NNC), an organization also accused of Communist leanings. Although Miller could not confirm Davis's membership in the Communist party, he claimed that Burke served as its executive secretary in Virginia.[28]

Others who discontinued open association with the Southern Conference included Senators Lister Hill of Alabama and Claude Pepper of Florida and Congressmen Luther Patrick and Brooks Hays from Alabama and Arkansas, respectively. As time passed, however, Hays and Pepper would realign themselves with SCHW. Hill and others, even though they may not have remained with the Conference, associated with individuals who did.[29] Hays remained active with the Southern Policy Committee, where SCHW members such as Barry Bingham, H. C. Nixon, and others still remained committed.[30] Miller, Hays, Patrick, and Pepper had been elected vice-presidents for SCHW in November 1938, and all four resigned almost immediately.[31]

The period from 1938 to the end of 1941 marked a time of uncertainty for the Southern Conference. Members found little to agree on. A more militant element wanted the Conference to be bolder in addressing racial equality; its less liberal element thought the Conference took too many chances by doing so. John B. Thompson, the interim president after Graham, advised the Southern Conference in 1941 that an organization with such a mixture of interests was bound to face difficulty, all the more reason why

we ought to demonstrate in this movement the strong, effective ways in which people who disagree on many political . . . topics can still work to-

Left to right: Joseph Johnson, Clark Foreman, and Claude Pepper in Washington, D.C., in June 1947. Courtesy of Archives and Special Collections, Robert W. Woodruff Library, Atlanta University Center, Atlanta, Georgia.

gether in a democracy for the basic things we sum up under the heading "human welfare." Despite all the excursions and alarms of the past twelve months I still can not see why all southerners who really believe in growing, advancing democracy can not unite their efforts around the anti-poll tax campaign, around the defense of labor's hard-won rights, and around the task of achieving more justice for the racial minority. For I have a deep feeling that the extent of one's real concern for actual democracy is only revealed by great emergencies.

Thompson had all the confidence that SCHW's program would be salvaged.[32]

The spectrum of problems that brought harmony to liberals at the founding of the Conference had for a while left little room for adjustment as each group grew less tolerant of the other's interest. Southern Conference liberals could not during this period agree on the solution to the region's racial problem.[33] Ultimately, however, SCHW must be praised because it at least made the attempt to solve a problem that many white southerners were unwilling to tackle. The anti-poll-tax campaign probably represented the one most important issue that cut across all classes and both races. The effort to organize workers ranked second for the Southern Conference. Its work in both areas would intensify in the next few years.

The race issue tied SCHW to alleged Communist-party control. If the race issue divided liberals in the 1930s, Communist allegations divided them in the 1940s and 1950s.[34] If members did not quit working in SCHW, they were guilty by association. Prominent leaders tried to discount the allegations.

Frank Graham, having accepted the presidency of SCHW despite opposition, began to question the allegiance of some members. He sent H. C. Nixon an urgent telegram November 19, 1939, "confidentially asking me to give him facts and opinion about the Southern Conference to be used in answer to attacks on the Conference and on Joe." Nixon replied that "the Southern Conference was neither pro-communist nor anti-communist, but democratic, American and Southern." As for Joseph Gelders, Nixon assured those who doubted him that "there is nothing subversive about Joe Gelders, and whatever radicalism attaches to him is constructive and human and has origin from mighty hard conditions in [the] U.S.A. He has done more for humanity on $120 a month than the other fellow did on $500 plus office expenses."[35]

The hearings conducted by the House Un-American Activities Committee (HUAC) did not help Graham put aside his suspicions. During the course of questioning Earl Browder, HUAC attempted to link several liberal organizations with the Communist party of the United States (CPUSA). It did so by getting Earl Browder to explain that "transmission belts" were Communists allegedly working among the masses in various organizations. HUAC identified several groups including the National Lawyers Guild, American Students Union, NNC, SCHW, Southern Negro Youth Congress, and the American Civil Liberties Union. The HUAC-prepared list also included "by coincidence" the names of governmental officials who gave the opening addresses or welcomes at these organizations' national conventions. President Roosevelt had sent written greetings to SCHW and the American Students Union. Secretary of Agriculture Henry A. Wallace had delivered the opening remarks at the National Convention of the International Congress of American Democracies and at the Consumers' National Federation convention. Secretary of the Interior Harold Ickes had done likewise at the conventions of the National Lawyers Guild, the NNC, and the American Civil Liberties Union. The First Lady had done no less at the World Youth Congress and the American Youth Congress.

With more input from its members than from Browder, HUAC concluded "that the New Deal is working along hand in glove with the Communist Party." Accordingly, SCHW was allegedly Communist because it embraced much of President Roosevelt's New Deal policies. By linking SCHW with American communism, HUAC also tainted organizations with which SCHW cooperated and received support.[36]

During the testimony of Robert William Weiner, financial secretary of the CPUSA, HUAC's questions led to Birmingham, the SCHW, and Joseph Gelders. Weiner maintained that the national office of the Communist party had contributed money to its financially troubled Birmingham group, but that none of the money had gone to sponsor SCHW's founding—which he repeatedly emphasized that the CPUSA discussed significantly only after SCHW's founding meeting in 1938. Subsequently, HUAC tried to show that Robert Hall, the Birmingham area's district organizer for the CPUSA, had known Joseph Gelders, implying that if the Communist party's national office had not sent money directly to SCHW or Gelders, that perhaps Robert Hall had. Weiner denied any knowledge of the alleged transactions.[37]

The attacks continued, but SCHW did little to meet them head on. As one member put it, "I do not mind a fight, but I hate to see the Southern Conference wasting its energies on this kind of petty squabble when it has such a large job to do." For the most part, other Conference officers believed that the "very idea [was] absurd."[38]

During 1941 SCHW members were harassed because of their association with the organization and their liberal views. In June the New York Signal Corps Procurement District, Army Base, Brooklyn, dismissed Margery De Leon, a clerk, from her job. De Leon had been an employee of the War Department for eighteen years, most of which had been spent in the Signal Office, 4th Corps Area, Atlanta. The charges against her, which had nothing to do with the quality of her work, stated that she had been "associated with or belong[ed] to an organization whose aims are inimical to the best interests of the Government. Your record shows that you are associated with persons whose ideas and beliefs are inimical to the best interest of the Government." Although De Leon found it extremely difficult to refute the vague and unsubstantiated charges, she did succeed in obtaining unofficial information that indicated the War Department considered her membership in three "Communist front" organizations—the North American Committee to Aid Spanish Democracy, the Atlanta League of Women Shoppers, and the Southern Conference for Human Welfare—as subversive activity. A congressman for De Leon's home state of Georgia, her unofficial source of information, sent her a confidential letter from Major General J. O. Mauborgue, Chief Signal officer of the army, in which he stated that the association with the three organizations was the only charge against her. Although prominent women throughout America had been members of and supported all these organizations, De Leon was singled out for harassment.

The activities of the Committee to Aid Spanish Democracy included raising funds to provide assistance to Spain, a victim of German attack at the orders of Adolf Hitler. The Atlanta League largely supported organized labor, requesting stores to stock only goods that bore a union label. De Leon served as secretary-treasurer of the Georgia SCHW. A board of review heard the De Leon case on July 29, 1941, and recommended that she not be reinstated. SCHW was called on to support De Leon, and Tarleton Collier and Frank Graham sent affidavits. On October 3, 1941, the War Department concurred in the recommendation of the board and considered the De Leon case closed. The United Federal Workers of America, a unit of CIO, fought for a reopening of the case and for a fair and impartial hearing, to no avail.[39]

At the time that Gelders received the plea for help in the De Leon case, he had to worry for the safety of his family, and indeed his own personal safety. He had been physically assaulted in the past, and the attacks had gone unpunished.[40] During Gelders's absence on the night of August 25, 1941, a cross similar to that used by the Ku Klux Klan was burned in his front yard. The scene attracted a crowd as Gelders's wife and others extinguished the fire, but no one identified the culprits or took precaution against another occurrence.

The next month in the early morning hours, shots were fired into the Gelderses' home from a moving car while Gelders, his wife, and fifteen-year-old daughter slept. The shots came through the front of the house, shattered the living room windows and lodged in the walls, but caused no injury. The Gelderses reported the incident to police, who never caught the guilty parties. The Gelderses lived on federal property that was part of the Farm Security Administration, but this did not prompt the Department of Agriculture or the Justice Department to launch an investigation into the shooting.[41] Both the Gelders and De Leon incidents showed SCHW's powerlessness. Its members were enthused about protecting the civil rights of all but, except for public awareness and seeking appropriate legislation, had little authority to punish culprits of violent acts.[42]

Considering that the United States was at war and that Communists, like Democrats, had to defend themselves against fascism, SCHW saw a short-lived decline of red-baiting during the World War II period. During the war, SCHW was bothered more with internal charges. Frequently, allegations about SCHW as a Communist-front organization developed after a SCHW biennial, but seldom did the charges come from within its ranks. The 1942 meeting proved different in this regard, as was evident in an editorial in the *Vanderbilt Alumnus* by a student participant who criticized SCHW because of Paul Robeson's remarks about his hope for Earl Browder's release from prison.[43]

Compared to charges from influential members and contributors, how-ever, the student's comments were minor. Roger Baldwin of the Robert Marshall Civil Liberties Trust Fund and Frank McCallister of the Southern Workers Defense League evinced disappointment over the April 1942 gathering and continued a debate with SCHW officers on the question of Communist allegations. The correspondence generated over this Baldwin and McCallister disruption mounted to such a volume that Foreman called himself "a sort of corresponding secretary with our opponents."[44]

One charge grew out of the other as McCallister, dismayed when Paul Christopher of the Labor Defense League was elected to the SCHW board instead of him, accused SCHW of being dominated and influenced by Communists. Nor could McCallister accept the fact that John P. Davis and John Thompson were elected to the SCHW board while he was not. Ob-sessed with the idea that SCHW was run by Communists and disap-pointed about not getting on the board, McCallister added Davis and Thompson to his list of Reds in SCHW. McCallister had little on which to base his charges, except that in accusing Davis of the NNC, he said that he based his conclusion on the action of A. Philip Randolph, who had refused reelection as NNC president in 1940 owing allegedly to its Com-munist domination. At first SCHW paid little attention to McCallister's accusations. But when he saw his attacks getting little Conference atten-tion, he wrote Baldwin—who had meanwhile accused John P. Davis, John B. Thompson (former SCHW president), Gerald Harris (president, Farmers' Educational and Co-Operative Union of America, Alabama divi-sion), and Dombrowski of being Communists or fellow travelers—to get Baldwin to push the issue.[45] McCallister understood that linking red-baiting to a financial contributor would demand serious SCHW consid-eration.

Foreman and Dombrowski had to take Roger Baldwin more seriously because of his affiliation with a foundation, and the Conference de-pended on financial support from such organizations. If the Marshall Fund thoroughly believed Baldwin, it could cut off its support and, more drastically, the rumor would more than likely spread to other foundations.[46]

The Marshall Fund did not support organizations "dominated by Com-munists," and herein lay the major problem with Baldwin. Before grant-ing the Southern Conference $1,000, it had requested the organization to give assurances that neither members of the executive board nor officers were Communist controlled, that Dombrowski be executive secretary, showing good faith in him, and that the money not be used for influenc-ing legislation. In May, Simon Gross of the Marshall Fund requested two reports, one on how SCHW used its money and one on the Nashville conference. Dombrowski reported that SCHW, in keeping with the terms of the grant, had used funds for relocating its central office and expenses for the April 1942 conference.

As far as Foreman and Dombrowski were concerned SCHW had met all the stipulations of the Marshall Fund. They believed that SCHW was a democratic organization and felt that Robert Marshall, who had contributed to it personally, would object to the exclusion of any Americans because of their political beliefs. Foreman said that he was just as amazed by Baldwin's accusation and ill feelings as Baldwin had claimed to be about the SCHW's defense of Communists.[47]

Foreman strongly believed that the Conference could make a big difference in the South, stating that he would welcome even Klansmen and anti-Semites who truly *wanted* to improve southern economic conditions, if they came to the organization on the basis of *equality* with blacks and Jews. The Conference absolutely would not be controlled by Baldwin and the Marshall Fund. Admittedly, this attitude meant that it would be controversial. Furthermore, Foreman knew that another trustee of the Marshall Fund, Gardner Jackson, did not agree with Baldwin's claims against SCHW, though Baldwin insisted his letters to Foreman met the approval of the Fund, Jackson included. When Foreman said he even had unofficial word that the Fund had granted another $1,000 since the Nashville conference, Baldwin disputed the claim.[48]

Dombrowski defended SCHW just as forcefully as Foreman, recalling that the Nashville conference significantly focused on the South's part in winning the war for democracy. He thought it a curious paradox for Mc-Callister and Baldwin to smear the biennial by seeking to deny SCHW a truly democratic policy. He reminded Baldwin that the exclusion of Communists in the Conference bylaws should have been sufficient. Dombrowski, who had in past years admired Baldwin, found his attitude hard to accept, especially since Baldwin supposedly fought for civil liberties. At the height of his frustration Dombrowski concluded that Baldwin's guilt-by-association theory was the same tactic used by Martin Dies of the House Un-American Activities Committee.[49]

The McCallister-Baldwin red-baiting controversy intensified as the summer progressed in 1942.[50] Eventually, even First Lady Eleanor Roosevelt entered discussions as a defender of SCHW. Oddly enough Gardner Jackson, a Baldwin colleague as one of the trustees of the Marshall Trust Fund, also came to the defense of SCHW. Both detractors and defenders in the situation agreed that at least a few fellow travelers might have been present at Nashville, but Foreman warned against giving a few people too much credit. Communist sympathizers had not, he said, acquired "extra powers" to dominate others. The general trend gave Communists excess credit, leaving the impression that one Communist had a dynamic influence over other people.[51]

Of the SCHW officials in question, John P. Davis was the most controversial. He, after all, had been largely responsible for Robeson's concert appearance at the April 1942 biennial but could not be blamed for Robeson's public appeal for Browder's release from prison. Davis even offered to resign from the board if it would help matters, but William Mitch convinced him not to.[52]

Foreman defended Davis because they agreed on what the South needed. Both believed civil and economic rights for blacks to be the absolute key solutions to the South's problems. Sincerely seeking to guarantee those rights did not make him or Davis of any particular "party-mind," he insisted. Foreman agreed with Davis's realization, despite what critics said, that if economic conditions of the South were to improve, blacks and whites had to set aside "petty differences" for the sake of the common goal. Regardless of party affiliations, Foreman willingly worked with Davis. He admonished McCallister for taking Randolph's word as president of the NNC against Davis, while refusing any consideration for Davis's defense by three SCHW presidents—Graham, Thompson, and Rainey. Foreman also reminded McCallister that Communists were allies with the United States in a war against fascism.[53]

Several of Davis's Southern Conference associates continued to defend his name. Lucy Mason, who had known Davis since 1933, weighed in on his side. She had no facts about his political views, but she admired his work in various liberal causes. Gerald Harris did not take McCallister's story seriously and found "it . . . very amusing . . . to think of anyone using undue influence on [Foreman] and Dr. Graham."[54]

When Lucy Mason confronted Baldwin about his accusations, she told him, "It is the inclusiveness, not the exclusiveness, of the Conference that gives it so much promise." Asking him to recall that she had frankly expressed the same sentiment at the 1942 biennial, she said that she had no reason to change her mind since then, and that subsequent events had strengthened her convictions.[55] On another occasion Mason retorted, "There are many people in the south who call you a Communist," and "your organization is widely branded as communist in this region." Mason added, of course, that she did not believe the charge, but she concluded, "you're doing to John Thompson [and the others] what ignorant people in this area do to you. It is unfair in both cases." Indeed, most southerners labeled subversive almost every cause associated with civil liberties and rights during this period.[56]

Foreman, in an attempt to break off correspondence with McCallister in June, tried to convince McCallister that his charges were insignificant. After an executive board meeting in Memphis, Foreman wrote to McCallister that "the meeting . . . was concerned with important matters, and so far as I can remember your name was not mentioned." But McCallister refused to give up his challenge to the Conference.[57]

It is not clear exactly what McCallister relayed to Baldwin about the SCHW's board and officers. But toward the end of the summer Baldwin's and Foreman's correspondence still included talk about Paul R. Christopher being elected to the board rather than McCallister. Both accusations from Baldwin and McCallister started around the same time in May.[58]

At least one trustee of the Marshall Fund cautiously agreed with Foreman and others from SCHW. Gardner Jackson was particularly wary of
the Conference's defense of John P. Davis. He did not doubt SCHW's high
regard for Davis's ability but was unconvinced about Davis's politics, concluding that, altogether, both Baldwin and SCHW had probably made too
much of factional differences.[59]

In reprimanding Baldwin, Jackson reminded him that the trustees had
agreed that he would submit his letter for their approval before sending it
to members of the Southern Conference, and Baldwin had failed to do so.
Jackson acknowledged that Baldwin had stated Marshall Fund policy correctly, but he also made it clear that the policy had not been intended to
force SCHW to exclude individuals because of political allegiance.[60] Ostensibly, Jackson and SCHW members differed in the interpretation of the
power of money as an exclusionary measure.

At first Jackson had accepted Baldwin's charge because he had not attended the conference as had Baldwin. SCHW correspondence, a talk
with the highly respected University of North Carolina President Frank
Graham, and an analysis of the board elected at Nashville made clear for
Jackson that non-Communist members dominated SCHW. With this revelation, Jackson recorded his full disagreement with the attitude Baldwin
expressed in his correspondence to Foreman. Jackson recounted Baldwin's blunders from the beginning:

> You yourself, asserted in the course of our discussions that there is no ques-
> tion that Jim Dombrowski is not a Communist and that the retention of him
> as secretary of the Conference is consequently not a violation of the stipula-
> tions we made when we gave the money. The most I think the situation war-
> ranted (if anything), judging by the further accounts I have heard from
> others than you, was a letter merely raising queries to Clark and Jim respect-
> ing Paul Robeson's remarks about Browder, John Davis'[s] role, John Thomp-
> son's attitude. . . . It seems to me fair to assess an individual's degree of
> sympathy for the Communist position by ascertaining that individual's
> known position on foreign policy prior to June 22, 1941 and his position im-
> mediately thereafter.

Jackson may have been convinced that Robeson, Davis, and Thompson
followed the CPUSA's line on foreign policy, but many Americans
changed their attitude toward Russia after the German attack on the Soviet Union, whereupon they aggressively favored President Roosevelt's
policy. Sometimes this meant that Americans so sympathized with
Russia that their views were indistinguishable from those of Communist
party members. Consequently, Jackson perhaps also saw how easy it was
to overstate the case against Communists.[61]

In the course of the chaos Baldwin altered the angle of his attack and
purported that SCHW must have been Communist because its board did
not include representatives from AFL, the Southern Electoral Reform
League, STFU, NAACP, and the National Urban League.[62] SCHW board

members, concerned about the harm Baldwin's accusation could have if he repeated it too often, discussed its damaging potential at the August 30 board meeting, where Dombrowski read his letter in which he had accused the Conference of not having represented on its board certain organizations that the Marshall Fund supported. A canvass showed that every organization named by Baldwin was represented except STFU, which had almost ceased operation.[63]

Eleanor Roosevelt, who was kept abreast of the SCHW-Baldwin situation, found Baldwin's accusation surprising. Having talked with members of the organizations that Baldwin claimed were not represented at Nashville and previous meetings, she concluded, "I have always understood that the Southern Electoral Reform League was somewhat socialistic and the Southern Tenant Farmers Union and the Workers Defense League somewhat Communist, but I imagine in cooperation with others they do effective work." Indeed Baldwin took the liberty to refute Eleanor Roosevelt. He wrote to her with the same charge he had made to Foreman and others, and informed the First Lady that "I think I can say with entire accuracy that none of the organizations [the ones that Baldwin claimed were not represented on the SCHW board] I mentioned are under the slightest Communist control."[64] Baldwin's talk about the executive board again linked him with McCallister, who wanted to replace Paul Christopher as representative of the Workers Defense League on the SCHW board. Roscoe Dunjee, who headed the NAACP in Oklahoma, was on the board, and so were representatives of the other organizations, but by Baldwin's analysis if the organization had not sent that person as a delegate to SCHW's 1942 biennial, he or she could not officially represent the respective organization. Although his conclusion was accurate, it amounted to no more than a mere technicality that was insufficient to warrant his alarm.[65]

Foreman, baffled by Baldwin's determination to prove that SCHW was Communist-controlled and that there was no southern collaboration of organizations on the part of SCHW, finally concluded, "I wonder if there is any use trying to straighten Roger Baldwin out." Foreman continued, "I hate to think that a man who has been so useful as he has in the past could deliberately distort the truth, but the only alternative seems to be that he is mentally deranged."[66]

Baldwin ended his dispute with SCHW members in September 1942, no doubt owing largely to Jackson's disagreement with him on the matter. Shortly thereafter Alva W. Taylor wrote to William F. Cochran of the Social Justice Fund to inform him that almost all southern organizations were represented on SCHW's executive board.[67] The SCHW wanted to make sure that if other contributors heard Baldwin's rumor, they should be informed that it was just that, a rumor.

Implications from the Dies Committee that the Marshall Fund was Communist-controlled, an issue that Lucy Mason had mentioned to Baldwin to make him more sympathetic toward SCHW, also prompted

Baldwin's decision to leave SCHW alone. The congressional committee established in 1938 and headed by the Texas Democrat Martin Dies investigated federal employees suspected of subversive activities or disloyalty to the government. It continued to suspect the Southern Conference of subversiveness. Dombrowski considered Representative Dies the equivalent of an "Axis stooge." On September 24 Dies presented to the House of Representatives the names of government officials he charged as Communists along with a list of checks that he claimed the Robert Marshall Fund had issued. Moreover, he charged that the foundation was Communist because it contributed to organizations that were. Dies's accusation, however, was against the Highlander Folk School in this regard; when news reporters confronted Dombrowski, he refused to make any statement about the Robert Marshall Fund.[68] Although the charges of the Vanderbilt student, the possibly concerted efforts of Baldwin and McCallister, and the Dies Committee forced the Southern Conference to be mindful of its association with Communists, the war and America's alliance with Russia lessened the impact on the public.

Red-baiting took its toll on SCHW officials, many of whom had ties with the academic world, which was less tolerant of leftist politics. In the midst of the McCallister-Baldwin charges and not long after the Nashville meeting, SCHW's newly elected president, Homer P. Rainey, resigned, and Dombrowski speculated that Baldwin's charges played a role in his decision—though Rainey claimed that the pressure of university work had gotten to be all he could handle. Dombrowski suggested that Foreman take Rainey's place, and he did, though at first only temporarily.[69]

Red-baiting plagued SCHW through 1948, and persisted with SCEF in the 1950s and 1960s. Loyal blacks, however, like Mary McLeod Bethune and Charlotte Hawkins Brown, were less susceptible to charges of communism. The strategy worked to divide the races in the movement.

In its early years the Southern Conference movement had difficulties, then, broadening the meaning of the 1930s and 1940s New South to include concerns of labor and blacks. This outreach, so necessary if real reform were to be accomplished, frightened many white southerners within and without the movement, which led to red-baiting and financial woes.

Making Poll Tax a National Issue

White southern Democrats had favored various ways of disfranchising potential political opposition since the Reconstruction period. In an attempt to eliminate blacks from the
political process they had devised the grandfather clause, lit-
eracy tests and, when all else failed, violence and intimidation. The poll
tax was simply another way to prevent blacks and poor whites who
threatened their control from voting. By 1908 every state that had been
part of the Confederacy had instituted the payment of a poll tax before a
person, otherwise qualified, could vote. Given the population propor-
tions, blacks were far more heavily affected than whites. Moreover, given
the economic discrimination against blacks, the disparity increased. But,
in an effort to reduce controversy, the Southern Conference for Human
Welfare emphasized that the poll tax had become an obstacle to a large
constituency of whites.[1]

With several representative interests to accommodate, in early 1939
SCHW began its effort to eliminate the poll tax, one of the more pressing
issues in the South. Partly because of President Franklin Delano
Roosevelt's suggestion and partly because of his concern with this problem, Joseph Gelders corresponded with several SCHW members in January 1939 about mounting a large campaign to end the process. He later
met with several persons and discussed plans to rid the South of the poll
tax. From the start, the abolition of the tax gained support from organized labor, especially the CIO unions. Representatives of these groups,
Lucy Randolph Mason and Bernard Borah, were among the first with
which Gelders discussed his plans.[2]

When the executive committee of the council met at Chapel Hill in February 1939, it established a Civil Rights Committee (CRC) of which Maury
Maverick, mayor of San Antonio, Texas, became chairman and Joseph

Gelders its executive secretary. James Morrison, law professor at Tulane University in New Orleans, and Virginia Durr also served on this committee. The Civil Rights Committee began to prepare a campaign against the southern poll tax, but not until August of that year would any evidence of its preparation materialize.[3]

In a report to Frank Graham, Gelders summarized in detail the strategy of the CRC for ridding the South of the poll tax. Primarily, the CRC believed that federal legislation and court action would produce "immediate success" as opposed to attempting the same task state by state. The passage of federal legislation would provide impetus for further suffrage reform. Gelders recounted the success of the committee in getting Lee Geyer to introduce its draft of H.R. 7534 into Congress, the *Pirtle* test case to show that the poll tax requirement was unconstitutional as it applied to federal elections, and that the CRC had secured a grant of an undetermined amount from the William C. Whitney Foundation to conduct a study of the entire suffrage situation in the South. Gelders expressed confidence that once the public knew the contents of the bill, it would demand passage of the Geyer bill.[4]

One of the major tactics that SCHW and CRC used to attract national attention to an issue involved making the public aware that the problem existed. If people only knew of the detriment the poll tax caused democracy, they would inevitably agree that the poll tax had to be eliminated. A prime tactic in this endeavor was Gelders's proposal of a test case in court. To make the point, CRC chose *Pirtle* v. *Brown*, a case that challenged the constitutionality of the poll tax solely as it applied to congressional elections. Henry Pirtle, a white resident of Tennessee and a qualified voter with the exception of not having paid his poll tax, sued for the right to vote for a member of Congress in his district. The CRC employed Crampton Harris, a former law partner of Hugo Black, to represent Pirtle. Gelders thought that the brief in the case was simple and short enough, only eighteen typed pages, and published it as a pamphlet to educate the public.

Some of the members of the CRC disagreed with proceeding with the test case because it would cost so much. "A $5,000 fee to test the poll tax laws is ridiculous," wrote Maury Maverick to James J. Morrison. Maverick and Morrison agreed that "there ought to be one patriotic lawyer in the United States who would" take the case "for practically nothing." Morrison doubted that Gelders and the committee could raise the $5,000 plus incidental expenses beyond that amount, but even if they could, Morrison was not sure that a test case was the best possible use of funds. He suggested that Gelders contact Victor Gettner of the National Lawyers Guild, whose subcommittee on civil liberties had been studying limitations on the exercise of the voting franchise.[5]

Gelders, however proceeded with the *Pirtle* case. The district court did not rule in Pirtle's favor, and the case ended unsuccessfully when the

Sixth Circuit Court of Appeals on March 8, 1941, upheld the district court decision, denying Pirtle the right to vote unless he paid his poll tax. The Supreme Court refused to hear the case.[6]

The CRC made significant progress on another front when on August 5, 1939, Representative Lee E. Geyer, a Democrat from California, introduced its version of an anti-poll-tax bill, H.R. 7534, before Congress. Geyer introduced the bill at the request of the CRC because no southern congressman would and read a letter from SCHW's committee on presenting his bill in the House. The letter told of how in November 1938 SCHW had adopted a resolution urging state and federal action to end poll taxes as a prerequisite for voting. The CRC expected Congress to pass the bill, but even if it were to fail, at least a larger segment of the American public would be aware that the poll tax was used to eliminate a great proportion of otherwise eligible voters.[7]

Gelders proposed that officers and members of the SCHW secure support for H.R. 7534 from other organizations to which they belonged and write to their congressmen and senators, especially to members of the House Judiciary Committee. For Graham's information Gelders included the names of the persons of the House Judiciary Committee. The CRC requested financial support as well from the SCHW and other organizations. Part of the educational campaign would include "Abolish the Poll Tax" seals (stamps) for envelopes and letters. The sale of these seals at one cent each would assure the involvement of "even the most underprivileged sections of the southern people." Organizations should begin their own campaigns by having their members write letters that could be placed in the newspapers; prominent leaders "should attempt to secure radio time over local stations—all to inform the public of the necessity of abolishing the poll tax." The successful effort on the part of SCHW, Gelders said, would "broaden . . . the influence of the Conference throughout the South and of preparing for an even broader South-wide conference when a call is issued by the Southern Council."[8] Gelders and the members of his committee would take the opportunity to discuss the poll tax at SCHW's next membership meeting, which would take place in spring 1940.

Gelders kept those who supported his efforts with the anti-poll-tax legislation informed about the procedures and the chances of success of Geyer's bill and the court case. He also kept them abreast of the isssue of finances, requesting even that the Marshall Fund contribute funds to the AFL and CIO because organized labor supported the CRC's efforts in abolishing the poll tax. CRC needed funds for staff salary, and, as Gelders pointed out, it "ha[s] to bring people to Washington for the hearings; organize a campaign of public education around the Geyer Bill." In another effort to raise funds and support for Geyer's anti-poll-tax bill, Gelders wrote individuals and organizations asking them to write congressmen to vote for the passage of H.R. 7534 and that they contribute

$25 each "for immediate expenses pending the development of a more adequate financial arrangement." In other instances Gelders urged anti-poll-tax supporters to show force by attending SCHW's 1940 conference in Chattanooga.[9]

Although several organizations had made the poll tax a national issue, no group in particular monopolized the campaign to abolish the pernicious system. About the time that Gelders mailed his letters, he received similar ones from some of the same organizations with like requests. Walter White of the NAACP sought the support of Gelders, CRC, and SCHW for Geyer's H.R. 7534 and "for authorization to circulate through your organization the anti–poll tax stamps on a mutually profitable basis," the same stamps that Gelders talked about in September 1939. Perhaps in an effort to get correspondence out quickly, White's staff had not noticed that Gelder's letter of March 1 had initiated this particular NAACP work. Gelders had dispersed the stamps with a letter explaining their purpose and urging individuals to order more as needed.[10] Roy Wilkins on March 13, 1940, sent Gelders the NAACP's $25 contribution toward eliminating the poll tax.[11]

By 1940 the SCHW board was attempting to diminish the large role that Joseph Gelders had begun to play in the fight against the poll tax. The Civil Rights Committee needed to raise funds for its cause, the poll tax, just as badly as the SCHW did for merely remaining operational. Leaders of SCHW reported that several persons indicated considerable dissatisfaction with Gelders. Even though no one had proof that he was a Communist, "there [was] certainly a widespread belief that his sympathies [were] strongly aligned with the Communist Party." These Conference leaders announced that they could not continue to regard the Communist charges as false when they themselves had begun to have doubts about certain members, particularly about Gelders. They argued that since the charges persisted, SCHW would remain forever under scrutiny for as long as these individuals did. Under the circumstances Gelders did not seem the likely person to lead the fight against the poll tax. Instead of gaining support and contributions Conference leaders thought Gelders would cause apprehension among its supporters. Only recently has research uncovered that Gelders, in fact, was a member of the Communist party, having joined after several attempts in 1935. Suspicions of Gelders lingered, but he remained a part of the liberal alliance in SCHW.[12]

Congressman Geyer still fought for the passage of H.R. 7534. In 1940, however, several organizations joined in his efforts and those of the CRC by forming a "loose committee." In addition to SCHW, groups represented included the AFL, CIO, Labor's Non-Partisan League, National Association for the Advancement of Colored People, National Negro Congress, American Civil Liberties Union, League of Women Shoppers, and the National Lawyers Guild. Geyer and Gelders sent out letters inviting many more to plan appropriate strategy to have Geyer's bill adopted.[13]

Gelders at this time had a desk in Geyer's office because the CRC did not have enough funds for its own office. Gelders correctly asserted that the lack of an office and staff caused the CRC's work to drag along slowly.[14]

CRC's efforts to eliminate the poll tax by no means ceased with the Geyer bill. Indeed, the struggle would continue beyond the 1940s and 1950s, and during this time, beginning about 1939–1940 the SCHW's CRC combined its efforts with those of several other organizations. Eventually the smaller efforts were turned into a national drive as SCHW members led in the formation of a National Committee to Abolish the Poll Tax (NCAPT).

Geyer initiated the formation of NCAPT in 1940 to muster support for his federal anti-poll-tax bill. The sole purpose of this nonprofit organization was to educate the public on the importance of abolishing the poll tax through the passage of federal legislation. To avoid competition between organizations aligned in this effort, as well as to pull the groups together in some centralized fashion, the NCAPT did not ask its members to pay dues; its activities would be financed through voluntary contributions. In addition to support from organized labor, thirty-three national organizations, including those already listed, joined the efforts of NCAPT.

Congressman Geyer served as NCAPT's first chairman until his death in June 1941. After his death, vice-chairs Virginia Foster Durr and Will Alexander took responsibility for a while. Later Jennings Perry, editor of the *Nashville Tennessean* and a leader in the fight to abolish the poll tax in Tennessee, headed the National Committee. The organization was governed by a national board composed of the officers plus one representative from each of the supporting national organizations. Only the executive secretary received remuneration for his services.[15]

Virginia Durr, sister-in-law of Justice Hugo Black, was typical of the large number of persons who would dedicate a great portion of their lives to the abolition of the poll tax. Durr's husband, Clifford, was a Roosevelt appointee to the Federal Communications Commission. When the Durrs moved to Washington in 1933, Virginia became active in the Women's Division of the Democratic National Committee, the vehicle through which she eventually met Lucy Randolph Mason, Eleanor Roosevelt, and others who would make up SCHW. Although Durr had learned of the Conference's first meeting in 1938 through Gelders, Mason, and others, she had attended that meeting at the request of Virginia Governor James H. Price, who asked her to represent the state.

Durr's involvement in public life started in her native Alabama where she served as vice-president of the Junior League of Birmingham and where she, too, actively sought to address local economic needs. This group organized motor pools and food centers for needy Birmingham families in 1931 and 1932. The New Deal, Durr said, "seemed to me to be the most marvelous thing in the world, because I'd come from Birmingham where half the population was starving, . . . and there was no public relief at all." The depth of deprivation that Durr and so many other southerners witnessed made it impossible for them to comprehend why anyone would not welcome Roosevelt's New Deal, which promised to alleviate much of the suffering.

After joining SCHW, Virginia Durr, a member of its Civil Rights Committee which made abolition of the poll tax its major goal when it was formed in 1939, became vice-chair of the NCAPT in 1940. She held that position until 1949. Durr, like so many of the other persons with whom she worked to end the onerous poll tax, "had the happy belief . . . that if people got to vote, they would have power enough to . . . change their conditions."[16]

In addition to NCAPT, Virginia Durr and Jennings Perry joined forces in another organization, the Southern Electoral Reform League, that also made the elimination of the poll tax its major goal. Perry was its chair and Durr its secretary. This group, organized early in 1941, shared several members in common with the Southern Conference, including Eleanor Roosevelt, Barry Bingham, Frank Graham, Clark Foreman, Claude Pepper, William Mitch, Dorothy Stafford, James J. Morrison, and others. Liberals were so few in number in the South that almost any organization that sought positive reforms was likely to have members common to other such groups, and the Southern Conference provided a place where all could come together. The Electoral Reform League issued a monthly bulletin to serve further notice to the public that the poll tax must go.[17]

After SCHW's 1940 membership meeting where certain members sought to undermine Gelders's leadership role in the anti-poll-tax movement, he sensed what was going on. He told Virginia Durr that "I hope after the next conference to have a clear mandate to proceed with conference activity without the usual interference from Foreman & Co. That would be a real pleasure." Forever dealing with financial difficulties, Gelders did not appreciate having to make decisions without Foreman's consent. Gelders despaired that he had to raise money for his own past-due salary.[18]

By August 1940 Gelders's enthusiasm for the anti-poll-tax campaign heightened as national attention focused on this issue, and the SCHW board authorized the opening of a CRC office in Birmingham. He aspired to strengthen the southern campaign for fear it might appear to involve fewer southerners than it actually had.[19] But by now Virginia Durr had become doubtful of Gelders's leadership in the poll-tax campaign and questioned him particularly about finances. Gelders assured her that he knew as little about finances as she since Clark Foreman supervised financial matters and that she should address questions about money to Foreman. Admitting that his excitement about the CRC's Birmingham office caused him to "rush . . . ahead with a program long overdue" without keeping in touch with CRC, Gelders vowed to stay in closer touch with Virginia Durr in the future. Despite his energetic efforts, however, he still struggled with finances as he proceeded with efforts to assure the passage of Geyer's bill and the hoped-for positive outcome in the *Pirtle* case.[20]

Others shared Durr's doubts or questions in regard to Joseph Gelders. They were especially concerned about his role in the *Pirtle* case. Eleanor Bontecou, involved in research to support the anti-poll-tax campaign, doubted that Crampton Harris would be successful with his brief for the case without seeking input and advice from the Department of Justice. She blamed Gelders for conveying the impression to the Department of Justice that its participation was not needed. As Bontecou saw things, two gains would result from the Department's input, the first of which included the use of its human and financial resources in the preparation of a long brief. The government, Bontecou reasoned, was given much wider latitude in the preparation of its briefs and in the selection of sources than would be permitted to a private attorney. Second, the benefit of advice and experience from officials at Justice in such a case would give it entirely new importance in the eyes of the Court. Moreover, by using information from the Department of Justice, expenses for SCHW and CRC would be reduced because neither group would need to expend resources for the same information.[21] In addition to the court case and efforts to obtain passage of legislation abolishing the poll tax on a national level, SCHW maintained an almost constant flow of material to educate the public. One such pamphlet, *The Poll Tax*, included articles by SCHW and its CRC members that addressed various aspects of SCHW's agenda.[22]

The poll-tax issue could not be separated from the wider issue of general concern for the poor economic conditions of the South. An inquiry made under the auspices of the New School for Social Research, which was funded by the Whitney Fund and directed by Eleanor Bontecou, found that low wages related directly to difficulties in paying poll taxes, which in turn reduced political participation. The findings rested on a report from George C. Stoney, who traveled through the South as a field worker paying special attention to wage labor and its relation to the ability of southerners to pay poll taxes. The general economic situation, particularly the poor prevailing wage scale, proved most helpful in an analysis of the suffrage situation in states such as Georgia, where the poll tax was cumulative. In this state failure to pay the poll tax for any number of years required, before the citizen could vote, the payment of a sum equal to the years missed.

Indeed, Stoney observed that in cases where people were able to pay poll taxes, their level of interest was higher for participation in local elections than national. Although they were aware of national leaders and issues, he said of this development:

For the most part[,] they don't seem to think that voting has anything to do with such things as the wage-hour law, which in Georgia seems to be regarded as manna from Heaven. Roosevelt, who they regard as responsible for the law rather than any Congressman or Senator, certainly does mean much to them.[23]

Because Stoney paid special attention to workers' wages, many laborers assumed that he had come from the wage and hour division of the federal government and expressed disappointment when they learned differently. County agents themselves reported that wage-hour standards were not enforced in McIntosh County, Georgia, where a recent suit suggested that perhaps the government knew about the conditions, but Stoney believed that to report his findings could bring improvements. He learned that conditions in McIntosh in the lumbering industries were worse than in other sections of southeast Georgia. For instance, in McIntosh County, Stoney observed that several sawmill employers did not always pay in cash, but instead handed out "babbitt," token money that could be spent only at local stores. Employers infrequently paid in cash, and even then workers earned only between $1.25 and $1.75 for a ten-hour workday. Stoney reported that these mill employers ran commissaries where the workers were forced to trade because they lacked cash and where basic necessities often cost twice as much as stores in town. Workers stood to be doubly cheated by the higher prices at the commissaries and often in the failure of employers to pay promised wages. They did not get a clear statement of what was earned, spent, or owed. The conditions that Stoney reported constituted a small portion of other such cases throughout the South.[24]

Women, a large percentage of those who were unable to meet the poll-tax requirement, and women's organizations contributed to focusing national attention on the issue. The southern representative of the Amalgamated Clothing Workers of America, Bernard Borah of Atlanta, reported that ninety-five percent of its members, who were women, could not pay poll taxes. Having struggled to gain suffrage only in 1920, women connected their early reform movement to the one at hand. On the twentieth anniversary of the Nineteenth Amendment, a delegation of women from poll-tax states went to Washington to deliver to Congress a statement bearing 100 signatures of women protesting the poll tax requirement. The activists argued in 1940 that even with a constitutional amendment, "we now realize that victory was only part won." Virginia Durr and at least thirty other women from SCHW signed the statement. As part of the ceremony in Washington, the women laid a wreath in the Capitol Building at the statue of Susan B. Anthony, a leading suffragist, and Senator Arthur Capper spoke of the statement from the Senate floor. Congressmen Geyer and Caroline O'Day addressed it from the House. O'Day cited the Department of Labor report that more than four million American women were denied the right to vote because of the poll tax and pointed out the hardship placed on lower-income families simply if one spouse chose to exercise the franchise. The women's expression received national press attention and added to a growing concern for abolition of the poll tax.[25] If the visit to Washington brought high moments to the poll-tax fight, it did just as much for other SCHW concerns.

SCHW found by 1941 that the civil rights description too broadly defined CRC's objectives. Acting on Gelders's recommendation that the Civil Rights Committee be abolished and an Anti-Poll Tax Committee be established in its place, the SCHW board elected Virginia Durr chair of the new committee. With Durr heading the committee, SCHW finally was granting the wish of some members who wanted Gelders less visible in SCHW. In summarizing the fight against the poll tax since 1938, Gelders cited the importance of recent Supreme Court decisions as they affected the constitutionality of anti-poll-tax legislation and emphasized that there be no laxity in the campaign. He also pointed out that CRC had practically restricted itself to the poll-tax fight but that other issues deserved attention. Thus, in addition to the Anti-Poll Tax Committee, Gelders asked that SCHW institute separate committees to fight against racial discrimination, lynching, and for academic freedom.[26] SCHW instituted the committees but kept anti-poll-tax work a top priority.

Sometimes poll-tax opponents feared that even some liberals shied away from full support of their fight. Anticipating the controversy that liberals would bring over the poll tax in SCHW's April 1942 biennial, Jennings Perry advised the board that he thought it best to postpone the meeting set for that spring until after August primaries. He worried that the few liberal southern politicians like Senator Claude Pepper of Florida stood the chance of defeat. Perry was convinced also that he would be more beneficial to SCHW by not being openly identified with it, requesting that the organization not mention him in any of its publicity. His fears, though, did not affect the board's plans for the biennial as it unanimously favored going ahead with it. At that meeting advocates for national anti-poll-tax legislation framed their appeal in World War II rhetoric that called for democracy at home and abroad.[27]

For the next several years support grew for the NCAPT's cause. By the end of 1942 total organizational affiliation numbered more than sixty-five, and after Geyer's death, Senator Pepper introduced another anti-poll-tax bill. In 1942 anti-poll taxers added yet another dimension to their fight when the NAACP attempted to get President Roosevelt to express strongly to the public what it understood him to advocate behind the scenes, abolishment of the tax. NAACP leaders made the poll tax a part of the ongoing concern for World War II, reminding the president that "[we] completely support your leadership to win the war," but "[we] believe that the Geyer-Pepper Bill is vital war legislation which must be enacted to unite the American people for winning the war."[28]

In a speech to the Senate, Claude Pepper also connected the fight against the poll tax with World War II, asking how Americans could "with the greatest war in history in progress" and as "the crusaders for democracy deny it to a large element of our people." More broadly Pepper's message to his colleagues described succinctly various reasons why the poll tax had to go. For one thing he reminded them that the attempt to abolish it had been long in the making, pointing out that northern states had called the tax "obnoxious" before the Spanish-American War, that Louisiana and Florida saw a tremendous increase in voter participation once the tax was repealed, and that even his part in the struggle to make democracy costless now reached its fifth year. To hear "the eloquent addresses which have been delivered in this body" against anti-poll-taxers, Pepper said, "one would think that some hideous monster under the guise of tyranny and dictatorship had attempted to protrude its head into this democratic and humanitarian assembly." Pepper understood that the supporters of the poll tax had declared political war against poor Americans, noting that the same senators who had voted against the Fair Labor Standards Act in 1937 (and legislation to eradicate slum areas and provide for adequate housing in the 1940s) now opposed anti-poll-tax legislation. Pepper's thorough knowledge of the history of the poll tax and his understanding of the situation in 1942 made him well aware that the few opponents became the major obstacle to anti-poll-tax legislation. A distinct minority of filibusters in the Senate would never allow that body to vote on the measure, and Pepper announced that he would lead a fight against the filibuster. For example, Mississippi Senator Theodore G. Bilbo was a noted filibusterer; he threatened to lead an eighteen-month filibuster to kill anti-poll-tax legislation in 1943. NCAPT and SCHW joined Pepper's fight to silence Bilbo and the filibusterers, and SCHW attempted to unseat him in 1946.[29]

Congressmen Vito Marcantonio of New York and George H. Bender of Ohio led other representatives and senators who joined Pepper and NCAPT efforts to eliminate the penalty on voting with the introduction of new legislation for the remainder of the 1940s. NCAPT campaigned against the filibuster, collected petitions in support of anti-poll-tax legislation, and lobbied Congress for anti-poll-tax legislation. The House of Representatives repeatedly voted to abolish the tax, but the Senate could never get past the filibuster or enough votes for cloture. Poll taxers even successfully killed the 1943 Green-Lucas bill that would have provided absentee ballots for Americans at war abroad to make the world safe for democracy. Anti-poll taxers found encouragement and even could claim partial credit in state repeals in Tennessee and Georgia in 1943 and 1945, respectively.[30]

If poll taxers did not hold up progress on poll-tax repeal legislation through the filibuster, they wrote NCAPT to voice complaints against its work. Their sentiments ranged from racism and the fear of black elected officials to advocacy for states' rights. Texas Senator W. Lee O'Daniel's letter expressed what most of his conservative colleagues and constituents voiced in other places when he wrote:

> A general impression is held by a great many people that by abolishing the poll tax, the main gain would be to permit the colored people to vote. That is not the case at all. If Congress should enact this Resolution abolishing the poll tax, it would have no effect whatever on the elections in my State of Texas, as far as the Negro vote is concerned . . . because the elections in Texas are generally determined in the Primaries, and not in the general election. Poll tax or no poll tax, colored people are not permitted to vote in the Democratic Primaries in Texas. The Democratic Party of Texas is an organization which has Members, the same as many other organizations, and consequently has the legal right to fix qualifications of its own Members, and this right has been upheld by the Supreme Court.

Fortunately, in *Smith v. Allwright* in 1944, the Supreme Court agreed with leaders of the NAACP in Texas when they successfully argued against the all-white Texas primaries.[31]

Although anti-poll-tax opponents proved more successful at maintaining the status quo, anti-poll taxers conceived various means in consciousness raising. The obvious method, educating the public, involved circulating leaflets with actual voter-participation figures. Using figures from the 1942 off-year election, NCAPT estimated that the poll tax assisted in disfranchising 11 million American citizens (7 million white and 4 million African-American) in seven southern states. It proposed the enforcement of the Fourteenth Amendment, section 2, which establishes representatives in the house proportionate to each state's population and that states which deny or "abridge" the right of a number of its citizens to vote suffer a corresponding reduction in its representatives. Section 5 of the Fourteenth Amendment empowered Congress to "enforce by appropriate legislation, the provisions of this article." According to NCAPT's calculations, the poll–tax states had sixty-nine Congressmen in the House when constitutionally they were entitled to only nine. In 1943 NCAPT produced several exhaustive poll-tax studies, sent out over 50,000 letters on the poll tax, and made over 350,000 pieces of poll-tax material, including its *Why the Poll Tax Is a National Issue*, available at various conventions. For fear that congressmen might ignore its letters, NCAPT depended on respective constituents to appeal (through mail or local office visits) to their representatives to support repeal of the poll tax. SCHW, in its continued belief in NCAPT and its cause, dedicated an entire issue of its *Southern Patriot* to the poll tax in 1943.[32]

Another NCAPT idea anticipated modern Election-Day television coverage. NCAPT executive secretary Katherine Shryver proposed documenting voter apathy with photography. On Election Day 1944, a corps of newspaper or amateur photographers in southern states would take pictures of the people not voting. Such a story would emphasize the large number of people who had grown indifferent to the political process because of the poll-tax hardship and help to make the point of the need for its demise.[33] NCAPT, however, failed to follow through with the suggestion.

Although no apparent evidence links him with the NCAPT or SCHW, noted historian Herbert Aptheker in 1946 published an article on the history of the poll tax in South Carolina. The longtime civil-rights advocate's message could not be distinguished from that of NCAPT; he called the poll tax an "undemocratic practice" that was "absolutely anachronistic and inexcusable." For a tax that so greatly impacted African Americans, it was fitting that Aptheker's essay appeared in the *Journal of Negro History*.[34]

Despite NCAPT's wide range of support, its financial shortfall interfered with its mission. A combination of financial instability and the relentless fervor of southern demagogues made NCAPT's goal seem almost impossible, and it struggled along until 1949. That year Jennings Perry called on various organizations and individuals to continue supporting NCAPT, but help was not forthcoming to see the anti-poll-tax group through the crisis. Individuals agreed to serve; Pepper accepted the chairmanship in 1949. Since many organizations could not contribute funds, NCAPT could not sustain the extensive educational campaigns in the next decade.[35] Only with the adoption of the Twenty-fourth Amendment to the Constitution in 1964 did poll taxes become a relic of the past. SCHW's CRC and the concerted effort of other groups continued to struggle for its end throughout the interim; even SCEF gave attention to the dreadful poll tax in its literature.

5

Southern Liberalism and the Search for Racial Justice during World War II

During World War II the Southern Conference for Human Welfare unified its strategy on the racial issue as campaign after campaign stressed the idea that an integrated society was the solution to southern ills. The organization took a firmer stand and took on a more direct approach to an integrated society as moderates deserted the group. But the shift did not come about easily, for SCHW members continued to hold differing views on the race issue. The war, more than anything else, provided a rallying point for liberals as the Southern Conference tied every feasible issue to the fight for democracy abroad and the plight of blacks at home. The Conference, as did African Americans in their Double V Campaign, raised a fundamental question: How could Americans fight for democracy abroad and not practice the same at home?[1]

By mid-1941 SCHW was financially strong and getting good media attention. World events quieted allegations of communism that opponents had leveled against SCHW leaders, which enabled them to further develop the financial base required to pursue a program of social and economic reform. In a seemingly providential manner the tragedy of World War II provided the backdrop against which the SCHW, under dynamic new leadership, could push its program. Already as early as June 22, 1941, when Adolf Hitler ordered the invasion of the Soviet Union and President Franklin D. Roosevelt extended the benefits of the lend-lease program to assist Russia, much of the sting about red-baiting had diminished. Within three days the president, under pressure from A. Philip Randolph and others loosely aligned in the March on Washington Movement, had signed Executive Order 8802, which outlawed discrimination in war-related industries and created the Fair Employment Practice Committee to guarantee compliance with his command. Executive Order 8802, though clearly a war document, marked the first time in the nation's history that the executive office had admitted that racial discrimination existed and that its elimination was in the country's best interest.

Highlighted by President Roosevelt's new but reluctant attitude toward reaching compromises with civil rights spokesmen on some of their demands, the 1930s and 1940s witnessed the beginning of changes in attitudes that resulted in gains of later decades. John P. Davis and other prominent blacks criticized the Roosevelt administration on the early New Deal programs that discriminated against blacks, but many of these same blacks, in turn, applauded Roosevelt in 1941 when he issued Executive Order 8802.[2] The Southern Conference and the attention it focused on the same issues for which blacks were becoming more outspoken add significantly to the high-water mark for civil rights in the period.

Under more favorable circumstances, SCHW pushed its position that the prevalence of racism was the most important single issue preventing the industrial and economic development of the South. It maintained that the South would progress only as much as all elements of the society were permitted to participate and to develop their talents.

In light of the United States involvement in World War II, the executive board immediately determined that defense, a theme already planned for the third biennial meeting, must be looked at from a different perspective. At a meeting in Washington in late 1941 the SCHW executive board set support of national defense as its major theme. The Conference would continue between 1942 and 1945 to nationalize previously local issues, largely through the labor movement and the anti-poll-tax fight. As its president John B. Thompson put it, certainly the country could be unified in efforts to defeat the Axis powers abroad, but "the old threats to true democracy in the South are not dead and our disfranchised millions and our minority groups must still use their imagination to realize fully the blessings of the democracy which we boast."[3]

When the Southern Conference attached itself to the Double V Campaign of national black organizations and the black press, it anticipated no less for the entire South. According to this theory, the war abroad was likely to increase the South's potential of finally becoming more equal to other sections of the nation. Other organizations concentrated their efforts largely in the North, but the Southern Conference, with the aid of a few northern white newspapers, directed attention to the southern population. The Conference stressed the waste of human resources involved when all Americans were not allowed equal opportunity, particularly in the war-production industries that created new areas of employment. The Conference also demanded that blacks be permitted to participate in politics and carried on an unprecedented national effort to end the poll tax and other evidence of a Jim Crow society. Southern liberals believed that the United States simply could not afford the risk of alienating millions of its citizens as the nation entered into a world war.

If SCHW expected no less from white southerners, "The South's Part in Winning the War on Democracy" became the theme for the 1942 SCHW meeting set for April 19–21 at the War Memorial Auditorium in Nashville. The world situation and American race relations became a major part of most discussions.

The "Urgent Call to the People of the South," the official call to the 1942 conference, brought up the positive conclusions of the 1938 National Emergency Council's *Report on the Economic Conditions of the South*, particularly the region's abundant resources. The defense of America, according to the Conference, depended on the South because other industrial areas had reached "productive capacity strained to the breaking point." The South had "the plant sites, the manpower—women as well as men, Negro as well as white—at decent living wages in a program of full production." In brief the South had a special contribution to make to the national strength, and SCHW's third conference would "stimulate practical actions to achieve these ends."[4] The Southern Conference, then, combined a Double V outlook with patriotic concerns.

Having decided after the attack on Pearl Harbor to support America's role in World War II, SCHW avoided attention to isolationism at the meeting. The choice of a keynote speaker for 1942 created controversy. Board member John P. Davis, national secretary of the National Negro Congress (NNC), opposed the suggestion of Mordecai Johnson, president of Howard University, because Johnson on recent occasions had urged against the full participation of African Americans in the war. Davis wanted Paul Robeson to appear and had already conferred with Robeson about it. Robeson, a black actor and singer and staunch advocate of civil rights, was drawn to SCHW for its insistence on integrated meetings and various other leftist and racial causes. Davis, who held similar beliefs, did not offer the name of another person; he simply did not like Dombrowski's choice of H. L. Mitchell of the Southern Tenant Farmers Union (STFU) to chair the agricultural panel because "he does not represent any substantial section of organized farmers in the South."[5]

Dombrowski respected Davis's suggestions. The major speakers for the meeting were the recipients of the Thomas Jefferson Award (Frank Porter Graham and Mary Bethune). Robeson appeared for a concert performance, and the group chose a member of the Roosevelt administration to chair the agricultural panel. As it happened, neither Mordecai Johnson nor Mitchell even attended the 1942 meeting. Thus, shunning Mitchell and the grass-roots people he represented in the STFU hurt the Conference's standing in the long run.[6]

The question of who should receive the Thomas Jefferson Award in 1942 presented another major problem for the board. John P. Davis suggested that two awards would be given, one to a black recipient and one to a white, and named Mary McLeod Bethune and Frank Porter Graham, respectively, as his choices. Subsequently, Dombrowski and others wanted Joe Louis, the boxing champion, substituted for Bethune. Clark Foreman agreed that Graham should receive an award and objected to giving a second award, but if that was to be, he favored Paul Robeson. Still others suggested that a southern African American receive only an "honorable mention" or that a black recipient get an award at the next biennial conference. This group contended that to present two awards the same year smacked of segregation. Davis strongly believed that since the country was at war it would be "ideal" that "we should point at this time . . . [to] Negro-white-unity—the unity of all Americans for victory." Contrary to the notion that awarding two medals was for the establishment of a separate one for blacks, Davis hoped that two awards would signify simply that two southerners of equal merit deserved the honor.

The board eventually decided to support Davis's idea of two awards. It then agreed unanimously on Frank Graham but wavered between Joe Louis and Bethune. The whites of the SCHW board were reluctant about Joe Louis because they knew little about him; Mrs. Bethune was well known.

By 1942 Mary McLeod Bethune's record in the struggle for racial equality and the betterment of all humankind was well established. She had distinguished herself as orator, executive, and educator. Her background as founder and president of Bethune-Cookman College had provided contacts through various members of her board of trustees and in fundraising efforts, which eventually led her to an involvement in federal affairs. Eleanor Roosevelt, who in 1924 had entertained Bethune at a luncheon for representative women leaders and who often worked with her in many causes afterward, sometimes helped Bethune in raising funds for her college and occasionally gave White House benefits for that purpose after 1933. Bethune was particularly noted as a counselor to Franklin Roosevelt on African-American affairs and as divisional director of the National Youth Administration. By 1940 Bethune had achieved formal recognition as "among the fifty most distinguished American women."[7]

Dombrowski finally favored Bethune and reasoned that she had given years of service to the South and the nation, while Louis had only won boxing matches. But Dombrowski and a few others still did not want to go against the opinion of African Americans in the matter. In the end the board settled on two awards, one to Graham and one to Bethune.[8]

SCHW arranged a meeting with black community leaders in Nashville to help ease the tension among several of the African-American board members that grew out of the board's disagreement in selecting recipients for the Jefferson Award. SCHW also wanted to increase black participation. The Southern Conference had always wanted black support, but it became all the more important as SCHW sought approval of its efforts in racial justice. Besides, a boost in black membership could only add to gains SCHW wanted to see continue. A larger black membership could also add to red-baiting. The red smear was waning, but the opposition of segregationists against the Conference continued as strong as ever. Dombrowski noticed by 1942 that many liberals, afraid of possible segregationist pressure, had failed to volunteer their services.[9]

SCHW moved to boost the morale of liberals and attract possible new members. It appealed to other sympathetic southern groups and expressed pride in the support it received from the three major labor organizations, the American Federation of Labor (AFL), the Congress of Industrial Organizations (CIO), and the Brotherhood of Sleeping Car Porters.

With the aid of representatives from organized labor, religious, and professional groups working with the local committee on publicity to boost attendance at the 1942 biennial, the Conference set a goal of 2,000 for delegates who would represent more than a million people. In order to entice them to come, the organizing committee set a sum of $2.10 to cover a year's membership, registration fee, and the Robeson concert, for which tickets to the public were $1.10. The projected figure was not fulfilled, however, as the third SCHW meeting ranked lowest with only 525 registered delegates on hand. Reportedly Robeson sang before an audience of over 2,000 people.[10]

Unity became the goal as the Southern Conference made final preparations for its April meeting. Board members agreed that organizational unity was important for conveying to other southerners the need to support every war effort to guarantee an Allied victory. Unity on the chosen theme would serve the Conference well. The theme of mobilizing southern people in the war effort would be lost if the Conference tried to address too many issues.[11]

In keeping with tradition and adding greater significance to the SCHW theme of how integration in the South could help the war effort, Franklin Roosevelt sent a letter in which he stated: "Victory over the Axis aggressors demands that neither man nor wealth be wasted, and that the privilege of participation in our great national undertaking be granted to every citizen. It also demands that our own democracy be maintained as a vital strengthening force." He hoped that the Conference message would convince most southerners how best to use all resources to the fullest.[12]

Southern Conference members and affiliates resounded the war theme in speeches and various sessions during the 1942 meeting. The SCHW president, John B. Thompson, opened the convention, speaking of the diverse makeup of the group assembled and its unity despite much adversity. After chronicling the organization's history, he focused on the various groups represented—"labor," "scholars," "intellectuals," "churchmen," "youth," and "Negro people." He noted that African

Americans still had faith in American democracy though they had suffered "untold indignities." But he added, "They know that all of us who
really care anything about victory cannot afford the stupid neglect and
waste of manpower that is requisite for victory." Thompson's speech
showed that by 1942 the Southern Conference, which had been founded
to address the economic disorders of its region, officially embraced the
pursuit of racial equality because it saw the race issue at the bottom of all
other problems.

SCHW members could not help but notice racial discrimination each
time they met, whether at biennial conferences or board meetings, since
segregated hotel facilities forced blacks to find housing with black families
in whatever communities they gathered, including Nashville in 1942. Occasionally a white member would stage an individual protest against this
reality. In one instance in Nashville at the James Robertson Hotel, the
person in charge of arrangements for an executive board meeting deliberately failed to tell the hotel management that blacks would be in attendance. The owner said that the meeting would not have been permitted
had he known beforehand that blacks would be present. Pretending that
he feared only for the harm that accepting an integrated party would
cause his business, he offered "to rent . . . a suitable place and pay for it
himself for any further such meetings."[13] Incidents such as this helped to
convince SCHW officials that most white southerners were determined
that the region would never willingly be integrated. Although the manager offered money for another place, he must have known that one was
not likely to be located.

The 1942 biennial provided a platform for vocal protest of racial injustice. In their acceptance speeches both Bethune and Graham advocated
the need to end discrimination against blacks. Bethune, like Thompson
earlier, emphasized that blacks still had faith in American democracy for
alleviating that discrimination. Graham, echoing the conference theme,
stated that "the discrimination against Negroes in the war industries is
damaging to our section, our national morale, and our democratic cause
in the world." The double victory theme continued in Graham's and Bethune's addresses as they both asked, "What Are We Fighting For?" Both
answered the question in basically the same way, calling for an extension
of democracy in the United States. Bethune declared: "We are fighting for
the perfection of the democracy of our own beloved America, and the
extension of that perfected democracy to the ends of the world." Graham
varied little in saying, "The three main issues before America are *first*, the
preservation of democracy *in America; second*, the defeat of the Axis in
Europe and Asia, and *third*, the organization of peace in the world."[14]

The presentation of the Thomas Jefferson Award to Bethune and Graham took place on Monday, April 20, the second day of the 1942 meeting.
Since they had spoken on Sunday, the night before they received their
awards, Paul Robeson's concert provided the major attraction on Monday
evening. Nashville Mayor Thomas L. Cummings introduced Eleanor

Roosevelt, who presented the awards during the intermission of the Robeson concert.[15] Graham later said of that night "it was . . . a high honor to be a co-recipient with Mrs. Bethune, who would add to the significance of any award of which she was a recipient."[16]

The inclusion of Robeson's concert in the 1942 conference program symbolized the unity within SCHW on the issue of civil rights. It was his first concert in the South and all the more a point of pride for the Southern Conference in having "the first public entertainment given in a public auditorium to an unsegregated audience."[17] Robeson's public statement at the concert that he would like to see Earl Browder, secretary of the Communist party USA, released from prison, convinced a few skeptics that SCHW used the racial issue "as a cover for its Communism."[18] Thus, Robeson also brought some unwanted controversy to SCHW.

The pride in the integrated Robeson concert was matched by SCHW's success in getting a large number of members of the Roosevelt administration in attendance and on panels. In other cases such persons as TVA Director David Lilienthal, Attorney General Francis Biddle, and Senator Claude Pepper, who supported the Southern Conference's ideas but were unable to attend, sent written messages. Along with die-hard supporters like Frank Graham and Clark Foreman, who also had official ties with the Roosevelt administration, the 1942 group represented the largest contingent from Washington, D.C., yet to attend a biennial meeting.

Four major panels—industrial production, agricultural production, the importance of youth to the military, and citizenship and civil liberties—held sessions on Monday, April 20. The panels on agriculture and youth also considered issues of health care and education. Panel discussions highlighted unity in winning the war and equated discrimination with "a waste of manpower" and a denial of the democracy for which World War II was being fought.[19]

Frank Graham chaired the industrial production panel, which focused on discrimination in war industries and cited specifically the shipbuilding industry at Mobile, where the Alabama Dry Dock Corporation used black laborers in skilled work but refused to classify them accordingly. Panelists noted many instances where black skilled workers trained white apprentices who became classified as skilled, while the black trainers continued to be only lower-paid helpers. The panel pointed out that the Gulf Shipbuilding Corporation, "as if to outdo its competitor in discrimination," refused to employ any blacks except for a few as janitors. All this took place in Mobile where city officials asked the federal government to build thousands of houses for its white laborers who had been brought into the area to fill jobs that blacks, already residing in the area, were capable of filling. The panel concluded that failing to recognize merit among all the workers was bound to retard production and hinder America's military forces. Moreover, the discriminatory conditions were "unfair and demoralizing to patriotic Negroes anxious to help their country" and, as so many of their own were humiliated, they reduced the number of blacks willing to fight in the war.[20] Nor were such conditions limited to the South. The shipbuilding industry, one of the nation's most important industries during World War II, received vast sums of money from the government. And yet despite the efforts of the Fair Employment Practice Committee, discriminatory practices in industries with government contracts remained a nationwide problem.

The industrial production panel had to note, however, that the South benefited from government contracts. Many problems, particularly unemployment, that had hampered the growth of southern industry before the war, had been lessened because of them. Unemployment had begun to dwindle as more men, especially displaced southern farmers, went into armed services and war production. Indeed SCHW believed all businesses, large and small, should be, where appropriate, converted to war production.[21]

The agricultural production panel, chaired by Arthur Raper, who in 1942 was senior social analyst for the U.S. Department of Agriculture/Bureau of Agricultural Economics, summed up agriculture's major dilemma: farmers produced too much. The panel concluded that "victory on the farm front . . . for 1942" meant the planning of nutritional needs and new agricultural knowledge, such as soil conservation and other innovations. The solution also involved developing a way to distribute more equally what had been produced. Addressing freedom from want, one of Franklin Roosevelt's four freedoms, panelists reasoned that "so long as one human being continues to suffer from hidden hunger, agriculture has not met its obligation to society." The panel also saw written tenant contracts as a major necessity. Such contracts would provide for "adequate shelter, home gardens, at least a living wage, as well as protection of the tenant['s] and landlord's share of the crop produced."[22] For those farmers whose conditions war productions and military services had not improved, the panel recommended that SCHW appoint a Fact-Finding Committee on Agricultural and Rural Conditions, which would in turn work with other groups and agencies dealing with the same problems.

Youth in the war effort was the focus of the third panel chaired by Homer P. Rainey, president of the University of Texas. Youths were needed "because theirs is the heritage of freedoms for which we are fighting, because only through them may we preserve the ideals of democracy, [and] we must prove to them in partnership the realities of freedom." This meant that young people, without discrimination based on class, creed, or color, must be given an equal part in the war effort through whatever necessary assistance and training. Panelists believed that the educational opportunities for all groups of southern youth had to be expanded. The panel considered federal agencies such as the National Youth Administration, the Civilian Conservation Corps, the Farm Security Administration, and the Tennessee Valley Authority that trained youth for war industries, conserved natural resources, and provided food for victory and power for industrial production as essential parts of the war program. These agencies were to be vigorously supported, and "any curtailment of their funds or program regarded as a form of sabotage."

To attract more southern youth to the war effort, the third panel also called on SCHW and other southern organizations to sponsor "a war mobilization day," on July 4 in different communities throughout the region. SCHW chose July 14, Bastille Day, to symbolize its attempt at mass unity for World War II support. On July 14, rather than Independence Day, Frank Graham, Josephus Daniels, some 250 other leading southerners, and various groups numbering at least 3,000 people convened a "Southern Win the War Mass Meeting in Raleigh, North Carolina." It is significant that racial integration occurred without any specific request for it. The program, which was also broadcast over the radio, featured speeches by U.S. Supreme Court Justice Hugo Black, Jonathan Daniels of the Civilian Defense Office in Washington, and President Frederick D. Patterson of Tuskegee Institute.[23] The July meeting demonstrated the Conference's ongoing and persistent efforts to publicize its liberal views.

The fourth panel on citizenship and civil liberties discussed Franklin Roosevelt's four freedoms: freedom of speech, freedom of religion, freedom from want, and freedom from fear. In a written statement for the panel, Attorney General Biddle summarized each category, adding that freedom from fear involved security, to be sure, "but not a security gained through the entrenchment of class over class, or of race over race." Senator Pepper's written message implied that perhaps the conferees had misplaced their priorities. He said that he understood that America had to mobilize to win the war in order to maintain the country and "our heritage." To this end the easy task had been effective mobilization; the more difficult and challenging task, that of preserving civil liberties, remained unresolved.

The panel recognized "certain evils" in America society that interfered with the rights of citizens and impaired civil liberties, and highlighted the poll tax and the denial of collective bargaining to workers as the worst among them. Its report warned:

> A failure to correct these evils not only indicates our failure to apply the principles of Democracy to every phase of life, but hampers the all out effort which victory in this war necessitates. Citizens . . . who are denied the right to vote without paying for that privilege are not likely to become the most determined opponents of political tyranny. Workers who are denied the right to organize and bargain collectively . . . may not be the most zealous advocates of respect for law in other parts of the world.[24]

In what became the essence of the black campaign, that in order to fight for democracy abroad rights had to be guaranteed at home, SCHW insisted that all Americans must share in the same goals.

By bringing such evils to the public's attention the Conference considered a large part of its task accomplished. It rested with each delegate to take the necessary next steps. Back in their respective communities they must lobby for bills abolishing voter restrictions and support only candidates who favored a free ballot for all citizens. So must they protest police brutality and fight manifestations of racism and religious intolerance in whatever form it appeared. They must guard against the Dies Committee's threat to civil liberties by lobbying that no further funds for the committee be allocated.[25]

In an assessment of the 1942 biennial, Dombrowski stressed that SCHW wholeheartedly supported the war effort but understood blacks' reluctance to support World War II. He also emphasized that the Conference was interracial and praised the Conference for "giving Negroes a platform from which to present their grievances."[26] But one sponsor, Ethel Clyde, in assessing the meeting, regretted the presence of few blacks at certain sessions, especially the lack of any blacks at the session for youth. Clyde believed that SCHW needed to have encouraged black students from nearby colleges to come and complained, without specifying anyone in particular, that the lack of compelling personalities as panel chairs may have been part of the problem.[27] Dombrowski's assessment pointed to SCHW's success in linking itself with the Double V Campaign, and Clyde hinted at its failure to reach a greater number in the black community and even a larger following.

The newly elected SCHW board member, Lillian Smith, criticized the meeting because youths were "segregated," set aside in a separate youth session. She suggested that at future meetings youth attend and participate on all panels rather than having one set aside for them. Smith held strong convictions about having all committees, just like any other aspects of SCHW, integrated, that is, whites and blacks as well as young and old together. She admonished Dombrowski, who had played a large role in arranging the program, for the youth segregation but praised him for the fact that African-American and youth problems crossed through all parts of SCHW's concerns. She said that his work in SCHW, "is the best act the Conference officials [could] take credit for."[28]

When Lillian Smith found that being editor of the Georgia magazine and taking care of her camp for girls and her farm would keep her too busy to participate actively in Southern Conference board meetings, she sent along her ideas for the Conference to Dombrowski, explaining that her suggestions were not to minimize the work the Conference had done. She emphasized that too much of the Conference's undertaking had been merely symbolic and called for a program that brought results. SCHW needed a program that would appeal to southerners with no special interests to promote. Smith thought it was legitimate for special interests to have representatives at the biennials and on the board and committees, but she believed that such bodies should include more southerners also who had the interests of all southerners at heart. To broaden regional vision she urged the more influential SCHW leaders to invite more social scientists, intellectuals, and persons from the professional groups, white-collar workers. If SCHW did not observe these guidelines, Smith predicted a stressed Conference would become filled with personal hostilities "and that horrible obsessional partisanship which besets all human beings but . . . none more than southerners." She hoped her suggestions would help SCHW grow into a different organization than what it had been in earlier years.

Smith, of course, was right about splintering as a result of many special interests.[29] Still, she had to be reminded that SCHW needed a membership with strong convictions about its various causes, most likely persons affected by specific problems. Tarleton Collier, SCHW member, chair of the penology committee, and an editor of the *Louisville Courier-Journal*, strongly resented her remarks about organized labor. He asserted his strong convictions, saying,"We are not going to do anything fundamentally in the South without organization of the little people, and that this is not going to be accomplished except through a widespread, democratic, and UNIVERSAL labor movement that will be strong [enough] to prevail against the red herrings of race, communism, [and the] CIO." Otherwise, he concluded, those people who will do anything to thwart reforms and changes would have the South return to "the same citadel of isolationism and nationalism [of] 1919 and 1920 under [the] leadership of Tom Watson and others." Collier's point was that southern whites had to be the major target for conversion because these were the people who would be more likely to say, "What the hell is all this hokum, and if the Four Freedoms mean ending the poll tax and letting the niggers vote or make two dollars a day and thus upsetting our folkways, then you can stick 'em you know where."[30]

Even young southerners proved Collier correct on his assessment of the race issue. Two white undergraduate students who had attended SCHW's Nashville meeting editorialized racial views in the *Vanderbilt Alumnus*. Both students agreed that the racial situation in the South was, next to the war, the most important issue in the region. One student wrote that having an interracial assembly without interruption "in the best meeting place of a Southern city," did not solve the problem, that even "having the most publicized woman in America [Eleanor Roosevelt] publicly present a Negro an award for being an outstanding Southerner isn't going to solve it either." The student considered such public display a condemnation of the majority of white southerners and advised that conservative groups instead of liberals deal with the race issue.[31]

Another student, because he favored all for which the Conference stood, condemned the first, defending Charlton, Graham, and others closely affiliated with the Conference. The second student pointed out, of course, that the racial issue had been in the hands of conservative groups long before the Southern Conference and that conservatives had done nothing except to worsen the situation for blacks. The editor of the school paper presented both views but sided with the first.[32]

Dombrowski took the various criticisms into consideration but publicly reported (with a larger membership in mind) uniformly enthusiastic letters from participants of the 1942 meeting. A few conferees wrote that the conference was a success; for example, Eleanor Roosevelt said that the Conference was the best that had been held thus far. Arthur Raper and others praised the Robeson concert for its unsegregated audience of over 2,000 and said it marked "a milestone in the regional cultural history." The National Committee to Abolish the Poll Tax, speaking specifically of the organization's fight against the poll tax, commended SCHW in its summary of the meeting.[33]

SCHW's third biennial marked the new direction the Conference was able to take under the leadership of Dombrowski and Foreman, two influential leaders foremost in solidifying pro-African-American sentiment within the organization and forcing the nation to take notice during the war years. Liberalism came at a cost, however. Southern congressmen who sought to undermine Roosevelt's innovations for liberal causes by chipping away at key persons who contributed to the president's liberalism targeted Foreman, a staunch advocate of racial equality, for elimination. Foreman, who had held important positions in the Roosevelt administration, found himself unemployed in early 1942. It was no coincidence that Foreman's dismissal as director of defense housing in the Federal Housing Authority came during the controversy over whether the Sojourner Truth Housing Project in Detroit, a project built for defense workers, would be integrated. Foreman insisted that blacks would live in the project and was dismissed the very day that housing officials announced that only whites would live there. In the interim that he was jobless, black leaders, particularly Walter White and Mary Bethune (convinced that Foreman's dismissal was based on his liberal racial views), urged Roosevelt to arrange another governmental position for him. Even Eleanor Roosevelt went to her husband on Foreman's behalf.[34]

In early June, Arthur Raper sought employment for Foreman at Black Mountain College in North Carolina. Foreman was impressed with the college and anticipated teaching political science there in the winter but, because of another job opportunity, he did not actually work there until 1943. Even when hired by Black Mountain College, he would not get along well because of his liberal racial ideas.[35] In July 1942 the U.S. Navy Department hired him.[36]

Foreman's dismissal from the federal job was just one of several examples where SCHW pointed to its strong stand for racial justice and World War II. The Southern Conference sought to turn around many negative situations by showing the connection between racial equality at home and victory in World War II abroad. In an address to the Kiwanis Club of

Bessemer, Alabama, on July 22, 1942, Horace G. Wilkinson, Birmingham lawyer and ex-leader of the Ku Klux Klan, attacked the Roosevelt administration, the Supreme Court, and the FEPC, and branded black World War I veterans as cowards who ran away from battles. He advocated the organization of a national League to Maintain White Supremacy. Two days later Alabama Governor Frank Dixon rejected a war contract for producing 1,750,000 yards of tenting material in a state institution because the contract included a nondiscrimination clause. The governor took the occasion to attack the administration, and Alabama Senator John Bankhead protested the placing of northern black troops in the South. Other incidents involved violence against blacks. For example, Roland Hayes, a distinguished African-American tenor, was beaten and jailed in Rome, Georgia; similar and worse incidents were reported in Texas and Missouri. In Alabama threats on advocates of organized labor incited violence between black and white mine workers, sometimes resulting in deaths among blacks.

The Southern Conference interpreted all the incidents as antilabor and as a resurgence of anti-Roosevelt sentiment since the principles of both organized labor and the administration created racial animosity. SCHW did not rule out the possibility that the perpetrators of racial violence sought to drive a wedge between the administration and the South, thus slowing down production in important war industries. Calling these disturbances interference with national security, SCHW requested Attorney General Francis Biddle to take action against "organized attempts to incite racial disturbances."

If U.S. victory over fascism depended on racial equality at home, SCHW asserted that racist actions against blacks amounted to treason. John P. Davis thought that Wilkinson should have been jailed for sedition. Davis and other SCHW members urged Franklin Roosevelt to make a statement, through one of his famous fireside chats, reaffirming constitutional guarantees of all citizens and clarifying the importance of racial equality in particular to global warfare. Davis recommended also that a federal grand jury investigate and prosecute inciters of racial violence and that the federal government reassert its intention to enforce fully and vigorously a policy of nondiscrimination.

SCHW members believed that most white southerners were not willing to jeopardize the entire war effort in the South because of their racism. On that principle the Southern Conference placed a full-page advertisement in the *Birmingham News*.[37] The August 16 advertisement received wide circulation as nonsouthern newspapers ran the statement. Its major point centered on race: "There has been artificially created in the South grave racial tension. . . . Violent speeches filled with Nazi ideas and phrases are inciting race hatred and conflict. . . . A widely advertised campaign to revive the K.K.K. is preparing the South for organized racial violence."[38] The *Atlanta Constitution* carried a statement inspired by and embodying the main line of that in the *Birmingham News*. The *Constitution* adapted its article to a racial disturbance Georgia Governor Eugene Talmadge incited, and greatly contributed to Ellis Arnall's successful campaign to defeat Talmadge for the governorship of Georgia.[39]

Like other Southern Conference endeavors, this ad campaign received mixed reviews. Several supportive individuals and organizations requested sometimes as many as 500 copies of the ad for distribution at meetings, and the United States Department of Justice even commended the Conference for its slogan "Don't Be Provoked."[40] The tear-off at the end of the ad commanded: " 'Don't Be Provoked!' Anyone who starts trouble acts as an Axis agent. Join us in supporting our commander-in-chief. Tear out and send to the President." The ad also provided a blank form for a pledge of support through Conference membership. One person used the tear-off to send a brazenly opposing reply in which the NAACP was given credit for the ad. Since the respondent's only concern centered on race, he automatically assumed that the NAACP, the oldest of blacks' civil rights organizations, had to be responsible. The response read:

> National Association for the advancement of colored People,
>   Your full page add in the Birmingham News today does not fool any Southern Man. Any body can read between the lines and tell you are made up of a lot of Coons[.]
>   Your are 100% correct in stating that the K.K.K. in [is] coming back and the impudent Negroes are bringing [this] on them selves. They are being taught in the High Schools and Colleges to demand their rights. that this is the oppertune time. Abandonment of race segregation just wont work in the South. read the attached clipping ["Negro Soldier Shot to Death in Mobile in Bus Driver Row"] and decid who you think is at fault. There are many more that will get the same dose[.]
>
> > Yours truly
> > Imma Southern Mann
> > Bugtussel. Alabama
> P.S.—Forward this on to your New York headquarters[.][41]

Some Americans remained concerned about Communists, but Foreman's reactions to the various summer disturbances spoke for that segment of southerners who adhered strongly to antifascism when he pointed out Hitler's prediction that the war would decide the world's fate for the next thousand years. An alarmed Foreman continued, "Yet there are those who act as if they would rather lose the war than to allow Negroes their Constitutional rights." Some southerners like William T. Couch at the University of North Carolina Press had concluded that Hitler's rise to power had been enhanced by a race problem. About Governor Dixon's refusal of the federal contract in July, Foreman thought it was "remarkable that in a democracy one should have to admit that the insertion of this clause in Government contracts is one of the real accomplish-ments of the New Deal." He expressed incredulity that such

activities which are known to slow down war production, injure morale and create confusion are allowed to go unchecked at such a crucial time in our history. The only possible explanation is that the people in the South and in the country as a whole do not yet believe that the war *is* a crucial strug-gle. . . . "Don't be provoked!" is a motto that should be printed in the news-papers and in every vehicle of public transportation, on the radio and in the movies. For self-control is now a form of patriotism.[42]

The racial disturbances intimidated some Southern Conference board members. Lucy Mason had supported and defended John P. Davis when Baldwin accused him of being a Communist, yet she did not want him to chair the civil liberties committee. It was not that the Conference lacked the courage, she said, but that there was no reason why the organization should incite trouble in an already troubled time. Her excuse centered on the racial unrest of July, and every time Davis's name was used in pub-licity in that regard, she cautioned, it would only act to give the reaction-aries more about which to become inflamed. She preferred "the appointment of a prominent [southern] white man."[43] Mason's analysis in this instance contradicted her otherwise liberal position on race. From her reasoning here, the Conference would have to remove all blacks from the board and from the SCHW, a development that Foreman and Dom-browski would never allow to happen.

Still racial violence brought condemnation from other SCHW leaders. The Southern Conference centered its attention on lynching, another problem that the black community sought to stop through federal legisla-tion. The Mississippi lynching of three persons, all taken from jail and two of whom were fourteen-year-old boys, occurred within one week in October 1942. Mississippi Governor Paul B. Johnson immediately con-demned the acts and had an investigator dispatched to Clarke County where the boys had been hanged. The governor also authorized the use of state guards in apprehending persons who allegedly had taken part in the lynchings. A number of arrests were made, but in Jones County, where the black adult male was lynched, the county grand jury, as of late 1942, had returned no indictments, not even after the incidents gained national attention and an investigation by the Federal Bureau of Investi-gation. In November at least seventy-five of the most prominent citizens of the state, including a large number of SCHW members, signed a letter to Governor Johnson that appeared as full-page statement in the *Jackson Clarion Ledger*. The letter commended the governor for his vigorous de-nunciation of the incidents but, unsatisfied with the outcome, the signers requested him to take further action.[44]

Praise for the Conference's stance came from as far away as New York, with one observer pointing out that "there is no doubt that the Southern

Conference is about the only bright sign that any of us can see in the South today."[45] Contrary to the actual outcome, the Conference claimed that the campaign contributed to getting federal indictments, which would have set a precedent in lynch law history.[46]

The racial turmoil that commanded national attention during the summer of 1943 presented yet another opportunity whereby the Conference could make its point on how the stressful situations could possibly harm America's chance for victory in World War II but not before Conference opposition would have its say. That June a West Virginian wrote to criticize basic Southern Conference principles—abolishing the tax, a democratic South, and a federal antilynching law. Commenting that "the South is democratic enough," the critic declared, "it is probably the case that you do not understand democracy." The writer claimed common interests with the Southern Conference on military victory in World War II, a lasting peace after the war, and human welfare in general, but did not see the necessity of including the issues of race, labor, and liberalism. The critic wrote:

> You run the danger of offending some of our noblest allies by your indication of colour-line fanaticism. . . . So far I think that ORGANIZED LABOUR has shown itself to be Democracy's enemy. . . . [Unions] are on the wrong track entirely. When a local one gets started out decently, it has to join one of these filthy national hook ups.

Finally, the opponent reasoned that the Conference's definition of liberalism meant "only those who agree with you in every way. That, to me, seems narrow," and added, "I hope you are properly insulted."[47] Dombrowski sent many such letters to Eleanor Roosevelt with the hope that she would pass them on to the president, giving him firsthand knowledge of what the Conference was up against in the South.[48]

During the summer of 1943 racial violence broke out in Newark; Detroit; Mobile; Beaumont, Texas; and Los Angeles, and SCHW took notice immediately, quickly pointing out that all areas were locations for important war-production industries and that disturbances of this kind hurt the war effort. Although SCHW and others could not prove it, they surmised the racial unrest to be the work of Axis spies, playing on the most pressing southern problem, racial discrimination. Dombrowski requested southern leaders to prompt individuals to write statements to Franklin Roosevelt, asking that he make a statement to improve race relations.[49] Responding to Dombrowski, several leaders pleaded with President Roosevelt to go before the American people, preferably in one of his fireside chats, and explain to them the seriousness of the situation, and to emphasize that victory depended on complete American unity. A typical message read:

I know no person in America who wields more influence with our people than you do. Knowing of your deep interest in our national unity, and knowing you do not want an epidemic of race riots to plague our nation, we want you to know that we feel you could do a great deal to erase and keep under control the prejudice against Negroes by a large portion of our white population in the south, if you would make a Fireside Chat over the radio to the American people on this grave and fundamental issue.[50]

Franklin Roosevelt, however, remained silent, and SCHW continued to focus on the disturbances in pamphlets and other publications.[51]

Because of its outrage over the lynchings and other vestiges of racial violence during the summer of 1942 and the increasing demand of its members to be better informed about the Conference's activities, SCHW had developed in 1942 the *Southern Patriot*, a monthly publication which appeared with the avowed goal of mobilizing people and resources for the war. The publication served to unify the war effort among organized labor, farmers, churches, and any liberal elements of the South. Moreover, the organization hoped that the distribution of a monthly publication would convince readers that SCHW supported ideas that all southerners would eventually embrace. Thus its distribution would attract new members, hopefully the unconverted mass of southerners.[52]

The first *Southern Patriot* had appeared in December 1942 with the front page headlined "It's a People's War," following through on SCHW ideas that had prevailed with the theme for its third biennial and emphasizing the need for total commitment from all Americans to assure an Allied victory.[53] A total commitment meant overcoming racism, and as the first issue made clear, SCHW would persist in publicizing racial injustice.

Conference members were not alone in their belief that public knowledge of injustices could work to a quicker solution. George Marshall of the Marshall Fund, which took great interest in improving racial relations, for instance, trusted SCHW's strategy and pointed out the Wellmon case to the Conference, a case about which Marshall had himself wired the governor of North Carolina. William Wellmon, a black construction worker, had allegedly attacked a sixty-seven-year-old white woman of Statesville, North Carolina, in 1941, and despite evidence that proved his innocence, he had been convicted and sentenced to be executed in December 1942. The SCHW plea sought pardon for Wellmon from North Carolina Governor J. M. Broughton, and the governor, convinced of Wellmon's innocence and having already granted him one reprieve, stayed the execution for another sixty days until March 5, 1943. Broughton planned to release him at the end of the second stay.[54] In another instance Louis E. Burnham of the Southern Negro Youth Congress reported that he and a white couple had been arrested, charged with disorderly conduct and violation of the segregation ordinance, and fined in court for eating together in a black restaurant in Birmingham. Burnham considered it hopeless to contest the fine but wanted the incident reported in the *Southern Patriot*.[55] SCHW's publication also carried stories frequently on violence against labor organizers in southern states. Because the Conference staff did not follow up many reports, readers often missed the inspiration that victories, however small, could bring.[56]

By 1943 the Southern Conference had become more uniform on its stand for racial equality, but several members, including African Americans, varied in opinion on how best to arrive at this ultimate goal. Embracing Roosevelt's New Deal principles as the solution to the South's major problems simultaneously provided an avenue of skepticism for black SCHW leaders who were quick to criticize shortcomings of the New Deal. Upon resigning as executive director of the National Negro Congress in 1943, SCHW leader John P. Davis continued to criticize the Roosevelt administration, particularly the ineffectiveness of the FEPC in its efforts to integrate African Americans into the war effort. FEPC's failure made Davis's conviction even stronger for the Conference's task of systematically articulating the need for more black involvement in World War II. Not all Conference leaders believed that public education would result in needed reforms. A. Philip Randolph advised blacks to demand equal rights through "civil disobedience," a tactic that Davis in 1943 called unreliable and cautioned would only lead to more violence against them. But in regard to the *Southern Patriot* Davis criticized the Conference for including information on too many other issues. Furthermore, he wanted the *Southern Patriot* to publicize positive actions, too, for example, the Louisiana governor's prosecution of the white murderer of a black soldier. Davis felt that public attention to the indictment, when it was returned, would have been of particular interest to Attorney General Biddle and other New Deal policymakers like Henry Wallace, who were sympathetic to causes for racial equality.[57] If Davis had been more amenable to civil disobedience, perhaps he could have convinced other SCHW leaders to add it to its paper campaigns in the 1940s.

Since the Conference sought racial equality, the lack of blacks in paid administrative positions proved awkward. One of Dombrowski's aims was to rectify the situation. He said the organization needed to do more than merely educational campaigns on this matter. But even Dombrowski experienced difficulty in this effort because he had to "prepare the field and smooth the way" with office neighbors in the Presbyterian Building where the SCHW office was located. He took so much time facilitating a smooth transition that the person he had wanted to work for SCHW took a job with Charles S. Johnson at Fisk University in the sociology department.[58] Dombrowski persisted in his plan, bringing it up frequently, but at least two years lapsed before the Conference would hire a black administrator. Dombrowski announced that Osceola E. McKaine had agreed in late 1945 to become the Conference's first black field representative and administrator as of January 1, 1946. McKaine, who would maintain an office in his home state of South Carolina, had long been involved in the struggle for racial equality. In the fall of 1940, the associate editor of the *Columbia* (South Carolina) *Lighthouse and Informer* initiated through that paper a movement that led to equal pay for black and white teachers in South Carolina. A champion of the working class, McKaine helped to organize Local 273 of the United Furniture Workers of America (CIO) in South Carolina. These activities placed him in the same stream of thought as SCHW leaders.[59] Because of travel limitations imposed during the war, the Southern Conference did not meet until November 1946, but in the meantime a few executive board meetings took place and the campaigns continued. The SCHW board decided unanimously in January 1944 to pay particular attention to repeal of the poll tax, a permanent FEPC, and the end of segregation.[60]

In the same meeting the Conference's board discussed the establishment of the moderate Southern Regional Council (SRC) and what its relationship with this newly formed organization would be. Since Howard Odum, SRC's first president, had already advised against a merger of any type, the matter was dropped.[61] Later developments revealed that the SRC and SCHW did not agree on a common racial stance, even though a few influential SCHW members, Will Alexander, for example, were active in the SRC.

SCHW, whose basic principles were founded on the belief that "a free and unfettered ballot" was the "cornerstone of democracy" and that thoroughgoing social and economic reforms must be predicated primarily on the democratic political process, aimed its work in 1944 on enlarging the electorate. On two fronts, the poll tax and the white primary, the Southern Conference, in cooperation with the National Committee to Abolish the Poll Tax, supported and mobilized others to H.R. 7, the poll-tax repeal measure, securing thousands of signatures for petitions. Although there was no success on the federal legislation, the Conference could claim partial credit for the favorable state action in Georgia.[62]

In the case of the white primary in Texas, SCHW secured signatures of outstanding southerners to a statement favoring its elimination and publicized the statement in the *Southern Patriot*. SCHW's position was justified when the Supreme Court outlawed the white primary in *Smith* v. *Allwright*. The organization also participated in voter registration campaigns in cooperation with the CIO-Political Action Committee (CIO-PAC) and the National Citizens Political Action Committee, in preparation for the presidential election, a campaign that encouraged people to vote by publicizing the registration dates in various states.[63]

At its Chicago convention in 1944 the CIO's executive board unanimously endorsed the Conference. In a follow-up meeting in Washington D.C., on December 7, presided over by its president Philip Murray and attended by representatives of CIO unions with special interest in the South, Clark Foreman, Lucy Mason, and James Dombrowski asked the unions to substantiate their endorsement of SCHW with financial aid. From August through November Dombrowski was on leave of absence and served as assistant director of public relations for CIO-PAC. The following year funds from CIO unions became the single largest income for the Conference.[64]

Although the group claimed independence, SCHW initiated and prepared material for an Editors and Writers Meeting, December 1944. At least fifty persons came together to discuss the restricted southern franchise. After extensive analysis of southern voting laws, the group unanimously agreed that the two obstacles causing the most restriction were the poll tax and the white primary.

SCHW's propaganda against the poll tax stirred many of those elected to office on a small number of votes who knew too well what to do to assure reelection. In 1945 Senator Theodore G. Bilbo of Mississippi spoke of the Southern Conference as "the South's No. One Enemy," a throwback to the 1938 National Emergency Council's *Report*, which referred to the South as the nation's number-one economic problem. The Conference, upon its founding, had centered attention on the *Report's* phrase, and now Bilbo captioned the Conference with similar language. His words along with derogatory remarks about the Conference, particularly its bold stand for racial equality, by Representative John Rankin of Mississippi, Representative Eugene Cox of Georgia, and Senator James O. Eastland of Mississippi provoked SCHW to begin its own campaign against these southern demagogues, a campaign that initially was only verbal. Conference President Clark Foreman, speaking to the Negro Newspaper Publishers Association on behalf of his organization, appealed for non-southern liberals' understanding and support in aiding southern liberals in the fight to "get rid of the Bilbo crowd."

If southern congressmen were not lambasting the Southern Conference specifically, many were browbeating programs that SCHW advocated—a permanent FEPC, for example. During the course of his filibuster in Congress in summer 1945 against FEPC, Senator Eastland said that "the Negro soldier was a[n] utter and abysmal failure in combat in Europe. . . . He has disgraced the flag of his country. He will not fight. He will not work." A few months later the SCHW conducted a survey that involved 255 white southern newspaper editors about Senator Eastland's statement, the results of which showed overwhelmingly that this segment of southerners opposed the recent expressions of racial prejudice in Congress. Foreman, though racial strife made his conclusion questionable, believed that the poll showed that the southern congressmen's statements did not represent "the true feeling of the South."[65]

Although all the southern demagogues equally disliked the Conference and expressed themselves just as forcefully, Bilbo became the epitome of their opposition toward SCHW. Many Conference leaders began to refer to Bilbo and his lot as "the Bilbonic plague." The Conference was good at making the best of a bad situation, and it led a campaign to raise SCHW funds "with Sen. Bilbo's help." It mailed out a postcard appeal at Christmas 1945 over Bilbo's signature with the message: "Please send a Christmas contribution to Bilbo's Enemy Number One—now." By May 1946 this appeal had brought in $1,000 as "public enemies of Sen. Bilbo responded." Southern Conference spokesmen continued publicly to denounce "Bilboism" in the South, and later their campaign took on a different character as they and other liberals sought actively the defeat of "poll-tax congressmen" in the 1946 election. When that strategy failed, they pursued efforts specifically to expel Bilbo, "the man," from the Senate but without success.[66] Suffering with cancer of the mouth, Bilbo agreed to step down until his health recovered. He never returned to the Senate; he died in the summer of 1946.

SCHW took every opportunity to combat prejudice, especially in the field of race and religion. The activities of Christian-front, anti-Semitic, and fascist groups were exposed through the *Patriot*. When the Christian American Association used religious and patriotic symbols to hide its "true fascist character," in promoting state legislation to destroy organized labor, the Southern Conference devoted the December 1944 issue of the *Patriot* exclusively to exposing the organization, and received orders for more than 100,000 copies.[67]

In 1944–1945 the Southern Conference pressured Congress to make the FEPC permanent. SCHW believed that when all southern citizens prospered the entire region prospered. Although many thousands of blacks found industrial employment in almost every southern city, in no southern city were blacks employed in numbers commensurate with their proportion of the population. SCHW was pleased by the inroads made against discrimination in hiring but still saw that a gigantic task was needed to break down discrimination on the job and in firing. Foreman further linked a permanent FEPC to national defense, reemphasizing before a Senate committee that such a measure would better protect America from practices that fostered disunity and hatred.[68]

The Southern Conference for Human Welfare, like so many of the newly formed race-relations groups of this period, spent a lot of money and energy in paper campaigns to address peace between the races, but Conference members continued for the rest of their lives searching for and working for solutions to the one problem that the majority of southern whites refused to consider, let alone address, unless in a negative vein. The Southern Regional Council (1944) became a new race-relations group in the South; in the North liberals created the Union for Democratic Action (1941) and the nonviolent-action-oriented Congress of Racial Equality (1942).[69] Many organizations sprang up in the midst of 1940s racial violence, but SCHW had been around since 1938 and since then, though at times it wavered, had sought to alleviate the problems that caused poor race relations. SCHW consistently supported major breakthroughs for the South—the elimination of the poll tax, the end of white primaries, the establishment of a permanent FEPC, and the end of segregation and discrimination—and included in its theme equal wages and better jobs for blacks, and higher wages for everyone. Aided by the war's elevation of civil rights to national prominence and a new, more sympathetic national administration in the years after the war, SCHW continued its efforts for racial justice. By the end of the war, however, SCHW found that the majority of white southerners still resisted as before efforts for racial justice.

Critical Years for SCHW

The history of the Southern Conference for Human Welfare (SCHW) is confounded by the apparent contradiction that 1946–1948 marked both its lowest and highest points. In the early part of this period SCHW created an educational arm, the Southern Conference Educational Fund (SCEF), in the hope that its tax-exempt status would free SCHW to speak more to political issues. All went well for a while, until old organizational troubles of finance, personal conflicts, and the continued onslaught of red-baiting took their toll. In an era that witnessed the beginning of the Cold War, charges of communism grew more serious, and the public reacted accordingly. Instead of improving its status and prestige, SCHW initially succeeded only in creating confusion for its members and interested financiers.[1]

Since SCEF and SCHW coexisted between January 1946 and November 1948, controversies arose over finances and administrative policies. SCEF, the component that now was allowed the tax-exempt status, received funds that SCHW needed for lobbying for legislation. Contributors, often following past procedures, mailed funds to SCHW only later to be informed that SCEF received SCHW funds because it held the tax-exempt status. Friction, therefore, developed between the Southern Conference and the Educational Fund in the absence of specific guidelines for the division of funds. The creation of more state committees added to the financial burden because these new auxiliaries spent more funds than they raised.

SCHW's attempt to find ways to resolve the race problem only added to the fervor with which reactionaries attacked the struggling organization. Nonetheless, during this difficult period SCHW's national administration provided major impetus to the pursuit of racial equality, setting into place a legacy that SCEF could carry forward even after its predecessor's demise. The Southern Conference for Human Welfare made it acceptable for respectable southern whites to speak openly about the desirability of an integrated, economically equal, southern society.[2]

SCHW, having dedicated much time and effort to racial equality during World War II, was even more vociferous at the war's conclusion in demanding equality for blacks. Indeed, during the war SCHW made its boldest stand for racial equality. As a result several black members, prominent among the many outstanding persons who had participated in and supported the Southern Conference movement since its beginning, became more deeply committed. Mary McLeod Bethune learned as an SCHW board member of its need to improve in membership and finances, and offered in late 1945 to make a southern speaking tour for the specific purpose of promoting the Conference's program, hoping to increase membership and boost finances in the process. Although Bethune specifically sought more southern black involvement in the Southern Conference, her tour would be used to reach a larger number of progressive members of the southern white community. The SCHW accepted Bethune's offer for a sponsored tour of the South.[3]

Once SCHW agreed to sponsor Bethune, Dombrowski, having reported SCHW's low financial status, urged the various state committee chairpersons to make every effort to assure the success of her speaking tour. The central office had been unable to meet its payroll for January, and he doubted whether it would be able to continue to subsidize state affiliates. The situation improved slightly when the Washington office became self-sustaining, and the New York office began to carry more of the financial load.[4] Part of the preparation for Bethune's tour involved sending letters to a number of members and contributors in the states where she would appear. SCHW always welcomed the cooperation of similar organizations. Although funds were low, it sent a small contribution to the Southern Negro Youth Congress and requested of Louis Burnham, its leader in Birmingham, that the group include SCHW material in its pamphlet to be ready for distribution in time for Bethune's address in that city.[5]

In order to reach larger audiences as well as to highlight that southerners still looked forward to an urban New South, the creation of which was a major goal when SCHW was founded in 1938, SCHW selected industrial areas for Bethune's speeches. By early January 1946 Bethune was scheduled to speak in about nine southern cities of Tennessee, Alabama, Florida, Georgia, and North Carolina, all between January 16 and 27. Before the tour she appeared at a fundraising party in New York on the 13th, and at the end, at a party in Washington, all for the Southern Conference.[6]

The Conference began immediately to publicize Bethune's appearances in various newspapers. It emphasized through the Bethune tour the major reason it had been established in 1938, repeatedly citing the indirect responsibility of Franklin D. Roosevelt, who solicited the *Report on the Eco-*

nomic Conditions of the South. Prominent southerners Lucy Randolph Mason, Frank Graham, Clark Foreman, and several others who developed the *Report*, also were founders of SCHW and had since remained strong supporters. Referring to itself as "friend and champion of the common man," SCHW reminded the South of the major issues it had been addressing since 1938. At each program where Bethune had been scheduled to speak the Conference kept participants biracial, even making sure that it used both black and white ushers. The printed programs included background information along with a similar statement for respective state committees, identification of the central office's executive board and of each state committee, and a long list of sponsors.[7]

Bethune was accompanied by Witherspoon Dodge, a newly employed, white field representative for SCHW and former director of the Fair Employment Practice Committee (FEPC) in Atlanta. The recently selected African-American field representative, Osceola McKaine, had originally been scheduled to tour with Bethune, but he worked instead in Alabama with a voter-registration campaign.[8]

The noted educator and civic leader began her ten-day tour in Nashville on January 17, 1946, at the Spruce Street Baptist Church, a black community church, in order to avoid Jim Crow ordinances. The issue was not whether Bethune could speak at only a black church but rather that the audience would be able to sit racially integrated without potential hostility from local authorities.[9] At this gathering Bethune appealed for a permanent FEPC and other important features of the Conference program. She told the overflowing church audience that "the ballot is the thing that will give you strength." Citing her efforts for over fifty years in the advancement of African Americans, she issued a special appeal for black women's political involvement and admonished that "brown women of America can only be counted as we unite" to make the SCHW's New South democracy a reality. If enough black voters would participate in Nashville politics, she believed the city would be forced to make changes inclusive of the needs of its black population, the first of which should be the employment of black policemen. She urged the city to rely on all of its human resources including the large number of qualified blacks from the several Nashville-area educational institutions. Bethune ended her speech with an appeal for membership and small contributions. Her efforts contributed to a 1946 projected budget of $100,000.[10]

Bethune's 1946 tour gained the support and involvement of leading African-American community leaders who were not necessarily Southern Conference members but whose belief in racial equality would cause them to work with the organization if only for a short time. Martin Luther King, Sr., pastor of the Ebenezer Baptist Church in Atlanta, offered his church for her speech there. In North Carolina, Charlotte Hawkins Brown, SCHW board member as well as founder and president of the

Palmer Memorial Institute, introduced Bethune when she spoke in Greensboro; President F. D. Bluford of North Carolina Agricultural and Technical College headed the arrangements committee. C. C. Spaulding, president of the North Carolina Mutual Life Insurance Company, chaired the committee for arrangements in regard to Bethune's visit in Durham.[11]

At the end of her speaking engagements for January, an exhausted Bethune was gratified by having reached thousands of people to tell them of the work of the Southern Conference. Her challenge was SCHW's success. The Conference did not prepare a summarized financial statement of the tour, but North Carolina alone reported 446 new members and donations of over $2,500, a favorable indication for what possibly came from other states.[12]

Bethune ended her speaking engagements in Durham, and as SCHW members vied for the biennials in their home states, Mary Price, chair of her native North Carolina committee, hoped that closing Bethune's tour there would make the state the choice for the next biennial. Despite Price's optimism, Foreman called a board meeting. The liberal North Carolina, then, missed having the Conference for its membership meeting as the larger event was postponed for later in 1946.[13]

Although the call urging board members to attend stated the subject of bylaws as the main business for discussion, the group also considered other pressing concerns.[14] Of the total thirty-six board members elected in 1942, only eleven attended the January 25 gathering in which they urged SCHW officers to work with other organizations toward the purposes of SCHW and to keep the board informed on such cooperative participation. In matters that concerned the working class and labor interests, the SCHW board adopted a resolution in support of the southern membership drive that was under way by organized labor and discussed the need for legislation that would increase hourly minimum wages, a major policy item that would improve standards of living in all fields of health, education, housing, and welfare. The board also adopted a resolution in support of Kentucky Senator Alben Barkley, a Democrat, who rebuked senators engaged in a filibuster to prevent action on the Permanent Fair Employment Practice Committee legislation. The SCHW endorsed Barkley's gallant condemnation of the other senators' tactics as "unjustifiable and indefensible." Defending James Dombrowski, the board denounced Mississippi Senator James Eastland, who had ridiculed the SCHW executive secretary because of his Polish name. SCHW declared Eastland, not Dombrowski, the un-American.[15]

The Southern Conference underwent a major, though hardly noticed, change at this January 1946 board meeting. Clark Foreman, SCHW president since 1942, proposed creating the Southern Conference Educational Fund, an idea that he and Dombrowski had worked on earlier in the month. Foreman persuaded the board to accept his recommendation, upon which it adopted a resolution.[16] Confusion for SCHW members arose, and with due cause, over the use of "changing the name" in the SCHW resolution, which was at best ambiguous, so that many members believed SCHW had simply become SCEF when, in fact, what occurred involved SCHW establishing a different organization to accept tax-exempt contributions and take on educational projects that would allow SCHW more freedom in political affairs.[17]

When the organization elected officers to serve temporarily until the general meeting that would be held later that year, Frank Porter Graham, who remained president of the University of North Carolina, was re-elected its honorary president. Dombrowski became dual administrator for SCHW and SCEF, being advised that he would spend at least one-third of his time with the Southern Conference. Foreman, however, reluctant to serve as president, preferred to serve only half-time, claiming that he had accepted a job, one that he did not identify, that would be effective as of February 1. This job, he said, would require more of his attention. Foreman assured the board that he still believed in the Conference's work, that the well-launched SCHW could do without his services, but he feared that SCHW could not afford to pay him a salary that adequately met his needs.[18]

Foreman's action had the effect, whether intended or not, of the board raising his salary, but his proffered resignation also involved the issue of his working relationship with Dombrowski. Foreman offered to resign only after Dombrowski became administrator; it is likely that he had now begun to doubt Dombrowski's effectiveness. Foreman also decided to remain president after the board asked him to reconsider and indicated that he would be provided an annual salary of $8,000 with an expense allowance of $2,000. The board set Dombrowski's salary at $2,500 per year as administrator and executive secretary, $500 less than what he had earned as just executive secretary.[19] Dombrowski's acceptance of such a smaller salary than Foreman's raises questions for which we do not have answers, especially since both held doctoral degrees.

As time passed and the two officials went about fulfilling their obligations for the Conference, Dombrowski did not seem to resent Foreman's higher salary. Nor did he ask for an increase in pay even though he had earlier considered teaching part time at the Garrett Biblical Institute, a graduate seminary of the Methodist Church at Northwestern University in Evanston, Illinois. Dombrowski's acceptance of less pay from SCHW made obvious his dedication to its program, particularly the civil rights aspect, a component of the SCHW program that he would spend the rest of his life trying to implement even though he would have other employment opportunities. But Foreman consistently criticized Dombrowski.[20] The board's action revealed that it considered Foreman indispensable for its program, possibly reinforcing what he had already concluded.

Furthermore, the confusion over responsibilities of the president and administrator eventually led to major differences and the beginning of an end for SCHW after the November 1946 membership meeting.

The process of gaining tax-exempt status for SCEF from the Treasury Department was simple enough. Dombrowski completed forms requesting tax exemption for SCEF and transmitted a certified copy of the amendment to the SCHW's charter on May 2, 1946, which stated that SCHW had changed its name to the Southern Conference Educational Fund. SCHW persisted in perpetuating ambiguity when a report that presented highlights of the SCHW activities for 1946 declared that the charter of the SCHW was amended to change the organization's name to SCEF at the January meeting, that a newly established SCHW was organized. To obtain tax-exempt status for educational work, then, the SCHW created SCEF, and for a time the two coexisted. But the board and officers did not make this clear for a long time. As for the Treasury Department, it worked with uncharacteristic speed and granted SCEF tax-exempt status in July 1946.[21]

In the future SCHW informed its contributors that it had established an educational fund to do purely educational work and to receive tax-deductible contributions and that "the Southern Conference for Human Welfare feels it necessary to keep itself free to participate in political and legislative work wherever necessary."[22] Although Foreman did not make it clear to potential contributors, they were to give all donations to SCEF and specify which group, SCHW or SCEF, was to use the funds.[23] As late as September the SCHW was still demonstrating incompetence. In applying for a grant from the William C. Whitney Foundation of New York City, Dombrowski wrote on SCHW stationery to ask for funds for the Southern Conference Educational Fund.[24] He was informed that the grant application needed to be presented to the Whitney Foundation on SCEF stationery if this was the organization that would actually receive the grant. Dombrowski later made the request on SCEF letterhead that included the names of officers typed in. The fact that SCHW and SCEF used the same stationery and the same people as officers confounded the situation even more.[25]

While the Southern Conference sought to obtain tax-exempt status and clarify the relative purposes of the Educational Fund and SCHW, Osceola E. McKaine, SCHW's only black field representative, and Witherspoon Dodge, a white field representative, attempted to recruit members and raise money. McKaine and Dodge visited various southern states and contacted prominent citizens of the local communities. They distributed SCHW literature and succeeded in involving some of the most active community and national leaders in SCHW activities.

In Virginia, McKaine traveled to Richmond, Portsmouth, Norfolk, and Suffolk. In Richmond, he met and talked with Luther P. Jackson, a prominent community leader and professor of history at Virginia State

College, who agreed to serve as vice-president of the newly formed Virginia Committee. Palmer Weber, a white southern liberal, was one of McKaine's contacts in Virginia, too. McKaine also met Virginia Beecher, who had been largely the organizer for the new state affiliate, and Vivian Carter Mason, executive director of the local National Council of Negro Women and secretary of the Virginia Committee.

McKaine was warmly received at several local gatherings in the Tidewater area of Virginia. He addressed ministerial alliances, political clubs, and organizations of business and professional men. He found blacks and organized labor groups in the Tidewater particularly interested in SCHW, and they urged him to return soon to help them in local elections. SCHW gained members and contributions through McKaine's work. P. B. Young, Sr., vice-president of the Southern Regional Council and publisher of the *Norfolk Journal and Guide,* made a sizable contribution, promising to give more later. The president of the Eureka Lodge agreed to serve on the executive board of the Virginia Committee.[26]

McKaine met Foreman in Charleston, South Carolina, where Foreman spoke on February 19 and 20. When the two left, enthusiastic members of South Carolina had begun to organize another state committee. As of February 20 McKaine was responsible for raising more than $1,000 in donations with a pledged membership of close to 2,000.[27]

McKaine proved most successful in voter-registration drives for the Southern Conference. Convinced his campaign would be greatly handicapped if conducted during a period that SCHW's work overlapped with that of another group, he assessed registration drives of various organizations prior to assignment. The Southern Aid Society of Virginia, pleased with his assistance and advice in local politics, sent high praises to Dombrowski and requested that McKaine return to assist in the campaign of an African American for councilman in Norfolk in June. Dombrowski was pleased for McKaine to cooperate.[28] McKaine's field work in Savannah, Georgia, between March 10 and March 24 raised the number of blacks registered to vote from 1,500 to approximately 7,000. Because of McKaine's outstanding achievement with the voter-registration drives in black communities, as of June 11, 1946, he had a full schedule of field-work assignments through August 5. He worked in Georgia, Tennessee, South Carolina, Virginia, and Florida.[29]

McKaine, like so many of the outstanding leaders from the black community, made numerous useful suggestions to SCHW officials on how SCHW could operate more smoothly and more efficiently. Based on his experiences McKaine drew up a set of plans that he sent to Dombrowski to facilitate fieldwork. He recommended that the secretary of each state committee prepare for assigned field-workers a list of names, addresses, and telephone numbers of persons in various organizations, including heads of ministerial alliances, heads of teachers associations, college fraternities, sororities, Elks, Masons, medical and dental associations, labor unions, and beauticians who might be of help to the Conference. Press notices in African-American and white newspapers that explained SCHW's activities should appear before the field representative arrived in the area. The representative also needed a quiet place to work while making local calls. Dombrowski heeded McKaine's advice and sent letters to committees expecting McKaine or Witherspoon Dodge setting forth desired preconditions.[30]

While McKaine was in Virginia, Dodge was in Florida, where he worked through the early part of March. In Jacksonville the African Methodist Episcopal ministerial association contributed $200 and promised continued support to SCHW. The reward in Tampa came in terms of prestige. University of Tampa President Ellward A. Nanee invited Dodge to speak at the University about SCHW. Nanee also asked Dodge to recommend a few liberal southern professors for lectures at the school. Dodge asked Dombrowski to send names to Nanee and to make sure to include Alva Taylor. Taylor, professor in the School of Religion at Vanderbilt University, epitomized Dombrowski's nineteenth-century heroes who combined social reform with religion.[31]

Dodge arrived in Savannah the week after McKaine's departure. Dodge appeared on the program at a mass meeting with the president of Georgia State College and two other influential persons in the community. He spoke to various clubs and Methodist and Baptist ministerial associations. He also worked on voter registration and participated in the League of Women Voters' radio program "Shall Democracy Restrict the Suffrage?"[32]

Between April and June Dodge covered the same states as McKaine, even visiting some of the same cities. Although Dodge was white, he appealed particularly to African Americans. In May he boasted about the enthusiastic crowds at his talks, many at black colleges in Atlanta. He also spoke proudly of the prominent blacks who promised to follow up on personal solicitation from the black community in the Atlanta area.[33] The Southern Conference had begun to expend more energy than ever before to build black membership. Although African Americans remained about a third of its members, SCHW work in black communities caused alarm later for its cooperative lifelong ally, the NAACP.

By June, Dodge believed that he saw the making for a mass movement. He had observed that many people wanted to join SCHW but simply could not pay for membership and tried to convince Dombrowski to get nonpaying members involved. Dombrowski reasoned that people ought to pay something in order to join the organization. He knew that the Southern Conference could not afford to mail literature for free, but literature informed members of SCHW's activities.[34] Dombrowski's hesitation cost SCHW members who stood to benefit the most from the reforms SCHW advocated. Dombrowski failed to act on advice similar to Dodge's in the 1950s when Fred Shuttlesworth, a leading civil rights activist, would broach the same idea. Consequently, Dombrowski's inability to reach poor southerners meant that the Conference would not attract a broad following. But the matter of free membership had less to do with this failing than with the Southern Conference's liberalism.

Dodge's fieldwork paid off for the Southern Conference; in July he reported having raised over $2,800 and having secured 547 members. He also had many stories to tell of his travels, one of which involved a soldier at a meeting in Knoxville, Tennessee, who endorsed his government check for $100 to the SCHW to cover membership of the fifty persons present and who told Dodge that he had done so because he was surprised to "find a fellow of your kind in the South."

McKaine and Dodge largely were well received in the states they canvassed, but white racism was a constant obstacle. Dodge noticed a strong hostility toward SCHW among whites in Alabama. Many people who had been referred to him, suspicious of the "radical reputation of the Conference," disagreed with one or another Conference principle, most frequently citing its alliance with organized labor and its bold stand for racial equality. After attempting to reply to their "evasions, excuses, and accusations," Dodge concluded that their opposition to SCHW pointed to major difficulties the Conference repeatedly had to confront in the South in its efforts to attract members. His observations convinced him of "how far in advance" SCHW was in comparison with "the pattern of southern thought, custom, and practice." Dodge noticed that particularly among the "best southern [white] people with wealth," few had a positive attitude toward blacks and were "pitifully undeveloped in an understanding of labor-management relations." Being less successful than he had anticipated, Dodge offered to resign at any time that Dombrowski wanted to call off the experiment.[35] Dombrowski did not agree with Dodge's assessment of his success, but insufficient funds with which to pay Dodge's and McKaine's salaries eventually ended their canvassing in late summer 1946.

The speaking tours, though concluded, had generated considerable publicity for the Southern Conference throughout much of the South. What SCHW needed now was some way by which to capitalize on the momentum that had developed and to keep its ideas before the public. As if preordained, the racial disturbances in Columbia, Tennessee, in late February 1946 again focused national attention on SCHW and its activities.

In part the difficulties in Columbia, Tennessee, developed out of the concern that SCHW representatives had expressed over the reception and recognition that black soldiers would enjoy when they returned home from the war. Only in the fall of 1945 the *Southern Patriot* had printed an article by President Benjamin E. Mays of Morehouse College in Atlanta and vice-chairman of the SCHW Committee for Georgia. He stated that African-American soldiers in World War I had fought in America's crusade to "make the world safe for democracy " only to return home to be

refused any semblance of democratic principles. Indeed, immediately after World War I black soldiers died unjustly, many still wearing Army
uniforms. SCHW, along with black people who hoped for progressive reforms at the war's end in 1945, demanded that the aftermath of World
War II be different. Black Americans had taken part in World War II for
the same reason as had white Americans, and in postwar America blacks
demanded an equal and just society. Mays's attitude represented the majority of his race who agreed with him that the days of gradualism had
ended; the violations against black people after the First World War must
not be repeated in post-World War II America.[36]

The events in Columbia brought into focus black people's notion of
democratic principles and the realities of a still unjust postwar South. On
Monday, February 25, 1946, at about ten o'clock in the morning Gladys
Stephenson and her son, James, a World War II Navy veteran, entered
the appliance section of the Castner-Knott department store to pick up a
repaired radio. Displeased with the service she had received, Gladys
Stephenson complained. Subsequently, a dispute developed between the
Stephensons and William Fleming, a Castner-Knott employee. The dispute erupted into violence when Fleming attacked Gladys Stephenson,
whereupon her son came to her defense. During the fight that ensued
between William Fleming and James Stephenson, Fleming received injuries as he fell or was pushed through a plate-glass window. Within minutes, four to six white men, drawn to the scene by the commotion, joined
in the attack against the Stephensons.[37]

When the police arrived, they too joined in the attack against the two
blacks, hitting Gladys Stephenson with a blackjack. They arrested the
Stephensons and charged them with breach of peace. Fleming, the initi-
ator of the altercation, was not charged. Although the Stephensons
pleaded guilty and paid a fifty-dollar fine, the Flemings were not satis-
fied. John Fleming, William Fleming's father, swore out a warrant for the
Stephensons' arrest on the charge of assault with the intent to kill. Later
the same day Julius Blair, a prominent black businessman who owned the
Blair Barber Shop, posted bond for the Stephensons' release.[38]

Before the Stephensons were released from jail, whites prepared to
lynch them. An African-American woman, present in the store when the
trouble began, overheard several whites discuss lynching plans. Whites
also intended to burn the blacks' homes and commit other destructive
acts. Rumors spread through Mink Slide, the local name for the black
business district, and whites, many of whom carried openly displayed
weapons, prepared "to get" the Stephensons. Sheriff Jim Underwood,
upon releasing the Stephensons from custody, advised that they should
leave Columbia for their own protection. Certain that the sheriff either
could not or would not protect the Stephensons, a group of local blacks
pirated James Stephenson out of town and transported him over back
roads to the relative safety of Nashville.[39]

Painfully aware of past lynchings in Columbia, blacks there knew that they could not depend on the police for protection. And just as the white mob had done in an earlier lynching, it went to the jail for the Stephensons in the same fashion, only this time the victims had fled to safety.[40] The Columbia police made no effort to disarm or disperse the mob, but Sheriff Underwood did attempt to disperse blacks who also gathered near the jail and in the Mink Slide district.

Unjustified racial violence in the past coupled with circumstances surrounding the arrest of the Stephensons, then, made the black community cautious. For self-protection it closed itself in, armed as best it could, and waited for an angry white mob. Whites fired randomly at blacks' homes as they drove through the neighborhood, but blacks did not fire back until whites had begun to invade on foot. Four policemen were shot during the exchange of gunfire.[41]

During the early part of the night Sheriff Underwood, fearful that Columbia was in for a major confrontation, called for assistance from Tennessee Governor Jim Nance McCord because Columbia's police force included only eight men, half of whom had been wounded. In response to Underwood's request, highway patrolmen, supervised by Tennessee Safety Commissoner Lynn Bomar, reached Columbia. Bomar's group made arrests of blacks in one home on East 8th Street and a few more who were leaving the area, all presumably charged with firing at police officers. The early morning dawn of February 26 brought destruction to Mink Slide at the hands of the white authorities.[42]

Governor McCord also ordered the Second Brigade of Tennessee State Guard, under the command of Brigadier General Jacob McGavock Dickinson, to go to Columbia to keep order. The state guard arrived between midnight and early dawn of the 26th. Dickinson, who reached Columbia ahead of the guardsmen, met with Bomar and Underwood, and all agreed not to take any further action until dawn and the arrival of other guardsmen. Dickinson expected guard support by 7:00 A.M., and the three men also decided that highway patrolmen and the guard would ask blacks to leave Mink Slide peacefully. If blacks refused, force would be used.

But about an hour before this agreement the Tennessee Highway Patrol marched into the Mink Slide district and forced blacks out. When Dickinson heard the disturbances, he immediately ordered the guard to the area, where it prevented the local white mob from entering. But the mob was not needed—the patrolmen did enough damage on their own.[43]

The highway patrolmen left a trail of destruction as if the mob itself had set upon this black business district. They smashed and ruined fixtures and furnishings of the funeral home and scrawled "KKK" on a casket. In the drugstore they destroyed equipment and looted the jukeboxes and cash register. This demolition-type group did the same in the doctor's office and the barbershop. Although they did not resist arrest, "men, women and children were lined up, cursed and beaten with blackjacks, fists and guns—then jailed."[44]

On February 26 the authorities arrested seventy persons—sixty-eight blacks and two whites who came with the mob to the jail the previous day to demand the Stephensons. But these two white persons were arrested for drunkenness, fined $9.25 and released after a few hours.[45] The *New York Times* report alludes that the Columbia police tried to dissuade the angry white mob and that what happened in Columbia was to be blamed on blacks. But the SCHW pamphlet describes the arrests by highway patrolmen differently. SCHW reported that blacks in the surrounded area were trapped and arrested, whether or not there was any reason to connect them with the shooting. Even veterans, some discharged so recently as to be still in uniform, had been kicked, cursed, and beaten with blackjacks upon their arrests. Persons arrested confirmed SCHW's story. Placing the blame where it was due, SCHW asserted, "It was the armed forces of the State of Tennessee who did the real rioting."[46]

News about the incident spread quickly. Walter White, secretary of the NAACP, in New York, immediately telegraphed Attorney General Tom Clark in Washington asking that the Department of Justice "act promptly and vigorously to safeguard constitutional rights of Negroes against State violation of those rights." He sent a similar appeal to Governor McCord.[47]

Although the initial arrests numbered sixty-eight blacks, state officials eventually arrested more than a hundred, all ostensibly in an effort to ascertain who shot the four white policemen on the night of February 25 and who fired the alleged shot from the barbershop at dawn on the 26th. They even arrested blacks who came to the jail to offer bail or inquire about those previously arrested. Immediately following the arrests, the state guard and highway patrolmen, under orders from the governor, conducted a house-to-house search for firearms in the black neighborhood. The sweep resulted in the confiscation of four hundred guns. NAACP lawyers claimed that the raid was conducted without regard for the United States Constitution or that of Tennessee, each of which contained provisions against unwarranted search and seizure.[48]

The most devastating in the series of incidents leading from the morning of February 25 occurred during a careless process of interrogating three of the prisoners on February 28. Highway patrolmen fatally shot two prisoners who allegedly attempted to escape. Although the patrolmen claimed the two men had enough time to locate ammunitions, load the guns, and shoot a patrolman, the patrolmen alone were responsible for the incident.[49]

When SCHW investigated the riot, especially the killing of the two prisoners, it raised some searching questions. SCHW found official attempts to explain the reasons and sequence of events leading to the killings "notably unconvincing." Rather than accept the official explanation, it placed the blame in the tradition of the long list of racial injustices for which the South was noted.[50]

As conditions began to settle, the NAACP sent Maurice Weaver, a white lawyer from Chattanooga, and Z. Alexander Looby, a West Indian-born attorney from Nashville, to Columbia to represent the black prisoners. Both worked under the direction of the NAACP general counsel, Thurgood Marshall. Weaver arrived in Columbia on February 26, but was not allowed access to any of the prisoners for several days.[51] Weaver and Looby succeeded in getting some prisoners free on bail quickly while they brought habeas corpus petitions to gain the release of others. The Maury County Circuit Court eventually indicted thirty-one blacks and four whites at the end of its regular session.

The injustice in Columbia, Tennessee, the major racial disturbance in the immediate postwar period, caused some leading civil rights groups to grow concerned lest the outbreak of hysteria against blacks at Columbia be allowed to set a pattern for postwar race relations.[52] These organizations formed national groups specifically designed to ensure that what had just happened there did not occur elsewhere. Initially, SCHW took part in a National Emergency Conference to Stop Lynch Terror in Columbia set up in early March by the National Federation of Constitutional Liberties (NFCL) to "help develop and coordinate" national activities on the issue. This group, like others that followed, outlined several civil rights violations of Columbia blacks including unwarranted arrests and searches, imprisonment without immediate access to counsel, and destruction of property. The group called for federal and state prosecutions of the law enforcement officers believed to be guilty of the crimes.[53] Thurgood Marshall and the NAACP did not take part in this first group because Marshall had begun busily preparing for the cases; the NAACP planned a similar conference of organizations in New York.[54]

By the end of March the SCHW, NAACP, NFCL, National Negro Congress, and a long list of others united forces in the National Committee for Justice in Columbia, Tennessee (NCJC).[55] The group, cochaired by Eleanor Roosevelt and Channing Tobias, gained wide recognition as a cross section of representatives from organized labor, civil rights leaders, Christian leaders, and other nationally known persons gave it full support. NCJC, following contemporary custom, sought solutions for an emergency situation through a national organization.

The National Committee set several priorities at its first meeting. Primarily all groups would work through a NCJC-policy steering committee and share in raising money for NAACP's Legal Defense Fund, maintain a national educational drive on racial injustice, and work to empower the black vote through registration drives in the South. The SCHW and NAACP, undoubtedly using the Columbia cases to draw attention to their work, never lost hope that blacks could improve their situation if only they could freely exercise the vote.[56]

NCJC became the sole national organization for justice in Columbia when the National Emergency Conference to Stop Lynch Terror met in late April, turned over its funds to the NCJC, and disbanded. NCJC leaders sighed relief because now they could provide undivided support to the NAACP. Since the NCJC functioned through the national office of the NAACP in New York and most of its leadership had come from Walter White, he was elected executive secretary.[57]

The National Committee for Justice in Columbia worked diligently to carry forward its purposes. But in so doing it faced formidable tasks. Numerous false stories printed by the white press, both northern and southern, had to be refuted. The white southern press, which seldomly carried a story about African Americans unless it centered on black crime or some other negative aspect of black life, was equally as diligent in preventing widespread dissemination of news on the attacks of blacks by whites. Blanket denunciation of all white Southern newspapers is unwarranted, but the volume of misrepresentation in those papers on the Columbia incident required a major effort on the part of SCHW and NCJC to correct the blatantly erroneous impressions.

After conducting their own investigations, the two groups published their findings, NCJC in 50,000 copies of its pamphlet, and SCHW in 200,000 copies of "The Truth about Columbia."[58] Competition for funds no doubt motivated separate publications also. Ads in selected newspapers such as the *New York Times*, the *Chicago Sun*, the *Nashville Tennessean*, and in the *Atlanta Constitution*, and radio programs over national networks, constituted a large portion of the NCJC- and SCHW-generated publicity. The two groups constantly protested to Tennessee Governor Jim McCord the violence of the state police and militia and urged prompt disciplinary action.[59]

Given the pressure from civil rights and other groups, Attorney General Tom Clark had a federal grand jury investigate the Columbia riot. The results from the grand jury reported in mid-June were disappointing. According to this investigation, the arrests did not involve irregularities; the threatening mob consisted only of unarmed teenagers. And the deaths of the two blacks in the Maury County jail were justifiable homicide. Furthermore, blacks had destroyed their *own* property before the arrests since there was no way to identify others who might have ruined property and stolen goods. Thus, this jury concluded the civil rights of African Americans had not been violated. As for the civil rights organizations, the grand jury charged that they had only increased racial tensions with their propaganda. Provided there had been an appropriate federal statute, the jury threatened to indict those groups responsible for various printed literature.[60]

After an unsuccessful attempt for a second grand-jury investigation, the thirty-one African-American defendants went on trial.[61] Their legal battles lasted through June 1947. The defense of the twenty-five charged with attempted murder of the four Columbia policemen ended in October 1946 with their exoneration. Their defense relied on witnesses who testified that they had not been in Mink Slide when the shooting occurred; other witnesses revealed that physical abuse and intimidation by Columbia police and highway patrolmen forced from them incriminating statements while imprisoned. The defense also demonstrated that blacks' memory of past lynchings created such fright that blacks had only acted in self-defense on February 25. Lloyd Kennedy and William Pillow stood trial in early November 1946 for shooting a highway patrolman during the raid in Mink Slide. Pillow was found innocent, but Kennedy was found guilty of attempted second-degree murder and sentenced to five years imprisonment. His case was appealed to the Tennessee Supreme Court on the ground that African Americans had not served on the jury that convicted Kennedy. Associate Justice Alan Presitt, upholding Kennedy's sentence in June 1947, ruled that "members of the Negro race have no right to trial by a mixed jury." The cases of the several other blacks never came to trial nor did those of four whites charged with attempted murder.[62] It is questionable whether there was ever any intent to bring the whites to trial since law enforcement agents had clearly sided with them from the very beginning. There is no indication that any of the white officials were released from their jobs for what occurred in Columbia, not even the officials responsible for the deaths of the two black prisoners. Nor were blacks ever reimbursed for property damage.

The postwar white South, which refused to tolerate progressive reform, included all the makings for an incident like the one in Columbia. The more militant African American exemplified the "New Negro" in his own defense at a time, like after World War I, when the Ku Klux Klan's membership also had begun to increase. The strong white-supremacist attitude came through clearly in the destruction of property in the black business district where the Klan's symbol was left in the funeral home.[63]

The SCHW took advantage of the Columbia incident and the many other situations of racial injustice during 1946 to spread the importance of its work. For instance, it attempted to distribute more of its literature on the need for organized labor. Racial disturbances were sure to hurt labor unions that sought to integrate black and white workers, like those affiliated with the CIO. The important SCHW pamphlet "Look Him in the Eye" emphasized the importance of the black soldier in World War II and racial equality for his people and challenged white southerners to look him in the eye and still believe that he deserved the status of second-class citizenship and substandard wages.[64]

While pressure from the components of NCJC prompted the grand jury investigation, which brought negative results, in the long run it helped to create positive efforts from President Harry S Truman. Partly as a consequence of the racial injustice in Columbia and various other localities across the country, Truman established a Committee on Civil Rights in

December 1946 that would research and report to him on legal safeguards for civil rights because, he said, "In some places, from time to time, the local enforcement of law and order has broken down, and individuals—sometimes ex-servicemen, even women—have been killed, maimed, or intimidated." Channing H. Tobias, who had cochaired NCJC, served on this fifteen-member committee along with a leading SCHW supporter, Frank P. Graham. Truman's creation of the committee, only one in many of his actions that profoundly declared civil rights a national issue, raised the hopes and expectations of African Americans and their counterparts in the struggle for democracy.[65]

The cooperative efforts of the various civil rights organizations in Columbia also revealed considerable competition among them. The organizations worked well on all fronts except finances, where trouble developed between the NCJC and the SCHW. The fact that the NAACP solely defended the legal cases while other groups also solicited funds created confusion. For instance Foreman, not George Marshall who actually was the leader of the National Federation for Constitutional Liberties, asked NCJC to reimburse NFCL for expenses incurred in sending out telegrams to raise money.[66] White replied that NCJC would not be held responsible for expenditures over which it had no control, especially since NCJC had not asked NFCL to raise the money.[67] Foreman probably acted for the NFCL because SCHW, his financially struggling group, was in the same situation. Shortly thereafter, he asked that the SCHW get reimbursed for funds it spent in helping to organize a Tennessee local of the NCJC. White mailed SCHW the requested amount in July. Although Dombrowski had assured him that SCHW would turn over all funds for legal defense to NCJC, White suspected that SCHW had raised money for legal defense of Columbia victims without actually reporting the money to the NCJC, and White requested a report from Dombrowski.[68] Dombrowski later reported that SCHW had raised around $3,000 with expenditures at about $2,500, thus SCHW had about $500 for the NCJC.

Dombrowski thought that White trusted the SCHW about which funds went to the NCJC, but White harbored suspicions from June through the remainder of 1946. One NAACP leader advised White in September to force SCHW, short of threatening public exposure, to give a detailed accounting of funds collected for the defense of the Columbia riot victims. White could not publicize that SCHW had allegedly raised funds under false pretext because to do so would allow enemies of both organizations to use their competition against the objectives sought by the NAACP and SCHW. The best possible solution, then, amounted to treating the SCHW not as a "counter organization," but instead to advise NAACP leaders in major southern cities that national NAACP officials mistrusted the Conference. Local NAACP branches were also advised that the best way to counter SCHW was through more diligent NAACP activity.[69]

By December Walter White, convinced that SCHW had held back funds owed the NAACP for legal defense in the Columbia cases, grew stern about the money. He informed Foreman that questions to the NAACP about SCHW's turning over the money had become "increasingly embarrassing to us." White told Foreman that various sources had claimed that SCHW raised as much as $50,000 for legal defense and that he had run out of excuses for the inquirers. Even though White had been a leading speaker at the SCHW membership conference in November 1946, he wrote Foreman in December that several NAACP branches opposed his making the speech at New Orleans until SCHW turned over its money for NCJC.[70] The SCHW received $4,525.64 and spent $4,024.48; thus SCHW turned over to the NCJC $501.16. When SCHW finally sent NCJC the remainder of money after expenses for printing and distribution of some 200,000 copies of its pamphlet, Dombrowski apologized for the delay and explained that his organization had not acted earlier because it had been "wrestling with a $25,000 deficit for some months."[71]

An unconvinced White still wanted an itemized statement from SCHW. He claimed that he wanted a list of names and addresses of contributors so that he could give due recognition to each in the fight at the conclusion of all cases but simply did not believe Dombrowski and Foreman.[72] White finally asked Daniel E. Byrd, executive secretary of the New Orleans NAACP Branch, conveniently located in the same city as the SCHW's recently moved central office, to determine the exact amount of money SCHW had collected without arousing any suspicion. Byrd, in his attempt to fulfill White's wish, only verified that Dombrowski's story was true. SCHW was running a large deficit, so "financially defunct" that the NAACP might not expect to get the money SCHW had promised.[73]

The NAACP's greatest concern over SCHW in the Columbia case concerned more than finances. It feared that SCHW would get involved in legal defense of civil rights cases or use the voter-registration drives in the South to get NAACP members to switch solely to SCHW membership. As NAACP fear mounted, some staff members deliberately refused to give information about SCHW; they simply referred inquiries to the New York office. A few NAACP staffers believed, however, that there was room for work by both SCHW and the NAACP and did make an effort to direct people to the Conference.[74]

Aware of the resentment at the NAACP, some Conference representatives tried to smooth over the differences. Dombrowski explained to White that SCHW's purposes differed from those of NAACP's, and that SCHW, cognizant of other groups that made legal aid their goal, never included "specific legal defense" in its work. SCHW worked to educate the public, make the facts known. The Southern Conference admitted its shortcoming in civil rights on the founding of the Civil Rights Congress in April 1946:

As you know, the SCHW is not a civil rights organization and cannot afford to divert funds and personnel from its own work to the defense of the numerous civil rights cases which are constantly arising in all parts of the South. The lack of an organization having civil rights as its specific and main function, and with a Southern office and Southern staff to handle this work, has therefore been a constant problem and handicap for the work of the Conference.[75]

SCHW cooperated in civil rights cases because this would "serve to complement" its work.[76] Moreover, the Conference hoped that through its program the cases that the NAACP defended could be prevented.

White's doubts about Southern Conference leaders were understandable given that he could not get the information he wanted. SCHW did receive large sums of money in 1946, largely because of its part in the Columbia incident. A great deal of money also came from its membership drive and from organized labor. And in fact, an analysis of SCHW's fundraising correspondence reveals that only one appeal mentioned the Columbia incident. In this instance SCHW stated that the incident had created a financial strain for SCHW, but if the CIO renewed its grant, the funds would be used to meet the Conference payroll. In March the CIO national office gave $1,000. Even though the group had financial trouble, it is improbable that Dombrowski and Foreman collected money for NCJC that was never turned over to it.[77] As for the switching of membership from NAACP to SCHW, evidence does not show that the NAACP had cause for fear. The fact that the NAACP noticed the growth of SCHW showed that the Conference finally had begun to gain recognition in the field of civil rights after operating for almost eight years.

The misunderstanding over finances in the Columbia incident did not hinder future relations for the two organizations. Clark Foreman, at the invitation of the NAACP, and Leslie Perry of the NAACP jointly chaired a meeting of a large number of organizations concerning civil rights legislation in December 1946. They agreed that an *"overall civil rights bill"* was not likely to pass but that each group would continue to lobby Congress for positive action on single issues, for example, legislation against lynching, the poll tax, the House Committee on Un-American Activities, Senate action to deny Theodore Bilbo his seat, and a civil rights bill for Washington, D.C.[78]

Given the overwhelming opposition to civil rights legislation, proponents of civil rights needed each other's support. Instead a few competed. Just as the NAACP grew concerned about SCHW competition, SCHW reacted in a similar way when northern-based groups like the Americans for Democratic Action, the National Citizens Political Action Committee, and the Progressive Citizens of America started local branches in the South.[79]

The Southern Conference had not held a membership meeting since the Nashville session in 1942. Having actively sought new members, it needed to bring them together to voice ideas for reforms in its hoped-for New South of democracy. At a September 1946 board meeting Dombrowski reported on preparations for a membership meeting set for November, and the board selected Georgia Governor Ellis Arnall to receive its Thomas Jefferson Award.[80]

SCHW held great expectations for the 1946 membership meeting. Dombrowski believed that New Orleans would welcome the organization's policies and reforms because the city supposedly was more liberal and progressive than most southern cities.[81]

Two incidents, however, soon made it evident that SCHW would not be welcome in the Crescent City. Immediately after the SCHW established an office in New Orleans, the Young Men's Business Club (YMBC) assigned itself the task of driving the organization out of town. The group based its entire opposition to SCHW on the allegation that the Southern Conference was a Communist front, largely because it held integrated meetings. The YMBC began publicly denouncing SCHW in mid-August and stepped up public opposition just before SCHW's November meeting, continuing in that vein far into 1947. YMBC opposition made it doubly difficult for SCHW to obtain a public facility in which to hold its integrated meeting.

Whatever the adversity, SCHW leaders struggled to make the best of it, and in the case of the YMBC, they dared the YMBC to prove that Communists dominated their organization. Leaders like Foreman and Dombrowski remained optimistic that the YMBC charge would attract to the Southern Conference those persons curious about learning what SCHW was all about, whether or not it was really Communist inspired. Dombrowski attempted to persuade members and interested persons to attend the 1946 biennial in New Orleans by promising that if the YMBC or any organization investigated SCHW thoroughly it would become only an ardent admirer and supporter.[82] A deluge of articles accusing SCHW became the YMBC's strategy to run the Conference out of New Orleans, a strategy that made the SCHW all the more determined to stay. Both SCHW and the YMBC voiced opposing views in the local newspapers— the *New Orleans Times-Picayune*, *New Orleans Item*, and *New Orleans States*—dating from August 1946. In addition to attacks in the press, leaders and members of both groups exchanged correspondence supporting the position each took. Leading officials of each group also voiced their views in public addresses where even former members of the YMBC opposed its persecution of SCHW.[83] The YMBC had to give up its verbal abuse of SCHW when after 1947 SCHW's central office remained in New Orleans.[84] SCHW officials, confident to have made their point, turned their attention to other priorities. The YMBC incident was just another in the long list of such accusations that usually came whenever SCHW announced its conventions, but in 1947, Foreman and Dombrowski prepared as never before to take on the YMBC in the hope to end the alleged accusation once and for all, though this was something they would never be able to do.

SCHW continued to fulfill its 1938 resolution, that future conventions would be held only in cities that allowed integrated meetings. Dombrowski arranged for the use of New Orleans's municipal auditorium on such grounds. But later the auditorium commission arbitrarily ruled that the meeting had to be segregated for use of the auditorium. Despite the fact that local attorneys advised Dombrowski that neither Louisiana nor New Orleans ordinances outlawed integration, SCHW did not push legal action because to do so would not gain access to the auditorium in time for its convention. Subsequently, SCHW arranged to have its conference in Carpenters Hall, owned by the Carpenters Union (AFL), which claimed to place no barrier in the way of democracy in spite of its barring blacks from joining. Since other integrated meetings had been held at the auditorium without incident, it appears that SCHW was turned down for other reasons.[85]

In the midst of financial troubles and the YMBC opposition Dombrowski finalized arrangements for the 1946 meeting. He mailed over 40,000 copies of the call or invitation to members and interested persons, inviting the usual die-hard liberals like Eleanor Roosevelt to speak. The former First Lady now had responsibilities with the United Nations, but SCHW leaders hoped that her interest in the South had not waned. In the event that she would be unable to attend, she was urged to send SCHW "a letter of greeting so that the inspiration we have received from your speeches, and President Roosevelt's letters in the last three Conventions will be continued."[86] SCHW also invited Florida Senator Claude Pepper to speak.[87]

Walter White, also invited, agreed to come only after the issue of racial segregation at the New Orleans Municipal Auditorium was settled.[88] White hesitated to attend SCHW's convention also because some NAACP leaders wanted him to attend various NAACP activities scheduled for the same weekend. White, however, went to New Orleans, asserting in his comments that he regretted having to miss his own organization's functions. White welcomed the opportunity to share the same platform with white liberal southerners and to have an audience such as the one that the Conference would bring together. He hoped to place the NAACP's work in the limelight and claim that it was the NAACP and not the SCHW that had done the job in the Columbia, Tennessee, cases and in other situations that required concrete effort and not rhetoric. Believing there to be competition between the two organizations, White refused to pass up an opportunity to do in part what many NAACP leaders accused the SCHW of doing. He tried to persuade SCHW members to switch their affiliation to the NAACP.[89] Although the two groups rivaled for members and contributions, each knew firsthand the importance of survival for both. Indeed, with the work of SCHW, the NAACP, the CRC, and the

Truman administration now voicing publicly the need to protect civil rights, the liberal southern minority could believe that a significant change would occur soon.

Supporters from as far back as 1938 attended SCHW's fourth biennial convention, but for the first time since its founding Eleanor Roosevelt was not there. She sent a telegram expressing her best wishes, but her absence indicated that she had begun to shift her interest to other projects. This fourth session also marked the first time that Frank Graham, who was ill, did not attend. The New Orleans conference marked the beginning of a changing of the guard in SCHW leadership.[90]

A postwar South that grappled with the same fundamental problems as in 1938 provided a theme for the New Orleans convention—"Free Democracy's Resources. The Southern Conference for Human Welfare Works for a Prosperous, Progressive South." Recognizing some gains in the South in recent years, SCHW still maintained that the region remained, in the historic words of Franklin Delano Roosevelt, "The Nation's Economic Problem Number One." As if rhetoric would solve many of the problems, SCHW adopted a thirteen-point program for 1947–1948, as it had done at all earlier biennials. SCHW also called its meeting a "Thanksgiving Convention" in which its members were especially grateful that the Allies were victorious over fascism in the war. Although it had not had a meeting since April 1942, SCHW had a sizable turn out in New Orleans where approximately 1,200 people attended the sessions and the program differed little from past ones, except now the registration fee had been raised from $1 to $3.

From the opening session on November 28 through the convention's end on November 30, prominent speakers, including former SCHW president John B. Thompson, Mary McLeod Bethune, Claude Pepper, Aubrey Williams, Lillian Smith, Osceola McKaine, Walter White, and Ellis Arnall, the liberal governor of Georgia, resounded SCHW's program for a democratic South. Thompson invoked the spirit of brotherly love and unity while Bethune, Pepper, and Arnall urged equal educational, economic, and political opportunities.[91] On the convention's final night, White, a speaker on the occasion of the presentation of the Thomas Jefferson Award to Arnall, returned to the theme of love for one's fellowman, placing the breakdown in regional morality at the root of all the South's social, economic, and political problems. White linked the South's backwardness to the moral degradation that had grown out of "the conviction among Southerners that the most ruthless, cruel and hate-creating individual is by those methods assured of being most successful."[92]

As in 1938 controversy surrounded the Conference's honoree for the Thomas Jefferson Award. Arnall received the Thomas Jefferson Award in the midst of much publicity that both praised and criticized him and SCHW before and after the meeting. The *Atlanta Constitution* and *Atlanta Journal* led in the negative reports of Arnall's accepting the award. These and other papers announced that Arnall would get "an empty honor," "a dubious honor," and that "Arnall [was] not the only good southerner." Editorials cited SCHW's alleged association with communism and its extreme stand on racial equality that led necessarily to a friendliness with the NAACP. Other papers praised Arnall and even questioned why the *Constitution*, a past Arnall supporter, came out as reactionary in this instance. Of course, Arnall denounced all the criticism in his speech at the convention.[93]

Some observers criticized SCHW because it gave Arnall the award in light of observations that Arnall allegedly soft-pedaled efforts to expose lynching in Georgia. During Arnall's tenure as governor, at least one lynching occurred in Georgia, and Arnall had done little to identify and prosecute the perpetrators. Nor had he even voiced strong opposition. The death was attributed to the familiar "parties unknown," and the crime went unpunished. Concerned citizens questioned SCHW's justification for giving Arnall an award for outstanding service to the southern people when he had not been effective in seeking justice in his own state.[94]

Thus, at its biennial SCHW had three fronts of opposition: the YMBC with the usual Communist charges, the Arnall controversy, and the mixup with the auditorium commission, none of which seemed to have kept supporters away. In 1946 SCHW boasted a meeting, its greatest and most worthwhile in terms of issues addressed since 1938, that gained at least as much attention as its founding one. Although the group did not know it, this convention marked its last.[95]

At the end of the November gathering the executive boards of SCHW and SCEF, still basically consisting of the same people for each group, met, and what had been an optimistic and unified convention in the last several days turned into a long and ugly squabble between two very diligent SCHW/SCEF leaders. SCHW now started to reap the consequence of its unforeseeable action in establishing the Educational Fund.

At the December 1 meeting the SCHW board attempted to separate SCHW and SCEF. The way in which SCHW's president Foreman pursued the change brought much disharmony among people who had been friends long before the Southern Conference existed. The group discussed its drastic financial situation and the inability to work out specific solutions; Foreman, who had gotten complaints from Eleanor Roosevelt, Frank Graham, and Lucy Randolph Mason about Dombrowski's management of the central office, blamed Dombrowski for much of the financial difficulty of the organizations. Foreman, Myles Horton, and Mason recommended that Dombrowski not remain as executive secretary of SCHW and administrator of both SCHW and SCEF. Members had only recently at the biennial convention elected officers who remained the same with the exception of Lewis Jones of Texas, who became parliamentarian, and a few new board members, which still made up a board of thirty-five.

Now, on December 1, the board, with a bare quorum of largely new members, adopted a change. Dombrowski would become the executive secretary of only SCEF; Branson Price, currently secretary of the New York Committee, would fill the position of administrator of SCHW as of January 1, 1947, on which date the position of assistant administrator would be eliminated. Foreman recommended Price because she had done a good job raising funds for the New York group. William Mitch objected to Branson Price simply because he did not want a woman to have the job.

When the SCHW board declared that Dombrowski's position would be with the SCEF, it essentially left Clark Foreman to run SCHW. Foreman denied premeditated thoughts about this move, but evidence reveals the opposite. Communication from the board members to him and Dombrowski indicated that the action taken by the board when it simultaneously created and filled a new position at SCEF opened a rift in the SCHW/SCEF board that would never be mended.[96]

Between December 1946 and February 1947 the board corresponded more than probably at any other point in the SCHW's history because of the Foreman-Dombrowski power struggle. Each administrator sought to prove a point and persuade board members in his favor. Initially, new board members claimed that placing Dombrowski in a new job would cause no ill feelings among the close-knit group of SCHW founders and other members. Once Mason (who had joined Foreman and Horton in proposing the change) and Dombrowski brought the strain to their attention, these members regretted having helped to move Dombrowski to SCEF. They now requested that Foreman, as president of SCHW, rescind the decision and call a board meeting for more discussion and further action, in an effort to keep Dombrowski at SCHW's central office.[97]

Several board members who had agreed with Foreman in December immediately thereafter advised that they disliked the action taken to displace Dombrowski. Mason reminded Foreman that Dombrowski had been overworked. She, too, wanted an emergency board meeting. Mason and others pointed out that it had largely been Dombrowski who had kept a struggling SCHW financially sound through some of its worst times.[98] Indeed, when Dombrowski came to SCHW in 1942, the organization had less than $100 on hand, but at the end of 1945, with Dombrowski as executive secretary, it grossed over $86,000, with at least $1,800 on hand. Margaret Fisher, chair of the SCHW Georgia Committee, in a seven-page letter to Foreman, expressed that she believed Dombrowski had been wronged.[99] The newly elected parliamentarian, Lewis Jones, even pointed out to Foreman that as he understood the bylaws, what had happened was not official, that SCHW did not have the authority to create and fill the job for SCEF. Mason, who "faithfully" stood by Dombrowski throughout the crisis, filled him in on Foreman's attitude about Jones's conclusion and the situation in general:

Sunday night Clark and I talked by long distance. I found he had not gotten Mr. Jones's letter, which was in Washington, so I read him my copy on the phone. It made him very angry and he wanted to argue each point with me, which I refused to do as I did not write the letter and am not parliamentarian. I rather think from what he said that he will not heed the letter any more than he has the protests from some of the board. But I could not pin him down on this, and he was very resentful of my part in the effort to get reconsideration. We had a hot talk, very hot.[100]

Foreman and Dombrowski tried to remain cordial, but Dombrowski never forgave Foreman for the action he spearheaded on December 1. Attempting to explain his position, Foreman pointed out that Dombrowski would be better suited for SCEF than to continue as head of SCHW. Foreman wrote to Dombrowski that:

the job of editing the Patriot, supervising publications and helping the state organizations with their educational program, as well as meeting with religious and educational groups, is one of tremendous importance. I feel that it is very fortunate that the Board has worked out an arrangement whereby you can devote your talents to the job of moral leadership in the South.

But if Foreman had been convinced of Dombrowski's talents, he might have insisted on keeping him in the position and working with him to solve organizational problems.

Dombrowski, shocked that the question of his tenure had ever been raised, was devastated by the board's action. He made clear why he felt he had been treated poorly. He did not think it right that he had been given no reason for the change of personnel nor the opportunity to defend himself. He had been sent out of the room for the duration of the discussion involving him, learning of his replacement when the board recalled him to the meeting. Regardless of whether he had been fired as administrator for relief of "arduous duties of managerial nature" or because of financial difficulties, Dombrowski questioned the change because too few board members had contributed to the decision. Only after he solicited advice from his close friends, Aubrey Williams and Palmer Weber, who advised in favor of Foreman's recommendation that they thought this was for the best interest of SCHW and SCEF, did he even consider the possibility that the board's action was appropriate. But even given their position, Dombrowski never accepted the board's decision.[101]

Despite his protestations, Foreman eventually had to give in to the wishes of the majority of the board when it insisted on deferring Branson Price's appointment until the full board could review the matter. The board met on January 5, 1947, with review of its action of December 1, 1946, as the primary agenda item.[102] In the interim between December and January, Dombrowski had hardened his position and was ready to present the board with an ultimatum; he would either remain as administrator of both SCHW and SCEF or the board would fire him. The board, recognizing the contributions Dombrowski had made to SCHW over the years, sustained his position. Price, who had been slated to take his place as head of SCHW, never came to New Orleans. Indeed, the board even raised Dombrowski's 1946 salary from $2,500 to $5,000 since he had spent as much as two-thirds of his time on SCHW work. Furthermore, Foreman's 1947 salary would be $8,000 as president, and Dombrowski's $7,500 as administrator.[103]

Dombrowski, as he had done when SCHW hired Osceola McKaine in 1946, insisted that SCHW and SCEF needed an African American at the administrative level. The board agreed, promising to hire such a person when funds permitted.[104] Dombrowski also brought back his white assistant, Frank Bancroft, and announced in early February that he had hired Edmonia Grant, fulfilling the commitment to hire a black executive. Grant, a Conference member since 1938, had done extensive work in race relations, coming to SCHW from the United States Office of Education on the National Project for the Adult Education of Negroes. The Tennessee native had earned an M.A. degree from Fisk University where she had done social research while on the staff of Charles S. Johnson, eminent sociologist and Fisk president since 1946. The studies on which Grant worked with Johnson became a substantial basis for Gunnar Myrdal's widely acclaimed *The American Dilemma*.[105] Now, at least with administrative positions filled, with the exception of a person in charge of only SCEF, SCHW attempted to resume its regular schedule of business. But the ill feelings between Dombrowski and Foreman endured.

To understand why Dombrowski felt especially disappointed in Foreman's action to place him at SCEF, one must understand that SCHW had been much more than a group of liberals coming together to produce progressive ideas and reforms for the region; these dedicated, personal friends had weathered earlier storms of organizational turmoil and disagreement. Virginia Durr described the group as a family, especially those who had been brought together for various assignments in the Roosevelt administration—the Durrs, Foreman, Graham, Aubrey Williams, Bethune, Supreme Court Justice Hugo Black, Virginia Durr's brother-in-law, whose association with SCHW was not by official membership but who supported the organization's principles by speaking at its first meeting and being present at various SCHW dinners in Washington. The group often partied together at fundraisers in different cities, especially Washington and New York. The various associations of people such as Eleanor Roosevelt, Lucy Randolph Mason, Mary Bethune, Channing Tobias, John P. Davis, Walter White, Modjeska Simkins, Charles Johnson, Palmer Weber, and George Marshall established a strong network of individuals among and between organizations like the NAACP, NFCL, SCHW, NNC, and CRC.

The relationship, then, between Dombrowski and Foreman before the December 1 board meeting had been close; whenever Dombrowski went to Washington, he frequently stayed with the Foremans. The two men had Ph.D. degrees from Columbia University, another shared interest along with their liberal ideas. But as individuals close to both attest, Foreman and Dombrowski, like so many other members of SCHW, had conflicting personalities. Foreman, described as headstrong and stubborn, seldom changed his mind about anything. He faced opposition head-on and was noted for even defying a racist sheriff with a loaded shotgun. When Foreman had made up his mind, then, that Dombrowski needed to be out of SCHW, out of his way, he was determined to see it through.

Dombrowski had a mild, easygoing personality, and if not to the extent for which Foreman was noted, also believed in sticking to his principles. The basic difference between the two, according to their close friend Weber, was that Foreman was a man of action and Dombrowski was a man for educating the public. Weber agreed with Foreman that Dombrowski would work better in the educational arm of SCHW and Foreman better with legislative lobbying for reforms.[106]

So when the dispute came up in December 1946, eventually those siding with either Dombrowski or Foreman split accordingly, with the majority in Dombrowski's favor. While the organization tried to maintain the regular order of business and to avoid publicity over its internal rift, much time was spent on dispensing with the Foreman-Dombrowski squabble.[107]

Dombrowski, feeling betrayed by a friend, never recovered from the December 1 decision. Foreman often questioned his efficiency and also became sensitive at the slightest criticism by Dombrowski. As late as April 1947 he wrote Dombrowski, "I am a little surprised at the implication in your letter that we are not unitedly pulling together at the present time. I wonder who you feel is not pulling his load?"[108]

The situation had not improved by June, and Dombrowski tried to explain his side to another SCHW officer, Virginia Durr:

> You know me well enough to know that I am never offended by a statement of fact and I do really appreciate your frankness in writing as you did about our problems. They are severe. I think most of it arises from the financial problem but there [are] other overtones and difficulties. I do not think the personality problem is insoluble, if a way could be found for Clark and I to work in the same office. A great deal of our trouble arises out of the simple fact of distance.
>
> One thing is certain, and you have stated it well, unless we find[,] and that right quickly[,] the formula for a united and cohesive organization, we will not survive.[109]

Durr agreed with Dombrowski's stance, adding also that she knew him well enough to know that he had "suffered over the situation in the Southern Conference." She continued, "I saw it coming long [ago], knew it would be fatal if you and Clark could not resolve your differences. . . . I tried to interpret one to the other and seemed to have failed utterly. . . .

I think when the July [meeting] comes[,] the dilemma must be resolved or we will be lost."[110]

The fight between Dombrowski and Foreman had repercussions on consistent contributors as well. For example, in late fall 1947 Ethel Clyde explained that she was "a bit uncomfortable" about SCHW. She wanted to know who had fired Dombrowski and why, after he had done what she called a magnificent job and had devoted years to it. She concluded, "The whole business makes me tired, to put it mildly."[111]

As would be expected, the organization transacted very little business during the Foreman-Dombrowski disagreement. In December 1946 Dombrowski had reported on finances, but except for one or two other matters that was all that got administrative attention.[112] By July 1947 Foreman willingly admitted SCHW-SCEF "work had suffered for seven vital months because of confusion and personalities."[113]

Since Dombrowski refused to accept the directorship of SCEF, the board began to search for someone after the January 5 meeting. When none of the possibilities accepted, Foreman agreed to serve temporarily as SCEF "director" without pay.[114] By July Dombrowski and Foreman continued to serve the two groups without a clear-cut separation. Dombrowski had become convinced, however, that for SCEF to survive it had to have its own president and director, that two individuals could do a better job raising money, that contributors would not be confused about separate requests of funds for both SCHW and SCEF.[115]

The power struggle between Foreman and Dombrowski affected the central office and its relationship with state committees. Trouble with the Georgia Committee developed because Foreman resented Margaret Fisher's boldness in disagreeing with his attempt to oust Dombrowski in December. The Georgia Committee complained about the small amount of money the central office had provided for its work and grew more concerned now that even less would be forthcoming. Foreman disputed the grievance, pointing out that the central office had provided the committee with $11,000 in 1945 and $25,000 in 1946, which took care of Fisher's salary and office expenses. Fisher further explained that the committee had spent money on projects that the Georgia group did not initiate; the state committee did not always agree with specific programs of the central office. Members of the committee voiced another complaint common with one that even the central office had expressed, that the New York Committee got too much credit for SCHW work. Southerners had not accepted northern interest in their problems in the past, and still were not ready to do so, even though they found it easy to spend money raised in New York and other parts of the country. Foreman expressed this response, explaining that "we would not want to do anything in New York that would offset the benefit received from the money." Quick to point out the faults of others, he blamed the poor state of the committee on Fisher. He concluded that the Georgia Committee's situation could be improved if "the proper person undertake the job in an organizational way." He welcomed Fisher's expected resignation, but wanted to keep the office open "in the calmness which I assume will follow Margaret's exit" and volunteered "personally" to underwrite the necessary amount of money for that purpose, "*provided* Margaret Fisher is out of the picture." Perhaps his conclusion about Fisher's work in Georgia resembled his assessment of Dombrowski's with SCHW.[116]

Although the group itself assessed its strengths and weaknesses and saw many shortcomings, it never overcame them. Lucy Mason, with intimate knowledge of the SCHW as a result of her close working relationship with it from its inception, offered reasonable and legitimate criticisms. Her insights revealed trouble spots that Witherspoon Dodge and others had pointed out before, but which had now become much more pronounced and potentially damaging to the organization's future. In a report on "What the Southern Conference for Human Welfare Cannot Be—And Why," Mason regretted that SCHW "cannot be a mass political organization. . . . We must recognize its limitations in public appeal." It had become such an "icebreaker," so identifiable with progressive reforms, that the "masses of people are not ready to follow it. Even if we were willing to give up an advanced program, the Conference has become so identified with such a program during its whole history that we could not escape association with it. The door to retreat is closed." Consequently, SCHW had led people to believe it could produce something circumstances made highly unlikely; she concluded, therefore, that unintentionally SCHW had "deceived the public as to the real possibilities."

The misconception caused other problems as well. SCHW in Mason's view suffered a loss of prestige and increased organizational indebtedness because of confusion in the public mind; that loss of prestige translated into a loss of funds, adding to further indebtedness. Even with the special appeals by field-workers, Mason pointed out, "the highest membership has been about 5,000 from all the southern states combined. Today the southern membership seems to be decreasing. If the Conference's entire southern membership was concentrated in one state it would not constitute a mass political movement in that state." The group had planned and proceeded with programs far in excess of financial resources and had moved ahead on anticipated income which had *not* materialized.

Although accurate in her assessment of SCHW's difficulties, Mason had little to offer in way of solutions for its troubles. She recommended that it could be a small, militant, progressive organization in the South and work aggressively on a *limited* number of issues. Then she turned to an old theme that SCHW's members had to be southern, which she thought had little to do with the Conference's problems. On the contrary, much financial support had come from other parts of the country, a contradiction that Mason sometimes acknowledged. She wanted other sections' money, but she wanted southerners to run SCHW. Realistically, if people from other sections contributed money, they would expect to help develop programs and have input in organizational matters. By early 1948, however, the New York Committee's expenses exceeded its fund-raising efforts and the central office asked that it close down. Then Mason advised the obvious, that SCHW not assume new financial responsibilities to any organization before it met its pledged contributions to the state groups. Finally, Mason wanted each board member to raise SCHW funds.[117] SCHW leaders did not heed Mason's analysis nor any of the other criticisms so that in the last two years of the Conference's history its progressive program received scant attention, and the organization began a slow journey into death.

Continued alleged charges of communism exacerbated the Conference's poor state. In June 1947 the House Un-American Activities Committee (HUAC) published its *Report* on SCHW in which it retold its charges against the organization dating back to 1938. The HUAC *Report* questioned Conference policies and attempted to show that SCHW was guilty by association, not only where individuals were concerned but in "joint activity with Communists Fronts" or "interlocking with Communist causes." The Conference-sponsored southern tour of Henry Wallace, which also started in June, became linked with charges in the HUAC *Report* because of Wallace's publicly expressed opposition to Truman's anti-Soviet stand on foreign affairs.[118]

SCHW defended itself against the attacks in the usual way, and this time gained the support of several persons not associated with it who helped to discredit the *Report*. Walter Gellhorn, a professor at the Columbia Law School, concluded:

> From semi-truths the committee has drawn conclusions which would be strained even if the factual assertions of the report were beyond challenge. The report demonstrates, not that the Southern Conference is a corrupt organization, but that the Committee has been either intolerably incompetent or designedly intent upon publicizing misinformation.[119]

Despite these well-founded refutations, Communist allegations against SCHW in 1947–1948 are cited by some historians as having caused the Conference's demise, but Communist charges did not kill SCHW.[120] No doubt so much talk about the Conference's alleged Communist domination hurt its prestige, but the organization's troubles actually resulted from its own faults and weaknesses. Indeed, if the organization had not been forced to deal with any false accusations, it would still have been in disarray by 1948. Moreover, the red-baited NAACP, even the SCHW-instituted SCEF, survived during the same period of Cold War hysteria. A long list of organizational problems led to the end of SCHW.

The organization never resolved internal problems, especially that of finances. Red-baiting may have restricted financing, but the confusion caused by SCEF's creation hurt SCHW's fund-raising efforts at the same time that SCHW lost financial support from organized labor. Foreman and Dombrowski went off payroll in July because of insufficient funds; Edmonia Grant became acting director. But finances did not improve under her guidance. She inherited Dombrowski's difficult task of working with Foreman and did not like it when the Washington Committee paid one-half of Foreman's salary without informing the central office. Not only had Grant accepted less pay based on the fact that Foreman agreed to work for none, but she sensed that the Washington Committee was beginning to take over the work normally done by the central office. SCHW lost important board members such as Mason, who resigned in October 1947 partly as a result of her loyalty to Margaret Fisher, who had left SCHW over her disagreement with Clark Foreman. Between summer 1947 and 1948 the organization lost other important, diligent persons either because of grave personal disagreements with other members or because some found another vehicle through which to seek their envisioned New South of democracy.[121]

The beginning of the Henry Wallace presidential campaign figured heavily in the problems of SCHW because it led to a widening of the rift between Foreman and Dombrowski. In May 1948 after already having worked with the Wallace campaign for several months, Foreman resigned from SCHW and SCEF altogether. He saw this campaign as "the most important movement in the country." In resigning from SCHW, he said that he understood that SCHW members probably would not share his belief that the Wallace candidacy offered "the South the greatest chance it has ever had to escape from the feudalism that has been such a curse to its people and to the rest of the country." When SCHW decided its role apart from the Wallace campaign, Foreman said that he had no choice but to depart from it. So many persons followed Foreman's example that the organization was left without leaders, as Dombrowski was spending his time and energy building up the Educational Fund and disassociating the *Southern Patriot*, at first SCHW's major organ, from the latter.[122]

In November 1948, owing to internal struggles and lack of money and leadership, a few persons on the SCHW board met and officially suspended its operation. In December 1948 Dombrowski and Foreman began to finalize the Conference's financial obligations with meager funds and the sale of office equipment. Under Dombrowski's leadership the Educational Fund's work would continue in the field of civil rights, particularly seeking the goal of a racially equal and integrated southern society. As one Conference member would later comment, "Thank goodness the Educational Fund has been established or all of the SCHW work would have been in vain."[123]

7

The Perpetuation of an SCHW Legacy

Two years before SCHW officially ended its work in November 1948, it had instituted SCEF, an offshoot that was initiated solely to provide a tax-exempt status for the parent organization. The Educational Fund took on more of the work of the SCHW. This was largely a result of a conflict between SCHW president Clark Foreman and SCHW-SCEF administrator James Dombrowski, and Foreman's enthusiasm and work in the Henry Wallace presidential campaign, which took away key influential SCHW leaders such as Virginia Durr. Unwittingly, when the SCHW established the Educational Fund, it had provided the means through which SCHW's decade-long struggle for democracy in the South could be carried forth. Palmer Weber, an SCHW advisory board member, said it best when he concluded, "The Southern Conference Educational Fund went right along. Thank God, we [had] separated them or it [too] would have been destroyed."[1]

The period between 1946 and 1948 best revealed how the Educational Fund acquired its SCHW-laden identity, an identity the Fund retained even into the 1960s. The most prevalent of these features became the lack of any major accomplishment in the fight for an integrated and just southern society.

The Educational Fund stood to reap good fortune from the defunct SCHW, particularly in gaining dedicated, influential leaders. James Dombrowski became the most important of the long list of individuals who had been a sustaining force in SCHW and who recognized the need to keep SCEF. After hesitation and indecisiveness, he finally accepted the executive directorship of SCEF in 1947, when it became obvious that SCHW was slowly dying. His dedication to the organization and all for which it stood became a lifetime preoccupation—he spent the next two decades in this same position, forever diligent to meet its challenges. If Foreman's doubts about Dombrowski's alleged inefficiency in SCHW administrative work were true, the latter's leadership capabilities and smooth operation of SCEF after 1947 did not support Foreman's charges. That Dombrowski directed only one organization after 1948, instead of both SCHW and SCEF as when Foreman issued his complaints, undoubtedly contributed to his greater efficiency during the later period. But he still faced grave difficulties raising funds.

Several other SCHW members and influential leaders initially remained active with the Educational Fund. With the exception of a few people, the SCHW and SCEF boards had been comprised of the same individuals. Shortly after SCHW disbanded, a few resigned from the SCEF board for various reasons, Clark Foreman among them. No one expected Foreman to remain with SCEF since he and Dombrowski had strained to make it through the last months of SCHW's operation. Few were surprised even when Foreman resigned as president of both SCHW and SCEF boards in May 1948, though he continued as a trustee of SCEF until he left to head the Wallace campaign. He could leave the movement but not the principles for which it stood. Before leaving, Foreman advised SCEF on what he believed were the major issues to which it might dedicate itself, and as late as 1957 he still pursued interests that SCHW had addressed. He became the executive director of the Emergency Civil Liberties Committee, a New York-based, civil liberties defense organization that many considered left of the American Civil Liberties Union.[2]

Virginia Durr had worked closely with the presidential campaign of Henry Wallace, but unlike Foreman, she stayed active with SCEF. In 1950, however, Durr resigned from the SCEF board because her husband, Clifford, took an appointment as counsel with the National Farmers Union (NFU), and the Durrs moved to Colorado. Yet she had become so closely acquainted with Aubrey Williams and James Dombrowski that she remained in touch with the organization. Even in the West, the issue of alleged subversives never subsided, and when Virginia Durr refused to answer questions associated with the claim that she was a Communist, NFU fired Clifford Durr. The Durrs moved back to Alabama, and by 1955 with new developments in Montgomery, both Virginia and Clifford became active in the Civil Rights Movement. Indeed, many SCHW members and officers continued in the struggle for equality and democracy for the South, but not necessarily with SCEF.[3]

Frank P. Graham supported SCEF as he had SCHW and agreed to serve on SCEF's board. His presidency of the University of North Carolina and other commitments prevented his involvement with SCEF, but he remained obligated in 1948 to the same causes that had kept him active with the Southern Conference. He became a member of President Harry Truman's Committee on Civil Rights, which in late 1947 reported what SCHW had advocated since the late 1930s—that segregation had become

Clark Howell Foreman in a picture taken by Mrs. Mairi Foreman, September 1972. Courtesy of Archives and Special Collections, Robert W. Woodruff Library, Atlanta University Center, Atlanta, Georgia.

a bottleneck to the South's progress. In March 1949 Graham gained political power with the possibility of making significant changes when North Carolina Governor W. Kerr Scott appointed him United States Senator to replace the late J. Melville Broughton.

Graham's appointment as a liberal southerner made the SCEF director and others of this liberal minority more confident that the South could be transformed sooner than they or segregationists had envisioned. Dombrowski, as most other liberal southerners, held Graham in high esteem. He praised the North Carolina governor for selecting Graham, concluding that the choice revealed a new type of chief executive emerging in southern politics. Dombrowski highlighted Graham's religious background in the *Southern Patriot* because he agreed with Graham's mixture of religion and social reform. Graham, wrote Dombrowski, believed in infusing human relationships with religious, ethical insights. Whenever he fought for better health, housing, and working conditions, Graham did not hesitate to do battle for minorities. Moreover, as administrator of a great state university dependent on the legislature for funds, Graham could have protected himself from criticism by being less outspoken on controversial issues but did not choose that route. Dombrowski was more impressed that when Graham's views on social legislation brought sharp criticism even the senator's critics admitted respect for him.[4]

Liberals were hard pressed to be successful in politics. Graham had a short-lived Senate career because when he ran for election in his own right in 1950 his opponent, Willis Smith, played up his liberalism, emphasizing Graham's role on Truman's Civil Rights Committee. Smith delighted in publicizing the 1947 House Un-American Activities Committee's report on the SCHW in which Graham, falsely of course, had been mentioned as one of the leading figures in "Communist-front organizations."

Graham's public life, then, took him away from the SCEF board in 1949 when he was appointed to the Senate. In 1954, when Dombrowski asked him to reconsider serving on the board, Graham replied that he was unable to do so because of his United Nations duties. Graham must have pleased Dombrowski, however, when he reported concentrating on the problem of racial injustice and discrimination in churches.[5] Graham's concern for integrated church worship pleased Dombrowski because of all the areas in which SCEF advocated racial equality—wages, politics, education, health care, library use—not one time had it launched a major campaign against segregated worship, a custom that predated legal segregation and endured long after segregation was outlawed in secular society.

Graham was not the only liberal who lost in the 1950 senatorial election. Claude Pepper, longtime advocate for SCHW, particularly its struggle against the poll tax, lost in Florida. The defeat of Graham and Pepper forewarned that liberalism was in for a great wave of resistance in the next decades.[6] These defeats symbolized only in a small way the turmoil associated with the creation of a different South in the 1950s and 1960s.

Throughout its history one of the great assets of SCHW had been the outstanding leaders from various social-reform organizations who served on its board and in other leadership roles. This became a liability when some of these individuals, because many had to divide their time among various groups, became less active. Seeing SCHW face tremendous difficulties, by 1948 several former leaders wanted nothing more to do with an organization created by SCHW, which in all probability stood to encounter similar circumstances. In this regard several persons sought to sever their relationship with SCEF in early 1948 though Dombrowski had begun already to work on making clear distinctions between the two organizations. Lucy Randolph Mason, who had painstakingly outlined major shortcomings of SCHW before it broke up, chose to confine her future activities to obligations with the Congress of Industrial Organizations. Harry Schacter, Paul R. Christopher, Frank Prohl, and Tarleton Collier followed Mason's departure from SCEF. Thus, the Educational Fund did not maintain the support of organized labor as had its predecessor. Since SCHW had placed so much emphasis on its members being southerners, former SCHW president John Thompson offered his resignation now that he was residing in Chicago. SCEF, not so southern bound, asked him to continue to serve. Under the terms of the bylaws Roscoe Dunjee, Percy Green, Charles S. Johnson, Lewis W. Jones, Mortimer May, William Mitch, Ira deA. Reid, and Lillian Smith had been dropped from the board automatically for having missed three consecutive meetings. But SCEF persuaded them to continue to serve by establishing only one annual board meeting, thereby making it easier for them to be present. These persons with the exception of Mitch, who officially resigned, stayed on the SCEF board. The organization's newest board members included Aubrey Williams, Luther P. Jackson, and E. Franklin Frazier.[7]

The resignation of William Mitch of the United Mine Workers of America in Birmingham represented in one instance several of the most serious SCHW problems that SCEF inherited, namely the charge of being a Communist organization. Understandably, organized labor was making a special effort to purge its locals of Communists and their sympathizers during this period when McCarthyism held sway. Mitch, then, disapproved of Sam Hall, who openly acknowledged that he headed the Communist party in Alabama. Mitch protested that people in the Alabama Southern Conference Committee had brought Hall into SCHW and promoted him to the chairmanship of the Alabama Committee despite his communism. Although his disagreement originated with SCHW, Mitch insisted on ending his service with it and the Educational Fund. Unaware of his contradiction, he said that the Southern Conference had outlived "its usefulness," but he still found it difficult to resign because he believed in SCHW's program and its attempt at transforming the South. He also regretted that the New York Committee carried the "bulk of the work . . . away from the South."[8] Mitch and a few other SCHW board members had wanted more support from southerners, but SCEF welcomed support from other parts of the country. Indeed, the Educational Fund came to accept that its survival depended on sources from outside the South.

The loss of Mason, Christopher, Collier, and Mitch signaled a major decrease in support from organized labor for the Educational Fund. Yet, the Fund could still rely on most of the African-American board members who had served for SCHW. The Southern Conference Educational Fund valued all its black supporters, but Mary Bethune was held in greater regard partly because of her national stature and her lifelong commitment and dedication to the fight for a just society. Bethune and Dombrowski, as so many individuals of SCHW and SCEF, had grown to be close friends by the late 1940s and early 1950s and this, too, accounted for the mutual high regard that she and the Fund shared. In 1950 Bethune invited Dombrowski to Florida for the celebration of her seventy-fifth birthday. Dombrowski did not attend but thanked her for the invitation, sending a telegram with greetings and a check for an unspecified sum "as a small token of my deep affection and respect for you."[9]

By the early 1950s Bethune became less active in the work of the Educational Fund and in other organizational activities owing to her age and frequent health problems. Dombrowski, however, convinced her to stay on the Fund's board in spite of the fact that she thought it best to resign. Bethune may have wanted and needed to limit her responsibilities, but instead of doing so she added more.[10]

Another outstanding black woman, Charlotte Hawkins Brown, founder and president of the Palmer Memorial Institute in North Carolina, had great influence with the Educational Fund. In 1955—by which time much had occurred toward the realization of the new democratic South that SCHW and SCEF had envisioned, though they had not been the prime movers in bringing it about—SCEF hailed Brown and Bethune as two of its most distinguished board members. Brown took pride in being "in at the beginning of the effort of the South to bring about interracial understanding and active good-will," and vowed that she did not "plan to ever forsake the organization in which I believe so firmly." Bethune, too, even in her last days, asked that she remain a part of the Educational Fund board "because of my deep and abiding faith and interest in all that the Fund is doing and hopes to do." Thus, Dombrowski credited Bethune and Brown for the part they played in the South's new beginnings when he said, "These beloved friends are two of the greatest women the New South has produced, or perhaps we should say that *have produced* the New South."[11]

Although one of the reasons the Educational Fund dissociated itself from the SCHW grew out of a conflict between Foreman and Dombrowski, when Dombrowski set up SCEF he did so with a keen eye toward avoiding the Conference's mistakes. Having experienced SCHW's difficulties and having offered many remedies to resolve them, Dombrowski saw to it that SCEF capitalized on SCHW's experiences. Because SCHW had met with much adversity, especially in regard to charges of communism from the House Un-American Activities Committee, the Educational Fund board discussed a name change for SCEF, in which "Southern Conference" would have been eliminated. But it failed to take action.[12] One of Dombrowski's first accomplishments for SCHW involved putting the organization on a sound, though temporary, financial base. Dombrowski's success with SCHW finances continued with SCEF as he kept the Fund free of major financial woes. Others from the SCHW group, including Aubrey Williams, Mary Bethune, Charlotte Hawkins Brown, Modjeska Simkins, and Benjamin Mays, had learned from the trouble spots in that organization and worked diligently with Dombrowski to prevent their recurrence in SCEF.

SCEF tried to avoid the negative aspects of SCHW, but its adoption of public education, an SCHW strategy, did have an adverse affect. SCEF's work that eventually consisted of publicity and moral persuasion resembled that of the old SCHW so much that the Internal Revenue Service ruled in 1949 against SCEF's qualification for tax exemption. The IRS concluded that SCEF's activities did not take it far away enough from political interests. Ironically, the organization that the Southern Conference established for tax-exempt purposes never attained that status after 1949, and this created some hardships for the group's finances. Between 1949 and 1953 Williams and Dombrowski worked to regain the Educational Fund's tax-exempt status but did not succeed.[13]

Although Dombrowski sought to convince the public that the SCEF differed from the SCHW, his attempt proved unsuccessful and understandably so. With the exception of a few people, SCEF included the same group who had been SCHW members. SCEF also resembled the SCHW on the matter of an office facility and how the organization operated. The Educational Fund decided to maintain the old Southern Conference office in New Orleans and did not move to another city until 1966. Occupying the same address as the Southern Conference at best caused confusion over what exactly the Educational Fund was and caused many people to believe that it was SCHW still in operation. The governing group, a board of directors of between 15 and 35 persons from southern and border states and the District of Columbia, met at least once per year at a time and place fixed by the board's president. SCEF officers, elected biennially, consisted of a president, one or more vice-presidents, a secretary, a treasurer (or the combined office of secretary-treasurer), and an executive director.[14]

The officers were familiar names from SCHW. Aubrey Williams, an active member of the Southern Conference since its founding in 1938 and who had been elected chairman of the SCHW Alabama Committee in 1946, became an SCEF board member the same year. Williams's most important and longest-served post with the Educational Fund began in 1947 when the group elected him as its first president. President Benjamin E. Mays of Morehouse College and Helen Fuller, an editor with the *New Republic*, were elected as SCEF vice-presidents, and Alva W. Taylor became secretary-treasurer.[15] The number of board members varied from time to time; in 1954 the number was increased from 25 to 52, and then to 58 in 1955. A few noted members included: L. C. Bates, publisher of the *Little Rock* (Arkansas) *State Press;* Jessie P. Guzman, director of the department of records and research, Tuskegee Institute; A. G. Gaston, President of the Booker T. Washington Insurance Company in Birmingham; Hal H. Lewis, professor of education, University of Florida; Bishop F. L. Lewis of the Colored Methodist Episcopal Church, Shreveport, Louisiana; and

Bishop Herbert Bell Shaw of the African Methodist Episcopal Zion Church, Wilmington, North Carolina.[16]

As the SCHW had done in previous years, SCEF had a board that represented a cross section of various organizations. Before 1955 the most notable of these groups included the NAACP. For example, Benjamin Mays served on the NAACP board of directors from 1950 to 1955, often expressing regret that his obligations as Morehouse College president interfered with attendance at the board meetings. His experience with SCEF duplicated much of this work with the NAACP, but the formidable task of transforming the traditional southern society made service in different organizations less important. Indeed, at the end of the 1950s, by which time direct action on the part of blacks was taking precedence over public education as a means of persuasion for legislative reform, many local and national leaders of civil rights organizations maintained ties with SCEF.[17]

From 1947 until the late 1970s, Dombrowski, the longest-serving official of the Educational Fund and also of SCHW before it disbanded, was the Fund's executive director. In 1947 the board set his salary at $4,000 and raised it to $7,500 the next year. It remained at that figure until 1951, when he earned $9,223.70. The president, Williams, received no remuneration. The Educational Fund gave no explanation for why Williams worked for the organization without compensation. He probably chose this arrangement because the organization operated on a small budget, and because his own business ventures in Alabama brought in substantial profits until the mid-1950s. He might have considered his services in the Educational Fund a major contribution to the organization. Dombrowski, who even received a salary, often contributed his own money to SCEF.[18]

Williams and Dombrowski did not begin their long years together in SCEF under the best of circumstances. Williams had been one of the few newly elected board members in 1946 to side with Foreman when he had initiated the procedure to move Dombrowski solely to work for SCEF, advising Dombrowski to agree to the arrangement. When Dombrowski eventually took Williams's advice, the two began almost immediately to dissociate SCEF from SCHW. Dombrowski and Williams, whose record in the field of social reform predated Dombrowski's, had much in common, especially their determination to create a just society. The two men sought early in their careers to rectify the second-class status of blacks. Dombrowski, for example, insisted on placing blacks in paid administrative positions in SCHW, and Williams did the same in the National Youth Administration, the New Deal agency he headed between 1938 and 1943. Moreover, the two men knew and associated with some of the same people between 1938 and 1947, particularly Eleanor Roosevelt, Walter White, and Mary Bethune, and shared in the causes for which these people worked. Working together in the SCEF seemed only natural. In their endeavor with the Educational Fund, Dombrowski and Williams attempted to build the strongest possible force against southern segregationists.[19]

The Southern Conference Educational Fund had problems, but unlike SCHW these came from without rather than from internal organizational struggles. One of the most important differences between SCHW and SCEF rested on the latter's approach to the demand for racial equality. From the time that SCHW formed in 1938 until its last meeting in 1948, certain members could not agree on how far to push for racial equality. The organization as a whole, however, saw segregation and discrimination as the root of the South's economic problems. In the Educational Fund the question never involved any hesitation about advocating total racial equality, but rather the group debated what area—education or transportation, for example—to tackle first. By placing attention on one broad topic, Dombrowski and the SCEF board believed much could be accomplished. Besides, national attention from the Truman administration on civil rights helped SCEF set its agenda.

The establishment of the Educational Fund did not gain the national and regional attention associated with the founding of SCHW, but the issues before it, or the ones it chose to address, were no less important. Indeed, much of the Conference's publicity between 1938 and 1948 helped to make civil rights a more important national issue. Although SCEF began with less publicity, it maintained a long existence, even into the 1970s, and became an important ally to blacks and mainstream black organizations in the Civil Rights Movement. It is significant that SCEF made it possible for the idealism of the New Deal liberals to impact the Civil Rights Movement decades later.[20]

The post-World War II era brought with it a heightened version of the racial tension that had occurred during the war. White veterans of World War II expected to regain jobs that blacks had filled while they were away, and blacks expected to keep those jobs. Moreover, blacks had developed a different attitude, and as SCEF vice-president Benjamin Mays concluded, a significant fallout of World Wars I and II was that blacks had learned to fight back. Mays asserted that blacks' new aggressiveness alone did more to improve their morale than any single factor.[21] The national administration's support for civil rights encouraged blacks even more.

Before Truman's advocacy for civil rights, black and white southern liberals had made it the center of national attention. For the first time in United States history liberal white southerners, though few in number, helped blacks capitalize on the two-front victory theme between 1941 and 1945. America had found itself in a dilemma, fighting for democracy abroad, on the one hand, and denying it to a large portion of its population, on the other. If this paradox gave cause for international embarrassment during the war, it became increasingly more shameful at war's end with the advent of the Cold War and Russia's propaganda about

America's racial inequalities. Indeed, the demand for racial equality by African Americans and their white liberal counterparts laid a groundwork on which President Truman could expand in the late 1940s. According to historian William Berman, the Truman administration placed civil rights in the national limelight. The president's efforts ostensibly ensured that he would get support from black voters. Truman had SCHW, the NAACP, and other social-reform groups to thank for their work in getting a greater number of blacks registered.[22] The Southern Conference for Human Welfare was no less genuine in its courageous and bold campaign that demanded an end to segregation and racial discrimination.

President Truman's appeals in the late 1940s represented the boldest of any national administration to that point in the twentieth century. The president's Commission on Higher Education reported in 1947 that "there will be no fundamental correction of the total condition [of African Americans] until segregation legislation is repealed."[23]

The Truman-appointed Committee on Civil Rights, in *To Secure These Rights*, called for a rectification of the "bad side" of the United States civil rights record. It recognized the occurrence of serious civil rights violations in every section of the nation, but pointed out that "much of it ha[d] to do with limitations on civil rights in our southern states." After a thorough analysis of past injustices, the Committee called for an end to segregation in order "to strengthen the right to equality of opportunity." It included among the several other specific recommendations the need for enacting a federal Fair Employment Practice Act, state and federal laws outlawing restrictive housing covenants, and federal legislation against lynching and the poll tax along with other safeguards to protect voting rights. The Committee's final recommendation included a task that the Southern Conference Educational Fund had already set for itself: "To rally the American people to the support of a continuing program to strengthen civil rights" through "a long term campaign of public education to inform the people of the civil rights to which they are entitled and which they owe to one another."

SCEF followed the Committee's guideline by giving the public examples of civil rights in operation. The Committee and SCEF concurred that "there still remain[ed] the job of driving home to the public the nature of our heritage, the justification of civil rights and the need to end prejudice."[24] When SCEF settled on the strategy for its program, it most resembled the old Southern Conference, which also believed it would be successful in ending discrimination and segregation with public educational campaigns.

Essentially, the Committee agreed with the basic program that SCHW had urged legislators to enact before 1948. In the general discussion of civil rights and social reform in the 1930s and 1940s, northern groups such as the Union for Democratic Action, the forerunner of Americans for Democratic Action, gained recognition for raising the consciousness of white Americans concerning the nation's minority populations. Since the SCHW and SCEF addressed the same issues and indeed held many of the same individuals within their ranks, the southern component of liberalism deserves more attention than it has been given in the past.[25]

Dombrowski placed major significance on the report from the President's Committee, especially since SCHW board members, Frank Graham and Channing Tobias, had been part of the Committee—which had formulated the strongest stance to date against the evils of segregation. Dombrowski concluded that "this report appears to be of the first importance, and probably will deserve to be ranked with the President's [Franklin Roosevelt] *Report on Economic Conditions of the South*, the publication of which gave rise to the Southern Conference for Human Welfare." But an editorial in the *Times-Picayune*, written shortly after *To Secure These Rights* appeared, was far more representative of the general reception the report could expect from the southern press. According to Dombrowski, the press objected based on traditional regional limitations. "If anything of a practical nature [was] to come of this report," he concluded, southern liberals had to be unrelenting in their endorsement and support.

What Dombrowski did not know was that Frank Graham believed in the essence of the Committee's report, that segregation needed to be eliminated from society. Graham disagreed with the Committee, however, that integration could be accomplished through legislation. Rather, he believed that the process would work best if white southerners voluntarily took the necessary steps, and he even issued a minority report in support of that view. The Committee had briefly discussed anonymously the minority opinion among its members. When the Committee presented its report to Truman, Graham was in Indonesia on another of the president's appointments. In the media coverage of the Committee on Civil Rights, Graham was simply mentioned while the positive recommendations from the majority of the group gained wider coverage. Dombrowski, therefore, had not learned of his part in the minority opinion.[26] Graham's position showed that Dombrowski's and Williams's theory about the "silent" majority of white southerners, who agreed with them but who were afraid to speak out because of the risk of reprisals from segregationists, was more complicated than they realized. Still, in the face of the most difficult circumstances, Dombrowski and Williams never gave up the Educational Fund's pursuits.

Almost no evidence revealed that SCEF's strategy to convince white southerners that segregation was morally wrong was working. On learning from the press that Goodrich C. White, who had taught Dombrowski as an undergraduate and who had become president of Emory University, objected to the majority opinion when he was on the Committee on Higher Education, Dombrowski was enraged. Dombrowski had no problem disagreeing with anyone in the fight for a democratic South and said that he felt obligated to ensure that Goodrich White knew firsthand of his and SCEF's disappointment about White's opinion. White and three other southern members of the Committee rejected the majority opinion on segregation as it applied to graduate and professional schools. The division on this question developed along regional lines with all the southern members of the Committee against integration and the majority, if not all, of the northern members for it. "This is where we stood 75 years ago," Dombrowski declared, hoping that southern leadership could soon "speak out as Christians and Americans and not as Southern-Christians and Southern-Americans." Recent experiences on college campuses led him to place the greatest hope on the younger generation of southern students. Dombrowski, gravely disturbed by the leadership they were receiving, deemed the students ahead of their leadership. He particularly noticed how the students at three unidentified southern universities spontaneously applauded when speakers there had boldly attacked racial discrimination and segregation.

Dombrowski eventually apologized halfheartedly to White, telling him that he wrote only "because of the high esteem in which I hold you and the gratitude that I feel for the stimulation of your classes and your teaching" and "because I feel so strongly about the issue in question." In a final effort to persuade White to change his opinion, Dombrowski sent to him a couple of his editorials from the *Southern Patriot* on integration.[27] White did not even reply to Dombrowski's letter. Not an isolated incident, Dombrowski's disappointment with White was one of many instances where SCEF supporters stood on the opposite side of influential people who had had a large role in their early development or careers. Indeed, they sometimes had to voice strong opposition to family members as in the case where SCEF field secretary Anne Braden's parents asserted in the 1950s that they despised her open advocation for an integrated society.[28] The effect of public education and persuasion became questionable in light of Dombrowski's unanswered letter to White and in light of Braden's antagonism with her parents.

While most white southerners ignored SCEF's efforts at moral suasion, the national administration brought about noticeably significant changes. President Truman acted on the last part of the request from his Committee, which called for the government's own immediate internal campaign for civil rights, particularly in the armed services where "efforts, already under way, [had begun] to develop genuinely democratic attitudes in officers and enlisted men." In 1948 Truman issued Executive Order 9981, initiating true integration, or as the committee put it, "equality of treatment and opportunity for the armed forces."[29] Truman's action provided strong support for Educational Fund leaders and encouraged their belief that their goal would be reached.

Through the earlier efforts of SCHW, then, and motivated by President Truman's actions on civil rights, the Southern Conference Educational Fund realized what major issue needed its attention. Before SCHW had officially disbanded in late 1948, its board had discussed potential issues that SCEF would address, issues that even Foreman had a hand in deciding.

Various SCEF members, especially Anne Braden, believed that Dombrowski alone decided to emphasize the issue of integration once he placed all his time and energy with the newly founded organization. However, Foreman had debated with the SCHW board this very issue the year before SCHW disbanded when he advised that the Southern Conference Educational Fund's program concentrate on one issue. Dombrowski initially suggested suffrage as *the issue*, but Foreman thought "that education would be more suitable" and that the whole question of teachers' salaries and "proper educational institutions in the South is something that we could arouse the maximum of interest in." The Alabama Southern Conference for Human Welfare Committee did publicize the need for equal salaries for white and black teachers in that state during 1945 and 1946; this struggle lasted into the 1950s. The NAACP led court battles for gains made in this area.[30] Foreman's prodding on the issue of southern educational institutions provided another example of how SCHW members influenced the direction of the Educational Fund's program. Nevertheless, most SCEF people, still harboring ill feelings over Foreman's attempt to displace Dombrowski in 1946, initially shied away from his proposal, only to return to it in the future as a major task.

For a brief period, the Fund directed attention toward fostering the development of interracial businesses in the South, assisting in providing for a free weekly service to all southern newspapers, and pushing a systematic educational drive in eleven southern states to promote voter registration. SCEF decided it would continue to support and cooperate with religious and organized-labor leaders but would not deal specifically with issues directly related to these general areas. Concluding that the business arena had long been a neglected field of interracial activity in the South, SCEF leaders proposed that they show the southern business community that segregation had been "wasteful and detrimental to the development of Southern business." The board then proceeded with the business component of its proposed guidelines for improvement in the areas of radio broadcasting, banking, and real estate.[31]

The organization recognized a need for interracial ownership of FM stations in every southern city with a population of at least 150,000. Citing the radio station WQQW in Washington, D.C., which was owned jointly by black and white businessmen, the Fund pointed out that this station had engaged actively in development of "interracial understanding in the Washington area." The Fund, therefore, saw this business venture as a way of increasing the positive dissemination of information on race relations and hoped that such stations would lead to a bridge for the black and white business communities that would help to "promote an approach to general community life and other business enterprises which would demonstrate the desirability of admitting Negro business capital to the development of Southern life."

The banking and housing industries presented major drawbacks for blacks. The Fund proposed reforms, in particular calling attention to the fact that few blacks were allowed to maintain accounts in banks in Miami, Florida. SCEF offered no specifics on how this situation could be remedied, suggesting only that "an effective and constructive manner" be used. In the development of unsegregated housing in the South, the group believed that this, too, could "be facilitated by joint Negro-white business housing enterprises." The organization again pointed to the Washington, D.C., area, where several black and white businessmen jointly owned apartment houses with the intention of making them into interracial dwellings. One apartment house on 16th Street, owned by the chairman of the Washington Committee of the Southern Conference for Human Welfare, was already interracial. In 1947 SCEF moved slowly toward realizing the magnitude of its work and concluded: "The quiet business development of such projects and the history of such projects in Southern communities will immeasurably assist in destroying certain Southern social myths which are today employed to support the segregation pattern."[32]

SCEF leaders considered communication, especially access to southern newspapers, a major need if an improvement in race relations in the South was to take place. And, optimistic to the end, they believed that the remedy to the problem of providing positive media coverage on race relations lay in the Educational Fund establishing a free weekly service to all southern newspapers. Indeed, despite the horrible coverage their side received in southern papers at the time of the Columbia, Tennessee, incident in 1946, SCEF officials claimed that reports would have been different if the editors of various newspapers had had adequate wire services through which to learn the truth. Convinced that excellent conditions for improved race relations in the South were at hand, they believed that many southern editors were "anxious and willing to have their news columns and editorial pages reflect a dignified, factual and constructive approach to the necessarily changing area of race relations," if only facts were reported through an unbiased source. Having observed and worked with a large number of southern editors, SCEF leaders found that a number of these editors throughout the region had acted with notable courage and conviction on the issue of racial equality and exemplified this in community and state life. It followed, at least to SCEF, that for each courageous, big-city editor, at least twenty-five to fifty more editors of county and weekly papers represented in smaller communities similar courage and integrity.[33]

Unquestionably, the political enfranchisement of African Americans in the South constituted one of the most important developments in southern social and political life during the first half of the twentieth century. It became the logical and necessary objective of all social-minded organizations in the region. SCEF continued to work for black suffrage as SCHW had done, especially identifying itself with registration drives and providing information as SCHW had done immediately after the Supreme Court's ruling against white primaries in 1944. But the Educational Fund, in the third and final section of its proposal, wanted to hire full-time staff members who would actively and systematically conduct voter-registration drives in the South.[34] SCEF did not act on any part of its new proposal, estimated to cost over $100,000, because the organization operated on such meager financial resources. SCEF had outlined goals that, if met, could have made a major improvement in race relations in the South. Inaction on the proposal had shown that the greatest of ideas was hardly worth the time and effort to formulate if it could not be carried through.

SCEF idealism could not be suppressed by financial constraints. The Fund's president took personal action on one aspect of the proposal. Aubrey Williams thought the need for blacks simply to have the opportunity to purchase homes was more important than integrated housing and proceeded to secure that opportunity in Montgomery and Birmingham, Alabama. Williams, who knew Alabama well, had long been concerned about the desperate need for improved housing for blacks. When he obtained information from the Federal Housing Authority (FHA) that only 61 houses that the agency had built in Alabama had been made available to blacks, he hardened his resolve to remedy that blatant discrimination in such a crucial sector of American life. In mid-1947 Williams established his own business venture, American Family Homes, Inc., to build 450 houses, mostly in Birmingham and all of which were to be sold to blacks. To show to what extent white southerners went to keep African Americans in dire straits, no banker in the Birmingham area would lend him money to begin building the units. Forced to start with a mortgage on his own home, loans from friends, and the financial support from northern liberals, Marshall Field in particular, Williams experienced another difficulty when insurance companies rejected the FHA-guaranteed mortgages because blacks would occupy the homes. The FHA itself discriminated when it allowed only a $5,100 guarantee on an $8,000 home in a black neighborhood but guaranteed $6,300 on an identical unit in a white neighborhood. Eventually, Lamar Life, a company in Jackson, Mississippi, took the mortgages and a Virginia bank loaned money to continue construction.

By the end of his business venture Williams had shown that blacks did not default on mortgages as often as whites of the same economic level, and he had made a small profit. Of the total 450 units sold, only five black buyers defaulted. In 1951 the business reported $96,000 from which Williams repaid in full his northern liberal friends, who by this time wanted their money back because of problems in placing mortgages, the fact that the project manager left in charge of daily operations embezzled money, and Williams's involvement in many other activities. At the same time that he started the housing business, Williams served as president of SCEF and the Alabama branch of the National Farmers Union; he also published and edited the *Southern Farmer,* a monthly from Montgomery. It is significant that Williams showed some of Birmingham's leading bankers that housing for black Americans was just as sound an investment as any other project.[35]

Since early in life, Williams had maintained an interest in racial equality, and his motive in the housing business was one of deep concern for raising the standard of living among Alabama blacks. The fact that Alabama was a state with almost a black majority lessened the impact of Williams's enterprise. If the state needed 29,000 units for whites, the number Williams learned FHA had built for whites, it needed even more for blacks.[36] But on another level Williams had revealed blatant discrimination on the part of a federal agency and had made a small effort to correct it. He had constructed more houses in Alabama for blacks in five years than the FHA, in operation since 1934, had built in thirteen.

Once the Educational Fund realized that its budget would not allow the implementation of its proposal, the organization reconsidered Foreman's suggestion, a major campaign on integration in educational institutions. Although Dombrowski basically agreed with Foreman, who saw one primary issue for a proposed project for SCEF, Dombrowski wanted to take on various issues of discrimination and segregation. In late 1947 Dombrowski concluded that "segregation in the 13 Southern states, having a population of almost one-third of the national total, confines one out of every four persons to an economic and political straight-jacket. It warps and impoverishes the cultural and spiritual life of all the people." He asked Foreman to "agree that segregation, with all of its implications— economic, political, social and ethical—underlies and complicates all basic problems confronting us in the South."

Dombrowski, mindful of the monumental task of trying to end all discrimination all at once, determined primarily that the time was right to push forward on abolishing segregation, but SCEF began work on equality in higher education, the area on which Foreman placed highest priority. The fundamental challenge involved turning public opinion against segregation so that state and federal discriminatory laws could be replaced with ones that would safeguard justice and equality for all.

For fear of taking on too much, an error the Southern Conference had made, the Educational Fund considered whether it might be more effective by tackling one state instead of taking on the entire South. If a state had to be selected, the choice would be determined largely on the basis of the most favorable conditions for success. Based on a general belief among southern liberals, SCEF surmised that Virginia and North Carolina were the two most favorable states. Ultimately, however, the SCEF, largely influenced by Dombrowski, broadened its program and targeted graduate schools, health facilities, and public libraries in all southern states as institutions in which definable results might reasonably be expected.[37]

SCEF and the Challenge of Desegregation

If a single issue from the SCHW policies and programs ran through the Educational Fund's history more fervently than that of its predecessor, it was increased emphasis upon efforts to achieve an integrated society. The young organization's leaders had not settled swiftly on whether to pay more attention to suffrage, politics, or economics; they grew more concerned about "concentrating on a challenge to the segregation pattern in Southern life." Yet these leaders, aware that the effort to achieve integration required encounters with the problems that SCHW had faced because the South had more than a few infamous instances of how determined it was to maintain its way of life, still took on the challenge.

The Educational Fund began immediately a campaign against discrimination and segregation in the October 1947 issue of the *Southern Patriot*, which graphically presented inequities in educational opportunities in seventeen states and the District of Columbia, where separate schools were maintained by law. Dombrowski considered "this Segregation in Education issue . . . the best by far . . . we have ever done and about the most timely, in view of the publication of the President's [Truman's] report on civil rights." SCEF's special *Patriot* issue showed that in states with mandated segregated schools, whites held the advantage in the value of school property per student enrolled, the amount spent per student in school, the length of the school term, the average salary of school teachers, the proportionate number of students transported to and from school, and the courses taught in state colleges and universities for teacher preparation. Indeed, the *Southern Patriot's* editor convincingly researched and showed that "there [was] no superior race; only superior opportunity." With charts and tables to support his conclusion Dombrowski revealed "that the general level of education in the low-income

South [was] so low that even the children of the more favored white group [did] not have as good an opportunity to develop as do all groups in the more prosperous states."[1]

While Dombrowski researched for data, he requested and received firsthand accounts of the hardship and disadvantages segregation caused for blacks in small rural communities. Lack of transportation to and from school for black students constituted a major problem. For example, Freeman Drake, Sr., of Roanoke, Alabama, described the hardship young children suffered as a result of not having transportation to and from school. Drake told of how the county provided some school buses for a portion of the schools. To reach the elementary community school in the upper part of Randolph County, for example, some children "have near 4 miles to walk over these hazard high ways with an improper passage for them to walk. The teachers comes near 20 miles and the building stays locked until the teachers come that distance. The tots after walking the 4 miles haves to stand out and take the winter weather."[2]

Under the heading "Professions in Proportion to the Population," Dombrowski showed an "appalling result" in seventeen states and the District of Columbia where African Americans lawfully were shut out of professional schools to maintain segregation. In thirteen southern states not one school supported by public funds allowed for the education of black doctors or dentists. This accounted largely for the fact that there was only one black doctor to every 8,000 blacks in Louisiana, for example; in the same state the ratio of white doctors to whites was one to 800. In general the relative poor health of the black population followed from the lack of adequate medical care. The mortality rate for blacks ranged 30 to 40 percent higher than that for whites, and the average life expectancy for blacks measured 10 to 12 years less than that for whites. Ultimately, the entire population, white and black, suffered from this situation, for as Dombrowski concluded, "disease germs observe no color line." It is important that when the Educational Fund protested discrimination against blacks in professional schools, it also demanded no less for Spanish Americans in the Southwest or Jews in the medical colleges in the North. Segregation and discrimination, the Educational Fund insisted, "wherever found, [made] a mockery of the Christian religion based on the universal brotherhood of mankind." SCEF, years before the *Brown* decision, predicted that "there can be little doubt that the Supreme Court sooner or later will declare segregation itself unconstitutional. When it does, all who love America, who love the South and who love their fellowman will say 'Amen.'"[3]

In making its case against segregated schools, SCEF anticipated arguments that attorneys would present before the Supreme Court when it heard presentations in the case of *Brown* v. *the Board of Education of Topeka, Kansas*. SCEF pointed out that segregation was so oppressive that "even if physical parity were achieved[,] equality would not exist. The value of a law degree, for example, rests in part upon the value it has in the eyes of the community." Basically, society tended to regard a degree from a small, separate black institution less highly than a degree from a large state university with a long legal tradition and thousands of distinguished alumni. On the issue of morale, Dombrowski's theory coincided with that of black SCEF board members, especially Benjamin Mays, whose views on this matter were published during the same period. Mays said that segregation became a "badge of inferiority" and stigmatized "every Negro child. The moment the Negro was segregated by law, prejudice and discrimination against him increased by leaps and bounds." Mays agreed with Dombrowski, saying also that "people who segregate and believe in segregation can hardly[,] if ever[,] make the Negro school equal to the white school even when both are accredited by the same agency."[4]

SCEF noticed some progress in equalizing the length of the school term and teachers' salaries for blacks and whites largely because of the success the NAACP experienced in its lawsuits against such blatant discrimination. In the basic matter of capital investment in schools and education in general and in transportation, however, the Educational Fund predicted "it would take 25 years at the present rate of progress for Negro schools to reach the point where white schools are now, and perhaps 100 years to reach parity."

The special "Segregation in Education" issue of the *Southern Patriot* had a wide distribution. The organization printed over 100,000 copies and had circulated over 70,000 copies by early 1948.[5] The special issue became the first in a long series of major, sustained propaganda campaigns directed from 1947 throughout the course of the Civil Rights Movement against all aspects of segregation and discrimination. Regrettably, the influential leaders of the organization did not realize the limited effect of idealism and liberalism without action or some kind of leverage. In the near future when changes began to occur, the NAACP, not the Educational Fund, could take sole credit.

A few encouraging signs had appeared in higher education in southern and border states. The Baltimore City Court ordered and the Maryland Court of Appeals upheld in *Murray* v. *Maryland* that the law school at the University of Maryland admit black students in 1935, and the State University of West Virginia had allowed blacks in its graduate programs since 1940. But these amounted to only a small beginning. The next several years offered more breakthroughs, one of which came in 1949 when the University of Kentucky voluntarily admitted blacks to its graduate school on a nonsegregated basis.[6]

Working on the premise that more southerners agreed with the SCEF program that advocated integration in higher education than would openly admit, James Dombrowski, on three occasions—spring 1948, fall 1948, and fall 1949—conducted surveys on the attitudes of a specific segment of southerners toward several proposed plans. In each case he surveyed a larger group, and in each group the majority opinion preferred integration.

The Educational Fund set out to ascertain in the late 1940s what was generally not recognized, namely that a large and growing group of southerners favored ending legal segregation. Results of the first of SCEF's surveys among southern sociologists indicated that three of four social scientists who replied favored dropping the racial bars in southern graduate and professional schools as a way to improve the overall quality of education for blacks. Only one in four favored the proposal of the southern governors' conference plan for segregated, regional schools. The first survey, then, reinforced Dombrowski's belief, and he simultaneously announced that it "should be a source of encouragement to liberal minded Americans everywhere." The Supreme Court's ruling in *Sipuel* v. *Oklahoma State Board of Regents*, whereby it ordered Oklahoma to provide Ada Lois Sipuel, who had sought admittance to the state's only law school, the University of Oklahoma, with an education in a state institution just as it did for applicants of any other group, continued to fuel Dombrowski's hope. This ruling, which required the extension to black students the same graduate and professional instruction offered by a state to white students, significantly affected the policies of southern institutions of higher learning. Yet Oklahoma insisted on circumventing the high court's decision by creating a separate and unequal law school for blacks.[7]

The determination of most white leaders of southern and border-state institutions to work around even the Supreme Court overshadowed the hope and idealism of SCEF leaders. Shortly after the *Sipuel* decision, southern institutions of higher education revised policies along four lines, largely to assure the maintenance of segregation. The first, Plan A, which the University of Delaware adopted, allowed African Americans to attend graduate schools on a nonsegregated basis, only when desired courses were not offered by a state-supported school for blacks. Plan B, as the University of Arkansas had adopted, admitted blacks to its law school "but with segregation." Plan C, adopted by the University of Oklahoma, created a three-teacher law school for blacks only. Plan D, the proposed Southern Governors Conference Plan, would establish segregated, regional graduate schools for blacks.

SCEF polled members of the Southern Sociological Society, an interracial organization of researchers whose interests centered on the South, to determine which of the four plans was most acceptable to what it considered one of "the most impartial and best informed group of experts that could be found in the South." It mailed 240 ballots with a cover letter explaining the four plans and asked the sociologists to indicate the plan of their choice. The ballot included space for a comment in favor of or against any chosen plan; no signatures were requested. Of the 240 ballots, 73 people, or 30 percent, replied. Of the 73 replies, 52 persons or 71

percent chose Plan A; 18 or 25 percent selected Plan D. Only 3 or 4 percent found all four plans unsatisfactory.

Dombrowski presented the results in the *Patriot* in tabular form by
states.[8] Among the reasons given for favoring Plan A, "more democratic"
and "more economical" became the most frequently cited answers from
the written comments. A response from Kentucky declared that it, like
Delaware, was "certainly ready for bi-racial graduate study; it will be
more efficient, less expensive, foster better citizenship." The University of
Kentucky became one of the first southern institutions to voluntarily integrate its student body in the summer of 1949. The liberal Frank Graham
as president of the University of North Carolina had recommended the
admission of blacks to that university in 1940, but moderates on the
school board would not allow it. A response from North Carolina expressed partly what SCEF hoped to accomplish. The respondent expected
that

> The mingling of qualified students of both races on the graduate level will be
> less fraught with menace to good interracial understanding than would an
> immediate introduction of interracial education on the lower educational lev-
> els of undergraduate and secondary school education. Let us demonstrate its
> success on the graduate level as a means of changing public opinion towards
> its acceptance more generally.[9]

The Educational Fund accepted the North Carolina response as most feasible though it wanted the complete elimination of segregation and
discrimination.

SCEF conducted a second survey later in 1948, this time mailing ballots
to the entire faculties of eleven state universities. From the 371 replies,
255 or 69 percent favored Plan A; 105 or 28 percent favored Plan D. Only
11 or 3 percent favored Plans B and C. Unlike the first survey, Dombrowski requested signatures of respondents. Of 371 replies (out of an
unstated total number), 205 persons signed and 165 did not. The argument in support of Plan A, as in the first survey, was that this plan appeared more democratic and more economical. The results of the second
survey permitted Dombrowski to calculate the school faculty least or most
favorable toward Plan A. He found that at the University of North Carolina, the state which SCHW believed to be more liberal than other southern states in the 1930s, the majority of faculty members who responded
favored dropping all racial bars. Mississippi led the three states that voted
in favor of segregated regional schools, followed by Georgia and South
Carolina, the other states in this category.[10]

The last survey of opinions toward integration in higher education conducted by Dombrowski revealed that seven of ten teachers who replied
favored immediate integration of African Americans into southern graduate and professional schools. Using names from school catalogs, Dom-

browski sent ballots to approximately 15,000 teachers in 155 institutions in 14 southern and border states and included black institutions for the first time. Of the total, he received 3,422 replies. Of the replies, 2,412 or 70.5 percent favored Plan A; 88 or 3 percent favored Plan B; 80 or 2 percent voted for Plan C; 842 or 24.5 percent for Plan D. He made a distinction between the responses from black and white institutions—3,134 or 91 percent were from teachers in 130 white institutions and 288 or 9 percent were from teachers in 25 black institutions. The trend in the third poll approximated the results of the poll of white state-university teachers of the previous year. Dombrowski noted that the inclusion of teachers from 25 black colleges, though they voted overwhelmingly for Plan A, made little difference in the trend of the data; of the total responses from white institutions, about 68 percent voted for Plan A. In the first and second surveys, which went to white faculty only, 71 and 69 percent, respectively, favored Plan A. Although the ballots stated that signatures were optional, 77 percent of the returns were signed, and 53 percent of those who replied gave written reasons for their choices. The recently integrated University of Kentucky reported no major catastrophe. From Kentucky came the response: "University of Kentucky tried Plan A this summer. Worked out o.k. as far as I learned. The sky did not fall, neither did any of the buildings fall down, nor did any of the students get contaminated," contrary to segregationists' predictions. A response from Maryland got to the essence of the matter: "In my opinion it is unconstitutional to tax citizens for a public service from which they receive no benefits."[11] The small number of people involved in the three surveys seems minor until considering the almost daily reporting of violence and other stories of racial injustice. The smallest positive factor became significant, and in this sense the Educational Fund found yet more hope for its region's eradication of discrimination in higher education. Dombrowski's surveys, however, had shown the sentiment of a few educated southerners, people who were not great enough in number to change the law. By conducting surveys, therefore, Dombrowski had made no major impact on the elimination of segregation from higher education.

Higher education was only one segment of life under segregation. In 1948 the actions of the southern governors on the proposed segregated regional school plan, the revival of the Ku Klux Klan, and the work of the Dixiecrats and white-supremacy elements presented resistance, hinting that it would take much more than favorable opinion to change southern society. Segregation laws of southern states, based on the premise that African Americans were inferior to whites, induced the belief among whites, in particular white policemen, that blacks had few rights that whites were bound to respect. Part of the fierce opposition of states' rights Democrats to any kind of federal civil rights program was the fear that these laws, and the pattern of segregation based on them, might be weakened. By opposing federal civil rights action, the southern "bolters," concerned primarily with the principle of federal versus states' rights, protested recognizing the civil rights of blacks at any level—national, state, or local. Birmingham had a noted character who bolted on the local level for the duration of the history of SCHW and SCEF. His opposition represented the perpetuation of a white-over-black syndrome and his determination to protect white southerners' way of life.

Racial violence and civil rights drew SCEF's Dombrowski to Birmingham in the spring of 1948. When a full-page advertisement appeared in the Birmingham newspapers asking citizens to vote in the May 1948 primaries for a slate of delegates and electors who would *not* support Harry Truman or anyone who favored civil rights for African Americans before or after the Democratic national convention at Philadelphia, City Commissioner of Public Safety Eugene "Bull" Connor's name appeared among the list of endorsers. Neither Connor's reputation nor that of the Birmingham police force consisted of protecting blacks or their rights. The month before the newspaper endorsement appeared, Birmingham police officers had shot and killed five blacks, the latest victim of police terror 19-year-old Marion Franklin Noble, killed on April 27. Allegedly, Birmingham police, in an attempt to intimidate NAACP members, had accosted them both physically and verbally and had even snatched off and stamped into the ground the buttons that they wore. The police had allegedly even beaten black businessmen.

Because of police brutality against blacks, the Southern Negro Youth Congress (SNYC) announced its plan for a meeting in Birmingham, whereupon Commissioner Connor "in his self-appointed role of censor of public meetings announced he would do everything he could to prevent the [SNYC] meeting from taking place." The commissioner called before him black ministers who had offered their churches for the meeting and threatened them with arrest if they allowed "the slightest infraction of the segregation laws." According to the press, Connor told one minister that the Klan had offered its cooperation to prevent the SNYC conference from being held. Connor's intimidation succeeded in part, as the conference's opening session could not be held because his coercion made it impossible for organizers to find a meeting place.[12]

SCEF, then, had its own confrontation with Birmingham's Bull Connor over segregation, much like the reception SCHW had experienced ten years earlier. This time the meeting had not been initiated by SCEF, but it involved SCEF leaders. On May 1, 1948, the SNYC opened a biennial meeting in Birmingham in a small black church, the Alliance Gospel Tabernacle. Four persons, including James Dombrowski, Doris Senk of New York, Edward Forrey, a representative of the Congress of Industrial Organizations' International Maritime Union, and the pastor of the church, Claude Herbert Oliver, were arrested—Dombrowski and two other whites for taking part in a meeting "not properly segregated" and Oliver for permitting an integrated meeting to take place in his church.

The arrests did not stop there. The main speaker for the occasion, Idaho Senator Glen Taylor, Progressive party candidate for vice-president, was arrested when he arrived and refused to follow police instruction that white people attending the meeting must use the rear entrance. To establish back-door entrance, police tacked a sign at the front to indicate the entrance was for blacks, and the previously nailed-shut back door had been opened for whites. When Taylor refused to comply with police orders, he was knocked to the ground and arrested, charged with resisting an officer, assault and battery, and disorderly conduct. On learning that the meeting had been segregated, he had decided not to speak and only wanted to go inside to make an announcement, an announcement that would have explained the Progressive party's campaign policy of its speakers' refusal to address segregated audiences.

When the cases came to trial, Recorder's Court Judge Oliver C. Hall went against his white-supremacy inclination and found four of the defendants not guilty. He concluded, "I believe these people who sponsored this meeting tried to create a separation of the races and abide by the law. . . . I would feel great pleasure in finding them guilty if the facts bore it out." That a white male, Edward Forrey, sat alone on a bench at right angles and about three feet away from benches used by the black audience, allowed Hall to rule that the "amount of space and the angle of the bench constituted the 'physical barrier' required by law." But unlike the other four, Senator Taylor was convicted, fined $50, and given a 180-day suspended jail sentence. He paid the fine but threatened to appeal the case on the ground that the segregation ordinance which the officer attempted to enforce violated the Fourteenth Amendment and United States civil rights statutes. He never did so. Perhaps segregationists were too smart to allow Taylor the opportunity by not charging the senator with breaking the segregation ordinance, going so far as to dismiss charges brought against the other four persons arrested on the same day as Taylor. If Taylor's arrest had done nothing else, for a brief period it had brought national, even international, attention to the South and segregation. According to a May 8 *New York Times* story, a Polish Communist party newspaper devoted its lead editorial to the arrest of Senator Taylor. The editorial pointed to America's contradictory democracy, saying that Taylor's arrest symbolized the same "anti-democratic" principles that the American government sought to "export" abroad.[13]

The Birmingham incident brought little revelation to Dombrowski. The SCEF leader concluded that "segregation and American democracy . . . cannot live together peacefully. . . . Under 'Bull' Connor civil rights of Negroes are protected about as well as they would be if the city were policed by the Klan."[14] This situation and others like it set the stage for the next decade, but still SCEF leaders insisted that there existed more southern whites who were sympathetic to SCEF's concern with racial equality than would openly admit their views. They clung to this belief despite the fact that white southerners found no difficulty consistently demonstrating the opposite.

SCEF made the most of promising new developments. The favorable responses for integration in higher education from the surveys that Dombrowski had conducted and Truman's focus on discrimination and segregation as a major national concern partly inspired the SCEF Declaration on Civil Rights Conference held in the fall of 1948. Just as when the National Emergency Council issued its *Report on Economic Conditions in the South* in 1938 and the controversy surrounding the report helped southerners decide to found SCHW, the report of Truman's Civil Rights Committee, similarly, gave impetus to the Southern Conference Educational Fund's greater interest in the elimination of segregation and discrimination. Dombrowski insisted that southern liberals not pass this most appropriate time and called for the conference in December 1947.[15] But the group, experiencing the disruption caused by the dying SCHW, decided not to hold its conference immediately. The 1948 Declaration of Civil Rights Conference coincided with SCHW's final board meeting, but the Educational Fund took the occasion to announce more clearly its purposes and goals.[16]

On November 20, 1948, fifty representatives of SCHW and SCEF met in Charlottesville, Virginia, and adopted a Declaration of Civil Rights to end segregation and discrimination, a document that at least 200 southern educational and professional leaders had signed previously. The group held discussions at the University of Virginia but departed to Thomas Jefferson's home at Monticello, where it formally adopted the Declaration and emphasized Jefferson's "all men are created equal" theme just as the SCHW had done on its founding. In part the Declaration read:

> We take these rights to include equality before the law, freedom from any discrimination bolstered by law; freedom of expression; and unrestricted access to all institutions supported by taxes for the public welfare, schools and hospitals not excepted; equal pay for equal work, and equal opportunity to receive training and to gain employment; and the right of unsegregated transportation, housing or assembly.[17]

The Educational Fund's proposed plan of action included three headings. First, it called on its members to speak out against discrimination and to guard against prejudice in work, thought, or deed. Second, members would inform and educate the public about present inequalities and injustices and seek to obtain approval of changes needed to remedy these wrongs. Finally, the Educational Fund called for legislation or repeal of existing laws violating these principles, notably laws enforcing public distinctions and the need for new legislation at all levels to shield the civil rights of all citizens.[18]

Aubrey Williams, in prefacing the discussion of the statement, saw this as a great beginning. He remained hopeful that there was "a growing feeling, even among the 'die-hards,' of the inevitability of the end of racial discrimination." As individuals in the Educational Fund saw it, President Truman's victory in 1948, despite his civil rights proposals, changed the climate of the South. SCEF leaders felt compelled to grasp the opportunity. Here, then, is one factor that made it possible for SCEF to be more outspoken on the issue of racial equality; it could capitalize on a different atmosphere. The liberalism of the national administration gave Dombrowski and Williams that extra sense of hope in a cause that they wanted to see achieved. SCEF recognized that the administration's commitment to ending discrimination, on the one hand, augmented by its determination to establish the United States as the moral leader of the world, on the other, would make it all the more difficult for southerners to continue to demand racial discrimination in contradiction to the ideals of American democracy.

After the first couple of years of deciding its strategy, putting its organization in order, and finding greater hope through Truman's Civil Rights Committee report, the Educational Fund determined that it could make a difference in the attitude of southern whites despite the South's past and present attitude toward race relations which stood to minimize that optimistic outlook. In the late 1940s, then, the Southern Conference Educational Fund reaffirmed the organization's goal of eliminating racial discrimination and segregation.[19]

The Supreme Court took up where the Truman Administration left off. SCEF wanted news of the breakthroughs spread far and wide, so it publicized in 1950 three major, unanimous decisions by the Supreme Court which established the legal framework whereby all segregation would eventually be outlawed. The cases included: *Henderson v. United States, Sweatt v. Painter,* and *McLaurin v. Oklahoma State Regents for Higher Education.* In the *Henderson* case the justices made segregation illegal in interstate railway transportation; in the *Sweatt* and *McLaurin* cases, Herman Marion Sweatt and George Washington McLaurin were admitted to the University of Texas and University of Oklahoma, respectively, on an integrated basis. In addition to publicizing the significance of these cases the Educational Fund prepared and submitted, though it was refused by the Court, an *amicus curiae* brief on behalf of *Sweatt.* It was no minor point that an interracial group of attorneys prepared the brief. Dombrowski marked the effort as a first for white southern lawyers to publicly support an attack against segregation.[20]

Although some progress was being made with a few court cases for which the Educational Fund could claim no credit, the organization recognized that the time had not yet arrived when it ought to focus less attention on integration. Thus, even before the final decision on the above cases, SCEF continued its campaign for integration in education with the initiation of a conference on Discrimination in Higher Education at Atlanta University in April 1950. The meeting was sponsored by 225 leaders from 116 southern colleges and universities. Based on the conference, SCEF published a 90-page pamphlet, "Discrimination in Higher Education."[21] A supportive message from Albert Einstein, who also had assisted the Southern Conference for Human Welfare and its efforts in the Columbia, Tennessee, incident in 1946, generated greater publicity for the gathering. He found segregation, the basis for perpetuating discrimination, a great evil and praised SCEF, saying:

> If an individual commits an injustice he is harassed by his conscience. But nobody is apt to feel responsible for misdeeds of a community, in particular, if they are supported by old traditions. Such is the case with discrimination. Every right-minded person will be grateful to you for having united to fight this evil that so grievously injures the dignity and repute of our country. Only by spreading education among all of our people can we approach the ideals of democracy.

While SCEF directed attention toward desegregation in higher education, it also targeted other inequities. It saw the need for desegregating public libraries and eliminating peonage and the poll tax. Preventing African Americans' use of public libraries was yet another part of the institution of segregation, but most white southerners also linked peonage and the poll tax to segregation, seeing them as obstacles to the economic and political well-being of blacks. By focusing attention on these areas, SCEF linked them with how segregationists tied them to segregation, the means of perpetuating white supremacy. To achieve an end to the entire southern tradition of segregation, the purpose of the piecemeal approach, SCEF also sought the inclusion of civil rights in the Democratic party's platform in the 1950s.

Aubrey Williams went before the platform committee of the Democratic party at its 1952 national convention in Chicago. Speaking on behalf of SCEF, the only southern organization which asked for an uncompromising civil rights plank, he reasoned, "I have long . . . come to the conclusion that the only way we will ever be able to give those members of the Negro race who are qualified a chance to secure decent employment is through a law, and I have had to reluctantly come to the conclusion that no Southern state will pass such a law." Except for a response from another white southerner, a Mrs. J. D. Alderman of Jacksonville, Florida, who admonished Williams, saying, "You can[not] legislate morals into people," his little-noticed request went unheeded. The Democratic party, however, adopted a compromised civil rights platform plank.[22]

SCEF began to center attention on the desegregation of public libraries in 1949. A couple of years later the organization reported that four cities—Forth Worth, Texas; Richmond, Virginia; Louisville, Kentucky; and Chattanooga, Tennessee—had abandoned segregated libraries. Louisville, though it had integrated its main library, kept other branches segregated. In 1952 it eliminated from its public library system the last vestiges of segregation. The next year SCEF reported that fourteen southern cities had integrated their public libraries.[23] The lack of court cases or acts of violence related to library integration up to 1953 helped SCEF leaders to believe (though falsely) that of all the areas of segregated society, the integration of library service might be achieved most easily. SCEF took library integration as a signal that many more white southerners were willing to end segregation in other areas, but the peaceful transition in the libraries gave way to arrests and trials of African-American students attempting to use all-white libraries in 1960.

Concessions from the Democratic party and from a few libraries did not make stamping out peonage and the poll tax any easier. Peonage lingered in the South in 1951 despite the fact that it had been invalidated by the Supreme Court in 1914, and SCEF was one of the few organizations to publicize its brutality. As in other instances where SCEF tried to correct a southern wrong, the white-supremacist South struck back, usually with violence. When Thomas W. Johnson, a Macon, Georgia, attorney and SCEF board member testified before Minnesota Senator Hubert Humphrey's Senate Subcommittee on Labor-Management Relations, the county sheriff later beat him. Johnson testified that Sheriff Carlus D. Gay of Laurens County, Georgia, had been an accomplice with local employers in placing black males in peonage by arbitrarily arresting them on trumped-up charges and releasing them to local employers for cheap labor, or sometimes for no pay. On learning from the sheriff of new arrests, the employers who ran sawmills, or naval stores, paid prisoners' bonds for release on the condition that they would work to repay the bond. If the black person's work proved unsatisfactory, the employer usually threatened to send the former prisoner back to jail or beat him, or both. The sheriff profited because part of his earnings came directly from a portion of fines and bonds paid. Investigators for the subcommittee who had gone into Laurens County found evidence in support of Johnson's observations; they even quoted the sheriff who explained how the system worked. For a hearing whose focus had been on the hostility against organized labor in the county, Johnson's testimony initiated the issue of peonage. Subsequent to the hearing, he went by the sheriff's office on a business matter, and the sheriff attacked him.[24] The sheriff went unpunished for the crime.

In 1953 SCEF's magazine carried a story about peonage in Sumter County, Alabama. This time seven white farmers, all of the same family, were indicted in federal court in Birmingham for forcing four black males into labor, one of whom died shortly after an oppressor brutally beat him. The federal court, however, made no indictment on the murder case, stating that this matter concerned the state jurisdiction. Since the farmers arrested were well off financially, it seemed improbable that they would have resorted to ransoming prisoners for work because the standard wage for black labor in the county averaged only two dollars per day, and the employers got the maximum amount of work for the day, which lasted from sunup to sundown. Aubrey Williams, aware that debt slavery was not unusual in the South, requested that Alabama Governor Gordon Persons investigate to what extent the practice prevailed in Alabama; the governor failed to act. An unidentified black lawyer in Sumter County had informed Williams that the practice was so prevalent that "the only unusual thing about this [reported] case is that a fuss is being made about it." Eventually, a year after indictments, two members of the Dial family, brothers Fred N. and Oscar Edwin, were convicted of peonage and sentenced to eighteen months in federal prison. But the state did not prosecute anyone for the murder.

The Educational Fund, keeping with tradition, believed that the brutality and the oppressive nature of peonage, if brought to the public's attention, could stir legislators to pass laws to eradicate it. But as Pete Daniel, the historian who has done extensive work on peonage, emphasized, local communities and the federal government ignored the practice even though more than 150 peonage cases were reported after 1958.[25]

The progress toward abolishing the poll tax was just as slow as attempts at wiping out peonage, especially since SCHW and other organizations had launched a major, decade-long national campaign against it between 1938 and 1948. Only in 1951 did the South Carolina and Tennessee legislatures eliminate the poll tax as a prerequisite to voting. Under a new constitutional amendment in 1953 Alabama discontinued requiring retroactive poll taxes, where conceivably an individual could have had to pay as much as $36 or more in back taxes before voting. Now the maximum assessment was set at $3. Although SCEF wanted to see the poll tax abolished completely, it admitted that at least "the most oppressive feature" of Alabama's law had been destroyed and continued to press for federal anti-poll-tax legislation.[26]

SCEF's drive against segregation and discrimination placed its survival in jeopardy as southern politicians took advantage of Cold War hysteria during the 1950s. Since to most white southerners working for racial justice became synonymous with being a Communist, SCEF became a target for further allegations. The atmosphere of the Cold War era, which brought with it greater suspicions of Communist sympathizers and infiltrators, forced the SCEF to deal with the Communist charges that now took on graver consequences. The usual messages from the House Un-American Activities Committee gave way to charges from the Senate Subcommittee on Internal Security of the Judiciary Committee, which initiated a hearing in New Orleans in 1954. Even though Senator William E. Jenner from Indiana headed the committee, only Mississippi Senator James Eastland and his aides actually showed up for the hearing. Probably Eastland conducted the hearing alone to prevent his possible defeat in the senatorial election in Mississippi; the attack on integrationists would give him greater leverage in his home state. Also the Dixiecrats seemed to be losing ground because of the few successes in courtroom battles favoring integration. Subsequently, McCarthyism became a way of intimidating white southerners who willingly established contact and became allies with blacks in their fight for civil rights. As one person called before the committee said, "Just as Joseph McCarthy saw a Red behind every government door, Eastland saw a Red behind every black."[27]

Whatever the reason, the committee brought Myles Horton, Aubrey Williams, James Dombrowski, and Virginia Durr before it to question their alleged communism. The major witnesses against them, Paul Crouch and John Butler, both later proved to be criminals. Their stories about the alleged charge against SCEF, therefore, were to be taken lightly. Eastland ably showed that he could make himself look foolish. One reporter conducted a survey among his colleagues covering this fiasco and concluded at the end of the hearings that based on what had been seen and heard, Eastland, out of the parties present during the entire hearing, proved to be the greatest threat to American ideals; Paul Crouch was second.[28] Eastland threatened other hearings but did not follow through on the threat.

One significant aspect of the Communist charges during this period that was not true in the 1940s was that reprisals became damaging to people's careers and personal lives. Clifford Durr, who represented Myles Horton at the hearing, suffered a slight heart attack on the last day of the proceedings. Durr, a frail man in 1954, might have suffered the heart attack anyway, but the intense drama of the hearings and the impugning of his wife's integrity probably brought it on. A few people faced economic reprisals, not to mention the emotional pressure that became more tense as a result of white supremacists' stepped-up militancy. In the line of economic reprisals some people lost their jobs simply because they were affiliated with SCEF. Williams and Dombrowski did not seek other employment, but in the event that they had, they probably would not have found jobs in the public sector after 1954. In 1959 the Tennessee legislature investigated Horton's Highlander Folk School and, based on spurious charges, which included among others the illegal sale of alcohol and the practice of integration in violation of Tennessee law, closed the school in 1961 in spite of Horton's appeals. The closer the South came to being democratic, the more intense racial violence grew.[29] Communist charges against SCEF persisted in the 1950s, forcing the organization to lead a major campaign in its defense in later years.

Between 1948 and 1956 probably the most difficult year for SCEF was 1954. But this year could also be called the most progressive. For the Supreme Court decision in *Brown*, though it addressed integration only in education, brought significantly broader consequences. For the first time since the late nineteenth century, integrationists worked with the law on their side.[30]

In some ways the most important immediate effect of *Brown* was psychological. It motivated blacks and liberal white southerners who otherwise might have been less willing to protest second-class status. SCEF's support of developments in Montgomery in 1955 illustrates the point. E. D. Nixon had grown close to Attorney Clifford Durr and his wife Virginia because Clifford Durr fought and won several cases that Nixon had brought to him. Nixon had even recommended Rosa Parks to Virginia Durr for part-time work as a seamstress, unknowingly creating a relationship that would change Parks's life and efforts at ending segregation. SCEF's influence and financial backing took Parks to workshops at the Highlander Folk School in Tennessee the summer before the precipitating incident that led to the Montgomery Bus Boycott and the gains that resulted from those activities. When Myles Horton informed the Durrs that a scholarship was available for a 1955 summer workshop, the Durrs urged Rosa Parks to accept it. Reluctantly, Parks consented to go when Aubrey Williams offered to pay her travel expenses to and from Tennessee.

Although she hesitated initially, Parks was influenced by the knowledge that the Durrs had been advocates for the end of segregation since the late 1930s. On numerous occasions they listened to Parks's complaints about segregation in the South, especially the situation involving Montgomery's public transit system. Parks deplored the custom of having to enter the front of the bus to pay to ride and then having to exit to reenter the back of the bus. Frequently, the white bus drivers pulled off and left black riders before they could board at the back. Moreover, Parks, secretary of the Alabama NAACP, kept the Durrs abreast of the efforts for a test case to end Montgomery segregated busing or at least to improve the present situation. Her hopes rose when Claudette Colvin, a fifteen-year-old high-school student, was arrested for refusing to give her seat to a white passenger. At Parks's invitation Virginia Durr attended an NAACP meeting concerning the incident, but Colvin's mother refused to allow her daughter to go through with the case.

Parks's knowledge, though it may have been subconscious, that she had someone to come to her rescue, added to her courage to balk at the bus driver's order that she give up her seat to a white male in 1955. She has said that she was simply too tired to move, but the Durrs accompanied E. D. Nixon to get Parks from jail. Indeed white southern liberal Clifford Durr assisted Fred D. Gray, her black defense attorney, after she was arrested for refusing to relinquish her bus seat. Virginia Durr supported the boycott, too, and provided transportation for blacks in this movement for change. Aid did not stop there, for Aubrey Williams helped E. D. Nixon, the principal organizer for the movement, to raise funds.[31] Although the gains from the boycott must be attributed largely to the many unsung black participants, the few local SCEF members provided personal and financial support to end one aspect of segregated life in Montgomery.

Anne and Carl Braden of Louisville did not need the psychological boost that *Brown* brought in 1954. This white couple made civil rights history by committing the crime of purchasing a home, in their name only, for a black couple, Andrew and Charlotte Wade, in a white section of the city. Anne Braden has since explained that when the Wades asked them to buy the house, it was not conceived as a big project. Neither she nor Carl foresaw the trouble that would follow; they simply wanted to help friends. In justifying their action, Anne explains: "We could do nothing else because we had never refused to help when a Negro took a stand against segregation and asked our assistance. I did not believe that I as a white person had a right to say to any Negro, 'Now is not the time.' " They had done as the Wades wished.

The white neighbors reacted immediately and demanded that the Wades move; they refused. Subsequently, the Wades' home was bombed twice without injury to the family, and they eventually had to give up the house and live elsewhere. The most harmful result became the nightmare that this created for the Bradens, whom the authorities accused of bombing the Wade's home. It did not make sense that the Bradens would bomb the house that they had bought for the Wades, but it made more sense to the local authorities than the accusation that the Wades bombed their own home. Things did not end there. The state eventually charged the Bradens with sedition by Kentucky laws that dated to the 1910s and the end of World War I, and Carl Braden served a year's prison term.[32] The incident helped to identify for SCEF two loyal soldiers in the fight for integration as the organization supported the Bradens with some finances during the early ordeal, and the Bradens became field secretaries for the Fund later when they could not find employment elsewhere.[33] The 1954 incident helped to clarify another reason why white liberals were called Communists—though the Bradens' activism made them more radical than liberal. Segregationists, the majority of southern whites, were convinced that "outsiders" or Communists had given blacks the notion that they wanted an integrated society, a reform that blacks lacked sophistication to demand on their own.

Despite the fact that many among its leadership advocated social equality during its history, SCHW placed major emphasis on economic equality and less on social equality. The line is a fine one, but SCHW is not to be blamed because it could have done more to promote social as well as economic equality. SCHW had worked diligently to eliminate discrimination, particularly during World War II. It had done no differently from SCEF, for which the Truman administration and its Civil Rights Committee had created more favorable circumstances in which to work. SCHW was ahead of its time in addressing equal economic opportunities for *all* because after everything was said and done, by the end of the 1960s even black-led civil rights organizations had come to understand that economic equality lay at the heart of the problem of equality of opportunity in America.

SCEF maintained itself specifically to eliminate racial segregation and discrimination in southern society. This task was a carry-over from SCHW, though SCHW never admitted this limited role. SCEF did not overlook the fact that education, health programs, and general health care for individuals could be improved by an upgraded southern economy that would increase the overall per capita income of all southerners. National civil rights leader Martin Luther King, Jr., made clear this necessity in 1968 during a major campaign in protest of American involvement in Vietnam.[34]

The important question, then, becomes: What had the Educational Fund accomplished by 1956? On many occasions SCHW and SCEF leaders talked about how "the Solid South ha[d] become the Fluid South." Leaders in both groups believed that both organizations played a major role in this progressive change. Their belief rested on the notion that southerners finally had begun to accept inevitable change, and to give support to those few individuals who at times felt isolated. In 1952, SCEF said, "if we were to choose a motto, it would be: You Are Not Alone!" But contrary to what SCEF leaders believed and given the outline of its activities, by 1956 no major accomplishments emerge for which the organization can take full credit. Yet, if the organization had done nothing else, it had provided moral and financial support to a few southerners who might have done nothing to change southern society. In that sense Williams appropriately termed SCEF's work as "keeping southern liberal sentiment mobilized."[35]

Using what it perceived as the most practical means, namely publicizing the horrors of segregation and racism in the *Southern Patriot* and on radio programs whenever that opportunity became available, the Educational Fund believed that it was helping to transform the South. It cannot be ascertained what percentage of people read the *Patriot* or heard radio broadcasts, but segregationists believed that SCEF had caused enough commotion that the organization should be stopped.[36] SCEF caused problems for the South's old guard and represented a major agent for change not because it had actually caused changes in southern society but because segregationists perceived it as an organization that could wholly disrupt the system of segregation.

White Southern Backlash and the High Price for a Just Cause

The idealism so prevalent in the Southern Conference Educational Fund (SCEF) had existed in earlier groups that marked significant historical periods. In their time the Abolitionists, the Radical Republicans, the Populists, the muckrakers, and the suffragists had envisioned an America that would offer equal footing to all citizens. Like these groups, SCEF relied on idealism and trusted the strategy of moral consciousness-raising that had worked well for its reform-oriented predecessors.

In the 1950s the Southern Conference Educational Fund began to observe the beginning of the fruition of its dream: segregation was ending and the eventual demise of overt racial discrimination was in sight. The most important of these breakthroughs, the Supreme Court decision in *Brown* v. *Board of Education of Topeka* (1954) and the Montgomery Bus Boycott of 1955–1956, made evident that blacks were taking charge of the struggle for civil rights. Individuals in the SCEF came to realize that the struggle for equality was changing in makeup; black civil rights leaders continued to welcome the help and support of whites sympathetic to their demands for a just society. The Supreme Court decision in *Brown* ended a long struggle for blacks and liberal whites in that for the first time since 1896 segregationists were placed on the defensive. But the *Brown* decision embraced only one aspect of racial equality, public education; blacks had yet many other obstacles to overcome, mainly those blocking the way to equitable economic and political opportunities.

Resistance and repression dominated the southern scene after the *Brown* decision and added to the already difficult task of blacks and their white liberal counterparts in the Civil Rights Movement. Mississippi

Congressman John Bell Williams labeled May 17, 1954, the day the Supreme Court announced the decision, as Black Monday and two months later he joined other staunch segregationists in forming the first White Citizens Council in Indianola, Mississippi. Throughout the 1950s southern legislators proceeded with various means to evade school integration, the most notable example of which was the Southern Manifesto whereby southern senators and congressmen pledged to use every means possible to reverse the decision. With the exception of three southern senators and twenty-four congressmen, all other southern congressmen signed the document. The legislators and the white southern majority proved quite successful in various strategies to prevent school integration. As late as the mid-1960s most public schools in South Carolina, Alabama, and Mississippi had not been integrated.[1]

Most white southerners, accustomed to the use of violence to maintain their superior status, proved no exception to this rule in the decades of the 1950s and 1960s. Indeed historians label this period the Second Reconstruction, in part because of the many violent attacks on blacks and white sympathizers by advocates of the status quo which occurred more intensely during the 1950s and 1960s than at any time since the end of the Civil War. Moreover, not since Reconstruction had southerners so avidly tested the strength of states' rights versus federal authority. Although the SCEF continued to expect that it could change the mentality of most white southerners through public awareness and condemnation, a few black leaders anticipated a massive resistance from segregationists.

In the aftermath of the *Brown* decision, then, blacks experienced both new hope and dread for tenser moments based on the reaction of die-hard segregationists. Roscoe Dunjee, editor of Oklahoma City's *Black Dispatch* and SCEF board member, pointed to evidence of developments in his native Oklahoma and concluded that in the mid-1950s the South faced another dark hour and that the era presented a major challenge simply because "white reaction will try to join with Negro Uncle Toms to defeat our objectives."[2]

Roy Wilkins, NAACP leader, agreed with Dunjee's assessment, and he too warned of the "dark before the dawn." Wilkins reasoned that a great many white people in the South were tremendously shocked, not because the NAACP and other civil rights organizations advocated the abolition of segregation, but because "for the first time since Reconstruction they are making absolute[ly] no headway with the old tested and tried techniques through which they have managed to stave off and defeat similar efforts in the past." Of course, blacks had resisted white scare tactics in the past, but far more blacks than in the 1950s had been easily intimidated by white violence and threats. During that period Wilkins observed that whites "only had to make their feelings known and to pass the word out to their colored people and a movement was stopped in its tracks, except for a persistent minority." Now that African Americans steadfastly proclaimed that segregation had to end, coupled with the promise of revolutionary changes evident by *Brown*, such action led white people to bond together in organizations like the White Citizens Councils and similar groups to fight desegregation, the NAACP, and other civil rights groups. Except for the Ku Klux Klan, before the 1950s they had not organized.

The end of the White Citizens Council movement began as soon as it started. Despite its success in the 1950s and early 1960s, its open use of methods already drawing national condemnation predicted its demise. The eventual death of the White Citizens Council movement summed up the importance of *Brown*. Many Americans, including blacks, lacked the confidence that the southern white majority would slowly convert as SCEF believed, but black leaders such as Wilkins and Dunjee valued "the silent condemnation and non-cooperation of important segments of the Southern white community."[3] The idealism of the Educational Fund and its efforts to make the American public aware of the horrors of segregation and discrimination remained a significant part of the Civil Rights Movement. Although the NAACP did not work closely with SCEF as it had in earlier years with the Southern Conference for Human Welfare (SCHW), it did not stop realizing the importance of the white southern minority.

Segregationists, as black leaders predicted, persisted in the violence that dominated the Civil Rights Movement and made condemnation stronger against them. When the White Citizens Council, White Knights, United Klans, and similarly organized segregationists did not commit murders and beatings, they resorted to anonymous, threatening telephone calls at odd hours, cross burnings, and other forms of harassment. The period between 1954 and 1965 became especially noted for bombings; Birmingham, because of the numerous bombings that occurred in that Alabama city, earned the sobriquet of "Bombingham." Even though the perpetrators of these acts clearly violated the law, almost all went unpunished even when the guilty parties were known and had been arrested in some cases. Similar stories can be told of Mississippi and other southern states. For example, in Mississippi two white men kidnapped a black youth, Emmett Till, beat him, tied his legs to an iron rod, and threw him into a river. Confessing to the murder only after a jury found them innocent, the two people went unpunished.[4] The Till murder simply became another incident that brought national and international attention to America's racial dilemma. Nationally and internationally publicized incidents continued.

In 1956 attention centered on Autherine Lucy when the University of Alabama at Tuscaloosa, after a three-year court fight, admitted her as its first black student. Mob violence of white segregationists, some from outside the Tuscaloosa area, disrupted school activities and compelled the university's board of trustees to expel Lucy for her own safety and because she accused the university of conspiring with the white mob.[5] The same year, Fred L. Shuttlesworth's home was heavily damaged by dynamite on Christmas night. The black minister and leader of the Alabama Christian Movement for Human Rights had staged a one-day defiance of Birmingham bus-segregation laws. When Shuttlesworth attempted to enroll four black youths at all-white Phillips High School in Birmingham in September 1957, segregationists again targeted him as an angry white mob beat him and threatened to kill him. In rare instances whites were punished for violence. When six white men attacked the black entertainer Nat King Cole as he performed for a white audience in Birmingham's Municipal Auditorium, police acted quickly to place the attackers in jail. The attackers, members of the White Citizens Council, got maximum jail sentences.[6]

Some blacks were threatened and abused, and sometimes murdered, for becoming registered voters. After numerous violent incidents in Mississippi in 1955, the minister G. W. Lee of Belzoni, the first black who registered in Humphreys County, was shot and killed while driving his car. The officials apprehended no one, and Lee's name was added to the long list of blacks who were killed "by hands unknown."

In a few instances the White Citizens Council used tactics similar to those of civil rights organizations. The group inserted a full-page advertisement in the Yazoo City, Mississippi, *Herald*, which listed the names and addresses of each person who petitioned for court-ordered school desegregation.[7] Many of the identified persons listed in the *Herald* were fired from their jobs; others were threatened.

In the midst of this turmoil it took a great amount of courage for liberal whites to rise above the dominant traditional trends of the 1950s and 1960s. Those who did suffered accordingly, but the Educational Fund continued as it had in the past to identify with blacks in the Civil Rights Movement.

Members of the Educational Fund urged the Senate Subcommittee on Constitutional Rights to hold hearings in Mississippi to investigate the infringements of citizens' rights. A delegation of twenty people from nine southern states presented a petition signed by a least 2,500 persons from "all states" to Senator William Langer, a member of the subcommittee. The delegation included Methodist Bishop Edgar A. Love of Baltimore, Aubrey Williams (SCEF president), James Dombrowski (SCEF executive director), Modjeska Simkins, and one of SCEF's most generous and dedicated financial supporters, Ethel Clyde of New York. The delegation reminded the subcommittee that in Mississippi white supremacy factions were defying the authority of the Supreme Court, denying justice in state institutions, condoning the murder of black citizens who attempted to exercise their civil rights, and driving fairminded white citizens into silence by economic reprisals and threats of physical violence. The fundamental confrontation, as Bishop Love emphasized, was clearly an insurrection against the Constitution and laws of the United States and, yes, it was also a continuation of past abuses.[8] The subcommittee did not investigate.

One of the most significant conflicts over the roles and powers of the federal government and those of a state occurred in Little Rock, Arkansas, between 1957 and 1959. The incident originated in the fall of 1957 when nine selected black children attempted to integrate Little Rock's Central High School. The forces of the state, under the direct and highly publicized leadership of Governor Orval Faubus, prevented their admission and precipitated a nationally and internationally observed drama. President Dwight D. Eisenhower eventually federalized the National Guard to guarantee the youths' attendance at Central High.[9]

Economic reprisal, an old tactic whites had used to quell black movements, again became an instrument of retaliation as they dared to challenge the traditions of white supremacy. Little Rock segregationists warned SCEF board members Daisy and L. C. Bates in 1957 of the economic damages they would suffer if they continued to push the integration issue. The Bateses, two black leaders instrumental in the development of the Little Rock crisis, in 1942 had invested their savings in a weekly newspaper, the *State Press,* and over the years they had begun to prosper. However, in October 1959, they were forced to watch as over sixteen years of their life's work dwindled away. Daisy Bates, willing to give her all, agonized over the thought of destroying her husband's investment and questioned the liberty to have him hurt along with her. L. C. Bates, who firmly believed in what his wife and Arkansas NAACP president was doing, constantly reassured her that their life's work was worth the cause. In 1959 business firms and advertising agencies canceled their contracts as they expired, eventually putting an end to the *State Press.* The Little Rock crisis had cost the Bateses a lot; not only were they forced to close their newspaper, they also incurred physical damages to their home and car, not to mention excessive tension.[10]

The Southern Conference Educational Fund supported the Bateses during this tragedy. In an effort to help compensate for the Bateses' advertising losses, the board sent financial support in a small amount as a "modest gift" to show appreciation for all that the Bateses had done, both in dedicated and courageous personal leadership, and through the pages of their paper, the *State Press,* "to strengthen the hands of those who were working for decency, democracy, and brotherhood. . . . You have been an inspiration to all of us who have been fighting to make these ideals a reality in the South and the nation." Daisy and L. C. Bates were grateful for the unspecified amount of SCEF money.[11]

The Educational Fund recognized the importance of editors and publishers, particularly black journalists, by adopting a resolution that read:

> Among the Southern men and women who have rendered distinguished service in the struggle for integration in the South, the Negro editors and

publishers are outstanding. None have shown more courage or rendered more distinguished service than Daisy and L. C. Bates, editors of the *Arkansas State Press*, Little Rock. Because of their leadership, they have suffered economic pressures forcing them to temporarily suspend publication of their newspaper.

The SCEF hails these brave citizens who prefer to suffer serious loss rather than compromise on their principles.[12]

The Bateses were consoled in the fact that they had made friends during the fight even though they had lost their sole means of support.[13]

The Educational Fund publicized the Bates tragedy in the *Southern Patriot*, and as a result readers sent contributions. The Bateses, then, continued to get unsought support after 1959.[14] The Educational Fund had demonstrated one of its most significant roles in the Civil Rights Movement, that of providing support to leading black figures who did the kind of work SCEF morally supported but in which it was not actively engaged.

White leaders of the Educational Fund paid for their alliance with blacks in the Civil Rights Movement. Its president, Aubrey Williams, did not escape economic reprisals. In 1957 he commented, "I am almost prostrate and finished so far as my *Southern Farmer* is concerned. I have lost money on it for the past nine years and have finally had to agree to kill it. . . . I simply was not able to get the big advertisers. They had me labeled as a bad guy from the start and I was never able to convince them that I was not even as radical as Jefferson." Later that year, on the same subject, a distraught Williams revealed to his close friend Dombrowski that his business was failing. He reported losing the *Southern Farmer's* largest account, which amounted to almost half his business. He reasoned that his poor business situation resulted because of this position with SCEF and his support of integrationists.[15]

Economic interests were just as important to the majority of southern whites as the continued hope to maintain white supremacy. Whites hoped to rob blacks of a chance at an education that would help them obtain better jobs. Whites were ahead economically, and the white southern majority would see to it that the situation remained that way. For example, they could allow black janitors, cooks, and other blacks in service occupations to enter Central High School to work for years before the 1957 incident, but would not allow black students to attend the school without creating major disturbances.

The question of integration over economics or vice versa plagued the entire Civil Rights Movement. Blacks were becoming more aware during the debacle of Little Rock and other massive resistance incidents of the importance of economic security, which had been a major concern of the Southern Conference for Human Welfare two decades earlier. But when the Southern Conference placed emphasis on equal economic opportunities in the late 1930s, few liberals, black or white, developed means for achieving that specific goal. The Little Rock incident, because the school desegregation effort created so much attention, caused many blacks to question whether the integration of schools was the most important aspect of African Americans' fight for first-class citizenship. P. B. Young, publisher and editor of the *Norfolk* (Virginia) *Journal and Guide* and a black leader who sought only integration as recently as the late 1950s, started to believe that equal employment opportunity constituted the most essential step to first-class citizenship. The cycle was catchy, however; in order to obtain high-status jobs, blacks needed education and training of high quality. Segregation also needed to be abolished, for it, like inferior education, prevented blacks from progressing to their full potential. Consequently, Young saw the *Brown* decision as the removal of the basic reasons for legal segregation and believed that it would enable blacks eventually to acquire better homes and jobs. Although integration was not entirely a school question, it remained the center of attention for most of the 1950s in terms of the Civil Rights Movement. The debate shifted back and forth, but by the late 1960s black leaders decided that equal economic opportunity was the key to equal treatment in all aspects of American society.[16]

In addition to the violence associated with the White Citizens Councils and other such groups, segregationists intensified the association of integration with communism during the 1950s. White southerners generally believed that blacks accepted, even expected, that the region would remain segregated and that little could be done about it. The expected norm between blacks and whites would be that of a master-servant relationship. Segregationists labeled as Communist anyone who refused to accept that general belief. The 1950s shattered that placid view and presented the white southern majority with the startling fact that a greater number of blacks than they realized no longer accepted a master-servant relationship between the races. Since blacks, according to southern white conservatives, had previously accepted that relationship, the change had occurred only because of the influence of outsiders, especially northerners and Communists, who led them to protest in the 1950s. This explanation, though simple, disposed at once all of the new and mysterious forces that threatened an Old South tradition.[17] Blacks who opposed segregationists were Communists, and so were their white allies in the struggle. Segregationists, however, generally attacked the liberal white integrationists on Communist charges. Anne Braden, white SCEF field secretary and a victim of Communist allegations, observed that "this, of course, was in line with the theory that Negroes on their own do not oppose segregation, that it is always the white radicals who pull the strings, and that if the white people so inclined could be silenced the whole disturbing problem would be eliminated."[18]

Thus it is not surprising that as demands for an end to segregation and racial discrimination increased, segregationists stepped up their attacks on SCEF and condemned its activities as Communist-inspired. And the charges always centered on the whites, apparently because no one thought blacks under its doctrines. Senator James Eastland, for example, a member of the Senate Subcommittee on Internal Security, called only whites from the Educational Fund to appear before his one-man New Orleans hearing in March 1954 despite the fact that blacks comprised at least half the SCEF board and the organization's officers included outstanding black leaders. Although unsuccessful in proving SCEF to be a Communist-front organization, Eastland, as liberals justifiably countered, capitalized on the hysteria of McCarthyism. Since he timed the New Orleans hearing during the same period in which the Supreme Court deliberated over school desegregation, some people, SCEF officers included, believed that by scrutinizing Virginia Durr, sister-in-law to Supreme Court Justice Hugo Black, Eastland hoped to cast doubt on the Court. Justice Black's liberal views varied little from those held by his friends in the Educational Fund, and his connection with the liberal organization went beyond the family connection with Virginia Durr. Black spoke in 1938 at the SCHW's founding meeting at which time the organization presented him with its Thomas Jefferson Award, but these facts in no way proved, as Eastland purported, that Durr and other white liberals influenced Black's opinions and those of others in the Franklin Roosevelt administration.[19]

In discussing Eastland's hearings from a contemporary perspective, historian Irving Brant surmised that "it may have been pure coincidence that the most vicious feature of the hearing was a slanderous assault upon the sister-in-law of one of the Supreme Court justices." That Durr had not been officially associated with the Educational Fund since 1950 makes Brant's theory more credible. Brant summarized the historical significance of the 1954 hearing when he said:

Call it pure coincidence. . . . That does not alter the fact that this New Orleans hearing, on account of its timing combined with its nature, will become a part of the history of the abolition of racial segregation in America—a chapter of history which will rank little below the abolition of chattel slavery in the forward march of American democracy and decency.[20]

When Senator Eastland called the hearing in New Orleans in 1954 to question the allegiance of SCEF members, he forced the Educational Fund to launch an attack of its own. In the next ten years integrationists, SCEF in particular, countered what had become a key weapon of segregationists, namely the accusation that they led Communist-front organizations. Whether in the American Legion *Firing Line* or other publications, those who attributed Communist ideas to SCEF actions specifically pointed back to the 1954 hearing in New Orleans, which one senator conducted, as their source of evidence. Aubrey Williams justifiably contended:

These Senators are shrewd enough to know that if a Senate Committee summons you before it with the announcement that it is probing into the "Communist activities" of your organization, that they can thereby get you branded by the newspapers and the radio as a "Red," with just as much effect as if you were a "Red." You are pronounced guilty by the press on the basis of the Committee's summons even before you testify.

The segregationist tactic must be credited at least as partly successful. Whenever people discussed the Fund, they applied the label or raised the question: "That is the organization, isn't it, that was investigated for Communist activities."[21]

Because of the battle between segregationists and integrationists over subversiveness, civil rights became increasingly linked to civil liberties. The Southern Conference Educational Fund, an organization founded specifically to cause social and economic integration of American society and to eliminate discrimination, and an organization that the Senate Subcommittee targeted as subversive, grew increasingly concerned about civil liberties during the 1950s and 1960s. Although SCEF's executive director, Dombrowski, contended for a while that the Fund's work in and of itself was enough to convince the public of its good intentions, Aubrey Williams, Carl Braden, and a few other SCEF officers argued that more was needed. Their conviction eventually led to their involvement in the establishment of a national organization to abolish the House Un-American Activities Committee and the Senate Subcommittee, and a full conversion of Dombrowski.[22] Williams pointed to the 1954 New Orleans hearing and how the key witnesses for the subcommittee had turned out to be liars and criminals, but Eastland had concealed these facts to make it appear that SCEF and its liberal leaders were Communists. Williams wanted articles published immediately disclosing the truth about tactics of Un-Americanism forces, but a few years passed before such publications appeared.[23]

Congressional committees and the Justice Department, including the Federal Bureau of Investigation (FBI), continued to seek out alleged Communists in the South in the late 1950s. The FBI, much as the white segregationists, considered persons subversive for the least thing, especially whites who entertained blacks in their homes. All of the SCEF associates were guilty of this, and sometimes a few whites joined SCEF's board after the FBI investigated them. Dombrowski related the story of a prominent New Orleans doctor who lived "at a rather fancy address" and occasionally entertained blacks. The doctor was not an affiliate of SCEF nor had he been identified with any liberal causes, but when the FBI began to question the doctor's neighbors about his activities, the man joined the SCEF board.[24] Such occurrences only made stronger Dombrowski's conviction that the Educational Fund became more widely known as a result of publicity related to Communist charges.

Even though on rare occasions the red-baiting tactic helped the SCEF's image, it had the most potential for adverse consequences. The bank, for example, where SCEF had held its account in New Orleans for eleven years and which had been friendly, "at least so it appeared," warned in 1958 that things would be different. But the Whitney National Bank did not require that SCEF close its account there.[25] Williams said that the FBI had harassed him, though he did not say how, while he attended the Educational Fund's May 1958 Conference on Voting Restrictions in the South in Washington, D.C. Growing weary at times because segregationist organizations never received the same treatment from the congressional Un-American committees as integrationists, Williams wanted to discontinue the fight "with regards to the FBI business in Washington." His consultation with Clifford and Virginia Durr and others about his decision persuaded Williams differently. Virginia Durr admonished that "no matter how wrong the FBI may be in hounding you[,] the fact that you are being watched by them will be something against you in many people[']s eyes." Williams similarly advised Carl and Anne Braden whose lives had been disrupted by the harassment of Communist charges since 1954.[26]

The false accusations from governmental agencies, especially HUAC, forced the Fund to join in the discussion of the late 1950s for the establishment of an organization specifically to eliminate the congressional committees. Williams believed "one of the most needed things at this juncture in the Civil Rights fight is to expose the informers and liars who are running over the South like rats . . . inciting legislators." The latest Un-American committee had been recently established in Florida. The other state with this infamous committee was Louisiana, and others were forming. Georgia had the so-called Research Commission, which served the same purpose of other states' Un-American committees. Williams suggested to Dombrowski the SCEF make a major project of discrediting the deceitful informers by publishing brochures on each one of them and on the persons responsible for so-called Un-American hearings. Williams added, "I can think of nothing I had rather do than spend the remaining days I have on this earth fighting J. Edgar Hoover and the undercover police he has established in this country."[27]

In 1958 the House Un-American Activities Committee called a hearing in Atlanta similar to the one Eastland headed in Louisiana four years earlier. With the exception of one black person, the Committee subpoenaed white integrationists, including Carl Braden from the SCEF, and the Fund again became the center of attention in the eyes of those seeking a Communist scapegoat for changes in the South. Braden refused to cooperate with the Committee by taking the Fifth Amendment. Because the HUAC hearings had created resentment and chaos in other sections of the country, many of the victims of the HUAC had begun the groundwork for a national committee to abolish both HUAC and its counterpart committee in the Senate. Frank Wilkinson, who formerly worked with the Los Angeles Housing Authority, lost his job because he refused to cooperate with HUAC hearings in California, and later an anti-HUAC group, the Citizens Committee to Preserve American Freedoms, chose him as its director. Anti-HUAC sentiments in California had been brewing since 1956, and since by 1958 Wilkinson had been dubbed "Mr. Abolition" by anti-HUAC forces, SCEF had asked him to be in Atlanta to observe the hearing there. When Wilkinson arrived, however, the Committee subpoenaed him. Wilkinson took the Fifth Amendment along with Braden, and Congress cited both for contempt but threatened only to imprison them. The two were free for the time because the Supreme Court's ruling in the June 1957 *Watkins* v. *United States* decision limited the powers of congressional investigating committees and declared that witnesses' Fifth Amendment rights take priority in hearings. The Court's ruling later favored the congressional committees, and almost every time the Court ruled differently, Braden felt the result immediately. Placed in prison in 1955 for sedition charges under an old Kentucky law, Braden, after serving eight months, gained freedom when the Court ruled in the 1956 *Nelson* case that voided the state law. In 1961 the Court reversed its stand on limiting the powers of the congressional committees, and Wilkinson and Braden then served ten months in prison on Congress's contempt charges.

The Atlanta hearing adversely affected the Educational Fund, but it provided the opportunity for Wilkinson and Williams to collaborate against the forces of Un-Americanism. With the help of black leaders the Fund began to work harder to link civil liberties to civil rights, and the connection became easier as state branches of the NAACP came under scrutiny of state HUAC committees. Southern state legislatures had begun to require organizations whose principal objectives included desegregation to provide a public listing of members and contributions.[28]

Since the Communist charges aimed at obstructing all groups who fought for integration, SCEF was not alone in counter-publicity against HUAC and the Senate Subcommittee. The Educational Fund, however, believed as never before that HUAC charges and those of the similar Senate Subcommittee harmed the Civil Rights Movement by especially keeping silent a great many white southerners, and some blacks even, who otherwise might have been a part of the crusade to create a new and different southern society.[29] By 1960 the anti-HUAC movement had been transformed into an official organization, the National Committee for the Abolition of the House Un-American Activities Committee (NCAHUAC). The NCAHUAC had a slow beginning that dated back to 1956 in California. But, in fact, the idea had been dormant since 1946 when the Southern Conference for Human Welfare and the NAACP in a cooperative effort discussed what should be done on the abolition of the House Committee on Un-American Activities. At that time, however, neither developed a strategy to rid the nation of HUAC.[30]

As Williams suggested, the NCAHUAC worked at converting congress-men to its side, and the many blunders of the HUAC kept it in the public consciousness, a development that also proved helpful to its eventual de-mise. Although the process took nearly twenty years, in 1975 the House eventually dropped what had become the House Internal Security Com-mittee (HISC) from its list of standing committees. As part of the many groups which kept up the campaign against HUAC/HISC, SCEF had con-tributed in a large way to the committee's end.[31]

The Louisiana Un-American Activities Committee (LUAC) made a grave mistake, making SCEF more determined to dismantle Un-American com-mittees, when its Chairman James H. Pfister inspired 100 New Orleans policemen and jail officials to raid SCEF offices and homes of two SCEF officers on October 4, 1963. The Committee boasted that it had planned the raid for 11 months, but the raiders first broke down the door of an empty room of the wrong office. Police seized personal and official prop-erty indiscriminately and arrested Dombrowski, Benjamin E. Smith (SCEF treasurer, labor and civil rights attorney, and American Civil Lib-erties Union counsel), and Bruce C. Waltzer, Smith's law partner, who had no official connection with SCEF. Charges against the three included violation of Louisiana Revised Subversive Activities and Communist Con-trol Law and the Communist Propaganda Control Act, both of which re-quired "subversive" individuals and organizations to register with the state. Authorities later released them on bond.

SCEF, of course, viewed the raid as one against the entire civil rights struggle and a major violation of civil liberties. If it could not spearhead a movement to dismantle all Un-American committee forces, other civil rights groups would suffer the same major infringements of constitu-tional rights. Immediately, SCEF appealed to the public to write protest letters to the U.S. Attorney General, the U.S. Commission on Civil Rights, Louisiana Governor Jimmie Davis, and New Orleans Mayor Victor Schiro. After the recent (1963) tragic murders of Mississippi civil rights leader Medgar Evers and the four girls killed by a bomb while in Sunday school in Birmingham, and the fire-hose episode in Birmingham streets, the public responded to the violations against SCEF in a big way. Most people responding to its appeal justifiably linked violations of civil liber-ties to the ongoing civil rights struggle. Between 1963 and 1965 LUAC published reports inclusive of correspondence between SCEF, the NAACP, the Southern Christian Leadership Conference (SCLC), the Student Nonviolent Coordinating Committee (SNCC), and various other civil rights organizations and leaders to prove SCEF's affiliation with communism.

On October 25, in a preliminary hearing, Judge Bernard J. Cocke of the Louisiana Criminal District Court for the Parish of Orleans dismissed the charges against Dombrowski, Smith, and Waltzer, citing lack of evidence and no probable cause for the issuance of the warrants. But because Senator Eastland had subpoenaed the SCEF records taken in the raid, Dombrowski had to spend the next two years in litigation to retrieve them. In the process he hoped to obtain a ruling that would declare unconstitutional the statutes that had allowed the raid and arrests in the first place. Eventually, the Supreme Court heard *Dombrowski* v. *Pfister* and ruled in January 1965 the Louisiana statutes unconstitutional, with Associate Justice William Brennan writing the majority opinion. The ruling by the Supreme Court gave civil rights groups leverage against segregationists and made it easier for Congress to abolish HISC in 1975. The entire episode left SCEF convinced, despite the action by the Supreme Court, that its long tradition of education and lobbying could lead to results.[32]

In the period between 1957 and 1963, during the time in which the establishment of the United States Civil Rights Commission provided valuable encouragement to civil rights adherents generally, the SCEF strategy and program changed slightly from what it had been since 1947. The organization's financial status remained about the same as in the past, and it still held conferences like the one in Washington, D.C., in 1958, which it devoted to blacks' voting rights. Having outlined, but not acted on, guidelines in 1947 for black voter registration drives, the Educational Fund in 1958 led a drive for voter registration, the effort of which netted a significant increase in black registrants. It likewise drew the attention of Congressman James Roosevelt of California who read Williams's introductory address at the conference to the House of Representatives. Evidently, James Roosevelt agreed with Williams and SCEF that African Americans' struggle for equality signaled the greatest challenge to American hypocrisy.

The Fund's most noticeable difference came when it provided on an individual basis bail money for a few leading civil rights figures like Shuttlesworth, white activist Robert Zellner, Robert Moses, and a few others. SCEF's support to these individuals, when no other organization would rescue them from jail, helped to bridge a gap between educational efforts and the grass-roots link to southern communities. SCEF's solicited advice from Ella J. Baker, former executive director of SCLC and SNCC founder, brought it closer to grass-roots activities. With the exception of Anne and Carl Braden and Dombrowski, few SCEF leaders could agree that payment of bail made the most appropriate use of its limited funds. Such skeptics did not want to support mass protest and continued to believe that the approach SCEF had taken all along, the public education and eventual conversion of white southerners, though this had shown little sign of success, would finally work. This view prevailed as SCEF also contributed to SNCC conferences on how to transform the South.[33]

Because SCEF leaders clung to past hopes and beliefs instead of going full force into the black-led Civil Rights Movement, the highly publicized activities of that movement overshadowed those of the Fund. Indeed the Civil Rights Movement made its publicity with a greater sacrifice than

Student Leadership Conference, Chapel Hill, North Carolina, May 4–6, 1962. Left to right: Ella Baker, unknown man in front row, Carl Braden (with hands clasped around knee), Anne Braden (in dark dress), Tom Hayden (?) (sitting on far right side, smiling). Courtesy of the Braden Collection, State Historical Society of Wisconsin, Madison.

financial cost to national civil rights organizations; participants paid the higher price through physical and mental abuse. The Educational Fund's efforts, however, got some media coverage and the Fund publicized in its own publications the havoc white segregationist lawbreakers were causing. But largely the organization continued its educational campaigns with newspaper advertisements and distribution of other literature.[34]

Two factors in 1958 added tremendously to the SCEF's publicity and notoriety. One was the publication of Anne Braden's book, *The Wall Between*, which included details about the decision she and her husband Carl made in 1954 to purchase a house for a black couple in a white section of Louisville and how segregationists had used the incident to disrupt the Bradens' lives. Second, Fred L. Shuttlesworth joined the Fund's board in 1958. Liberals, north and south, read Braden's account; Shuttlesworth stayed in the news from 1958 throughout the Civil Rights Movement. He encountered in Birmingham, where he and his family began protest for integration in the late 1950s, the infamous Theophilus Eugene "Bull" Connor. Connor by this time had become as much a representative for segregationists as SCEF had become for integrationists.

Shuttlesworth became a major link between SCEF and the larger Civil Rights Movement. In late 1958 he gained national attention when he and

Carl and Anne Braden, Charleston, West Virginia, April 7, 1963. Courtesy of Braden Collection, State Historical Society of Wisconsin, Madison.

his family attempted to integrate the public school system in Birmingham where his family received physical abuse and the school system remained segregated. Next Shuttlesworth attempted to change the segregated seating policy on Birmingham's public transit system. In each instance the local authorities met him with violence, and the systems remained unchanged. Shuttlesworth especially had become an important figure in Alabama because he had devised a way to keep the NAACP functional in the state by creating the Alabama Christian Movement for Human Rights (ACMHR) after the state legislature made it illegal for the NAACP to operate. Ultimately, Reverend Shuttlesworth also represented the importance religious leaders brought to the movement as he and many others preached on Sunday mornings, "we are not just interested in the buses. The big thing we're interested in is that we do not have to clear our sermons with city officials."[35]

Between 1958 and 1963 Shuttlesworth went on speaking tours for SCEF and his ACMHR, and the groups divided the money raised from these engagements. In 1959 Shuttlesworth advised SCEF executive director

James Dombrowski that the work of SCEF could probably be carried out better if the organization developed a grass-roots following. Shuttlesworth, who commanded the attention of leading black ministers, offered to enlist the aid of his congregation and to have other black ministers do the same. But Dombrowski, who had not heeded similar advice from field-worker Witherspoon Dodge during the days when he served as SCHW executive secretary, did not take Shuttlesworth's advice in the late 1950s. And the lack of a mass following became just as much a detriment to SCEF in the late 1950s as it had been to SCHW in 1948.[36]

In between the appearances for speeches to arouse public sentiment for civil rights and fundraising Shuttlesworth went back to Birmingham to lead boycotts against white merchants who refused to hire blacks and who practiced other forms of discrimination. He also headed protest marches, which usually led to his arrest by Bull Connor. Connor went so far as to send detectives to church meetings to spy on Shuttlesworth and other civil rights leaders. In the process of his work in Birmingham, Shuttlesworth became a close associate of the nationally acclaimed civil rights leader Martin Luther King, Jr., who agreed with Shuttlesworth's approach. By 1963 the two were spending time together in Birmingham's jail. SCEF leaders such as the Bradens, Williams, and Dombrowski did not spend time in jail, but they raised bail money for Shuttlesworth and Zellner and other activists who chose direct action.[37]

By 1960, when the sit-ins and freedom rides had taken the Civil Rights Movement to yet another level and people like Virginia Durr and her husband encountered almost "daily insanities," the situation grew so desperate that when the *New Yorker* carried a story about the white liberal couple in Montgomery with changed names, most people of that city knew the people in question. In the article the Durrs had been interviewed and told of verbal and other abuses they suffered from segregationists. Because of the article many readers felt compelled to encourage the Durrs by sending supportive letters. A correspondent from a southern state who had since moved to Pennsylvania doubted the comfort a distant friend could bring but wanted the Alabama couple to know that white liberals did make a difference. Ultimately, the writer hoped that the offer of friendship might provide "some feeling that your courage isn't wasted. It spreads more seeds than you may ever realize. And it enables you to live with yourself. I wonder how many of the people who snub you on the street envy you that?"[38] The episode helped the SCEF members to understand that their idealism and liberalism did not constitute wasted courage. The problem, however, was that SCEF sympathetic correspondents were those persons already convinced of the need for major changes. If segregationists ever were convinced otherwise, they remained silent.

What was it about the few white southerners that drove them to ally with blacks in the struggle? One liberal white southerner, Anne Braden, described the intensity of the southern white majority as neurotic, and segregationists described that of the liberals in the same way. Braden said that she "grew up in a sick society, and a sick society makes neurotics— of one kind or another, on one side or another. It makes people like those who could take pleasure in killing and mutilating Emmett Till, and it makes people like me." Braden believed that when the Supreme Court outlined in 1954 its decision on the effects of segregation on the black child, it might have included some discussion about what segregation did to the white child. If neurotics were what liberals ought to be called, Braden concluded that even if the name applied there were many neurot- ics like herself in the South and that the answer did not rest with the group who called themselves "saner and more practical and more mod- erate" who insisted that change occur at a slower pace. As long as segre- gation remained a fact in the South, blacks and people like Braden would be compelled to struggle against it. Braden's metaphor for an integrated and just society depicted a world without walls, and she saw the interra- cial movement of SCEF and that of the leading civil rights organizations as a tearing down of the wall of segregation and discrimination. Speaking of the decision she and her husband took to help the Wades in 1954, she wrote:

> But who can ever say for sure what unconscious motives make him act? How can I say for sure that the purchase of the house did not also fulfill a need in me: a need to fling a dramatic challenge to a community I thought was mov- ing too slowly, to a society too satisfied with its sins—to fling it like an an- swer back through the years of my own life . . . to the throbbing of my own conscience as I felt the decadent white world closing around me—to fling it like prophecy, impractical perhaps but hopeful, of a New World that could come, a world that I had seen through a glass darkly, a world without walls.[39]

For over two decades the members of the Southern Conference for Hu- man Welfare and its successor, the Southern Conference Educational Fund, publicized the appalling effects of segregation and discrimination in the South. Finally in the 1960s television coverage of such tragic events as Birmingham's Police Commissioner Bull Connor's use of police dogs and fire hoses on civil rights demonstrators in that city demanded na- tional and international attention. The greater media coverage garnered by black civil rights leaders and mass protesters made widespread the declaration that America treat all its citizens equally. What southern white and black liberals had attempted to do in twenty-five years through the distribution of literature, the direct-action approach of black activists had accomplished almost immediately. In the final analysis, then, SCEF, founded specifically to eliminate segregation and racial discrimination, could not take credit for the attention the Civil Rights Movement now received. Because the struggle for equality in the South had been so long and had involved so many individuals, no single group could take complete credit for the resulting reforms.

The decades of efforts on the part of SCEF, however, chronicled an evolution from the time, 1946–1963, when a few white southerners did an about-face on race relations, to an era when blacks used direct action to demand total equality, a method that finally resulted in more tangible, lasting reform. This evolutionary transition, which always had involved interracial cooperation, by 1963 became almost solely organized and coordinated by blacks. Even in SCEF black leaders filled a larger number of the administrative positions.

Although southern white liberals could take little credit for the revolutionary changes that occurred in 1964 and thereafter, their willingness to advocate change during the time when most southerners shunned the race issue entitles them to consideration in the discussion of civil rights. The 1938 protest for integrated seating at SCHW's founding meeting in Birmingham, when Eleanor Roosevelt stubbornly refused to move her center-aisle seat, represented a sit-in of sorts, and the act gained national attention. But because no other deliberate protests followed the First Lady's challenge, it was not until 1960 that the method became a celebrated tool of the movement.[40]

Birmingham, a city in the headlines in 1938 because of the race issue, had changed little by 1963. Both in 1938 and in 1963 Birmingham became a focal point for change although in the former case the First Lady's action proved more symbolic than reformative. No one dared arrest Eleanor Roosevelt in 1938, but twenty-five years later when blacks marched and demonstrated in the streets of Birmingham and other southern cities to demand that Jim Crow must go, white authority met them with violence. Just as segregationists forced liberals in 1938 to confront the race question more directly, violent confrontations with black demonstrators in 1963 led to revolutionary changes in society. Indeed, many of the same individuals participating in the cause for equality in 1938 remained committed to it in 1963.

Between the 1930s and the 1960s various local, state, and national organizations such as the NAACP, the Commission of Interracial Cooperation, the Southern Conference for Human Welfare, the Southern Regional Council, the Fellowship of Reconciliation, the Educational Fund, SCLC, SNCC, and the Congress on Racial Equality addressed issues associated with civil rights. Each group had worked hard and long on the road to equality and justice that paved the way to federal action in the 1960s, but with the exception of NAACP members, the members of the Educational Fund and its predecessor had been in the struggle the longest. For instance, Congress did not abolish the poll tax with federal legislation until 1964 with the Twenty-fourth Amendment to the Constitution, though the SCHW and a few liberal legislators had demanded federal action in a concerted effort since 1939.

Most white southerners remained adamant about maintaining white supremacy as their way of life and were willing to see the entire region languish in order to do so. The more loudly black and white southern liberals demanded equality, the more determined the southern white majority grew about denying civil rights and racial equality. But by the 1960s another segment of southern society stepped forward in the interest of the region's economy. Southern white businessmen made an important contribution to changes wrought by the Civil Rights Movement. Although most southern white businessmen tried to remain loyal to their past tradition of white supremacy, economic factors determined that they reluctantly accept "inevitable change."[41] The violence and disruption that accompanied civil disobedience and boycotts carried out by black protesters made the South less attractive for the establishment of new business enterprises from other parts of the nation. Southern liberals had been right to associate the region's economic success with social reform. It had been the 1938 *Report on Economic Conditions of the South* and the controversy it created that provided the impetus for southern liberals concerned with civil liberties and economic issues to establish the SCHW.

With the passing of each decade the white liberals in SCEF became more vocal and radical, particularly after 1956 when they allied with the direct action of Martin Luther King, Jr., and SCLC, and later SNCC. The eventual close association between King and Fred Shuttlesworth initially made this possible. Past black leaders of SCEF largely included NAACP members who did not wholeheartedly welcome the direct-action technique of black protesters. The Montgomery Bus Boycott of 1955–1956 had identified a national leader, and for the first time the moving feet and dogged determination of black masses placed the fight for equality beyond even the legal tactics of the NAACP.

Yet when white liberals believed that they had become militant, their efforts kept them in the background away from the dynamism created by blacks and their leaders. We learn much from well-known playwright Lorraine Hansberry, whose literary works, many of which were written in the 1950s, rely on personal experiences related to tragedies of racism.[42] An activist, Lorraine Hansberry worked as reporter for Paul Robeson's journal, *Freedom*. In that capacity she met Louis E. Burnham of the Southern Negro Youth Congress, the *Freedom's* editor, and a person who greatly influenced the young artist. Other activists Hansberry met while with *Freedom* included W. E. B. Du Bois, Modjeska Simkins, and Anne Braden. Hansberry understood well the Civil Rights Movement and the struggle of her people, and during May 1963 when Attorney General Robert Kennedy met with her and other leading black activists, Hansberry set the tone and predicted that the dialogue between national white leaders and black protesters seemed meaningless without action. The leaders wanted Robert Kennedy to persuade his brother, President John Kennedy, to escort to school a black child already scheduled for school integration in the South. The black leaders were convinced that if any white spit on the child, a common defiant act by white southerners, while escorted by the president, the act would symbolize spitting on the nation. But when Robert Kennedy referred to the scheme of the black leaders as a "meaningless moral gesture," Hansberry retorted that the Civil Rights Movement needed a moral commitment from the Kennedys. Hansberry, during that meeting, likened the Civil Rights Movement to the struggle for the emancipation of slaves in the nineteenth century. She said that whites like John Brown had died for that cause, and in the twentieth century the need remained for blacks to "encourage the white liberal to stop being liberal and become an American radical." Only when enough white liberals became radical would the basic organization of American society change.[43] Hansberry placed the hope for America's future democratic principles on the militancy of whites. After all, the fundamental task blacks confronted still hinged on convincing enough whites in positions of power that blacks were right in demanding equality. Hansberry's insight provided a clue to the major importance of the idealism of the Southern Conference Educational Fund; its white leaders grasped the urgency of the Civil Rights Movement and their alliance with blacks in the struggle made them radicals. But blacks also needed the moral gestures from white SCEF leaders; they wanted whites marching and willing to go to jail.

By 1963 outstanding SCEF leaders, especially Aubrey Williams and Virginia Durr, began to express bitterness that they had put in years with the struggle for equality in their native region but had little to show for their efforts. Williams's bitterness, partly a result of his physical condition (he was dying from cancer) and of a resentment of support he sensed blacks shared within their communities, overwhelmed his view of the Civil Rights Movement in the late 1950s and early 1960s. In the late 1950s blacks publicly supported the Educational Fund by condemning the congressional hearings, but Williams did not think black leaders had done enough. When he said that he realized "that there have been all too few white Southern liberals and perhaps they have not been too meaningful nor too courageous," he thought the blacks, "especially the Northern leaders, have done very little to help them." He emphasized that regardless of "how hard a time the Negro has, at least he does have a community to support him with encouragement and praise and backing, he does have people to associate with and in his own community he is not a pariah, but the southern white liberal has only a handful of people to give him any backing at all, he must live a stranger among his own people and the Negroes often give him little backing or none at all."

Williams, though he did not specify what more blacks could have done, believed that local blacks could have supported the Durrs in Montgomery, for example. And, indeed, the Communist hysteria of the 1950s had targeted whites so that Williams's opinion represented the complaint of a southern white liberal as a result of red-baiting smears. He believed that northern blacks disassociated from southern white liberals such as Dombrowski and himself because they had been accused of being Communists. Feeling alienated and concerned that the future would indeed include young white southern liberals, Williams welcomed Robert Zellner's communication with white southern youth to stir their interest in the civil rights struggle.[44]

Perhaps Williams could have understood that blacks needed a stronger showing of support than the educational campaigns. As Hansberry put it, some act of moral gesture was needed. Moreover, when it had become evident that segregationists showed no signs that they would sympathize with any of what SCEF hoped to accomplish, it seemed contradictory that Williams would want to be accepted by these members of his own race whose racial attitudes he opposed.

But at times Williams seemed to have a clear understanding of the developing situation in the Civil Rights Movement, and he frequently praised individual black leaders. In 1960 he summarized the role and importance of some of these individuals when he wrote:

There are . . . three kinds of leaders; there are the shock troups, the expendibles, these bear the burden of making the attacks upon the enemies of free men, they also must take any new ground gained for mankind. Modjeska Simkins belongs to this group.

Then there are the proclaimers, who once new ground is taken and they view the situation as having been accepted by society, emerge and give voice and sanction to the new areas of rights and justice. These are the Ralph McGills, the Harry Ashmores.

Then there are the politicians, who once the additional ground has been won, and the proclaimers have set their seal upon it, about face and to make legal what they had only recently denounced as the wild schemes of radicals and impractical idealists.

Modjeska Simkins has been for the span of her life of the shock troups and the expendibles. Tho[ugh] she is still far from being expended. One might steal a title from a Broadway play now in favor, The Indistructible Molly Brown, and say no more appropriate title could be found for Modjeska.[45]

That SCEF had achieved no dramatic breakthrough by 1963 was not because its leaders lacked outstanding ideals and great expectations for the southern region. When the Educational Fund is realistically assessed, we find that the leaders failed because they never developed a plan to execute their great ideals. The partially successful strategy of transforming society through the legal system had made it difficult for most white southern liberals to appreciate more fully the physical protest of the 1950s and 1960s. They relied on newspaper advertisements, radio broadcasts, and the organization's monthly publication, all of which resembled the turn-of-the-century belief held by the muckrakers that if people could

Anne Braden and Modjeska Simkins at an Emergency Civil Liberties
Union dinner in New York, December 1955. Courtesy of the Braden
Collection, State Historical Society of Wisconsin, Madison.

learn of the ills of society, they would clamor for a change. The one dramatic difference between Progressive era muckrakers and SCEF and its
white liberals is that the latter included blacks in the entire scheme of all
changes advocated. Indeed, African Americans remained SCEF's major
concern. SCEF leaders can also be likened to the Abolitionists, who could
not take credit for the emancipation of slaves, though that was their purpose. But Abolitionists, few in number as the southern liberals of SCEF,
predicted slavery's end and published large quantities of literature with
such announcements. Not unlike the Abolitionists, SCEF fulfilled an important mission by the role it played in the Civil Rights Movement.[46]
It kept issues of equality and the promise of the American ideal before
the nation for decades to see the ultimate accomplishment brought about
as a consequence of the massive civil rights demonstrations and media
coverage, President John F. Kennedy's assassination, and President
Lyndon B. Johnson's appeal to Congress for civil rights legislation.

Conclusion

Public awareness campaigns have long been a mainstay of reform-oriented organizations. Much of the reform legislation of the early twentieth century resulted indirectly, or directly in a few instances, as a consequence of the public attention muckrakers drew to issues. For example, the Food and Drug Act of 1906 addressed the concern for healthy food consumption after public outrage associated with vivid fictitious food packing scenes in Upton Sinclair's *The Jungle* (1906). In keeping with muckrakers of the Progressive era, the Southern Conference for Human Welfare (SCHW) and the Southern Conference Educational Fund (SCEF) unwittingly used the same strategy of public awareness to address major social, economic, and political problems of the South. The questions then arise: What did this muckraking strategy involve? How successful were SCHW and SCEF at raising the national consciousness toward creating a new and democratic South and the more specific issue of civil rights?

In answer to the first question the SCHW and SCEF printed large quantities of material and participated in radio talk-show debates. The organizational magazine of both groups, the *Southern Patriot*, reached an audience of an undetermined number of readers. The estimated SCHW mailing list at its highest in the mid 1940s reached approximately 10,000 people, sometimes close to 30,000 when specific crisis events occurred. In response to the race riot in Columbia, Tennessee, in 1946 SCHW mailed about 100,000 pieces of literature. SCEF's mailing list peaked at 3,000 persons or groups by 1955. Yet, given these figures, it is difficult to gauge exactly who read the literature. For instance, individual subscribers to the *Southern Patriot* probably shared one copy with other persons, especially family members. Likewise organizational subscribers may have circulated the magazine among their members. And, of course, the reading audience included users of major university libraries. For an entire decade the Southern Conference's Civil Rights Committee and its single-issue National Committee to Abolish the Poll Tax printed various pamphlets about the undemocratic practice of the poll tax. It also printed its own *Poll Tax Repeal*.

The newspaper advertisements that the SCHW generated during World War II demanding a just society played more than a minor role in the systematic public-education process. Moreover, the SCHW and SCEF had the support of major southern-newspaper editors including Mark Ethridge, Barry Bingham, Jennings Perry, Roscoe Dunjee, Percy Green, and even Ralph McGill, briefly, in the 1940s. Other intellectuals included Lillian Smith, the author of *Strange Fruit*, and the great scientist and humanitarian Albert Einstein. James Dombrowski and Clark Foreman, both of whom had doctoral degrees from Columbia University, spent their lives working for causes as outlined by the SCHW and the SCEF.

Southern Conference leaders and supporters failed to understand, however, that educational material and written protest could easily be ignored.[1] It is one thing to be knowledgeable about disturbing facts and situations for a region and yet another to be able to make a significant impact on situations—the southern business community, for example— by staging a boycott, sit-in, or some other form of direct-action protest. Labor organizer and Communist party leader Hosea Hudson's work in Birmingham in the 1930s, the large number of black people who physically left the South to protest white supremacy, and other pre-1955 activity testify to the preparedness of southern black communities for activism.[2] Understandably, blacks knew well their precarious circumstances as SCHW and SCEF described them. Action, not literature, would motivate their participation in the civil rights struggle.

Because the Southern Conference and the Educational Fund focused so much public attention on various issues with the written word while the leading black organizations took a new and different approach by the late 1950s, SCHW and SCEF are to be judged not so much by what they accomplished but for the leadership role they set in outlining what could and should be done. In these instances SCHW and SCEF created much commotion by addressing major issues that southern politicians, especially demagogues, consistently spoke about in Congress. The public grew to know Mississippi Senator Theodore G. Bilbo, Mississippi Congressman John Rankin, Georgia Congressman Eugene Cox, and Mississippi Senator James Eastland for their strong opposition to the SCHW and later the SCEF because the organizations, according to the conservative politicians, worked to wreck southern culture by calling for an integrated society. The Southern Conference and the Educational Fund campaign against those southern demagogues increased public awareness of the causes the two organizations addressed. Indeed the move to unseat Senator Bilbo in the mid 1940s became a major national issue. Other opportunities for SCHW ideas to go before Congress came when Foreman, during his tenure as SCHW president, addressed that body about major southern problems.

SCHW and SCEF radio talk shows during the 1940s and 1950s represented one of the most widely used methods of publicity of the time. These talk shows during the war included the Win the War Campaign in North Carolina in 1942, the talk shows about unseating Senator Bilbo in the mid 1940s, and talk shows about civil rights by SCEF affiliates in the

1950s. Aubrey Williams debated Eugene Talmadge in Georgia on school desegregation in the 1950s, and Talmadge's comments put the nation on notice that many white southerners were willing to close the whole public school system rather than to agree to integrate the schools. In addition to talk shows, newspaper advertisements, and other literature, Dombrowski, Foreman, Mary McLeod Bethune, and other Conference and Fund members made numerous speeches around the country. Other significant publicity centered on conferences, the biennials of the SCHW between 1938 and 1948, and the specific-issue gatherings, such as the Civil Rights Declaratory Conference in 1948 or the Discrimination in Higher Education Conference in 1950. The organizations' sustained concern for racial justice more so than the few Communists within their ranks made them targets for red-baiting by the conservative opposition.

Neither SCHW nor SCEF could sever itself from the Communist charges leveled against them. Although in some cases people shunned the organizations because of the charges, the very charges kept both organizations in the public eye. A few individuals even joined the Educational Fund's ranks because they felt the charges were unjustified and wanted to work with the organization to prove the point. In fact SCEF used the most severe cases of red-baiting to keep its major goal at the center of media attention.

The basic cooperation that both SCHW and SCEF shared with other leading civil rights organizations—the National Association for the Advancement of Colored People, the Southern Christian Leadership Conference, and the Student Nonviolent Coordinating Committee—gave a tremendous morale boost to African Americans. At times they publicized the importance of the southern conference movement's support. In 1959, for instance, Jessie P. Guzman (Tuskegee Institute archivist) noted in a speech to the Tuskegee Civic Association that legal actions taken by blacks had resulted in substantial gains. But she also emphasized that blacks must not forget the small body of white southerners who had supported that effort. The easily identifiable group she said believed in equality for all Americans. She named Aubrey Williams; James Dombrowski; Lillian Smith; Carl and Anne Braden; Judge J. Waties Waring, who ruled the white primary in South Carolina unconstitutional; the leaders of Koinonia Farm, an interracial, religious community near Americus, Georgia; and numerous others.[3] Consequently, SCHW and SCEF played a major role in raising the national consciousness on the issue of civil rights and other related issues for the creation of a new democratic South and a national democratic society in general. Given that civil rights did not gain national recognition and federal support until President Harry S Truman's administration, the Southern Conference's exposures about its region become increasingly important.

SCHW tied together all the basic issues that would have eliminated segregation and discrimination in the 1930s and 1940s. Namely, its leaders placed economic equality as the single most important issue for

eliminating all the South's major ills. Ultimately, these same issues surfaced during the latter phase of the Civil Rights Movement. In the late
1960s Martin Luther King, Jr., pointed to economic equality and concluded that the bottom line to total equality rested on one's opportunity
to enjoy the benefits provided by access to an adequate income.

If the Southern Conference was ahead of its time, as it so rightly
claimed in the 1930s and 1940s, the Educational Fund operated during a
time when national circumstances demanded more than public education
and awareness if the South's racial problems would ever be solved. The
Conference and the Fund had major important, idealistic goals for the
southern region, but these objectives did not materialize as a direct consequence of their public educational campaigns. Henry Wallace's 1948
presidential campaign showed that the Southern Conference's goals specifically had failed to materialize. This same election serves the purpose
for another major point. That the Progressive party adopted the policy
that its leaders speak only to integrated audiences was a protest itself.
Wallace based his campaign on protest, protest of the very thing that he
believed blocked southern and national progress, segregation. Indeed,
Wallace's 1948 presidential campaign signaled the attention that protest
demanded. Furthermore, Wallace's unsuccessful campaign revealed how
the political process sometimes provoked the least amount of change or
social reform. Perhaps SCHW's biggest failure was its split in 1948 and
the fact that SCEF did not go along with SCHW members who supported
the Progressive party. As civil rights commissioner and historian Mary
Frances Berry concludes, "Electoral politics is not considered the only
route to empowerment. 'Protest is a necessary ingredient of political involvement.' It fuels political change by dramatizing intolerable inequities.
When we [African Americans] stopped the direct-action campaigns and
relied solely on the electoral process, our issues got lost. And we lost the
high moral ground they were based on."[4]

The 1930s and 1940s marked a historical period when social-reform organizations believed in litigation as the key to equality and a just society.
Only in the 1950s did this method gain major breakthroughs with still
others following in the 1960s, but these changes resulted from the work
of the NAACP and predominately black organizations. By the 1960s,
however, largely youth led direct-action campaigns greatly aided the process. A few SCEF leaders during this time acknowledged the general difference in age of themselves and many of the people who actively
protested.[5] It is to the foot soldiers who carried out those campaigns that
the major credit must go for breakthroughs in civil rights although the
southern conference movement played major supportive roles to the predominately black organizations and their leaders.

In 1963 Southern Conference leaders commemorated the founding of
SCHW; the year marked twenty-five years of their participation in the
struggle for justice and equality. It also marked the one-hundredth anni-

versary of the Emancipation Proclamation. Yet, 1963 did not leave Americans, particularly those working for a societal transformation, much to hope for. The year turned out to be a shocking one. A leading crusader for justice, Eleanor Roosevelt, died. Segregationists murdered Mississippi civil rights leader Medgar Evers and four young girls at a church in Birmingham, and randomly beat numerous others. Near the end of 1963 an assassin's bullet killed President John F. Kennedy. The turmoil-filled year, however, brought Americans to a turning point as the violence and tragedies helped them, even southerners, reluctantly accept major changes. Perhaps the historical lesson from the destruction of the Civil War one hundred years before to the bombings, murders, and beatings one hundred years later taught that violence made Americans more amenable to change.

That many southern white liberals dedicated a great part of their lives to creating an integrated and nondiscriminating society in itself became significant. It took a great amount of courage to call for changes that guaranteed ostracism by one's own race. Except for the questionable use of a mild-mannered strategy in the 1960s, white liberals whose idealism led them to believe in the basic human decency of their fellowman are to be credited for their righteousness. But in all probability, if public awareness alone had continued in the 1950s and 1960s, the 1964 Civil Rights Act and the 1965 Voting Rights Act might have come much later, if at all.

BIBLIOGRAPHICAL ESSAY

Abundant primary sources, many of which have not been previously used, constitute the basis of this thematically and chronologically developed study. Much of the information found in the various collections overlaps and requires careful listing and the raising of specific questions to prevent a great amount of repetitive work. The Southern Conference Educational Fund (SCEF) Papers (1938–1963) and the National Committee to Abolish the Poll Tax Papers (1943–1948) are available at the Tuskegee University Archives, Tuskegee, Alabama. The Southern Conference for Human Welfare (SCHW) Papers and Papers of Clark Foreman (1938–1967) are housed at the Robert W. Woodruff Library, Atlanta University Center, Atlanta, Georgia. At Tuskegee the guide for the papers refers to them as SCHW Records, but the boxes are labeled as SCEF Papers. For purposes of making a distinction between records at Tuskegee and Atlanta, I refer to the papers at Tuskegee as SCEF Papers. The Anne and Carl Braden Papers deposited at the State Historical Society, Madison, Wisconsin, include a wealth of SCHW and SCEF files. The greater part of Clark Foreman's incoming correspondence is at Atlanta, and James Dombrowski's is at Madison. Official files of the SCHW and SCEF include minutes, financial records, correspondence, memoranda, drafts of speeches, press releases, and printed matter. SCHW, for instance, began the monthly publication of the *Southern Patriot* in 1942, and SCEF continued to publish it throughout the 1970s. The material reflects on SCHW/SCEF's principal activities, in particular Henry W. Wallace's presidential campaign, both groups' attitude toward and relations with labor organizations, and the investigation of the SCHW in 1947 by the U.S. House Un-American Activities Committee for evidence of alleged Communist domination. Among the various correspondents are Mary McLeod Bethune, Charlotte Hawkins Brown, Eleanor Roosevelt, Hugo L. Black, Lillian Smith, and many others.

The Virginia Foster Durr Papers are housed at the Alabama Department of Archives and History, Manuscript Division, Montgomery. When SCHW instituted the National Committee to Abolish the Poll Tax in 1938, Durr became its vicechairperson. For this dedicated service and her early fight for a just society the National Council of Negro Women gave her an award in 1946. Durr became an active participant in the Civil Rights Movement, and her papers contain much information about her political and civic activities in this development of the 1950s and 1960s. Although the papers of her husband, Clifford Durr, are housed at the state archives, too, Virginia Durr's papers include some information about his political life.

The Frank Porter Graham Papers are part of the Southern Historical Collection at the University of North Carolina, Chapel Hill. The bulk, from 1928 through the 1960s, chronicles Graham's public interest and activities in race relations, organized labor, and human-welfare questions. As president of the University of North Carolina, Graham became a prominent figure in the state, and his liberal ideas, sometimes a liability, helped to carry that preeminence throughout the southern region and the nation.

The National Association for the Advancement of Colored People (NAACP) Papers, located at the Library of Congress in Washington, D.C., contain information on the cooperative efforts of the NAACP, the SCHW, and SCEF. Several parts of the papers provide much insight into the competitive nature of the work between the NAACP and groups like the SCHW and SCEF as they went about the business of developing a just society. These groups almost always sought financial support from the same northern liberal foundations and individuals, a factor that increased competition between them.

The Federal Bureau of Investigation Files on SCHW and SCEF promise to provide an abundance of information on the alleged Communist charges against the organizations in question and several individuals, but after an almost two-year attempt to obtain a portion of these records through the Freedom of Information Acts, the Records Management Division of the Department of Justice only recently has begun the process of declassifying a few files.

Although the primary source material abundantly provides for a different approach and interpretation of SCHW and SCEF, two earlier studies must be a basic starting point for research on the two organizations. These studies provide a separate look at each organization; see Thomas Krueger, *And Promises to Keep: The Southern Conference for Human Welfare, 1938–1948* (Nashville: Vanderbilt University Press, 1967) and Irwin Klibaner, "The Southern Conference Educational Fund: A History" (Ph.D. dissertation, University of Wisconsin, 1971). Krueger contends that SCHW did very little in addressing the issues most pertinent to African Americans. He bases his theory on the fact that the organization did not establish itself for the sole purpose of addressing civil rights issues. He concludes that with the Henry Wallace presidential campaign in 1948 SCHW generally lost public attention and accomplished little because the Progressive party refused to address segregated audiences. Klibaner agrees with Krueger's assessment and concludes that SCEF was more successful simply because its major goal centered on civil rights.

Several dissertations about various SCHW and SCEF leaders and some of the organizations to which they belonged have been useful for background information. These include: Pat Bryan Brewer, "Lillian Smith: Thorn in the Flesh of Crackerdom" (University of Georgia, 1982); Cicero Alvin Hughes, "Toward a Black United Front: The National Negro Congress Movement" (Ohio University, 1982). Hughes's thesis helped to explain partly why some blacks did not trust white organizations like SCEF. He attributes the early phase of separateness of black organizations to A. Philip Randolph's call for independent black protest in the 1940s. Other useful dissertations are: Anthony Lake Newberry, "Without Urgency or Ardor: The South's Middle-of-the-Road Liberals and Civil Rights, 1945–1960" (Ohio University, 1982); Clarence G. Newsome, "Mary McLeod Bethune in Religious Perspective: A Seminal Essay" (Duke University, 1982); Patricia Ann Sullivan, "Gideon's Southern Soldiers: New Deal Politics and Civil Rights Reform, 1933–1948" (Emory University, 1983). Sullivan's work includes some coverage of the Southern Conference for Human Welfare but concentrates on the 1948 presidential campaign of Henry Wallace. Henry Lewis Suggs, "P. B. Young and the Norfolk *Journal and Guide*, 1910–1954" (University of Virginia, 1976) tells of the importance of one of the most significant southern black newspaper editors and the role of the black press for southern liberals.

Much biographical work remains to be done on presenting the lives of the large number of outstanding individuals who gave decades of service in the fight for human welfare for all Americans, particularly southerners. A few of the stories already told by and about these individuals include: Warren Ashby, *Frank Porter Graham: A Southern Liberal* (Winston-Salem, N.C.: John F. Blair, 1980); Wilma Dykeman and James Stokely, *Seeds of Southern Change: The Life of Will Alexander* (Chicago: University of Chicago Press, 1962); Richard Henderson, *Maury Maverick: A Political Biography* (Austin: University of Texas Press, 1970); Lucy Randolph Mason, *To Win These Rights: A Personal Story of the CIO in the South* (New York: Harper and Row, 1952); Anthony P. Dunbar, *Against the Grain: Southern Radicals and Prophets, 1929–1959* (Charlottesville: University Press of Virginia, 1981), a collective biography about many people involved with SCHW and SCEF; John Salmond, *A Southern Rebel: The Life and Times of Aubrey Willis Williams, 1890–1965* (Chapel Hill: University of North Carolina Press, 1983). Through Salmond's work it became clear that Williams seemed unwilling to understand how or why some blacks mistrusted white leadership in the fight for civil rights. Although the question of trust became the greater concern, Williams believed that blacks should have welcomed white support and even felt bitter and betrayed by 1960 because he thought blacks could have provided more support to white liberals in their work. Virginia Durr's life and background most recently are developed through her own account in *Outside the Magic Circle: The Autobiography of Virginia Foster Durr*, ed. by Hollinger F. Barnard (University: University of Alabama Press, 1985). John Hope Franklin and August Meier, eds., *Black Leaders of the Twentieth Century* (Urbana: University of Illinois Press, 1982), inform us with more information of a few of the leading black leaders, many of whom were SCHW and SCEF members, of this century and leave room for much general work on the general subject of black leadership collectively in this century. Any study of the Civil Rights Movement must touch on the life of Martin Luther King, Jr., and the most recent studies about King include David J. Garrow, *Bearing the Cross: Martin Luther King, Jr., and the Southern Christian Leadership Conference* (New York: William Morrow, 1986) and Stephen B. Oates, *Let the Trumpet Sound: The Life of Martin Luther King, Jr.* (New York: Harper and Row, 1982).

General studies are helpful for the broad picture of African Americans and their relation to American history. The most useful references in this category include: Mary Frances Berry and John W. Blassingame, *Long Memory: The Black Experience in America* (New York: Oxford University Press, 1982). Berry and Blassingame make the dismal conclusion about the general progress of African Americans when they predict that not until the twenty-first century will blacks reach parity with mainstream America. The other work is by John Hope Franklin, *From Slavery to Freedom: A History of Negro Americans* (New York: Knopf, 1974).

Throughout the history of the Southern Conference and the Educational Fund the issue of the poll tax and voting rights remained a major concern. Few scholarly works discuss the specific topic of poll tax; therefore, the works by Steven F. Lawson, *Black Ballots: Voting Rights in the South, 1944–1969* (New York: Columbia University Press, 1976) and Frederic D. Ogden, *The Poll Tax in the South* (University: University of Alabama Press, 1958) constitute the bulk of work on the issue. One of the sources that the SCHW relied on in the 1940s that still proves helpful is that by Eleanor Bontecou, *The Poll Tax* (Washington, D.C.: American Association of University Women, 1942). The leading work in southern politics in general is that by V. O. Key, Jr., *Southern Politics in State and Nation* (New York: Knopf, 1949). Key argues from the basic premise that "in its grand outlines the politics of the South revolves around the position of the Negro," a conclusion that SCHW draws about blacks and most southern issues. Two additional recent studies must be consulted on the southern political development: Paul Kleppner, *Who Voted? The Dynamics of Electoral Turnout, 1870–1980* (New York: Praeger, 1982), and Steven F. Lawson, *In Pursuit of Power: Southern Blacks and Electoral Politics, 1965–1982* (New York: Columbia University Press, 1985).

Government publications played major roles in the history of SCHW and SCEF. In 1938 one report, U.S. National Emergency Council, *Report on Economic Conditions of the South* (Washington, D.C., 1938) laid the groundwork that pointed to the need for an organization like SCHW. Another government analysis, *Report on the Southern Conference for Human Welfare: Investigation of Un-American Activities in the United States* by the House Committee on Un-American Activities, 80th Cong., 1st sess., June 16, 1947, created much controversy for the SCHW over alleged Communist domination. Finally, from the U.S. President's Committee on Civil Rights, *To Secure These Rights: The Report of the President's Committee on Civil Rights* (New York: Simon and Schuster, 1947) lent national acclaim to the very issue of civil rights, the major concern of the SCEF.

Other significant studies provided background information on specific aspects of the twenty-five year history. William C. Berman, *The Politics of Civil Rights in the Truman Administration* (Columbus: Ohio State University Press, 1970), claims that Truman's civil rights maneuvers were strictly for political expedience in 1948 and in 1952 to keep the Democratic party intact. Yet Berman makes too much of Truman's politics; Truman himself said that he was "dead earnest" about civil rights and that he would work for civil rights legislation as long as he lived. The list continues: Carl M. Brauer, *John F. Kennedy and the Second Reconstruction* (New York: Columbia University Press, 1977); Judith Caditz, *White Liberals in Transition: Current Dilemmas of Ethnic Integration* (New York: Spectrum, 1976); Frank Freidel, *F. D. R. and the South* (Baton Rouge: Louisiana State University Press, 1965); Paul M. Gaston, *The New South Creed: A Study in Southern Mythmaking* (New York: Knopf, 1970); William H. Harris, *The Harder We Run: Black Workers since the Civil War* (New York: Oxford University Press, 1982); William H. Harris, *Keeping the Faith: A Philip Randolph, Milton P. Webster, and the Brotherhood of Sleeping Car Porters, 1925–37* (Urbana: University of Illinois Press, 1977); William H. Harris, "A. Philip Randolph as a Charismatic Leader, 1925–1941," *Journal of Negro History*, 64 (Fall 1979); John B. Kirby, *Black Americans in the Roosevelt Era: Liberalism and Race* (Knoxville: University of Tenn. Press, 1981); Lester C. Lamon, *Black Tennesseans, 1900–1930* (Knoxville: University of Tennessee Press, 1977); Anthony Lewis and *The New York Times, Portrait of a Decade: The Second American Revolution* (New York: Random House, 1964); Katherine DuPre Lumpkin, *The South In Progress* (New York: International, 1940); Gunnar Myrdal, with Richard Sterner and Arnold Rose, *An American Dilemma: The Negro Problem and Modern Democracy* (New York: Pantheon, 1972); Anne Moody, *Coming of Age in Mississippi* (New York: Laurel, 1968); Mark Naison, *Communists in Harlem during the Depression* (Urbana: University of Illinois Press, 1982); Howard W. Odum, *The Way of the South: Toward the Regional Balance of America* (New York: Macmillan, 1947); Harvard Sitkoff, *A New Deal for Blacks: The Emergence of Civil Rights as a National Issue*. Vol. I: *The Depression Decade* (New York: Oxford University Press, 1978). Sitkoff argues that civil rights, as an idea and a movement, was critically stimulated by certain political, cultural, constitutional, and attitudinal developments in the Depression decade. Contrary to most recent interpretations, he asserts that the groundwork for the civil rights revolution was laid during the New Deal era.

A few other significant studies which added to my understanding of the South and southern liberalism include: George B. Tindall, *The Emergence of the New South, 1913–1945* (Baton Rouge: Louisiana State University Press, 1967); Arthur I. Waskow, *From Race Riot to Sit-In, 1919 and the 1960s: A Study in the Connections between Conflict and Violence* (Garden City, N.Y.: Doubleday 1966); C. Vann Woodward, *The Strange Career of Jim Crow* (New York: Oxford University Press, 1955); C. Vann Woodward, *The Burden of Southern History* (Baton Rouge: Louisiana State University Press, 1968); C. Vann Woodward, *The Origins of the New South, 1877–1913* (Baton Rouge: Louisiana State University Press, 1951); Nancy J. Weiss, *The National Urban League, 1910–1940* (New York: Oxford University Press, 1974).

Significantly, C. Vann Woodward and John Hope Franklin, two preeminent present-day historians, participated in SCHW activities in the 1930s and 1940s. Many of the SCHW and SCEF officials themselves were also intellectuals, and some of their works which follow address many of the very issues for which they sought solutions in southern society. They presented their ideas as trained scholars in such works as: *The Shore Dimly Seen* by Ellis Arnall. Two administrators had even obtained the Ph.D. degrees from Columbia University, and their doctoral dissertations appeared in book form. See James Dombrowski, *The Early Days of Christian Socialism in America* (New York: Columbia University Press, 1936), and Clark Foreman, *Environmental Factors in Negro Elementary Education* (New York: W. W. Norton, 1932). Mark Ethridge, in *America's Obligation to Its Negro Citizens* (Atlanta: Conference on Education and Race Relations, 1937), is paternalistic in this address, but does offer some constructive suggestions for economic equality. Finally, Arthur F. Raper and Ira DeA. Reid, in *Sharecroppers All* (Chapel Hill: University of North Carolina Press, 1941), advise "for the real meaning of the term 'sharecropper' look to such matters as low wages, insecurity, and lack of opportunity for self-direction and responsible participation in community affairs." The book describes poor economic conditions in the South during the late 1930s and early 1940s.

Many useful sources listed in the notes have not been relisted here, and for a fuller bibliography, readers should use this essay with the notes.

APPENDIX

Statement of Principles for Action

Unanimously Adopted, Nashville, April 21, 1942

The Southern Conference for Human Welfare was organized in 1938 by Southerners who were determined to study the social and economic problems of the South and to pool their best resources of intelligency and energy to remedy the South's ills. People from all walks of life and of all shades of opinion were brought into a working unity by the desperate needs of the South. They came together, and have continued to work together, determined to make the South an integral part of the United States and to eliminate the South's many handicaps (in economics, education and health) by the development of our democratic institutions.

Today in April, 1942, the very interests and institutions of democracy are in jeopardy because the independence of our country is threatened. Neither the strength nor the speed essential to win the war is possible without the full use of all the South's material and all the South's human resources—Negro and White alike. Many of the goals the Southern Conference set for the fulfillment of democracy three years ago are now the requisities of victory. Without this victory no further progress will be possible and no work for human welfare will go on. All our goals are unified by the sweeping threats of this war.

Therefore, we resolve to give our renewed and united strength to winning this war by organizing the cooperative efforts of Southerners on the following basic principles:

I. The resources of the South can play a major role in speeding our victory. Management must meet with labor so as to use to the fullest extent contributions which labor can make to efficient operation. We must have the fullest use of our productive capacities. Small industries and idle plants must be converted at once to war production. All our machinery must be in continuous use, three shifts a day, one hundred and eighty hours a week. Each local community must develop its own resources on its own initiative and translate the President's leadership into production now.

II. With the urgent necessity of rationing food and clothing it is imperative that Southern agriculture be geared to produce abundantly for freedom, as requested by our Commander-in-Chief. Our manpower—both military and civilian—is now too priceless to be limited by underproduction, underconsumption, or by neglect of the vast resources of farm production represented by small farmers, tenants, and sharecroppers who can with government help, make great contributions to maximum farm production for ourselves and our allies. Farm-labor unity is also essential for such maximum production. The work of the Farm Security Administration is proving invaluable in the food-for-freedom program and should be extended. We support a policy of government encouragement to the organization of co-operatives among the Southern farmers.

III. The equal obligation of all citizens to give their full strength to our democratic offensive call upon us to provide adequate facilities for health and training of all our youth—Negro and White—for the important jobs that await and to cooperate fully in our national government's efforts at balanced price control and rationing of essential commodities.

IV. The requisities of victory demand action by approved government agencies and citizens of communities to remove all infringements of the civil liberties and democratic rights of all the American people, regardless of race, color, creed or national origin. Every effort to maintain and extend these freedoms here in the South will strengthen the basic faith of our people and will hasten the victory for these freedoms abroad.

THESE ARE THE METHODS OF VICTORY
AND THIS IS THE ORDER OF THE DAY!

The Southern Conference for Human Welfare urges all Southerners—farmers, laborers, businessmen, women, and youth—to share fully in a united common effort to help win the victory by utilizing all the resources of the South. We must match the effort and sacrifice of the brave people of Britain and China, of the Philippine Islands and Russia, free peoples fighting in exile, and of all other sections of our own country, with the united will of the Southern people to win this war and to win the peace for democracy. Only thus can we fulfill the hope of our Commander-in-Chief "for the full utilization of our resources within the principles of our democratic faith." The commands of today are: to join in a great offensive now; to work, to produce, to sacrifice, to win! We now say to each other, as our father who gave us our freedom said, "Awake—arise—or be forever fallen!"

Source: Proceedings of the Third Meeting of the Southern Conference for Human Welfare (Nashville: SCHW, April 19–21, 1942), 4–5. A copy of the *Proceedings* may be found in folder 84, box 4, SCEF Papers.

"Lend a Hand in Dixieland"*

Theres a lot that happens in the land of cotton
The bad sticks out and the good's forgotten
Lend a hand, lend a hand, lend a hand to Dixieland
In Dixieland they are beginning
Voting and the people winning
Shake a can, shake a can, shake a can for Dixieland

Chorus

Oh it's not so easy in Dixie
To vote To vote
In Dixieland you can help us stand for democracy
In Dixie
Do away, do away with the KKK
In Dixie

The people South come in whites and colors
But all of them are really brothers
Lend a hand, lend a hand, take a stand for Dixieland

With rights to vote and decent living
Put an end to fascist lynching
Fill a can, fill a can, fill a can for Dixieland

*This song included protests against lynching and voter restrictions, two reforms SCHW advocated.

Source: Branson Price to James Dombrowski, September 16, 1946, folder 38, box 2, SCEF Papers, where song is attached to letter.

Prominent Members of National Committee for Justice in Columbia, Tennessee

Elsie Austin
Roger N. Baldwin*
Edward L. Bernays
Mary McLeod Bethune*
Hon. Andrew J. Biemiller
Hon. Jane M. Bolin
Charles G. Bolte
Charlotte Hawkins
 Brown*
Oscar C. Brown
James B. Carey
Colonel Evans F. Carlson
Rev. Allan Knight
 Chalmers
Leo M. Cherne
Dr. Nathan K.
 Christopher
Norman Corwin
Bartley Crum
Russell W. Davenport
Jo Davidson
Bette Davis
Hon. William L. Dawson
Hon. Hubert T. Delaney
Earl B. Dickerson
Hon. Helen Gahagan
 Douglas
Melvyn Douglas
Roscoe Dunjee*
Albert L. Einstein*
Edwin R. Embree*
Dr. W. J. Faulkner
Justin Feldman
Marshall Field*
Mrs. Marshall Field*
Clark Foreman*

Lewis S. Gannett
Frank P. Graham*
David M. Grant
William L. Green*
Thomas L. Griffith, Jr.
Oscar Hammerstein II
John Hammond
Hon. William H. Hastie
George E. C. Hayes
Helen Hayes
Dr. George E. Haynes
Rev. Charles C. Hill
Rev. John Haynes
 Holmes
Langston Hughes*
Robert M. Hutchins
Harold L. Ickes*
Lillie M. Jackson
Dr. D. V. Jemison
John Johnson
Rev. John H. Johnson
Freda Kirchwey
Fiorello H. LaGuardia
Hon. Charles M.
 LaFollette
Hon. Herbert H.
 Lehman
Leo A. Lerner
Max Lerner
Ira F. Lewis
Sinclair Lewis
Joe Louis*
Rev. A. A. Lucas
Henry R. Luce
George Marshall*
Newbold Morris

Hon. Wayne L. Morse
Carl Murphy
Philip Murray*
T. G. Nutter
James G. Patton
Clarence E. Pickett
Charles Poletti
Hon. Adam C. Powell,
 Jr.
A. Philip Randolph*
Dr. E. I. Robinson
Bishop William Scarlett
William Jay Schieffelin
David O. Selznick
John Sengstacke
Artie Shaw
Bishop Bernard J. Sheil
Hilda Simms
Lillian E. Smith*
Edward J. Sparling
Arthur B. Spingarn
Frank P. Stanley
Mabel K. Staupers
Nathan Straus
Herbert Bayard Swope
Dr. J. M. Tinsley
Mrs. Robert L. Vann
Bishop W. J. Walls
Leon H. Washington
Palmer Weber*
Carter W. Wesley
Beulah T. Whitby
Jane White
Walter White*
Dr. Stephen S. Wise
P. B. Young, Sr.*

*Members or supporters of SCHW

Source: Eleanor Roosevelt and Channing Tobias to "Dear Friend," June 25, 1946, "Columbia, Tennessee" folder, box 4, SCEF Papers.

NOTES

Introduction

1. Aubrey Williams, "Gradualism Effective—or Necessary?" *Southern Patriot*, 8 (January 1950), 2; "New Orleans Integration Petition Proves Decency's Strength," ibid., 13 (October 1955), 1; ibid., 12 (April 1954), 4; Paul Tillett (of Rutgers University and the Wells Phillips Eagleton & Florence Peshine Eagleton Foundation) to Williams, September 26, 1958, folder 5, box 17, Carl and Anne Braden Papers (State Historical Society, Madison, Wis.).

2. Aldon Morris, *The Origins of the Civil Rights Movement: Black Communities Organizing for Change* (New York: Free Press, 1984), xi.

3. Frances Fox Piven and Richard A. Cloward, *Poor People's Movements: Why They Succeed, How They Fail* (New York: Pantheon, 1977), esp. 20–21 where the authors discuss the difficulty of uniting across class lines. Robert J. Norrell, *Reaping the Whirlwind: The Civil Rights Movement in Tuskegee* (New York: Knopf, 1985).

4. *Plessy v. Ferguson*, 163 U.S. 537, 1896; Wilma Dykeman and James Stokely, *Seeds of Southern Change: The Life of Will Alexander* (Chicago: University of Chicago Press, 1962); John T. Kneebone, *Southern Liberal Journalists and the Issue of Race, 1920–1944* (Chapel Hill: University of North Carolina Press, 1985); Charles Eagles, *Jonathan Daniels and Race Relations: The Evolution of a Southern Liberal* (Knoxville: University of Tennessee Press, 1982).

5. William H. Harris, "Trends and Needs in Afro-American Historiography" in *The State of Afro-American History: Past, Present, and Future*, ed. by Darlene Clark Hine (Baton Rouge: Louisiana State University Press, 1986).

6. Morton Sosna, *In Search of the Silent South: Southern Liberals and the Race Issue* (New York: Columbia University Press, 1977). Sosna defines stages of liberalism, noting that between 1880 and 1900 liberals allowed that segregation could stay but that blacks needed to be treated humanely. Between 1900 and 1938, similar circumstances existed with a few ambiguous voices against segregation. By 1938 a few southerners could call for equality, but quite a number could not accept social equality along with economic and political equality. Where liberals stood on the question had become very complex by then. See also William E. Ellis, "Catholicism and the Southern Ethos: The Role of Patrick Henry Callahan," *Catholic Historical Review*, 69 (January 1983), 42–50. Ellis sees the southern liberal as a supporter of religious toleration and labor unions, and intolerant of racial prejudice.

7. Ellis applied the term *individualistic progressive* for people who worked independently of group efforts. See Ellis, "Catholicism and the Southern Ethos," 50.

8. Anne Braden, *The Wall Between* (New York: Monthly Review Press, 1958).

9. Jessie P. Guzman (SCEF board member and archivist at Tuskegee Institute) to James Dombrowski, July 5, 1959, microfilm 306, reel 4, Carl and Anne Braden Papers (State Historical Society, Madison, Wis.); Dombrowski to Guzman, August 3, 1960, ibid.; Guzman to Dombrowski, August 5, 16, 1960, ibid. Guzman acknowledged seven cases of SCHW and SCEF records on August 16.

10. *Our Land Too: The Legacy of the Southern Tenant Farmers' Union*, a documentary film; *Eyes on the Prize: America's Civil Rights Years, 1954–1965* (Boston: Blackside, 1987).

1. A New Answer to the Old Questions of
Southern Poverty and Backwardness

1. See Paul M. Gaston, *The New South Creed: A Study in Southern Mythmaking* (New York: Knopf, 1970), on the creation of the idea of New South, and esp. 4–5 for other meanings of the term.

2. C. Vann Woodward, *Origins of the New South, 1877–1913* (Baton Rouge: Louisiana State University Press, 1951), 318. This volume by Woodward and the one by George Brown Tindall, cited below, are vols. 9 and 10, respectively, of the well-received History of the American South Series. Gavin Wright, *Old South, New South: Revolutions in the Southern Economy since the Civil War* (New York: Basic Books, 1986), offers a more recent study.

3. George Brown Tindall, *The Emergence of the New South, 1913–1945* (Baton Rouge: Louisiana State University Press, 1967). See Woodward, *Origins of the New South*, 291–320, for details on the southern economy.

4. Gaston, *New South Creed*, 79.

5. Ibid., 93–94.

6. Joel Chandler Harris, ed., *Joel Chandler Harris' Life of Henry W. Grady: Including His Writings and Speeches* (New York: Cassell, 1890), 100.

7. Henry W. Grady, *The New South: With a Character Sketch of Henry W. Grady by Oliver Dyer, Author of "Great Senators"* (New York: Robert Bonner's Sons, 1890), 239, 240–41.

8. Ibid., 244.

9. *Race Problems of the South: Report of the First Annual Conference Held under the Auspices of the Southern Society for the Promotion of the Study of Race Conditions in the South at Montgomery, Alabama, May 8, 9, 10, A.D. 1900* (New York: Negro Universities Press, 1969 [1900 by the B. F. Johnson Publishing Co.]), 5, 24.

10. Ibid., 5, 12, 21, 22–23, 24, 27, 42; Woodward, *Origins of the New South*, 353.

11. Wilma Dykeman and James Stokely, *Seeds of Southern Change: The Life of Will Alexander* (Chicago: University of Chicago Press, 1962); John T. Kneebone, *Southern Liberal Journalists and the Issue of Race, 1920–1944* (Chapel Hill: University of North Carolina Press, 1985), xiii, xvi, 74–75, 133; Charles Eagles, *Jonathan Daniels and Race Relations: The Evolution of a Southern Liberal* (Knoxville: University of Tennessee Press, 1982), 23–24. The Commission sought to end police brutality and lynching, urged racial equity in wages, and encouraged greater publicity for achievements by blacks. Although CIC did not protest vigorously against segregation, it provided a proving ground for a few southern liberals who later would devote years doing so—for example, Clark Foreman.

12. Gaston, *New South Creed*, 189–90, 222–23; C. Vann Woodward, "New South Fraud Is Papered by Old South Myth," *Washington Post*, July 9, 1961, p. E-3.

13. Wallace Strowd to Frank Graham, July 12, 1938, folder 65, Frank Porter Graham (FPG) Papers, Southern Historical Collection (University of North Carolina, Chapel Hill). Graham to "Wallace," July 12, 1938, ibid.; Fitzgerald Hall to Lowell Mellett, Executive Director of the National Emergency Council, September 7, 1938, folder 70, FPG Papers. The papers are in unnumbered boxes with separate-numbered folders by years. Fitzgerald Hall protested against many aspects of the 1938 NEC *Report* on behalf of the Southern States Industrial Council, Inc. There are several other negative responses, see 1938, folders 66–70, ibid.; Gaston, *New South Creed*, 222–23.

14. Lowell Mellett to Frank Graham, June 25, 1938, folder 65, FPG Papers; Newspaper clippings, Clark Foreman Scrapbook, 1938–1939, Southern Conference for Human Welfare Papers (Robert W. Woodruff Library, Atlanta University Center, Atlanta). Hereafter, SCHW Papers; Thomas A. Krueger, *And Promises to Keep:*

The Southern Conference for Human Welfare, 1938–1948 (Nashville: Vanderbilt University Press, 1967), 11–13; Frank Freidel, *F.D.R. and the South* (Baton Rouge: Louisiana State University Press, 1965), 1, 35–36, 47, 64–70, 99.

15. Mellett to Graham, June 25, 1938, folder 65, FPG Papers; telegram, Graham to Mellett, June 30, 1938, ibid.

16. U.S. National Emergency Council, *Report on Economic Conditions of the South* (Washington: U.S. Government Printing Office, 1938), 3; Krueger, *And Promises to Keep,* 13–19.

17. David R. Coker to Graham, July 7, 1938, folder 65, FPG Papers; Graham to Coker, July 29, 1938, folder 66, ibid.; Henry A. Wallace to David R. Coker, June 30, 1938, folder 65, FPG Papers; Clark Foreman to Graham, August 1, 1938, folder 67, ibid.

18. U.S. National Emergency Council, *Report,* 4, 6, 8, 61–64; Frederick Shelton of the Kiplinger Washington Agency to Graham, August 15, 1938, folder 67, FPG Papers on when the *Report* became available. See also Krueger, *And Promises to Keep,* 14–16.

19. U.S. National Emergency Council, *Report,* 7, 12, 19, 21–22, 26, 27, 39, 41, 43, 47, 54.

20. Ibid., 1–2.

21. Fitzgerald Hall to Lowell Mellett, Sept. 7, 1938, folder 70, FPG Papers; Gaston, *New South Creed,* 222–23; Guy B. Johnson, "Does the South Owe the Negro a New Deal?" *Social Forces,* 13 (October 1934), 100–103; Frank L. Owsley, "A Key to Southern Liberalism," *Southern Review,* 3 (Summer 1937), 28–38; H. Clarence Nixon, "Farm Tenancy to the Forefront," *Southwest Review,* 22 (October 1936), 11–15; J. Phil Campbell, "The Government's Farm Policies and the Negro Farmer," *Journal of Negro Education,* 5 (January 1936), 32–39.

22. Graham to Clark Foreman, July 18, 1938, folder 66, FPG Papers; Palmer Weber interviewed by Linda Reed, Nov. 13, 1983; Freidel, *F. D. R. and the South,* 35, 98.

23. Coker to Graham, July 7, 1938, folder 65, FPG Papers; Barry Bingham to Graham, July 23, 1938, folder 66, ibid. Bingham "was disturbed to see what an unfriendly reaction there was . . . on the part of a number of Southern newspapers."

24. "Roosevelt Appoints a Slumming Commission," *Textile Bulletin,* July 7, 1938, pp. 14–15, in folder 65, FPG Papers. The Clark Publishing Company of Charlotte, North Carolina, published the paper every Thursday.

25. Barry Bingham to Graham, July 23, 1938, folder 66, FPG Papers.

26. Arthur Raper and Ira DeA. Reid, "Old Conflicts in the New South," *Virginia Quarterly Review,* 16 (Spring 1940), 226.

27. Fitzgerald Hall to Graham, August 26, 1938, folder 69, FPG Papers; Hall to Mellett, September 7, 1938, folder 70, ibid.; report, Fitzgerald Hall, "Comments on the Report of Economic Conditions of the South," September 7, 1938, ibid.; Hall to Graham, September 12, 1938, ibid.; Arthur Goldschmidt to Graham, September 14, 1938, ibid.

28. Mellett to Hall, September 19, 1938, folder 71, FPG Papers; Raper and Reid, "Old Conflicts in the New South," 223.

29. Graham to Clark Foreman, July 18, 1938, folder 66, FPG Papers; Frederick Shelton of the Kiplinger Washington Agency to Graham, August 15, 1938, folder 67, ibid.; Katherine Lackey, Graham's secretary, to Mellett, August 15, 1938, ibid.; Lackey to Mellett, August 24, 1938, folder 69, ibid.; Alexander Heard to Graham, September 11, 1938, folder 70, ibid.; Rowland Allen, director of L. S. Ayres & Co., to Graham, September 12, 1938, ibid.; D. McL. McDonald of the South Carolina Conference of Social Work to Graham, September 14, 1938, ibid.; Graham to McDonald, September 21, 1938, folder 71, ibid.

30. McDonald to Graham, September 14, 1938, folder 70, FPG Papers; program, "Duke University Centennial Celebration, Trinity College—Duke University, 1838–1839—1938–1939," "Symposium on the Changing Economic Base of the South," November 17, 18, 1938, folder 72, ibid.; Raper and Reid, "Old Conflicts in the New South," 226.

31. Joseph Gelders to Virginia Foster Durr, July 30, 1938, folder 7, box 31, SCHW Papers. Joseph Gelders tells Virginia Durr of his recent meeting with Lucy Randolph Mason in Atlanta and relates to Durr also Mason's enthusiasm for the Conference.

32. *Who's Who in America: A Biographical Dictionary of Notable Living Men and Women of the United States* (41 vols. Chicago: A. N. Marquis, 1892–), XX, 1077; Warren Ashby, *Frank Porter Graham: A Southern Liberal* (Winston-Salem, N.C.: John F. Blair, 1980), 43, 81–86, 141–50.

33. Lucy Randolph Mason, *To Win These Rights: A Personal Story of the CIO in the South* (New York: Harper & Brothers, 1952), 5–17, 19–20. A more recent biography on Mason is John A. Salmond, *Miss Lucy of the CIO: The Life and Times of Lucy Randolph Mason, 1882–1959* (Athens: University of Georgia Press, 1988).

34. Mary Braggiotti, "Southern Progressive," *New York Post*, March 3, 1945, p. 1; *Southern Patriot*, 3 (March 1945), 7; Weber interview, November 13, 1983. The *Southern Patriot* became the monthly publication for the SCHW in 1942.

35. *Who's Who in America*, XXV, 828; Braggiotti, "Southern Progressive."

36. Weber interview, November 13, 1983; Gunnar Myrdal, *American Dilemma: The Negro Problem and Modern Democracy* (New York: Harper & Brothers, 1944), 471.

37. Graham to Henry A. Foscue, July 28, 1938, folder 66, FPG Papers; Graham to "Forman," July 18, 1938, ibid.; Cicero Alvin Hughes, "Toward a Black United Front: The National Negro Congress Movement" (Ph.D. dissertation, Ohio University, 1982), 63–64.

38. Joseph Gelders to Virginia Durr, July 30, 1938, folder 7, box 31, SCHW Papers; Louise O. Charlton and Luther Patrick to Virginia Durr, August 13, 1938, ibid.; Louise O. Charlton, "The Southern Conference for Human Welfare," in *Report of Proceedings of the Southern Conference for Human Welfare* (Birmingham, Ala.: n.p., Nov. 20–23, 1938), 3–6, folder 103, box 9, Southern Conference Educational Fund (SCEF) Papers (Hollis Burke Frissell Library, Tuskegee, Ala.) Note that SCHW records are in Atlanta, SCEF in Tuskegee. Sarah Newman Shouse, *Hillbilly Realist: Herman Clarence Nixon of Possum Trot* (University: University of Alabama Press, 1986), 79–81, 91.

39. Charlton, "The Southern Conference for Human Welfare," 3–6, folder 103, box 9, SCEF Papers.

40. Virginia Durr interviewed by Linda Reed, December 29, 1982; Krueger, *And Promises to Keep*, 16–19. Durr's account coincides with Krueger's on the Gelders and Mason collaboration. Unaware of Nixon's and Gelders's meeting, Durr could not comment about it. Daniel Joseph Singal, *The War Within: From Victorian to Modernist Thought in the South, 1919–1945* (Chapel Hill: University of North Carolina Press, 1982), 293. Krueger's and Singal's accounts differ in that Singal says that Gelders played no significant part in calling the SCHW's November meeting, that his name did not even appear on the letterhead. Krueger gives Gelders much credit. A recent study, Shouse, *Hillbilly Realist*, 102–3, esp. 210 (n. 18), also gives Gelders credit for pulling together forces for SCHW. Alabama native H. C. Nixon is noted for *Forty Acres and Steel Mules* (1938) and his contribution to the Twelve Southerners, *I'll Take My Stand* (1930). See Charlton, "The Southern Conference for Human Welfare," 3–4, for more details about the Southern Policy Committee and the Alabama Policy Committee.

41. "Outline of the History of the Southern Conference," n.d., folder 18, box 1, SCEF Papers; W. Bert Johnson to Graham, September 1938, folder 70, FPG Papers;

Joseph Gelders to Graham, October 8, 1938, folder 76, FPG Papers; Gelders to Graham, October 25, 1938, ibid.; Gelders to Graham, November 8, 1938, folder 77, ibid.

42. Shouse, *Hillbilly Realist*, 132–33; Singal, *The War Within*, 291.

43. Krueger, *And Promises to Keep*, 3–6. Many white southerners vigorously opposed any advocacy group that might interfere with the status quo of southern society.

44. Gelders to Graham, October 8, 1938, folder 76, FPG Papers. The letter is written on the National Committee for People's Rights' letterhead. Krueger, *And Promises to Keep*, 4–5; Singal, *War Within*, 293.

45. Louise O. Charlton, "A Conference on the South," *New Republic*, September 28, 1938, p. 216. Charlton, a former school teacher, could also count on contacts from that pool to help in this crusade for southern improvement. Unidentified newspaper clipping, July 7, 1965, folder 2.55, Hill Ferguson Papers (Birmingham Public Library Archives, Ala.).

46. *Report of Proceedings of the Southern Conference*, 5; copies of forms sent out for SCHW participation, October 15, 1938, folder 76, FPG Papers. The reverse side of the forms included excerpts from the NEC's report. Addison T. Cutler to Graham, October 31, 1938, folder 72, ibid.; Joseph Gelders to Virginia Durr, May 28, 1940, folder 7, box 31, SCHW Papers. Gelders's letter reveals that William F. Illig, residing in Erie, Penn., in 1940, contributed $1,000 to the SCHW in 1938. Krueger, *And Promises to Keep*, 25.

47. *Report of Proceedings of the Southern Conference*, 7; Charlton, "A Conference on the South," 216; Graham to Hugo Black, October 25, 1938, folder 76, FPG Papers; telegram, Black to Graham, November 2, 1938, folder 77, ibid.

48. Will [Cholment] of Lancaster, Penn., to Graham, November 11, 1938, folder 78, FPG Papers. Virginia Van Der Veer Hamilton, *Hugo Black: The Alabama Years* (University: University of Ala. Press, 1982, pbk. ed.), esp. 32–33, 98–100, 111–12, makes clear Black's acceptance of Klan support but that he did not practice Klan philosophy when given the opportunity to defend justice for all.

49. Press service of the National Association for the Advancement of Colored People, New York, September 15, 1937, NAACP Papers, microfilm reel 15, Indiana University Library; Anne Celeste Butt, secretary to Justice Black, to Thurgood Marshall, September 13, 1937, ibid.; Butt to Walter White, September 13, 1937, ibid.

50. Mary McLeod Bethune to Walter White, October 19, 1938, Special Correspondence, 1910–1939, NAACP Papers, microfilm reel 15.

51. Weber interview, November 13, 1983.

52. *Report of Proceedings of the Southern Conference*, 5, 7–9. Krueger and others place the figure of delegates at between 1,200 and 1,500 although the proceedings set it at 1,200. Krueger, *And Promises to Keep*, 25. Charles Granville Hamilton, "South Faces Its Own Race Issue," *Christian Century*, December 7, 1938, pp. 1520–21. Hamilton sets the number between 1,000 and 2,000. W. T. Couch, chairman of the program committee, sets the figure for the general audience even higher, 3,000 to 5,000, for some of the sessions when persons such as Graham, Eleanor Roosevelt, and Hugo Black spoke. W. T. Couch, "Southerners Inspect the South," *New Republic*, December 14, 1938, pp. 168–69.

53. "Outline of the History of the Southern Conference," n.d., folder 18, box 1, SCEF Papers.

54. Hamilton, "South Faces Its Own Race Issue," 1520; *Report of Proceedings of the Southern Conference*, 7–9, 30–31; *Pittsburg Courier*, December 3, 1938, pp. 1, 4. Alabama Governor Bibb Graves also had Ku Klux Klan ties but did not get any reaction like that given Justice Black. Hamilton, *Hugo Black*, 127, 287; Nell Irvin Painter, *The Narrative of Hosea Hudson: His Life as a Negro Communist in the South* (Cambridge, Mass.: Harvard University Press, 1979), 290–91.

55. Franklin D. Roosevelt to Louise O. Charlton, November 19, 1938, in *Report of Proceedings of the Southern Conference*, 2.

56. *Report of Proceedings of the Southern Conference*, 29.

57. Gilbert Osofsky, *The Burden of Race: A Documentary History of Negro-White Relations in America* (New York: Harper & Row, 1967), 328–29, 401–2. During the early days of World War II white southerners would create the myth of "Eleanor Clubs" where blacks, especially domestics, supposedly met to discuss racial equality and praise the First Lady. Rumors varied from state to state about how black domestics behaved differently as a result of being members of Eleanor Clubs. See Howard W. Odum, *Race and Rumors of Race: Challenge to American Crisis* (Chapel Hill: University of North Carolina Press, 1943), for detailed rumors about the Eleanor Clubs.

58. Couch, "Southerners Inspect the South," 168–69; Durr interview, December 29, 1982; Krueger, *And Promises to Keep*, 26.

59. Ashby, *Frank Porter Graham*, 157; Durr interview, December 29, 1982.

60. *Report of Proceedings of the Southern Conference*, 13; *Pittsburgh Courier*, December 3, 1938, pp. 1, 4.

61. *Report of Proceedings of the Southern Conference*, 29.

62. Ibid., 25–27; Shouse, *Hillbilly Realist*, 59.

63. *Report of Proceedings of the Southern Conference*, 13–21; "F. D. R. Hit before Dies Committee," *Atlanta Constitution*, November 6, 1938, p. 7–A; Athan Theoharis, *Spying on Americans: Political Surveillance from Hoover to the Huston Plan* (Philadelphia: Temple University Press, 1978), 196–97; Dan Carter, *Scottsboro: A Tragedy of the American South* (Baton Rouge: Louisiana State University Press, 1969). A resolution on the NEC *Report* expressed gratitude that President Roosevelt, the NEC, and the advisory group had devoted concern for the South.

64. "The objectives of this organization shall be to unite the Southern people and their organizations, to

1. Promote the general welfare
2. Improve the economic, social and cultural standards of the Southern people
3. Advance Southern functional growth in accordance with American democratic institutions and ideals
4. Initiate and support progressive legislation in Congress and the states in harmony with the principles and program of the Southern Conference . . .
5. Continue and expand activities started at the Southern Conference . . .
6. Secure the cooperation and coordinate the activities of other organization[s] now existing in the Southern States.

To this end, the Southern Conference shall endeavor to secure unity of action and maximum cooperation of all Southern progressives, individuals and groups, from church and school, from all labor, farm, industrial, fraternal and civic organizations, regardless of race, creed or color, who support or are in sympathy with the aims and program of action adopted at the Southern Conference for Human Welfare." *Report of Proceedings of the Southern Conference*, 11.

65. Ibid., 11–12, 30–32.

66. Ibid., 14, 18.

2. How the Southern Conference Movement Operated

1. Mark Ethridge to Frank Graham, November 30, 1938, folder 78, Frank Porter Graham Papers, Southern Historical Collection (University of North Carolina, Chapel Hill).

2. *Report of Proceedings of the Southern Conference for Human Welfare* (Birmingham, Ala.: n.p., Nov. 20–23, 1938), 20; "Outline of the History of the Southern

Conference," n.d., folder 18, box 1, Southern Conference Educational Fund (SCEF) Papers (Hollis Burke Frissell Library, Tuskegee, Ala.).

3. Clark Foreman to Frank Graham, July 10, 1939, folder 1, box 35, Southern Conference for Human Welfare (SCHW) Papers (Robert W. Woodruff Library, Atlanta).

4. George C. Stoney to Clark Foreman, August 15, 1939, folder 1, box 35, SCHW Papers; Stoney to Foreman, September 13 and 14, 1939, ibid; minutes, SCHW executive council meeting, October 6, 1939, ibid.; "Outline of the History of the Southern Conference," folder 18, box 1, SCEF Papers.

5. Minutes, SCHW executive council meeting, October 6, 1939, folder 1, box 35 SCHW Papers; Daniel Joseph Singal, *The War Within: From Victorian to Modernist Thought in the South* (Chapel Hill: University of North Carolina Press, 1982), 293; Thomas Krueger, *And Promises to Keep: The Southern Conference for Human Welfare* (Nashville: Vanderbilt University Press, 1967), 41.

6. Roger N. Baldwin, director of the American Civil Liberties Union, to Virginia Durr, July 27, 1938, folder 7, box 31, SCHW Papers; H. C. Nixon to Virginia Durr, November 29, 1939, ibid.; Lucy R. Mason to Clark Foreman, January 24, 1940, folder 2, box 35, ibid.; Barry Bingham to Howard Lee, November 16, 1939, folder 240, box 20, SCEF Papers; Bingham to Lee, January 25, 1940, ibid. See Robin Davis Gibran Kelley, "Hammer n' hoe: Black Radicalism and the Communist Party in Alabama, 1929–1941" (Ph.D. dissertation, University of California, Los Angeles, 1987), 589, and Singal, *The War Within*, 293 on Gelders's and Lee's membership in the Communist party.

An organization dependent solely on voluntary contributions, SCHW stood to lose financial support if its opposition proved convincing to the public. Aside from their concern over possible damages from allegations of Communist involvement with SCHW, Mason and Bingham wanted assurance that an integrated meeting would take place.

7. Barry Bingham to Howard Lee, February 5, 1940, folder 240, box 20, SCEF Papers.

8. Lucy Randolph Mason to Clark Foreman, January 24, 1940, folder 2, box 35, SCHW Papers; Barry Bingham to Howard Lee, January 25, 1940, folder 240, box 20, SCEF Papers; Bingham to Lee, November 16, 1939, ibid.; H. C. Nixon to Virginia Durr, November 29, 1939, folder 7, box 31, SCHW Papers.

9. Barry Bingham to Virginia Durr, November 18, 1940, folder 7, box 31, SCHW Papers.

10. Frank Graham to Eleanor Roosevelt, January 22, 1940, folder 2, box 35, SCHW Papers; Lucy Randolph Mason to Clark Foreman, January 24, 1940, ibid.; Lee to Bingham, January 28, 1940, folder 240, box 20, SCEF Papers.

11. "Outline of the History of the Southern Conference," n.d., folder 18, box 1, SCEF Papers; program, "A call . . . the Second Southern Conference for Human Welfare: 'Democracy in the South,' " folder 85, box 5, ibid.; Howard Lee to William Mitch of United Mine Workers of America, March 30, 1940, folder 250, box 20, ibid.; Krueger, *And Promises to Keep*, 51, 54.

12. "Memberships, Southern Conference," n.d., folder 2, box 35, SCHW Papers. A note about the 1940 meeting reveals that 62 of the 108 sponsors sent cash.

13. Randolph and John P. Davis held opposing political views in the National Negro Congress, forcing Randolph to resign as its president in 1940. Davis was a great part of SCHW, where at least for a time individual differences could be set aside to help it reach its goals. See William H. Harris, "A. Philip Randolph as a Charismatic Leader, 1925–1941," *Journal of Negro History*, 64 (Fall 1979), 309. Howard W. Odum's name also appeared on the list of sponsors, but it is doubtful that he actually sponsored the 1940 Conference or any other. Odum claimed consistently to have not supported SCHW since its beginning. Odum to James A.

Dombrowski, November 13, 1952, microfilm 306, reel 4, Carl and Anne Braden Papers (State Historical Society, Madison, Wis.). Sponsors' names appear on the last page of 1940 Conference program, folder 85, box 5, SCEF Papers.

14. 1940 Conference program, folder 85, box 5, SCEF Papers; Krueger, *And Promises to Keep*, 56; Wilma Dykeman and James Stokely, *Seeds of Southern Change: The Life of Will Alexander* (Chicago: University of Chicago Press, 1962), 281.

15. Dykeman and Stokely, *Seeds of Southern Change*, 12, 18, 29–30, 78, 172–76, 184–85, 214–23; George Brown Tindall, *The Emergence of the New South, 1913–1945* (Baton Rouge: Louisiana State University Press, 1967), 177–83, 423–25; Lester C. Lamon, *Black Tennesseans, 1900–1930* (Knoxville: University of Tennessee Press, 1977), 19, 83.

16. "Resolutions Adopted, Second [SCHW] Meeting, April 14, 15, 16 [1940], Chattanooga, Tennessee," folder 18, box 1, SCEF Papers. It is interesting that even in early 1941 when President Franklin D. Roosevelt urged Congress to help him to aid Britain with the Lend-Lease Program, many Congressmen balked.

17. "Resolutions Adopted, Second Meeting," folder 18, box 1, SCEF Papers.

18. Ibid.

19. Minutes, SCHW executive board meeting, August 2, 1941, folder 7, box 31, SCHW Papers; Harvard Sitkoff, *A New Deal for Blacks: The Emergence of Civil Rights as a National Issue*, Vol. I: *The Depression Decade* (New York: Oxford University Press, 1978), 319–23; "Resolutions Adopted, Second Meeting," folder 18, box 1, SCEF Papers. Perhaps some leading white SCHW officials might not have agreed with A. Philip Randolph's threatened March on Washington as a reasonable strategy in 1941, but they certainly supported the results.

20. Ibid. See chapter 4 for more on SCHW's fight against the poll tax.

21. Lillian Smith to Dombrowski, June 1, 1942, folder 236, box 19, SCEF Papers. Smith's proposal brought up what John P. Davis and Joseph Gelders had set forth in 1941.

22. Minutes, SCHW executive board meeting, August 2, 1941, box 7, box 31, SCHW Papers. Joseph Gelders, speaking at length to the board about the need for separate committees, shared personal experiences about academic freedom as he had had difficulties as professor of physics at the University of Alabama. The board's last order of business touched on plans for the 1942 meeting whereby Foreman came up with a theme, "The South in National Defense." The board voted approval, but the time and place would be decided later. In 1941 authority rested in the SCHW board, not its Southern Council, for organizational decisions.

23. Smith to Dombrowski, June 1, 1942, folder 236, box 19, SCEF Papers; Foreman to Charles S. Johnson, June 23, 1942, folder 4, box 35, SCHW Papers.

24. SCHW executive board meeting, April 16, 1940, folder 13, box 18, Braden Papers; Dorothy Stafford to Howard Lee, April 18, 1940, folder 2, box 35, SCHW Papers; William Mitch to Howard Lee, July 23, 1940, ibid. Dorothy Stafford requested that SCHW not make her letter public.

25. Alton Lawrence to SCHW executive board, September 13, 1941, folder 235, box 19, SCEF Papers. Lawrence received self-addressed postcards that had been sent out with his memo in favor of Nashville. Minutes, SCHW board meeting, October 31, 1941, folder 5, box 18, Braden Papers. "Human Welfare Conference May Move to New Orleans," *New Orleans Times-Picayune*, August 16, 1946, in folder 16, box 1, SCEF Papers.

26. Executive board meeting, August 2, 1941, folder 7, box 31, SCHW Papers; see other letterhead in 1941. One cannot rely on letterhead for exact months of transitions, however, as SCHW hesitated to change stationery because of its precarious financial situation.

27. John B. Thompson to SCHW executive board, January 16, 1942, folder 235, box 19, SCEF Papers. Dombrowski's union card located in folder 2, box 17, Braden

Papers; Anthony P. Dunbar, *Against the Grain: Southern Radicals and Prophets* (Charlottesville: University Press of Virginia, 1981), 217.

28. James Dombrowski to Virginia Durr, October 28, 1940, folder 7, box 31, SCHW Papers; *Christian Century*, December 7, 1938, p. 1520.

29. James Dombrowski to Virginia Durr, October 28, 1940, folder 7, box 31, SCHW Papers; Paul R. Christopher to James Dombrowski, August 13, 1942, folder 231, box 19, SCEF Papers; "Report on Conditions in Nashville [to Highlander Folk School]," January 1, 1941, folder 2, box 17, Braden Papers; "Report on Tennessee Conditions," ibid.

30. "Biographical material, 1897, on James Anderson Dombrowski," folder 1, box 17, Braden Papers; Dombrowski to Harold W. Stokes, President of Louisiana State University in 1949, April 7, 1949, "Segregation in Education" folder, box 8, SCEF Papers; Dunbar, *Against the Grain*, reviewed by Thomas A Krueger in *Journal of American History*, 69 (June 1982), 199–200; James Dombrowski, *The Early Days of Christian Socialism in America* (New York: Columbia University Press, 1936), vii. After 1946, when the newly instituted Southern Conference Educational Fund made integrated education its major goal, Dombrowski many times used his religious, educational, and southern background to try and persuade key officials like Harold Stokes to integrate white universities.

31. James Dombrowski, "Highlander Chairman Terms It School for 'Democratic Living,'" *Nashville Tennessean*, November 19, 1939; Dunbar, *Against the Grain*, 43–45; George Brown Tindall, *Emergence of the New South* (Baton Rouge: Louisiana State University Press, 1967), 633. See also Bill Moyers, "The Adventures of a Radical Hillbilly: An Interview with Myles Horton," *Appalachian Journal*, 9 (Summer 1982), 268, 273. For greater details of the Highlander Folk School see Frank Adams and Myles Horton, *Unearthing Seeds of Fire: The Idea of Highlander* (Winston-Salem, N.C.: John F. Blair, 1975). The most recent study on Highlander and Horton is John M. Glen, *Highlander: No Ordinary School, 1932–1962* (Lexington: University Press of Kentucky, 1988).

32. John B. Thompson to Dombrowski, January 19, 1942, folder 235, box 19, SCEF Papers; Dombrowski to Eleanor Roosevelt, March 6, 1942, folder 4, box 35, SCHW Papers; Clark Foreman to Eleanor Roosevelt, July 26, 1942, ibid. Dombrowski and Eleanor Roosevelt grew to be close friends. She sent him a picture of herself soon after he took the job with SCHW, and he said that he would place it on his office wall and "consider it one of my principal treasures."

33. Simon Gross of the Robert Marshall Civil Liberties Trust to Clark Foreman, May 19, 1942, folder 3, box 1, SCEF Papers; Dombrowski to Gross, June 9, 1942, ibid.

34. James Dombrowski to SCHW executive board, February/March 1942, folder 5, box 31, SCHW Papers; Moyers, "The Adventures of a Radical Hillbilly," 268.

35. Memo, Thompson to Virginia Durr, Foreman, John P. Davis, Dombrowski, January 18, 1942, folder 234, box 19, SCEF Papers.

36. *Proceedings of the Third Meeting of the Southern Conference for Human Welfare* (Nashville: SCHW, April 19–21, 1942), 2, 6. Copy of *Proceedings* in folder 84, box 4, SCEF Papers; "Southern Conference for Human Welfare, Some Achievements of the Liberal South in 1942," folder 5, box 35, SCHW Papers; "Members of the Executive Board," April 27, 1943, ibid.

37. "By-Laws of the Southern Conference for Human Welfare . . . Adopted April 21, 1942," folder 4, box 35, SCHW Papers; *Proceedings*, 6.

38. See chapter 7 for more details surrounding SCHW's creation of SCEF.

39. Foreman to Henry A. Wallace, October 4, 1946, folder 10, box 35, SCHW Papers; Irwin Klibaner, "The Southern Conference Educational Fund: A History" (Ph.D. dissertation, University of Wisconsin, 1971), 243.

40. Dombrowski to Williams, October 15, 1958, folder 5, box 17, Braden Papers; Dombrowski to Robert Palmer, November 3, 1960, microfilm 306, reel 5, ibid.

41. Dombrowski to Albert E. Barnett, May 2, 1958, microfilm 306, reel 4, ibid.; Dombrowski to Charlotte H. Brown, May 1, 1960, ibid.; "Resolution Adopted by the Board of Directors of the SCEF," June 11, 1960, ibid; Wilhelmina M. Crosson to Carl and Anne Braden, Jan. 6, 1961, ibid. The board meeting in Atlanta on June 11, 1960, took place on Brown's birthday, and the officers adopted the resolution in honor of her and thanked her for years of service and support. The letter dated January 6, 1961, which the Bradens mailed to Dombrowski, included a note relating Brown's death.

42. Williams to Johnson, May 27, 1957, folder 5, box 17, ibid.; Dombrowski to Barnett, May 2, 1958, microfilm 306, reel 4, ibid.; Dombrowski to Williams, October 15, 1958, folder 5, box 17, ibid.

43. Williams to Barnett, March 5, 1958, ibid.; Dombrowski to Barnett, October 9, 1959, microfilm 306, reel 4, ibid.; Dombrowski to Williams, November 18, 1959, folder 13, box 17, ibid.

44. Telegram, Williams to Dombrowski, September 26, 1961, folder 7, box 21, ibid.; SCEF board to Williams, October 29, 1961, ibid.; Dombrowski to Edgar Love, November 14, 1962, microfilm 306, reel 5, ibid.; Love to Dombrowski, December 3, 1962, ibid. The board elected Williams as SCEF's president emeritus. Everett W. MacNair, informal notes on SCEF board meeting, April 26, 1963, ibid.

45. "Outline of the History of the Southern Conference," folder 18, box 1, SCEF Papers.

46. Treasurer's report, October 5, 1939, folder 1, box 35, SCHW Papers. SCHW paid H. C. Nixon $552 and George C. Stoney $150.

47. "From the desk of Lucy Randolph Mason" [to Foreman, 1940], folder 2, box 35, ibid.

48. Lee to Bingham, January 8, 1940, folder 240, box 20, SCEF Papers.

49. Howard Lee to Clark Foreman, April 22, 1940, folder 2, box 35, SCHW Papers.

50. Maury Maverick to Virginia Durr, January 16, 1940, folder 5, box 31, SCHW Papers; Joseph Gelders to Ethel Clyde, February 27, 1940, folder 2, box 35, ibid.; SCHW executive board meeting, April 16, 1940, folder 13, box 18, Braden Papers.

51. Financial statement as of June 15, 1940, folder 2, box 35, SCHW Papers; financial statement as of August 1, 1940 to February 15, 1941, ibid.

52. Alton Lawrence to Clark Foreman, June 3, 1941, folder 7, box 31, SCHW Papers; minutes, SCHW executive board meeting, August 2, 1941, ibid.; ibid., October 31, 1941, folder 5, box 18, Braden Papers.

53. Lucy Mason to Clark Foreman, February 29, 1940, folder 2, box 35, SCHW Papers; Alton Lawrence to Clark Foreman, June 3, 1941, folder 7, box 31, ibid.; Foreman to Lawrence, May 24, 1941, ibid.; minutes, executive board meeting, August 2, 1941, ibid.; Warren Ashby, *Frank Porter Graham: A Southern Liberal* (Winston-Salem, N.C.: John F. Blair, 1980), 142.

54. Gelders to Clark Foreman, September 11, 1941, folder 7, box 31, SCHW Papers; minutes, SCHW board meeting, October 31, 1941, folder 5, box 18, Braden Papers.

55. Clark Foreman to Lucy R. Mason, March 4, 1940, folder 2, box 35, SCHW Papers. SCHW kept names of its membership on 3 x 5 index cards with current addresses, telephone numbers, and information about an individual's membership to other organizations and contributions to SCHW. Only a small fraction, approximately 60, were found in folder 5, box 31, ibid.

56. Minutes, SCHW executive board meeting, August 2, 1941, folder 4, box 31, SCHW Papers. Virginia Durr, who served on the finance committee, reported that the Christian Social Justice Fund and the Whitney Fund had each given $1,000. Gerald Harris's farm committee had received $1,500 also, but records do not indicate which foundation contributed the money.

57. "Suggestions for Setting up State Committees of the Southern Conference for Human Welfare," n.d., folder 35, box 2, SCEF Papers.

58. See case of Margery De Leon, August 6, 1941, folder 7, box 31, SCHW Papers for Georgia affiliate; "Committee for Virginia, Affiliated with the Southern Conference for Human Welfare," n.d., unidentified folder, box 6, SCEF Papers. This pamphlet establishes that the Virginia committee organized January 22, 1942.

59. Each committee deserves its own history and awaits scholarly pursuit. For information on all committees see "Description," SCEF Papers.

60. Dombrowski to Gardner Jackson, February 21, 1942, folder 7, box 1, SCEF Papers; memo, Dombrowski to the Trustees of the Robert Marshall Fund, ibid.; Dombrowski to Durr, March 9, 1942, folder 234, box 19, ibid. SCHW applied for financial support from various foundations: Christian Social Justice Fund, William C. Whitney Foundation, American Peoples' Fund, Robert Marshall Civil Liberties Fund, all of New York City, and Julius Rosenwald Fund of Chicago. For letters and more information about contributions from foundations see folders 4, 6, 9, 10, box 1, SCEF Papers.

61. Clark Foreman to Elizabeth Gilman of the CSJF, March 14, 1942, folder 4, box 1, SCEF Papers; Dombrowski to William F. Cochran, May 4, 1942, ibid.; William F. Cochran to Dombrowski, May 26, 1942, ibid.

62. Dombrowski to Foreman, March 6, 1942, folder 4, box 35, SCHW Papers; Dombrowski to Foreman, March 25, 1942, folder 7, box 31, ibid.; Foreman to Dombrowski, March 30, 1942, folder 4, box 35, ibid.; "The Field Foundation, Inc.: Information," folder 12, box 17, Braden Papers.

63. "State of Tennessee, Charter of Incorporation . . . Southern Conference for Human Welfare," March 5, 1942, folder 8, box 35, SCHW Papers; Dombrowski to Foreman, March 6, 1942, folder 4, box 35, ibid.; Dombrowski to Foreman, October 7, 1942, ibid. Jennings Perry, Edward T. Ramsdell, H. C. Nixon, Julius Mark, Paul R. Christopher, and George N. Mayhew signed the charter.

64. Dombrowski to George Marshall, November 23, 1942, folder 7, box 1, SCEF Papers; "A Special Memorandum for the Marshall Fund," December 1942, folder 7, box 1, ibid.; "Summary of the Outstanding Achievements of the Southern Conference for Human Welfare during the Present Year," ibid. Same application to Christian Social Justice Fund, folder 4, box 1, SCEF Papers.

65. Minutes, SCHW executive board meeting, Chattanooga, August 30, 1942, folder 13, box 18, Braden Papers; "Summary of the Outstanding Achievements of the Southern Conference for Human Welfare during the Present Year," folder 7, box 1, SCEF Papers; Tarleton Collier and Dombrowski to "Dear Friend," 1943, folder 84, box 4, ibid.

66. Minutes, SCHW executive board meeting, Atlanta, February 7, 1943, folder 13, box 18, Braden Papers. The few members present discussed a few things informally and recommended their findings to the other board members by correspondence.

67. "Southern Conference for Human Welfare Plans for 1943," folder 4, box 1, SCEF Papers; Singal, *The War Within*, 293.

68. See chapter 5 on WWII for more details.

69. "Statement on the South and a Program for the Southern Conference," 1942, folder 1, box 1, SCEF Papers; Dombrowski to Gardner Jackson, September 5, 1942, folder 7, box 1, ibid.; John C. Granberg of the *San Antonio Emancipator* to Foreman, September 25, 1942, folder 4, box 35, SCHW Papers.

70. Foreman to Dombrowski, September 20, 1942, folder 4, box 35, SCHW Papers; *Southern Patriot*, 1 (December 1942), 1. Alton Lawrence had proposed that large orders would be requested by unions if bundle orders went for 25 cents, thereby making the publication affordable for workers and giving it more exposure. Dombrowski to Foreman, October 6, 1942, folder 4, box 35, SCHW Papers; Dombrowski to Foreman, October 7, 1942, ibid. Dombrowski studied the lists carefully, going over them state by state, and noted that SCHW had two mail files: (1) a file of 3 x 5 cards containing the names of persons who attended the

conferences and other contacts made in preparation for the conferences; (2) address plates of the Southern News Almanac list. The 4,700 names on cards and 6,400 names on plates totaled over 11,000. See "Analysis of SCHW Mailing Lists, Oct. 6, 1942," folder 11, box 1, SCEF Papers. For letters appealing for subscribers to the *Southern Patriot,* see folder 84, box 4, SCEF Papers.

71. Mrs. F. R. Earnshaw to *Southern Patriot,* n.d., "Poll Tax-Washington, D.C.," folder, box 11, SCEF Papers; E. [Erwin] to SCHW, December 20, 1943, folder 128, box 11, ibid.; Clark Foreman, chairman of the editorial board, to "Dear Friend," October 30, 1942, folder 84, box 4, ibid.; *Southern Patriot,* 1 (December 1942). Fred Sweet became the first editor of the *Southern Patriot,* and other board members included Will W. Alexander, Helen Fuller, Ira DeA. Reid.

72. Dombrowski to Gardner Jackson, May 15, 1943, folder 7, box 1, SCEF Papers. Dombrowski's estimate of SCHW membership stood between 12,000 and 15,000 in 1943. See Dombrowski to Milton C. Rose, Secretary at William C. Whitney Foundation, March 15, 1943, folder 10, box 1, SCEF Papers; Dombrowski to Edwin H. Embree, president of Julius Rosenwald Fund, April 13, 1943, folder 9, box 1, ibid.

73. "Financial Statement as of December 31, 1944," folder 5, box 1, SCEF Papers.

74. "Nashville Office, Southern Conference for Human Welfare, Summary of Receipts and Disbursements—January 1 through December 31, 1945," folder 18, box 1, SCEF Papers. In 1945 Alabama, Florida, Georgia, North Carolina, Tennessee, Virginia, Washington, D.C., and New York made the list of SCHW state committees or affiliated chapters.

75. " 'Lend a Hand for Dixieland,' " *New York Post,* August 29, 1946, in folder 10, box 35, SCHW Papers. A copy of the campaign song is included in appendix; *New York Times,* September 19, 1946, p. 17, ibid., September 20, 1946, p. 27. SCHW's records do not reveal the total amount of all the gatherings, and the *Times* does not include other coverage.

76. Minutes, SCHW board meeting, Richmond, Va., September 26, 1946, folder 6, box 18, Braden Papers. It does not seem reasonable that the board could justify paying Bancroft $6,000 while it had raised Dombrowski's salary to only $4,999.91 as administrator of both SCHW and SCEF. Dombrowski informed Bancroft of SCHW's precarious finances. Document 016312, October 1946, folder 3, box 18, ibid. Foreman and Dombrowski may have believed McKaine would no longer have anything to do with the Conference, and McKaine may have even said so, but he did participate in the November 1946 convention.

77. Minutes, SCHW board meeting, Nashville, May 28, 1946, folder 6, box 18, Braden Papers; Foreman to Lucy Mason, October 7, 1946, folder 3, box 18, ibid.; minutes, SCHW board meeting, December 1, 1946, folder 6, box 18, ibid.; Foreman to Dombrowski, October 3, 1946, folder 10, box 35, SCHW Papers; minutes, NCAPT, Washington, D.C., January 2, 1949, folder 6, box 31, ibid.; Jennings Perry to Dombrowski, January 3, 1947, folder 1, box 36, ibid.

78. Dombrowski to Foreman, October 25, 1946, folder 3, box 18, Braden Papers; Financial Records (1946–1948), folder 100, box 8, SCEF Papers, show the following income for 1946 by month:

Jan.	$ 577.41	July	$25,587.14
Feb.	7,930.07	Aug.	5,265.58
March	8,993.10	Sept.	15,548.38
April	11,111.62	Oct.	24,405.90
May	13,647.87	Nov.	9,770.53
June	10,932.31	Dec.	10,902.39

SCHW did not indicate which funds came through SCEF for the entire year, but from July to December, according to Dombrowski's later report, it took in over $34,000. Between these records and a report Dombrowski prepared in December 1946 a discrepancy shows up: total for the above, $144,222.98; the amount in Dombrowski's report, $116,844.97. See memo, Dombrowski to SCHW board, re: finances-analysis of revenues 1946, December 24, 1946, folder 11, box 35, SCHW Papers. Krueger, *And Promises to Keep,* 144, uses the $116,844.97.

79. My discussion of the Columbia, Tennessee, race riot is included in chapter 6. Dombrowski to Foreman, November 6, 1947, folder 3, box 18, Braden Papers; minutes, SCEF board meeting, January 30, 1948, November 21, 1948, folder 2, box 22, ibid.

80. "Southern Conference Educational Fund Summary, Auditor's Report, 1947," folder 2, box 22, Braden Papers; see chapter 7 for information on the loss of SCEF's tax exemption.

81. Dombrowski to Bethune, June 23, 1950, Dec. 4, 1950, microfilm 306, reel 4, Braden Papers; Bethune to Dombrowski, January 16, 1951, ibid.

82. Contributions and Subscriptions, SCEF, year ending December 31, 1951, folder 2, box 22, Braden Papers; Dombrowski to Robert A. Childers of Childers Manufacturing Co., Houston, Tex., November 16, 1955, microfilm 306, reel 4, ibid. In 1955 Childers was SCEF treasurer.

83. Virginia Durr interviewed by William D. Barnard, 1974, p. 158, transcript in Columbia Oral History Collection (Columbia University, New York).

84. *Southern Patriot,* 14 (September 1956), 1, 4; Aubrey Williams to C. K. Steele, December 20, 1956, microfilm 306, reel 5, Braden Papers.

85. See John Finnegan (a student at Midwood High School in Brooklyn) to SCHW, November 18, 1943, folder 134, box 11, SCEF Papers; Alfred Young of N.Y. to SCHW, n.d., ibid.; Dombrowski to Young, November 29, 1943, ibid.

86. "For Your Children, Too," 1945–1946, box 7, SCEF Papers; "Look Him in the Eye," 1945–1946, ibid.; Claude A. Taylor of Oakland, Calif. to James Dombrowski, January 4, 1944, folder 134, box 11, SCEF Papers; Opal Sargent (Mrs. H. M. Sargent) of Stibnite, Idaho, to SCHW, January 5, 1944, ibid.

3. Alienation, Fear, and Red-baiting

1. Louise O. Charlton to Aubrey Williams, December 1938, folder 7, box 31, Southern Conference for Human Welfare (SCHW) Papers (Robert W. Woodruff Library, Atlanta University, Ga.); *Emancipator,* 1 (March 1939), 15; Thomas A. Krueger, *And Promises to Keep: The Southern Conference for Human Welfare, 1938–1948* (Nashville: Vanderbilt University Press, 1967), 36–37; Charles H. Martin, "The Rise and Fall of Popular Front Liberalism in the South: The Southern Conference for Human Welfare, 1938–1948," *Perspectives on the American South,* 3 (1985), 119–44. Keeping in mind Hosea Hudson's observation about tensions between educated and noneducated blacks in the Birmingham National Association for the Advancement of Colored People (NAACP) in the 1930s, one has to believe that class also created strains within SCHW. See Nell Irvin Painter, *The Narrative of Hosea Hudson: His Life as a Negro Communist in the South* (Cambridge, Mass.: Harvard University Press, 1979), 271.

2. Palmer Weber interview with Linda Reed, November 13, 1983, transcript, Alderman Library (University of Virginia, Charlottesville); Warren Ashby, *Frank Porter Graham: A Southern Liberal* (Winston-Salem, N.C.: John F. Blair, 1980), 160.

3. *Report of Proceedings of the Southern Conference for Human Welfare* (Birmingham, Ala.: n.p., November 20–23, 1938), 13–22. Thomas Krueger argues that SCHW, concerned with the fear of running off members if it pressed too strongly

for racial equality, was not serious about the social equality for African Americans in the South. The basis of the argument is that white conferees feared that if they were too insistent on integration, members who lacked a mutual concern would be alienated and disassociate themselves from SCHW despite its other endeavors. Thomas Krueger argues in *And Promises to Keep*, 29–30, 148. I disagree with Krueger's assessment, given the various SCHW resolutions addressing racial issues.

4. "Interracial. A composite report of all resolutions of the Panel on Interracial Groups was submitted by the Resolutions Committee.

To urge the positive extension of the franchise to all our citizens of proper educational qualifications, in primaries and general elections;

To urge the abolition of poll-taxes as a prerequisite to voting;

To endorse and support federal and state anti-lynching legislation;

To oppose the practice of wage differentials between racial groups;

To recommend that appropriations for public education be based upon school populations and that we give encouragement to every effort for adult education for all racial groups;

That interracial meetings in the future be characterized by sincerity, understanding and intelligence;

To recommend that adequate appropriations be made by the states for negro graduate work in Southern state-supported negro institutions."

Report of Proceedings, 14; speech of Walter White, executive secretary of the NAACP, annual conference, July 7, 1939, NAACP Papers, microfilm reel 10 (Indiana University Library, Bloomington).

5. Gunnar Myrdal, *An American Dilemma: The Negro Problem and Modern Democracy* (New York: Harper & Brothers, 1944), 879–907.

6. Ibid., 469, 470.

7. Thus, Krueger's perception of the SCHW simply emphasizes the precaution that the new organization took to try and convince the white southern majority that equality for all could work.

8. Louise O. Charlton to Aubrey Williams, September 20, 1938, folder 7, box 31, SCHW Papers.

9. W. C. Henson to Virginia Durr, November 23, 1938, folder 7, box 31, ibid.

10. "Intelligent Discussion vs. Social Hand Holding," unidentified newspaper clipping, November 1938, folder 78, Frank Porter Graham (FPG) Papers, Southern Historical Collection (University of North Carolina, Chapel Hill); Clarence Poe to Frank Graham, December 10, 1938, folder 80, ibid.; Harvard Sitkoff, *A New Deal for Blacks: The Emergence of Civil Rights as a National Issue*, Vol. I: *The Depression Decade* (New York: Oxford University Press, 1978), 9–10; Morton Sosna, *In Search of the Silent South: Southern Liberals and the Race Issue* (New York: Columbia University Press, 1977), 185. Mark Ethridge and Virginius Dabney, for example, could not support desegregation; Joseph Gelders, Lucy Mason, Virginia Durr, Foreman, Graham, and Dombrowski wholeheartedly denounced segregation. Ethridge revealed his views in a speech he delivered, "America's Obligation to Its Negro Citizens," August 1937, esp. p. 11, at the fourth Southwide Conference on Education and Race Relations, Blue Ridge, North Carolina. The Commission on Interracial Cooperation made it available through its bulletins on race relations. See chapter 7, note 33, for more on moderates.

11. O. L. Browne to Frank Graham, November 25, 1938, folder 78, FPG Papers; unidentified report, 1938, folder 76, ibid.; L. A. Crowell, Jr., to Frank Graham, December 1, 1938, folder 79, ibid.

12. *Christian Century*, December 7, 1938, pp. 1520–21.

13. Frank Graham to L. A. Crowell, Jr., December 22, 1938, folder 83, FPG Papers.

14. Louise O. Charlton to Frank Graham, November 26, 1938, folder 78, FPG Papers; Earl Long to Frank Graham, November 26, 1938, ibid.; Clara G. Bruce to Graham, December 2, 1938, folder 79, ibid.; Norman Thomas to Graham, December 22, 1938, folder 83, ibid.; Margaret Sanger to Graham, December 12, 1938, folder 80, ibid.; Louise O. Charlton to Aubrey Williams, December 1938, folder 7, box 31, SCHW Papers.

15. Margaret Sanger to Graham, December 12, 1938, folder 80, FPG Papers; Norman Thomas to Graham, December 22, 1938, folder 83, ibid.; *Report of Proceedings*, 20.

16. Clara B. Bruce, executive secretary of the National Council of Negro Women, to Graham, December 2, 1938, folder 79, FPG Papers.

17. George Brown Tindall, *The Emergence of the New South, 1913–1945* (Baton Rouge: Louisiana State University Press, 1967), 583–86.

18. Howard W. Odum to James A. Dombrowski, November 13, 1952, microfilm reel 4, Carl and Anne Braden Papers (State Historical Society, Madison, Wis.); Tindall, *Emergence of the New South*, 586; Krueger, *And Promises to Keep*, 24–25.

19. Telegram, Howard W. Odum to Graham, November 21, 1938, folder 78, FPG Papers.

20. Mark Ethridge to Graham, November 30, 1938, folder 78, FPG Papers; Wilma Dykeman and James Stokely, *Seeds of Southern Change: The Life of Will Alexander* (Chicago: University of Chicago Press, 1962), 137, 282–85; Tindall, *Emergence of the New South*, 719–20; Krueger, *And Promises to Keep*, 119–20; Sitkoff, *New Deal for Blacks*, 23. Sitkoff informs us that the CIC shunned controversy at all costs, especially refusing to insist on racial equality. Officially the Southern Conference as an organization said that SRC was too moderate, but individuals such as Will Alexander and others served on the board of SRC and worked with the SCHW at the same time, illustrating in large measure how the Conference wavered on advocating total elimination of segregation. Although many members of the Conference agreed that segregation was morally wrong, those within this segment did not consent to an all-out campaign against it.

21. "Welfare Officials No Reds, Dr. Raper," *Atlanta Constitution*, November 27, 1938, p. 6–A; Krueger, *And Promises to Keep*, 64–65. Raper, who often worked with Ira DeA. Reid, a noted black sociologist, wrote several publications on the southern economic problems and the plight of the tenant farmer: Arthur F. Raper and Ira DeA. Reid, *Sharecroppers All* (Chapel Hill: University of North Carolina Press, 1941); Arthur Raper and Ira DeA. Reid, "Old Conflicts in the New South," *Virginia Quarterly Review*, 16 (Spring 1940), 218–29.

22. Lucy Randolph Mason, *To Win These Rights: A Personal Story of the CIO in the South* (New York: Harper & Brothers, 1952), 19–20.

23. John Hope Franklin to Linda Reed, May 16, 1984, letter in possession of author; Sitkoff, *New Deal for Blacks*, 154.

24. Hubert Baugh to Graham, November 26, 1938, folder 78, FPG Papers. No evidence in Graham's correspondence indicates a reply to Baugh. Baugh probably had in mind Gelders and Robert Hall, both active in CPUSA in Birmingham in 1938, but the SCHW records do not bear out any large financial contributions from them.

25. George Londa to Mr. (Bruce) Bliven of the *New Republic*, November 27, 1938, personal correspondence, 1938–1939 folder, Virginia Foster Durr Papers (Alabama Department of Archives and History, Montgomery). Hereinafter VFD Papers. These papers do not include box numbers. Londa's article never appeared in the *New Republic*.

26. Londa to Bliven, November 27, 1938, VFD Papers; Louise O. Charlton to Aubrey Williams, December 1938, folder 7, box 31, SCHW Papers.

27. Londa to Bliven, November 27, 1938, VFD Papers; "Welfare Officials No Reds, Dr. Raper," *Atlanta Constitution*, November 27, 1938, p. 6–A; Krueger, *And Promises to Keep*, 37–39.

28. Francis P. Miller to Frank Graham, December 21, 1938, folder 82, FPG Papers; John Salmond, *A Southern Rebel: The Life and Times of Aubrey Willis Williams, 1890–1965* (Chapel Hill: University of North Carolina Press, 1983), 195; Bankhead quotation from Krueger, *And Promises to Keep*, 38; Cicero Alvin Hughes, "Toward a Black United Front: The National Negro Congress Movement" (Ph.D. dissertation, Ohio University, 1982), 63–64, 113, 241.

29. Hill, for example, agreed with Aubrey Williams, a strong supporter of SCHW, on many issues and voted in his favor for becoming head of the Rural Electrification Administration in 1945 when most southern senators would not. For information on later involvement of Senator Pepper, particularly in the abolition of the poll tax, see SCHW and SCEF Papers, Atlanta and Tuskegee, respectively. See Salmond, *Southern Rebel*, 179–97; Ashby, *Frank Porter Graham*, 161; Krueger, *And Promises to Keep*, 38. Pepper, elected to the Senate in 1936, was defeated for reelection in 1950, but he later returned to the Congress as Florida representative, and he still served in that capacity for the remainder of his life. He died May 30, 1989.

30. H. C. Nixon to Virginia Foster Durr, November 29, 1939, folder 7, box 31, SCHW Papers.

31. *Report of Proceedings*, 30.

32. John B. Thompson to Virginia Durr, April 28, 1941, folder 5, box 34, SCHW Papers.

33. Raper and Reid, "Old Conflicts in the New South," 225, 228.

34. Sara Alpern, *Freda Kirchway: A Woman of THE NATION* (Cambridge, Mass.: Harvard University Press, 1987), 179.

35. H. C. Nixon to Virginia Durr, November 29, 1939, folder 7, box 31, SCHW Papers.

36. U.S. Congress, House, Special Committee on Un-American Activities, *Investigation of Un-American Propaganda Activities in the United States*, 76 Cong., 1 sess. (13 vols., Washington, D.C.: GPO, 1939–1940), VII, 4482–84; File 66-3286-641, "List of Subjects on which Index Cards Have Been Destroyed," 1953–1955, Federal Bureau of Investigation, U.S. Department of Justice (Freedom of Information Act photocopies in author's possession). List included Communist party, National Negro Congress, Southern Conference for Human Welfare, and many others. If the FBI destroyed the cards in the 1950s, it is possible that the cards had been started in the 1930s.

37. U.S. Congress, House, Special Committee on Un-American Activities, *Investigation of Un-American Propaganda Activities*, VII, 4765–67.

38. Bingham to Lee, November 16, 1939, folder 240, box 20, SCEF Papers; W. T. Couch to Virginia Durr, March 21, 1940, folder 5, box 31, SCHW Papers.

39. The case of Margery De Leon, dismissed War Department Employee, August 6, 1941, folder 7, box 31, SCHW Papers; Margaret Sirugo, Chairman of the Defense Committee, to Joseph Gelders, October 19, 1941, ibid.

40. See details of physical attack on Gelders in chapter 1.

41. Laurent Frantz to National Federation for Constitutional Liberties, September 11, 1941, folder 7, box 31, SCHW Papers.

42. See Frances Fox Piven and Richard A. Cloward, *Poor People's Movements: Why They Succeed, How They Fail* (New York: Pantheon, 1977), who argue that protest movements have a limited time frame in which to make their impact.

43. *Vanderbilt Alumnus*, April 1942, 16.

44. Dombrowski to Simon Gross, May 21, 1942, folder 3, box 1, SCEF Papers; William R. Cochran to Dombrowski, May 26, 1942, folder 4, box 1, ibid.; Foreman to Dombrowski, May 28, 1942, folder 4, box 35, SCHW Papers. Correspondence

between McCallister, Baldwin, Dombrowski, and Foreman continued for several months, until September. Foreman sent Dombrowski and later other board members their letters.

45. Frank McCallister to Foreman, May 4, 1942, folder 4, box 35, SCHW Papers; Foreman to Dombrowski, May 19, 1942, folder 4, box 35, ibid.; Mason to Baldwin, July 4, 1942, folder 4, box 35, ibid. See William H. Harris, "A. Philip Randolph as a Charismatic Leader, 1925–1941," *Journal of Negro History*, 64 (Fall 1979), 309; Hughes, "Toward a Black United Front," 113, 241, on Davis's and Randolph's differences within NNC. Baldwin had suspected Gelders (not mentioned in the 1942 summer) of Communist affiliation since 1938; Baldwin to Mrs. Clifford (Virginia) Durr, July 27, 1938, folder 7, box 31, SCHW Papers.

46. Foreman to Dombrowski, May 19, 1942, folder 4, box 35, SCHW Papers. Minutes of executive board meeting of SCHW, Chattanooga, Tenn., August 30, 1942, folder 13, box 18, Braden Papers.

47. Foreman to Baldwin, May 19, 1942, folder 4, box 35, SCHW Papers; Foreman to Eleanor Roosevelt, July 26, 1942, ibid.; Gross to Dombrowski, May 19, 1942, folder 3, box 1, SCEF Papers; Dombrowski to Gross, June 9, 1942, ibid.

48. Foreman to Baldwin, May 26, 1942, folder 4, box 35, SCHW Papers; Baldwin to Foreman, May 29, 1942, ibid.

49. Dombrowski to Foreman, May 25, 1942, folder 4, box 35, SCHW Papers; Dombrowski to Baldwin, May 27, 1942, ibid. Baldwin implied that Alva Taylor, too, was a Communist but never openly accused him as he did the others. See Anthony P. Dunbar, *Against the Grain: Southern Radicals and Prophets* (Charlottesville: University Press of Virginia, 1981), 205, 211, 242, for details about Taylor, who was a federal labor mediator in 1942.

50. Foreman to Bishop Paul Kern, May 16, 1942, folder 4, box 35, SCHW Papers; Mason to Baldwin, May 28, 1942, folder 4, box 35, ibid.

51. Clark Foreman to McCallister, May 1942, folder 4, box 35, SCHW Papers.

52. Mason to Baldwin, July 4, 1942, folder 4, box 35, ibid.

53. Foreman to McCallister, May 1942, folder 4, box 35, ibid.

54. Gerald Harris (president, Farmers' Educational and Co-Operative Union of America, Alabama division) to Foreman, June 5, 1942, folder 4, box 35, ibid.; Atlanta University President Rufus Clement to Foreman, June 5, 1942, folder 4, box 35, ibid.; Mason to Baldwin, July 4, 1942, ibid. The question of Davis's possible Communist party membership remains unanswered. Mark Naison asserts that Davis may have been secretly a Party member and cites evidence by Richard Wright biographers that when Davis dealt with Wright, an avowed Communist, he was acting for the Party. See Mark Naison, *Communists in Harlem during the Depression* (Urbana: University of Illinois Press, 1983), 178, 190n.

55. Mason to Baldwin, May 28, 1942, folder 4, box 35, SCHW Papers.

56. Mason to Baldwin, July 4, 1942, folder 4, box 35, ibid. Mason defended all the Baldwin-accused persons, Thompson, Davis, Dombrowski, and Gerald Harris. See also John Hope Franklin to Linda Reed, May 16, 1984, possession of the author. Franklin was a member of the SCHW during the 1940s.

57. Foreman to McCallister, June 8, 1942, folder 4, box 35, SCHW Papers; McCallister to Foreman, July 25, 1942, ibid.

58. Foreman to Baldwin, August 4, 1942, folder 4, box 35, ibid. For the mention of McCallister in May, see Foreman to Baldwin, May 19, 1942, ibid.

59. Gardner Jackson to Foreman, June 2, 1942, folder 4, box 35, ibid. Having received the Foreman and Baldwin correspondence that Foreman had earlier sent him, Gardner Jackson sent a copy of his letter from Baldwin to Foreman.

60. Gardner Jackson to Roger Baldwin, June 2, 1942, folder 4, box 35, ibid.

61. Gardner Jackson to Roger Baldwin, June 2, 1942, folder 4, box 35, ibid. Genuine isolationists, SCHW leaders had supported World II only after the Japanese had attacked Pearl Harbor. See my discussion in chapter 1.

62. Baldwin to Foreman, July 14, 1942, folder 4, box 35, SCHW Papers; Mason to Baldwin, July 14, 1942, ibid.

63. Minutes of executive board meeting of SCHW, Chattanooga, Tenn., August 30, 1942, folder 13, box 18, Braden Papers; Alva W. Taylor to William F. Cochran, September 4, 1942, folder 4, box 1, SCEF Papers.

64. Eleanor Roosevelt to Baldwin, June 23, 1942, folder 4, box 35, SCHW Papers; Baldwin to Eleanor Roosevelt, June 26, ibid.

65. Foreman to Eleanor Roosevelt, July 9, 1942, folder 4, box 35, SCHW Papers; Foreman to Baldwin, August 4, 1942, ibid.; Baldwin to Foreman, September 2, 1942, ibid.

66. Foreman to Eleanor Roosevelt, July 9, 1942, folder 4, box 35, SCHW Papers. I have not checked health records to see if Baldwin was in fact ill.

67. Baldwin to Foreman, September 2, 1942, folder 4, box 35, SCHW Papers; Alva W. Taylor to William F. Cochran, September 4, 1942, folder 4, box 1, SCEF Papers; Dombrowski to Gardner Jackson, September 5, 1942, folder 7, box 1, ibid.

68. Dombrowski to Foreman, September 25, 1942, folder 4, box 35, SCHW Papers; "Former Highlander School Head Silent on Dies Charges," *Nashville Banner*, September 25, 1942, clipping in ibid.

69. Dombrowski to Foreman, June 2, 1942, folder 4, box 35, SCHW Papers; Foreman to Ralph McDonald, June 9, 1942, ibid.; Foreman to Charles S. Johnson, June 23, 1942, ibid.

4. Making Poll Tax a National Issue

1. National Committee to Abolish the Poll Tax, "Poll Tax Fact Sheet," n.d., folder 126, box 11, Southern Conference Educational (SCEF) Papers (Hollis Burke Frissell Library, Tuskegee, Ala.); Eleanor Bontecou, *The Poll Tax* (Washington, D.C: American Association of University Women, 1942), 9–13; Frederic D. Ogden, *The Poll Tax in the South* (University: University of Alabama Press, 1958), 1–31. See also Steven F. Lawson, *Black Ballots: Voting Rights in the South, 1944–1969* (New York: Columbia University Press, 1976), esp. 55–85.

2. "Joe" (Gelders) to Virginia Foster Durr, January 3, 1939, folder 7, box 31, Southern Conference for Human Welfare (SCHW) Papers (Robert W. Woodruff Library, Atlanta University Center).

3. Joseph Gelders to Frank Graham, September 20, 1939, folder 7, box 31, ibid.; "Outline of the History of the Southern Conference," folder 18, box 1, SCEF Papers; Thomas A. Krueger, *And Promises to Keep: The Southern Conference for Human Welfare, 1938–1948* (Nashville: Vanderbilt University Press, 1967), 42.

4. Gelders to Graham, September 20, 1939, folder 7, box 31, SCHW Papers.

5. James J. Morrison to Joseph Gelders, July 10, 1939, folder 6, box 31, ibid.

6. Gelders to Virginia Durr, January 3, 1939, folder 7, box 31, ibid.; Ogden, *Poll Tax in the South*, 272–73.

7. *Congressional Record: Proceedings and Debates of the 76th Congress, First Session* (Washington, D.C.: GPO, 1939), vol. 84, pt. 14, appendix, pp. 4123–24; Lee E. Geyer, "The Poll Tax: Says Democracy," n.d., folder 10, box 32, SCHW Papers.

8. Gelders to Graham, September 20, 1939, folder 7, box 31, SCHW Papers.

9. Gelders to Lincoln Kirstein, February 27, 1940, folder 2, box 35, SCHW Papers; Gelders to George Marshall, February 27, 1940, folder 1, box 32, ibid.; Gelders to American Civil Liberties Union, March 1, 1940, ibid.; Gelders to W. C. Curott of Corpus Christi, Texas, March 16, 1940, ibid. Gelders sent letters to American Federation of Labor, Congress of Industrial Organizations, NAACP, National Urban League, and other groups.

10. Gelders to W. C. Curott, March 16, 1940, folder 1, box 32, SCHW Papers; Margot Gayle to Virginia Durr, July 30, 1940, folder 7, box 31, and Gelders to Durr, July 17, 1940, ibid. The envelopes were sealed with anti-poll-tax stamps. The organization also had poll tax buttons that read "100% Democracy/Abolish Poll Tax."

11. Telegram, Walter White to Gelders, March 11, 1940, folder 1, box 32, SCHW Papers; Roy Wilkins to Gelders, March 13, 1940, ibid.; Gelders to Wilkins, March 15, 1940, ibid.

12. Couch to Virginia Durr, March 21, 1940, folder 5, box 31, SCHW Papers; Barry Bingham to Virginia Durr, May 27, 1940, folder 5, box 34, ibid.; Robin Davis Gibran Kelley, "Hammer n' hoe: Black Radicalism and the Communist Party in Alabama, 1929–1941" (Ph.D. dissertation, University of California, Los Angeles, 1987), 365–74, 500, 543–44, 589. Kelley's work gives a fuller treatment of Gelders's life and points out that the Communist party aligned closely with the New Dealers during the 1930s and 1940s, and that this accounts for Gelders's interest in it. Gelders's hopes blended well with SCHW's New Deal-like agenda.

13. Howard Lee to Congressman Lee E. Geyer, February 19, 1940, folder 1, box 32, SCHW Papers; Geyer to Judge W. C. Hueston, February 27, 1940, folder 1, box 32, ibid. This same letter went to several other persons and organizations. Gelders to (John) Carson, February 27, 1940, ibid.

14. Gelders to Ethel Clyde, February 27, 1940, folder 2, box 35, SCHW Papers; Gelders to George Marshall of the Marshall Fund, February 27, 1940, folder 1, box 32, ibid.

15. "History of the National Committee to Abolish the Poll Tax," n.d., folder 6, box 33, SCHW Papers; folder 5, box 34, ibid. contains a blank sheet of stationery that identifies the officers and sponsors of the National Committee to Abolish the Poll Tax; *Congressional Record: Proceedings and Debates of the 77th Congress, Second Session* (Washington D.C.: GPO, 1942), A2561 on Geyer's death; Ogden, *Poll Tax in the South*, 250.

16. W. M. Kemper (Governor Price's executive assistant) to Virginia Durr, November 17, 1938, folder 8, box 31, SCHW Papers; Virginia Durr to Ann Durr, July 1940, family and political correspondence folder, Virginia Foster Durr Papers; *Birmingham News*, March 26, 1976, p. 19; Virginia Foster Durr interview with Linda Reed, December 29, 1982, transcript Lilly Library (Indiana University, Bloomington). Durr has told her life's story also in *Outside the Magic Circle: The Autobiography of Virginia Foster Durr*, ed. by Hollinger F. Barnard (University: University of Alabama Press, 1985).

17. *Democracy for Dixie*, 1 (June 1941), a news and information bulletin published by the Southern Electoral Reform League, folder 8, box 31, SCHW Papers; Ogden, *Poll Tax in the South*, 250–51.

18. Gelders to Virginia Durr, n.d., folder 7, box 31, SCHW Papers.

19. Gelders to Virginia Durr, August 6, 1940, folder 7, box 31, ibid.

20. Ibid.; Gelders to Durr, November 11, 1940, folder 7, box 31, ibid.

21. Eleanor Bontecou to Virginia Durr, August 6, 1940, folder 5, box 31, SCHW Papers; Ogden, *Poll Tax in the South*, 272–73.

22. *The Poll Tax* (n.p.: SCHW, 1940), contents: Frank Graham, "Challenge for Democracy"; Barry Bingham, "Americans without Votes"; George C. Stoney (member of staff of the "Suffrage in the South," a project under the auspices of the New School for Social Research), "Tool of State Machines"; James J. Morrison, "Obstructing the Constitution"; H. C. Nixon, "Influences of the Past"; and Tarleton Collier (vice-president of Georgia SCHW affiliate), "Southerners for Suffrage Reform." Pamphlet may be found in folder 1, box 32, SCHW Papers.

23. Eleanor Bontecou to Clark Foreman, July 20, 1940, folder 2, box 35, SCHW Papers. Stoney reported that the practice of peonage, forced labor without pay

because of owed debt, continued in McIntosh County sawmills. On another note of interest, however, Stoney witnessed that McIntosh County had higher than average agricultural wages than the rest of central Georgia because "apparently . . . most of the negroes in this county are small landowners" and tended to pay their laborers well. The advisory research committee of the New School for Social Research consisted of H. C. Nixon, Arthur Raper, C. Vann Woodward, Ralph Bunche, Francis W. Coker, and Max Lerner.

24. Eleanor Bontecou to Clark Foreman, July 20, 1940, folder 2, box 35, ibid.

25. Gayle to Virginia Durr, July 30, 1940, folder 7, box 31, SCHW Papers; Bernard Borah to Virginia Durr, September 20, 1940, ibid.; Gayle to Virginia Durr, October 5, 1940, ibid.; Barry Bingham to V. Durr, November 18, 1940, ibid.; *Congressional Record: Proceedings and Debates of the 76th Congress, Third Session* (Washington D.C.: GPO, 1941), vol. 86, pt. 17, appendix 5236, 5247, 5310. Borah's group had received a copy of the women's statement and wrote Durr to commend the effort.

26. Minutes, SCHW executive board meeting, August 2, 1941, folder 7, box 31, SCHW Papers. Virginia Durr remained one of the few who continued to work with Gelders. In 1942 when SCHW prepared for its biennial meeting, Durr wanted Gelders to be a civil rights and civil liberties panelist, but James Dombrowski, the executive secretary, thought less of the suggestion. Gelders, who seldom worked with SCHW after 1941, did not appear with the panel. See Virginia Durr to James Dombrowski, March 6, 1942, folder 234, box 19, SCEF Papers; Dombrowski to Durr, March 9, 1942, ibid.; *Proceedings of the Third Meeting of the Southern Conference for Human Welfare* (Nashville, Tenn,: SCHW, April 19–21, 1942).

27. Dombrowski to Foreman, March 14, 1942, folder 4, box 35, SCHW Papers; Foreman to Dombrowski, March 16, 1942, ibid.; Dombrowski to Foreman, March 17, 1942, ibid.; "Southern Conference Calls for Tax Removal to Aid War Effort," *Poll Tax Repealer*, 1 (April 1942). This one fold-out page of the *Repealer* is located in "National Committee to Abolish the Poll Tax, 1943–45" folder, group II, series A, box A410, National Association for the Advancement of Colored People (NAACP) Papers (Library of Congress, Washington, D.C.).

28. Catherine T. Freeland (Walter White's administrative assistant) to Virginia Durr, October 19, 1942, "National Committee to Abolish the Poll Tax, 1942" folder, ibid., NAACP Papers; Sylvia Beitscher (executive secretary of NCAPT) to Freeland, October 21, 1942, ibid.; NAACP News Release for NCAPT, November 20, 1942, ibid.; NAACP Telegram to President Franklin D. Roosevelt, ibid.; James J. Morrison to Senator John Overton, November 5, folder 6, box 31, SCHW Papers.

29. "A Plea for Democracy: The Anti-Poll Tax Bill," Speech of Hon. Claude Pepper of Florida in the Senate of the United States, November 21, 1942, copy in folder 132, box 11, SCEF Papers; Virginia Durr to James Dombrowski, June 22, 1943, folder 126, box 11, ibid.; NCAPT and SCHW started a Bundles for Bilbo Club in 1942 in which they sold a bundle of 100 *Repealers* for $1; the money would be used to "bundle Bilbo and his bully boys" in the poll tax states. See "Bundles for Bilbo," in *The Poll Tax Repealer*, 1 (December 1942), part of "NCAPT, 1943–1945" folder, box A410, NAACP Papers. See chapter 5 for details on SCHW's strategy to unseat Bilbo.

30. Congressman George H. Bender to James Dombrowski, June 9, 1943, folder 126, box 11, SCEF Papers; Dombrowski to Katherine Shryver (executive secretary of NCAPT), November 16, 1943, folder 125, box 11, ibid.; "The Anti-Poll Tax Bill— The Soldier Vote Bill, The Fight for Democracy," 1943, ibid.; NCAPT News Release, October 1944, ibid.; telegram, Jennings Perry to Virginia Durr, February 1, 1943, folder 8, box 31, SCHW Papers; "Chronology of Anti-Poll Tax Legislation in Congress [1939–1947]," folder 11, box 32, SCHW Papers; "Georgia Kills the Poll Tax," *The New Republic*, February 26, 1945, pp. 291–92.

31. Texas Senator W. Lee O'Daniel to "Dear Friend," (with 1943 material) folder 131, box 11, SCEF Papers. In several instances of racism conservatives equated intelligence with a person's ability to earn the money to pay the tax; their remarks resembled those of Henry Grady in the 1890s. See folders 130–34, box 11, ibid., for a bulk of letters against the NCAPT cause. The definitive study on the demise of Texas's all-white primaries is Darlene Clark Hine's *Black Victory: The Rise and Fall of the White Primary in Texas* (Millwood, N.Y.: KTO Press, 1979).

32. The constitution of the United States of America, Amendment XIV, Section 2, Section 5; NCAPT "1942 Election" material, folder 126, box 11 SCEF Papers; Report of Katherine Shryver to NCAPT executive board, September 28, 1943, folder 126, box 11, ibid.; *Why the Poll Tax Is a National Issue: The Poll Tax Repeal Handbook* (Washington, D.C.: NCAPT, September 1943), copy found in folder 127, box 11, ibid.; NCAPT form letter, November 2, 1943, folder 125, box 11, ibid. *The Southern Patriot*, 1 (October 1943). The seven poll tax states in 1942 were: Alabama, Arkansas, Georgia, Mississippi, South Carolina, Texas, and Virginia. NCAPT noted among the many poll-tax-related misfortunes that Mississippi, the poorest state in the union, required the highest poll tax, $2. Furthermore, poll-tax states were the poorest in per capita income.

33. "Kit" (Katherine Shryver of NCAPT) to Marge (Gelders, Joe Gelders's daughter), October 20, 1944, folder 125, box 11, SCEF Papers.

34. Herbert Aptheker, "South Carolina Poll Tax, 1737–1895," *Journal of Negro History*, 31 (April 1946), 131–39.

35. NCAPT appeal letter, December 22, 1942, "NCAPT, 1943–45" folder, box A410, NAACP Papers; minutes, NCAPT, Washington, D.C., January 2, 1949, folder 6, box 31, SCHW Papers; William Green (president of AFL) to Jennings Perry, January 18, 1949, folder 6, box 31, ibid.; A. F. Whitney (president of Brotherhood of Railroad Trainmen) to Perry, ibid.; Robert J. Silberstein (executive secretary of National Lawyers Guild) to Perry, January 28, 1949, ibid.; Walter White to Joseph H. B. Evans, January 28, 1949, ibid.; NCAPT minutes, February 2 and 9, 1949, ibid.; Claude Pepper to NCAPT, February 21, 1949, ibid. Like SCHW, NCAPT depended on individual and organizational contributions, and NCAPT also received a major share of its income from organized labor.

5. Southern Liberalism and the Search for Racial Justice during World War II

1. Walter White, "Decline of Southern Liberals," *Negro Digest*, 1 (January 1943), 43–46; Lee Finkle, "The Conservative Aims of Militant Rhetoric: Black Protest during World War II," *Journal of American History*, 60 (December 1973), 692–713.

2. Thomas Cripps, "Movies, Race, and World War II: *Tennessee Johnson* as an Anticipation of the Strategies of the Civil Rights Movement," *Prologue*, 14 (Summer 1982), 49–67; Harvard Sitkoff, *A New Deal for Blacks: The Emergence of Civil Rights as a National Issue*, Vol. I: *The Depression Decade* (New York: Oxford University Press, 1978), viii–ix, 58–59, 317–23. Historians specializing in race relations termed the 1930s and 1940s a "watershed" owing to national attention brought to civil rights issues.

3. John B. Thompson to SCHW executive board, January 16, 1942, folder 235, box 19, Southern Conference Educational Fund (SCEF) Papers (Hollis Burke Frissell Library, Tuskegee, Ala.); Thompson to Dombrowski, January 19, 1942, ibid.; Dombrowski to Gardner Jackson, February 21, 1942, folder 7, box 1, ibid.

4. "An Urgent Call to the People of the South," 1942, folder 5, box 31, Southern Conference for Human Welfare (SCHW) Papers (Robert W. Woodruff Library, Atlanta University Center).

5. John P. Davis to Dombrowski, March 10, 1942, folder 234, box 19, SCEF Papers; Sitkoff, *New Deal for Blacks*, 164. Martin Bauml Duberman, *Paul Robeson* (New York: Knopf, 1989) is the most recent scholarship on Robeson.

6. Later, when the organization would realize its many shortcomings, one regrettable awareness was its failure in its early years to attract and maintain a large grass-roots membership.

7. *Who's Who in America: A Biographical Dictionary of Notable Living Men and Women of the United States* (41 vols., Chicago: A.N. Marquis, 1899–), XX, 310; *Who's Who in Colored America: A Biographical Dictionary of Notable Living Persons of African Descent in America* (Brooklyn, N.Y.: Who's Who in Colored America, 1940), 53; Clarence Genu Newsome, "Mary McLeod Bethune in Religious Perspective: A Seminal Essay" (Ph.D. dissertation, Duke University 1982), 189–90, 191–92, 267; Mary McLeod Bethune, "Clarifying Our Vision with the Facts," *Journal of Negro History*, 23 (January 1938), 10–15; Mary McLeod Bethune, "My Secret Talks with FDR," *Ebony*, 4 (April 1949), 43–48.

8. John B. Thompson to Dombrowski, March 30, 1942, folder 234, box 19, SCEF Papers; Dombrowski to V. Durr, April 5, 1942, ibid.; Virginia Durr to Dombrowski, April 8, 1942, ibid.; Davis to Thompson, April 8, 1942, ibid.; Dombrowski to V. Durr, April 10, 1942, ibid.; Frank Graham, who was now with the National War Labor Board, to Foreman, May 1, 1942, folder 4, box 35, SCHW Papers.

Thompson admired Louis for donating the purses from both his knockout fights of January 9 and March 27, 1942, to the Naval Relief Fund, which provided aid for families of servicemen killed in action. Louis, born in a sharecropper's shack in Chambers County, Alabama, in 1914, had earned fame through professional boxing and became heavyweight champion in 1937. See Harry A. Ploski and James Williams, comps. and eds., *The Negro Almanac: A Reference Work on the Afro-American* (New York: John Wiley, 1983), 930, 953.

9. Memo, John B. Thompson to Virginia Durr, Foreman, John P. Davis, and Dombrowski, January 18, 1942, folder 234, box 19, SCEF Papers; Dombrowski to Thompson, March 15, 1942, ibid.; Dombrowski to Foreman, March 2, 1942, folder 4, box 35, SCHW Papers.

10. Dombrowski to Edwin R. Embree, President of Julius Rosenwald Fund, March 20, 1942, folder 9, box 1, SCEF Papers; "Report of Representation at the Third Meeting, Nashville, Tennessee, April 19–21, 1942," folder 232, box 19, SCEF Papers; Dombrowski to Simon Gross, May 21, 1942, folder 3, box 1, SCEF Papers. A note about SCHW, 1942, folder 4, box 35, SCHW Papers placed membership at about 1,000.

11. Thompson to V. Durr, April 7, 1942, folder 234, box 19, SCEF Papers; John P. Davis to Dombrowski, April 1942, folder 234, box 19, ibid.

12. Franklin D. Roosevelt to Frank P. Graham, honorary chairman, SCHW, March 28, 1942, in *Proceedings of the Third Meeting of the Southern Conference for Human Welfare* (Nashville: SCHW, April 19–21, 1942), 7. Copy of *Proceedings* in folder 84, box 4, SCEF Papers; telegram, Thompson to Franklin Roosevelt, April 20, 1942, in ibid., 8.

13. Paul R. Christopher to James Dombrowski, October 21, 1942, folder 247, box 20, SCEF Papers.

14. *Proceedings of the Third Meeting of the Southern Conference*, 6, 9–11, 12–13, 16, 17.

15. Memo, Dombrowski to trustees of the Robert Marshall Fund, 1942, folder 7, box 1, SCEF Papers; *Proceedings*, 6; *Nashville Tennessean*, April 19, 1942, pp. 1, 4, 8, 6–B.

16. Perhaps Graham and Bethune received empty boxes because as late as October 1942 Dombrowski wrote them explaining the delay in their getting the med-

als. The awards were not actually mailed to the recipients until December of that year. Graham to Foreman, May 1, 1942, folder 4, box 35, SCHW Papers; Dombrowski to Graham, September 29, 1942, folder 247, box 20, SCEF Papers; Dombrowski to Bethune, September 29, 1942, ibid.; Dombrowski to Bethune, December 11, 1942, ibid.; Dombrowski to Graham, December 14, 1942, ibid.

17. "Summary of the Outstanding Achievements of the Southern Conference for Human Welfare during the Present Year," 1942, folder 7, box 1, SCEF Papers; *Nashville Tennessean*, April 19, 1942, p. 6–B.

18. *Vanderbilt Alumnus*, April 1942, 16; Duberman, *Paul Robeson*, 258–59.

19. Bryce Holcomb, commissioner of conciliation, U.S. Department of Labor; Frederick B. Sweet, consumers division, Office of Price Administration; and Robert C. Weaver, chief, Negro Employment and Training Branch, Labor Division, War Production, showed up for the industrial production panel. David E. Lilienthal, chairman, Tennessee Valley Authority, sent a written statement. *Proceedings of the Third Meeting of the Southern Conference*, 6, 21.

Administration representatives on the agricultural production panel included: C. E. H. Daniel of the Farm Security Administration; Milo Perkins, executive director, Board of Economic Warfare; but M. L. Wilson, director of extension work, U.S. Department of Agriculture, sent a written statement. *Proceedings*, 23.

Bethune, director of the Division of Negro Affairs, National Youth Administration, and Eleanor Roosevelt were part of panel III, Youth and Training: Civilian and Military. Brigadier-General Frederick Osborn of the War Department sent a written statement. *Proceedings*, 27.

United States Attorney General Francis Biddle and Senator Claude Pepper of Florida sent written statements to the fourth panel on citizenship and civil liberties. *Proceedings*, 30.

20. *Proceedings*, 22–23.

21. Ibid., 22–23, 24–25; William H. Harris, "Federal Intervention in Union Discrimination: FEPC and West Coast Shipyards during World War II," *Labor History*, 22 (Summer 1981), 325–47. It is not certain if labor disputes were involved in the cases SCHW cited in Mobile. Harris's article explains the difficulty the FEPC found in enforcing nondiscrimination in war production industry.

22. *Proceedings*, 24–25.

23. Ibid., 27–29; Jonathan Daniels to Foreman, June 20, 1942, folder 4, box 35, SCHW Papers; Foreman to Charles S. Johnson, June 23, 1942, ibid.; "Report on the Southern Win the War Mass Meeting, Raleigh, North Carolina, Bastille Day, July 14, 1942," ibid.; Dombrowski to William F. Cochran, July 15, 1942, folder 4, box 1, SCEF Papers; Cochran to Dombrowski, July 21, 1942, ibid.; "Summary of the Outstanding Achievements of the Southern Conference for Human Welfare during the Present Year," 1942, folder 7, box 1, SCEF Papers. SCHW established variously southern-located win-the-war committees.

24. *Proceedings*, 30–31.

25. Ibid., 31; see Appendix: "Statement of Principles for Action, Unanimously Adopted, Nashville, April 21, 1942," *Proceedings*, 4–5. This document summarizes the conclusions of all the panels.

26. Memo, Dombrowski to trustees of the Robert Marshall Fund, 1942, folder 7, box 1, SCEF Papers.

27. Ethel Clyde, of Huntington, N.Y., to Dombrowski, June 1, 1942, folder 235, box 19, SCEF Papers. Ethel Clyde gave large sums of money to SCHW in the 1940s and 1950s. See Durr interviewed by William D. Barnard, 158.

28. Lillian Smith, editor of *North Georgia Review*, to Dombrowski, May 19, 1942, folder 236, box 19, SCEF Papers. Smith, in a later letter to Dombrowski states that she had had to find another printer for her magazine because the previous one refused to print her liberal racial views. Smith to Dombrowski, June 1, 1942, folder

236, box 19, ibid. In 1944 Smith gained notoriety for her novel, *Strange Fruit*, which examined segregation and white supremacy. See also Morton Sosna, *Southern Liberals and the Race Issue: In Search of the Silent South* (New York: Columbia University Press, 1977), 188–89.

29. Chapter 3 of this study, on alienation of moderates, is one example of this.

30. Tarleton Collier to Foreman, June 12, 1942, folder 4, box 35, SCHW Papers; see Foreman to Charles S. Johnson, June 23, 1942, folder 4, box 35, ibid. Thomas "Tom" Watson of Georgia, in the late 19th and early 20th centuries, argued strongly for racial equality but later supported white supremacy. Collier also held SCHW executive reins as acting president in 1942–43 while Foreman went abroad with the U.S. Navy. Foreman to "My dear friend," November 21, 1942, folder 4, box 35, SCHW Papers; Foreman to Charles S. Johnson, August 13, 1943, folder 5, box 35, ibid.

31. *Vanderbilt Alumnus*, April 1942, 16.

32. Ibid.

33. Dombrowski to Simon Gross, May 21, 1942, folder 3, box 1, SCEF Papers; Lillian Smith to Dombrowski, May 19, 1942, folder 236, box 19, ibid.; "Southern Conference Calls for Tax Removal to Aid War Effort," *Poll Tax Repealer*, 1 (April 1942). This one fold-out page of the *Repealer* is located in "National Committee to Abolish the Poll Tax, 1943–45" folder, group II, series A, box A410, National Association for the Advancement of Colored People Papers (Library of Congress, Washington, D.C.).

34. Patricia Ann Sullivan, "Gideon's Southern Soldiers: New Deal Politics and Civil Rights, 1933–1948" (Ph.D. dissertation, Emory University, 1983), 61–66; Dombrowski to Foreman, May 18, 1942, folder 4, box 35, SCHW Papers. Here Dombrowski inquired about news of Foreman's appointment. Foreman to Dombrowski, May 28, 1942, folder 4, box 35, ibid. See also Charles S. Johnson, *To Stem this Tide: A Survey of Racial Tension Areas in the United States* (Boston: Pilgrim Press, 1943), 50–59, which places the Sojourner Truth housing incident in national perspective, i. e., shortage of housing for blacks in general.

35. Arthur Raper to Foreman, June 3, 1942, Foreman to Raper, June 8, 1942, folder 4, box 35, SCHW Papers; Sullivan, "Gideon's Southern Soldiers," 66, 108.

36. Foreman to Lucy Randolph Mason, July 9, 1942, folder 4, box 35, SCHW Papers.

37. "Statement on the South and a Program for the Southern Conference," n.d., folder 1, box 1, SCEF Papers; memo to executive board of SCHW from Dombrowski, August 11, 1942, folder 231, box 19, ibid.; open letter of appeal from SCHW, August 20, 1942, folder 18, box 1, ibid.; John P. Davis to Dombrowski, n.d., folder 247, box 20, ibid.; Dombrowski to Foreman, August 16, 1942, folder 4, box 35, SCHW Papers. Other material that document same racial violence, Graham et al. to Senator (Elbert) Thomas, August 12, 1942, folder 18, box 1, SCEF Papers; "Negro Soldier Shot to Death in Mobile in Bus Driver Row," newspaper clipping, folder 229, box 19, ibid.

38. For a full copy of the ad see "To Our Commander-in-Chief, Franklin D. Roosevelt," *Birmingham News*, in folder 112, box 10, SCEF Papers. SCHW also ran the ad again in the December issue of the *Southern Patriot*, back page. "U.S. at War," *Time*, August 31, 1942, p. 23. This article also carried parts of the news ad and spoke of the various acts of violence against blacks, and in answer to the remarks about cowardice of black soldiers the *Time* article mentioned U.S. General Douglas MacArthur's awarding three black soldiers with medals for acts of bravery. For information on the northern paper that ran the ad see: Chester Bowles, State Director of Office of Price Administration, Hartford, Conn., to Dombrowski, September 21, 1942, folder 229, box 19, SCEF Papers; James Dombrowski to Leigh Danenberg, publisher, *Bridgeport* (Conn.) *Herald*, October 7, 1942, folder 229, box

19, ibid. The *Bridgeport Herald* had a circulation of approximately 92,000. Leigh Danenberg to Dombrowski, October 5, 1942, folder 229, box 19, SCEF Papers.

39. Dombrowski to William Cochran, September 8, 1942, folder 4, box 1, SCEF Papers; *Atlanta Constitution*, September 3, 1942, p. 2, "What's the Matter with this State" in support of Ellis Arnall warned, "anyone who causes dissension in the ranks by either disloyalty to our Commander or by appeals to race hatred gives aid and comfort to the enemy." See also, "Don't Be Misled by Partial Poll," *Atlanta Constitution*, September 7, 1942, p. 7 in support of Arnall.

40. Dombrowski to "Mrs. Tilley," October 7, 1942, folder 229, box 19, SCEF Papers; Victor W. Rotnem, " 'Don't Be Provoked': Department of Justice Official Praises SCHW Slogan," *Southern Patriot*, 1 (December 1942), 2. See folder 229, box 19, for an assortment of letters about ad.

41. Reply to August 16, 1942 newspaper ad, n.d., folder 229, box 19, SCEF Papers. The pledge over which this note was typed read: "Mr. President: We pledge to preserve Southern unity, free from race conflict, behind the war effort."

42. Clark Foreman, "Axis Accent in the South," September 1, 1942, folder 7, box 31, SCHW Papers. Daniel Joseph Singal, *The War Within: From Victorian to Modernist Thought in the South, 1919–1945* (Chapel Hill: University of North Carolina Press, 1982), 294.

43. Lucy Mason to Dombrowski, July or August 1942, folder 231, box 19, SCEF Papers. See the discussion about Roger Baldwin in chapter 3.

44. "Summary of the Outstanding Achievements of the Southern Conference for Human Welfare," 1942, folder 7, box 1, SCEF Papers; *Jackson Clarion Ledger*, October 13, 1942, p. 1; ibid., October 14, 1942, p. 1; ibid. October 20, 1942, pp. 1, 10; ibid., October 21, 1942, pp. 1, 3; ibid., November 11, 1942, p. 5.

45. John Hammond (lover of music and sponsor of the 1938 concerts that brought blues to New York City) of New York City to Dombrowski, November 18, 1942, folder 2, box 17, Carl and Anne Braden Papers (State Historical Society, Madison, Wis.).

46. "Southern Conference for Human Welfare, Some Achievements of the Liberal South in 1942," folder 5, box 35, SCHW Papers.

47. Elizabeth McMillin Jones to "Dear Friends" (SCHW), June 22, 1943, folder 134, box 11, SCEF Papers.

48. Dombrowski to Eleanor Roosevelt, June 24, 1943, folder 106, box 9, SCEF Papers. This entire folder contains mostly race-related letters to Eleanor and Franklin Roosevelt.

49. Dombrowski to "Dear Friend," June 1943, folder 106, box 9, SCEF Papers. Some of the letters sent to Franklin Roosevelt at Dombrowski's urging included those from: Paul R. Christopher, president of Tennessee State Industrial Union Council (CIO), June 29, 1943; R. O'Hara Lanier, acting president of Hampton Institute, June 29, 1943; P. E. Thomas, Chairman of Library Board, Clarendon, Ark., June 29, 1943; the Memphis Provisional Council, International Woodworkers of America (CIO) adopted a resolution and sent it to the President, all ibid.

50. Paul R. Christopher to Franklin Roosevelt, June 29, 1943, folder 106, box 9, SCEF Papers.

51. Harvard Sitkoff, "Racial Militancy and Interracial Violence in the Second World War," *Journal of American History*, 58 (December 1971), 661–81.

52. Foreman to Dombrowski, September 20, 1942, folder 4, box 35, SCHW Papers; Dombrowski to Foreman, October 6, 1942, ibid.; "Summary of the Outstanding Achievements of the Southern Conference for Human Welfare during the Present Year," 1942, folder 7, box 1, SCEF Papers.

53. *Southern Patriot*, 1 (December 1942).

54. Dombrowski to George Marshall, December 16, 1942, folder 7, box 1, SCEF Papers; appeal letter, "Save the Life of William Wellmon, Condemned to Die

December 18th," 1942, folder 5, box 34, SCHW Papers; *Greensboro Daily News*, December 7, 1942, p. 11; ibid., December 16, 1942, sec. 2, pp. 3, 8.

55. Louis E. Burnham of the Southern Negro Youth Congress to Dombrowski, December 21, 1942, folder 1, box 1, SCEF Papers.

56. Dombrowski to George Marshall, March 24, 1943, folder 7, box 1, SCEF Papers.

57. John P. Davis to Dombrowski, January 27, 1943, folder 249, box 20, SCEF Papers. Davis's opposition to civil disobedience may have been due to the Communist party line during World War II, opposing all militant activities perceived to detract from the war against fascism.

58. Dombrowski to John P. Davis, February 21, 1943, folder 249, box 20, SCEF Papers; Dombrowski to Charles S. Johnson, March 24, 1943, ibid. Dombrowski discussed plans with Johnson to hire a "Mrs. Wesley."

59. Newspaper clipping, *Columbia* (S.C.) *Lighthouse and Informer*, January 6, 1946, misc. folder, box 6, SCEF Papers; unidentified newspaper clipping, n.d., ibid.; leaflet inviting "5,000" to be present to hear Field Representative McKaine speak on behalf of SCHW, March 31, 1946, ibid.

60. "Minutes, Executive Board Meeting—Black Mountain College," January 22–23, 1944, folder 13, box 18, Braden Papers; Foreman to Charles S. Johnson at the Julius Rosenwald Fund, May 6, 1944, folder 9, box 1, SCEF Papers. See also chapter 3 for more on SCHW and SRC.

61. "Minutes, Executive Board Meeting—Black Mountain College," January 22–23, 1944, folder 13, box 18, Braden Papers; George B. Tindall, *The Emergence of the New South, 1913–1945* (Baton Rouge: Louisiana State University Press, 1967), 719.

62. "Report of the Executive Secretary for 1944," folder 9, box 32, SCHW Papers; Clark Foreman, "Georgia Kills the Poll Tax," *New Republic*, February 26, 1945, pp. 291–92.

63. "Report of the Executive Secretary for 1944," folder 9, box 32, SCHW Papers; see also Darlene Clark Hine, *Black Victory: The Rise and Fall of the White Primary in Texas* (Millwood, N.Y.: KTO Press, 1979).

64. "Report of the Executive Secretary for 1944," folder 9, box 32, SCHW Papers; Palmer Weber interviewed by Linda Reed, November 13, 1983 (Manuscripts Division, Alderman Library, Charlottesville, Va.).

65. Julius J. Adams, "South Spearheads Drive to Oust Negro-Baiters," *New York Amsterdam-News*, August 4, 1945, p. 1–A; "Eastlands and Bilbos Don't Speak for South, Say Southern Editors," *Southern Patriot*, 3 (August 1945), 7; "Southern Editors Poll Reveals Opposition to Eastland Statement," *Southern Farmer*, October 1945, in folder 112, box 10, SCEF Papers; New York Committee of SCHW to "Friend," 1945, folder 112, box 10, ibid.

66. "James Dombrowski Gets Hot Letter from 'Rev.' Bilbo," *Nashville Globe*, January 4, 1946; *New York Times*, February 1, 1946, p. 19; copy of Bilbo postcard appeal, misc. folder, box 6, SCEF Papers; action report, SCHW New York Committee, May 27, 1946, ibid.; unpublished manuscript of radio broadcast in answer to assertions made by Sen. Theodore G. Bilbo, August 22, 1946, in folder 112, box 10, ibid.; "The Negro to Bilbo—An Answer," radio broadcast, August 29, 1946, in folder 103, box 9, ibid.

67. "Report of the Executive Secretary for 1944," folder 9, box 32, SCHW Papers; *Southern Patriot*, 2 (December 1944).

68. "Report of the Executive Secretary for 1944," folder 9, box 32, SCHW Papers; "Statement of Dr. Clark Foreman, President, Southern Conference for Human Welfare, to Senate Committee on Education and Labor, March 13. Hearings on FEPC Legislation" with 1944 material, folder 112, box 10, SCEF Papers; John A. Davis (Director of Review and Analysis of FEPC) to Dombrowski, July 8, 1944, folder 112, box 10, ibid.; Dombrowski to John A. Davis, July 17, 1944, ibid.; A.

Philip Randolph and Allan Knight Chalmers, cochairmen of the National Council for a Permanent FEPC, August 16, 1944, ibid.; Randolph and Chalmers to Dombrowski, August 29, 1944, ibid. In these letters SCHW received information on employment of blacks and instructions on activities to push for the permanent organization.

69. Sitkoff, "Racial Militancy and Interracial Violence in the Second World War"; Peter J. Kellogg, "Civil Rights Consciousness in the 1940s," *The Historian*, 42 (November 1979), 19.

6. Critical Years for SCHW

1. *To Secure These Rights: President's Committee on Civil Rights* (New York: Simon and Schuster, 1947), 49. The Committee on Civil Rights concluded that the reaction to national interests and international politics in regard to communism had reached a state of hysteria.

2. Southern Conference or Conference refers to SCHW, and Educational Fund or Fund is in reference to SCEF.

3. James Dombrowski to Mary McLeod Bethune, December 12, 1945, folder 6, box 4, Southern Conference for Human Welfare (SCHW) Papers (Robert W. Woodruff Library, Atlanta University Center); Margaret Fisher to Ralph Mark Gilbert, December 21, 1945, folder 6, box 4, ibid.

4. Dombrowski to Fisher, et al., January 13, 1946, folder 6, box 4, ibid.

5. [Dombrowski] to Louis Burnham, December 21, 1945, folder 6, box 4, SCHW Papers; Mary Price to Charlotte Hawkins Brown, December 20, 1945, folder 5, box 4, ibid.

6. Carolyn Lehman Goldberg to Lucia Pitts (Clark Foreman's secretary in Washington, D.C.), December 31, 1945, folder 5, box 4, SCHW Papers; Pitts to Dombrowski, January 2, 1946, ibid. Bethune's tour for January included: 16–17, Memphis and Nashville; 18–20, Birmingham and Mobile; 21, Jacksonville; 22–23, Savannah and Atlanta; 24–27, Greensboro, Durham, and Winston-Salem.

7. Georgia press release, January 10, 1946, folder 6, box 4, SCHW Papers; memo, Lucia Pitts to Dombrowski et al., January 11, 1946, folder 5, box 4, ibid.; Margaret Fisher to Bethune, January 11, 1946, folder 6, ibid.

8. Memo, Dombrowski to Margaret Fisher, Polly Dobbs, Mary Price, O. E. McKaine, Witherspoon Dodge, and Lucia Pitts, January 13, 1946, folder 6, box 4, SCHW Papers.

9. Announcement, "SCHW Presents Mary McLeod Bethune . . . Nashville, Tennessee, Jan. 17, 1946," folder 103, box 9, Southern Conference Educational Fund (SCEF) Papers (Hollis Burke Frissell Library, Tuskegee, Ala.); "Public Meeting for Mrs. . . . Bethune, 'Making Democracy Live,' " January 17, 1946, misc. folder, box 6, ibid.

10. *Nashville Banner*, January 18, 1946, p. 1 in untitled folder, box 6, ibid. The article did not indicate how much money Bethune raised here. Membership was now $2 each year.

11. Margaret Fisher to "Dear Atlanta Member," January 7, 1946, folder 6, box 4, SCHW Papers; memo, Mary Price to Dombrowski and Lucia Pitts, January 10, 1946, folder 5, box 4, ibid.

12. Bethune to Dombrowski, January 30, 1946, folder 6, box 4, SCHW Papers; Ethel S. Berry to Mary Price, January 31, 1946, folder 5, box 4, ibid.; Mary Price to Bethune, February 9, 1946, ibid.; Berry to Price, February 13, 1946, ibid. Of the money raised in various states from the Bethune tour, everything above the $2 membership fee remained with state affiliates.

13. *Southern Patriot*, 4 (January 1946), 7; Mary Price to Dombrowski, January 2, 1946, folder 5, box 4, SCHW Papers; Foreman to Price, January 13, 1946, folder 10, box 4, ibid.; Price to Foreman, January 16, 1946, ibid.

14. "A Call to Meeting Jan. 26, 1946 to Adopt New Set of By-Laws," January 1946, folder 112, box 10, SCEF Papers; O. E. McKaine Report, Period: January 31–February 20, 1946, folder 31, box 2, ibid.

15. Minutes, meeting of the SCHW executive board, Durham, January 25, 1946, folder 8, box 35, SCHW Papers; *Durham Morning Herald*, January 27, 1946, p. 1, in untitled folder, box 6, SCEF Papers.

16. "The Charter of SOUTHERN CONFERENCE FOR HUMAN WELFARE be amended as follows: (1) By changing the name of the corporation to SOUTHERN CONFERENCE EDUCATIONAL FUND, INC. (2) By substituting for the statement of the purposes of the corporation the following: To improve the educational and cultural standards of the Southern people in accordance with the highest American democratic institutions, and ideals; and for the support of any literary or scientific undertaking, as a college or university, with powers to confer degrees; an academy; a debating society; lyceum; the establishment of a library or libraries; the support of a historical society; the promotion of painting, music or the fine arts." See minutes, executive board meeting, January 25, 1946, folder 8, box 35, SCHW Papers.

17. Minutes, executive board meeting, January 26, 1946, folder 8, box 35, SCHW Papers.

18. Minutes, executive board meeting, January 26, 1946, folder 6, box 18, Carl and Anne Braden Papers (State Historical Society, Madison, Wis.); *Durham Morning Herald*, January 27, 1946, p. 1; Clark Foreman to James Dombrowski, February 18, 1946, folder 8, box 35, SCHW Papers. Enclosures included Foreman's version of the January 26 minutes because he said the earlier version included mistakes by Dombrowski. Tarleton Collier was elected secretary; Alva Taylor, treasurer; and vice-presidents included Paul R. Christopher, Roscoe Dunjee, Virginia Durr, William Mitch, and Hollis V. Reid. Except for a few changes, the board remained the same. Louise O. Charlton, the prominent judge from Birmingham, is listed as a board member while every year since 1938 she had been an honorary chairperson. After 1942, however, not much notice is given to Charlton who became less active in SCHW in the 1940s. The same is true of John P. Davis who may have been forced away because of his alleged communism. Joseph Gelders became noticeably less active in the 1940s probably for the same reason. On Charlton's distance from SCHW see Morton Sosna, *Southern Liberals and the Race Issue: In Search of the Silent South* (New York: Columbia University Press, 1977), 142 (note 3). Despite Gelders's remoteness in the 1940s, the Southern Conference Educational Fund created a Joseph Gelders Memorial Fund upon his death in March 1950. See Emma Gelders Sterne to Dombrowski, January 30, 1951, folder 1, box 21, Braden Papers.

19. Clark Foreman to James Dombrowski, February 18, 1946, folder 8, box 35, SCHW Papers.

20. Murray H. Leiffer to Dombrowski, February 2, 1946, folder 2, box 17, Braden Papers. Dombrowski had turned down a job offer from the biblical institute on January 23, only a couple of days before the board meeting.

21. Memo, Foreman to Dombrowski, January 18, 1946, folder 2, box 1, SCEF Papers; Monroe Oppenheimer to Foreman, January 23, 1946, folder 8, box 35, SCHW Papers; Oppenheimer to Dombrowski, March 5, 1946, ibid.; J. O. Jermigan, Deputy Collector, to James Dombrowski, May 16, 1946, folder 2, box 1, SCEF Papers; Monroe Oppenheimer to Treasury Department, July 9, 1946, ibid. Copy of a completed form 1023 is attached to Oppenheimer's letter; Southern Conference for Human Welfare, Some Highlights of 1946 Program, 1946, folder 103, box 9, ibid.; Dombrowski to Milton C. Rose, October 5, 1946, folder 10, box 1, ibid.

22. Clark Foreman to William Cochran, April 30, 1946, folder 9, box 35, SCHW Papers.

23. Foreman to E. I. Kaufman, June 1, 1946, folder 9, box 35, SCHW Papers; Foreman to Oscar Cox, ibid. SCEF was identified under a separate column in the financial records for July 1946, but total receipts for months thereafter were not separately entered. See financial records, 1946–1948, folder 100, box 8, SCEF Papers.

24. James Dombrowski to Milton C. Rose (Secretary, William C. Whitney Foundation), September 13, 1946, folder 2, box 18, Braden Papers.

25. Rose to Dombrowski, September 27, 1946, folder 10, box 1, SCEF Papers; Dombrowski to Rose, October 5, 1946, ibid.

26. Mary Price to Foreman, January 13, 1946, folder 10, box 4, SCHW Papers; O. E. McKaine Report, Period: January 31–February 20, 1946, folder 31, box 2, SCEF Papers. Employees and the director of the Norfolk branch of the Virginia Mutual Aid Society made individual donations, and the president of the Lodge, a benevolent association with 1,700 members, gave $500 earmarked for a continued permanent FEPC campaign and $200 specified for the anti-poll-tax drive. The group promised to involve the Lodge fully in SCHW's work.

See also Henry Lewis Suggs, *P. B. Young Newspaperman: Race, Politics, and Journalism in the New South, 1910–1962* (Charlottesville: University Press of Virginia, 1988).

27. McKaine Report, folder 31, box 2, SCEF Papers. McKaine suggested that SCHW literature be placed at a booth or made available in some way at the halls of all county and state teachers meetings. His success prompted Mary Price, head of the North Carolina Committee, to request his help in that state. It is not clear if he went, but he did send names of prominent liberals, both black and white, for Price to contact in Wilmington and Winston-Salem, "some sold on SCHW 100%." See O. E. McKaine to Mary Price, February 19, 1946, folder 31, box 2, SCEF Papers.

28. S. H. Bell to Dombrowski, February 20, 1946, folder 31, box 2, SCEF Papers; Dombrowski to Bell, April 6, 1946, ibid.; memo, McKaine to Dombrowski, n.d., folder 31, box 2, ibid.

29. McKaine to Dombrowski, March 20, 1946, untitled folder, box 6, SCEF Papers; Dombrowski to Georgia Mitchell, Secretary of Committee for Louisiana, June 11, 1946, folder 31, box 2, ibid.

30. Memo, McKaine to Dombrowski, n.d., folder 31, box 2, SCEF Papers; see March 22, 1946 letters, folder 29, box 2, ibid.

31. Witherspoon Dodge to Dombrowski, February 4, 1946, folder 29, box 2, SCEF Papers; Dodge to Dombrowski, March 10, 1946, ibid.; Anthony P. Dunbar, *Against the Grain: Southern Radicals and Prophets* (Charlottesville: University Press of Virginia, 1981), 29. Dodge's letters, written on hotel stationery, made clear the difference between his accommodations and those of McKaine, who had to abide by Jim Crow laws.

32. McKaine to Dombrowski, March 20, 1946, untitled folder, box 6, SCEF Papers; Dodge to Dombrowski, March 26, 1946, folder 29, box 2, ibid.

33. Dodge to Dombrowski, May 4, 1946, folder 29, box 2, SCEF Papers; Dodge to Dombrowski, May 17, 1946, ibid.

34. Dombrowski to Dodge, June 6, 1946, ibid.

35. Dodge to Dombrowski, July 3, 1946, ibid.; an additional letter same day, ibid.

36. Benjamin E. Mays, "It Must Not Happen Again," *Southern Patriot*, 3 (October, 1945), 5; Rayford W. Logan, *What the Negro Wants* (Chapel Hill: University of North Carolina Press, 1944).

37. "Report of S. Neuberger re: Columbia, Tennessee," March 4, 1946, "Columbia, Tennessee" folder, box 4, SCEF Papers; "Facts in the Columbia, Tenn.,

Cases," March 18, 1946, ibid.; SCHW, "The Truth about Columbia, Tennessee Cases," n.d., ibid.; Dorothy Beeler, "Race Riot in Columbia, Tennessee, February 25–27, 1946," *Tennessee Historical Quarterly*, 39 (Spring 1980), 49–61. Beeler's analysis is to be taken lightly as her argument favors the white local, state, and federal authorities. Many of her facts involving the initial development of the incident are misrepresented in light of the various testimonies and investigations done by SCHW, NAACP, the newly formed Civil Rights Congress, and the National Federation for Constitutional Liberties, all of which include the perspective of the victims. See also Guy B. Johnson, "What Happened at Columbia," *New South*, 1 (May 1946), 1–8. According to Johnson, Gladys Stephenson's radio had been left at the store for about two months, and Fleming sold it. She demanded it back; he sent for it. In the meantime the two exchanged bitter words.

38. Beeler, "Race Riot in Columbia," 50. Columbia had recently elected as sheriff Flo Fleming, one of William Fleming's brothers, but Flo Fleming had not started his new post when the riot occurred. See Gail Williams O'Brien, "Return to 'Normalcy': Organized Racial Violence in the Post–World War II South," in *Violence in America*. Vol. 2.: *Protest, Rebellion, Reform*, ed. by Ted Robert Gurr (Newbury Park, Calif.: Sage, 1989), 254.

39. Untitled, undated document that gives the perspective of a black male intimately involved in activities in the black community and this incident, "Columbia, Tenn." folder, box 4, SCEF Papers; SCHW, "The Truth about Columbia, Tennessee Cases," ibid.; National Committee for Justice in Columbia, Tennessee, minutes of meeting, April 24, 1946, folder 9, box 35, SCHW Papers; Agnes E. Meyer, "The Untold Story of the Columbia, Tenn., Riot," *Washington Post*, May 19, 1946, reprint made specifically for SCHW distribution. Sheriff Jim Underwood may have sympathized with blacks who had supported his candidacy for the recent election in Columbia. See O'Brien, "Return to 'Normalcy,' " 249.

40. Untitled, undated document, "Columbia, Tenn." folder, box 4, SCEF Papers; SCHW, "The Truth about Columbia, Tennessee Cases," ibid.; Meyer, "The Untold Story of the Columbia, Tenn., Riot."

41. Untitled, undated document, "Columbia, Tenn." folder, box 4, SCEF Papers; SCHW, "The Truth about Columbia, Tennessee Cases," ibid.; Meyer, "The Untold Story of the Columbia, Tenn., Riot"; see Arthur I. Waskow, *From Race Riot to Sit-In, 1919 and the 1960s: A Study in the Connections between Conflict and Violence* (Garden City, N.Y.: Doubleday, 1966), 210–18, on how police brutality and police partiality forced blacks to fight back, instances where the only defense of African Americans was self-defense.

42. Untitled document in "Columbia, Tennessee" folder, box 4, SCEF Papers; Beeler, "Race Riot in Columbia," 51.

43. Beeler, "Race Riot in Columbia," 51–52, states the facts clearly but concludes that the state authority helped to prevent destruction. The officials' actions were not to protect the victims but added excitement and confidence to the white mob that intended to do the damage. SCHW, "The Truth about Columbia," box 4, SCEF Papers.

44. "Report of S. Neuberger re: Columbia, Tennessee," March 4, 1946, "Columbia, Tenn." folder, box 4, SCEF Papers; Civil Rights Congress, "Columbia, Tennessee, February 26, 1946: Will America White-Wash This?" group II, series A, "Columbia, Tenn. . . . 1946" folder, box A206, National Association for the Advancement of Colored People Papers (Library of Congress, Washington). All of the information prepared by SCHW, NAACP, CRC, and other civil rights groups emphasized the damage to blacks' property and the fact that all persons arrested went without resistance though according to Beeler and the police shots were fired across the street from the barber shop. Beeler, "Race Riot in Columbia," 52.

45. *New York Times*, February 27, 1946, p. 44; "Report of S. Neuberger," SCEF Papers.

46. SCHW, "The Truth about Columbia," box 4, SCEF Papers; untitled, undated document, "Columbia, Tenn." folder, ibid.

47. *New York Times*, February 27, 1946, p. 44.

48. "Report of S. Neuberger"; SCHW, "The Truth about Columbia"; Beeler, "Race Riot in Columbia," 52.

49. "Report of S. Neuberger"; SCHW, "The Truth about Columbia"; Beeler, "Race Riot in Columbia," 52.

50. SCHW, "The Truth about Columbia."

51. "Report of S. Neuberger," SCEF Papers; Beeler, "Race Riot in Columbia," 57.

52. Telegrams, Foreman and Dombrowski to Tom Clark, March 2, 1946, untitled folder, box 6, SCEF Papers; Foreman and Dombrowski to Harry Truman, ibid.; "Report of S. Neuberger"; Beeler, "Race Riot in Columbia," 54–55.

53. Foreman to Thurgood Marshall, March 9, 1946, group II, series A, "Columbia, Tenn. Riot, Southern Conference on Human Welfare, 1946" folder, box A206, NAACP Papers; Foreman to Thurgood Marshall, March 10, 1946, ibid.; Foreman to Walter White, March 14, 1946, ibid.; all are telegrams. "Resolution on Police Violence against the Negro Community in Columbia, Tenn. Adopted by Representatives of Sixty Organizations Joined in a National Emergency Conference to Stop Lynch Terror in Columbia, Tenn., Washington, D.C., March 13, 1946," folder 8, box 35, SCHW Papers; SCHW, "The Truth about Columbia," box 4, SCEF Papers.

54. Thurgood Marshall to Foreman, March 11, 1946, group II, series A, "Columbia, Tenn. Riot" folder, box A206, NAACP Papers. Marshall may have hesitated to participate in the Emergency Conference to Stop Lynch Terror in Columbia for fear of association with several organizations that had been labeled Communist. Furthermore, the NAACP may have wanted to raise its own money over the tragedy.

55. Foreman to Walter White, March 20, 1946, group II, series A, "Columbia, Tenn. Riot" folder, box A206, NAACP Papers; White to Foreman, March 21, 1946 ibid.; Minutes, National Committee for Justice in Columbia, Tenn. (NCJC), April 4, 1946, folder 9, box 35, SCHW Papers.

56. NCJC minutes, April 4, 13, 1946, folder 9, box 35, SCHW Papers. A partial list of members is included in the appendix.

57. NCJC minutes, April 24, 1946 and May 8, 1946, folder 9, box 35, SCHW Papers; *Word from Washington*, 1 (April 1946) in untitled folder, box 6, SCEF Papers. NCJC had its own stationery by May 8, 1946 and listed the NAACP's telephone number for official use.

58. Oliver W. Harrington, NAACP public relations director, to "Dear Friends," April 25, 1946, folder 9, box 35, SCHW Papers; NCJC minutes, May 15, 1946, ibid.; Dombrowski to White, December 7, 1946, group II, series A, "Columbia, Tenn." folder, box A206, NAACP Papers.

59. SCHW action: postcard and letter of appeal to McCord, untitled folder, box 6, SCEF Papers. L. Marcella Pope, Washington branch of the National Negro Congress, to Virginia Durr, March 19, 1946, folder 8, box 35, SCHW Papers. Included with this letter was a copy of statement of protest to McCord signed by leading labor leaders and various civil rights groups from the D.C. area.

60. See Z. T. Osborn, Jr., Assistant U.S. Attorney, Department of Justice, to Dombrowski, April 11, 1946, folder 2, box 17, Braden Papers; Dombrowski to Osborn, April 13, 1946, ibid.; Dombrowski to J. F. Richardson, May 21, 1946, ibid.; Z. T. Osborn, Jr., to Dombrowski, May 24, 1946, ibid.; Foreman to J. F. Richardson, May 29, 1946, ibid.; *Word from Washington*, 1 (April 1946) in untitled folder,

box 6, SCEF Papers, a publication by the Washington SCHW Committee; *New York Times*, June 15, 1946, p. 25; Beeler, "Race Riot in Columbia," 55–56. Although Beeler begins her article with an exoneration of the law officials, she ends by defending blacks, a contradiction she never resolves in the article.

61. Dombrowski to White, July 8, 1946, group II, series A, "Columbia, Tenn." folder, box A206, NAACP Papers. See correspondence between NAACP and CRC, dated July 11, 1946, through August 28, 1946, group II, series A, "Columbia, Tenn. . . . Riot" folder, box A206, NAACP Papers.

62. Foreman to White, Oct. 7, 1946, group II, series A, "Columbia, Tenn. . . . 1946" folder, box A206, NAACP Papers; *New York Times*, November 19, 1946, p. 35; ibid., June 27, 1947, p. 5; Beeler, "Race Riot in Columbia," 59–60.

63. Agnes E. Meyer, "Columbia (Tenn.) Riot: Social and Economic Background," *Washington Post*, May 20, 1946 in "Columbia" folder, box 4, SCEF Papers; NCJC minutes, May 15, 1946 and May 22, 1946, folder 9, box 35, SCHW Papers; Gilbert Osofsky, *The Burden of Race: A Documentary of Negro-White Relations in America* (New York: Harper & Row, 1967), 425–31. Meyer's article highlighted socioeconomic factors that the NCJC had not publicized; the organization had at least 100,000 copies of it printed for distribution.

64. Foreman to Julius Schreiber of the American Jewish Committee, April 4, 1946, folder 9, box 35, SCHW Papers; James A. Dombrowski, "The Southern Conference for Human Welfare," *Common Ground*, 6 (Summer 1946), 14–25.

65. *New Orleans Times-Picayune*, Dec. 7, 1946, p. 7; *To Secure These Rights*, vii; William C. Berman, *The Politics of Civil Rights in the Truman Administration* (Columbus: Ohio State University Press, 1970), 41–78.

66. Clark Foreman to Walter White, April 30, 1946, group II, series A, "Columbia, Tenn. Riot" folder, box A206, NAACP Papers; Foreman to Channing Tobias of the Phelps-Stokes Fund, April 30, 1946, ibid.; NCJC minutes, May 29, 1946, folder 9, box 35, SCHW Papers.

67. Walter White to Foreman, May 1, 1946, group II, series A, "Columbia, Tenn. Riot" folder, box A206, NAACP Papers.

68. NCJC minutes, May 29, 1946, folder 9, box 35, SCHW Papers; White to Foreman, June 10, 1946, group II, series A, "Columbia, Tenn. Riot" folder, box A206, NAACP Papers; Dombrowski to White, June 21, 1946, ibid.; White to Dombrowski, June 26, 1946, ibid.; White to Dombrowski, July 2, 1946, ibid. The SCHW's pamphlet sold for 1¢ each, $1 per hundred, $7.50 per thousand. See back cover, "Truth about Columbia." Having printed 200,000 pamphlets, the group stood to make approximately $2,000, provided that each copy sold for 1¢ and not in bundles of 1,000 for $7.50.

69. Memo. G. B. Current to White, September 20, 1946, group II, series A, "Columbia, Tenn." folder, box A206, NAACP Papers.

70. White to Foreman, December 4, 1946, group II, series A, "Columbia, Tenn." folder, box A206, NAACP Papers.

71. Dombrowski to White, December 7, 1946, ibid.

72. White to Dombrowski, December 20, 1946, ibid.

73. Byrd's willing person from within the SCHW central office could not produce a list of contributors because the SCHW books were locked up, and she could not justify her wanting to check back to the time when SCHW had received large sums of money. Besides, the informer had learned that amounts had been entered under one entry; there was no way of discerning who gave what amount. Furthermore, the informer confirmed the story about SCHW's financial woes; she would be leaving at the end of January 1947 because of insufficient funds for her salary. White to Daniel Byrd, December 9, 1946, group II, series A, "Columbia, Tenn. Riot," folder, box A206, NAACP Papers; Daniel Byrd to White, December 12, 1946, group II, series A, "Leagues, Southern Conference for Human Welfare,

1945–46" folder, box A366, ibid.; Byrd to White, January 27, 1947, group II, series A, "Southern Conference Educational Fund, 1947–49" folder, box A514, ibid.

74. Byrd to White, December 12, 1946, group II, series A, "Leagues, SCHW, 1945–46" folder, box A366, NAACP Papers; Branson Price, executive secretary of SCHW, New York Committee, to White, December 19, 1946, ibid.; White to Price, December 26, 1946, ibid.; memo, Julia E. Baxter of the NAACP to White, December 27, 1946, ibid.; Byrd to White, January 27, 1946, ibid., "SCEF, 1947–49" folder, box A514, ibid.

75. Memo, Dombrowski to SCHW staff members, April 18, 1946, folder 10, box 4, SCHW Papers.

76. Ibid.

77. Financial records, 1946–1948, folder 100, box 8, SCEF Papers; Dombrowski to Lee Pressman, March 21, 1946, folder 8, box 35, SCHW Papers.

78. Summary of minutes—meeting on Civil Rights Legislation, Dec. 23, 1946, folder 11, box 35, SCHW Papers.

79. Foreman to Aubrey Williams, January 21, 1947, folder 3, box 18, Braden Papers. In 1947 Williams, the former Roosevelt administrator from the National Youth Administration, was back in Montgomery, Ala., where he published and edited the *Southern Farmer*.

80. Dombrowski to Foreman, August 31, 1946, folder 10, box 35, SCHW Papers; minutes, SCHW board of representatives at Richmond, Va., September 26, 1946, folder 6, box 18, Braden Papers.

81. "Human Welfare Conference May Move to New Orleans," *New Orleans Times-Picayune*, August 16, 1946, in folder 16, box 1, SCEF Papers.

82. Dombrowski to "Dear Friend," n.d., folder 39, box 2, SCEF Papers.

83. The SCHW filed a massive amount of material pertaining to the YMBC charges. See New Orleans YMBC material folders 116, 117, 118, 119, box 10, SCEF Papers. This material contains correspondence between SCHW and YMBC; folder 15, box 1, ibid. includes article clippings from the three papers mentioned here.

84. See folders 120–22, box 10, SCEF Papers for information on January–July 1947 and folder 123, box 11, ibid.

85. Newspaper clipping, "May Sue for Right to Use Auditorium," n.d., folder 17, box 1, SCEF Papers; *New Orleans Times-Picayune*, November 28, 1946, p. 1; *Southern Patriot*, 4 (December 1946), 2, 5; Dombrowski to Millard U. Schindler (manager of the municipal auditorium), January 2, 1947, folder 1, box 36, SCHW Papers; Foreman to Dombrowski, January 13, 1946, ibid.

86. Foreman to Dombrowski, October 3, 1946, folder 10, box 35, SCHW Papers; Foreman to Eleanor Roosevelt, October 4, 1946, ibid.

87. Foreman to Claude Pepper, October 4, 1946, folder 10, box 35, SCHW Papers.

88. Foreman to Walter White, October 4, 1946, group II, series A, "Speaker—Walter White—Southern Conference of Human Welfare, 1946–47" folder, box A545, NAACP Papers; White to Foreman, October 31, 1946, ibid.; Foreman to White, November 7, 1946, ibid.

89. Walter White to Thurgood Marshall, November 19, 1946, "Speaker . . . SCHW" folder, box A545, NAACP Papers; Daniel E. Byrd to White, November 18, 1946, ibid.; White to Byrd, November 19, 1946, ibid.; Byrd to White, November 23, 1946, ibid. Krueger, *And Promises to Keep*, 151, states that White agreed to address the New Orleans convention out of gratitude for SCHW's cooperation in the Columbia incident. On the contrary, White concluded that SCHW had been a sore spot where the cases were concerned and did not always agree with SCHW literature on the matter.

90. Helen Reynolds (Graham's secretary at UNC) to Foreman and Dombrowski, November 14, 1946, folder 10, box 35, SCHW Papers; Eleanor Roosevelt to "Mr.

Jones," November 7, 1950, group II, series A, "Board of Directors, Eleanor Roosevelt, 1946–55" folder, box A139, NAACP Papers. Krueger, *And Promises to Keep*, 152, asserts that Roosevelt did not go to New Orleans because she had become "disillusioned" with SCHW over its association with "known Communists," but Krueger probably makes too much of this disillusionment theory because Roosevelt continued her association with SCHW (even served on the board of the New York Committee) and SCEF leaders in the 1950s, especially with Aubrey Williams, who by then was SCEF president. Moreover, as she ceased helping to raise funds for SCHW, she did the same with the NAACP.

91. *Southern Patriot*, 4 (December 1946), 1–8, SCHW devoted the entire issue to the New Orleans convention. A tentative program for the convention listed the registration fee at $3, see folder 39, box 2, SCEF Papers; SCHW 1946 Convention Program, folder 38, box 2, SCEF Papers; Krueger, *And Promises to Keep*, 152–55. Krueger sees the attendance as skimpy, largely comprised of African Americans; yet he asserts that SCHW was still not as strong as it should have been on racial equality. According to the *Patriot* SCHW raised $3,400 at the convention—with a registration fee of $3 at least 1,133 people were there.

92. Address by Walter White, November 30, 1946, "Speaker . . . 1946–47" folder, box A545, NAACP Papers.

93. *Atlanta Constitution*, November 19, 1946; ibid., November 25, 1946; ibid., November 26, 1946; *Atlanta Journal*, November 26, 1946; *New Orleans Item*, November 1946. It is ironic that Foreman and his organization would become the target of criticism for the *Atlanta Constitution*, a paper founded by his maternal grandfather, Clark Howell. The *New York Herald Tribune*, November 18, 1946; the *New York Age*, November 23, 1946; *Louisville Courier-Journal*, December 2, 1946; all praised Arnall. See copy of Arnall's speech, "Freedom in the South," group II, series A, "Speaker . . . SCHW, 1946–47" folder, box A545, NAACP Papers; "Governor Arnall Condemns 'Ism,' " *New Orleans Times-Picayune*, December 1, 1946, p. 24, where Arnall speaks out against communism and fascism. It is interesting that Arnall, like Bethune and Graham in 1942, got an empty box at the biennial. On seeing Arnall at a SCHW fund raiser dinner the next month in New York, Foreman "was quite embarrassed to have to explain to him that the box was empty." See Foreman to Dombrowski, December 18, 1946, folder 11, box 35, SCHW Papers.

94. Broadus Mitchell (Consulting Economist, Research Department, International Ladies' Garment Workers' Union, AFL, New York) to Foreman, November 18, 1946, folder 1, box 36, SCHW Papers. Mitchell also telephoned the NAACP and urged it to pressure Arnall to state publicly what obstacles prevented state action. Roy Wilkins agreed with Mitchell and evidently was one of the persons who wanted White to stay away from the SCHW convention. Wilkins advised White to pressure Arnall "inasmuch as 'you people participated in giving him an award.' " Mitchell believed "the NAACP and others who had honored Arnall owed it to the rest of the country to smoke him out." See Memo, Roy Wilkins to White, December 20, 1946, group II, series A, "Speaker—Walter White—1946–47" folder, box A545, NAACP Papers.

95. There is no indication that John P. Davis or Louise Charlton attended the 1946 Conference. The board had assessed its membership and decided according to bylaws adopted at the January Durham meeting that members missing three consecutive meetings be automatically dropped. Thus, letters were sent to F. D. Patterson, Hollis V. Reid, John P. Davis, A. T. Mollegan, M. C. Plunk, Ira deA. Reid, and Lillian Smith to that affect, but the Conference invited them to attend the 1946 convention and to "continue to take an active interest in the work of the Conference." See Dombrowski to F. D. Patterson, October 30, 1946, folder 10, box 35, SCHW Papers, which contains a notation that he sent the same letter to the others.

96. Minutes, meeting of board of representatives SCHW, December 1, 1946, folder 6, box 18, Braden Papers; Mason to Foreman, December 8, 1946, folder 11, box 35, SCHW Papers, in which Mason asserts that "apparently only two board members [Horton and herself] and the one associate member [Palmer Weber] knew in advance that it would be proposed to dispense with the services of Dombrowski." Foreman to Dombrowski, December 9, 1946, ibid.; Foreman to Paul R. Christopher, December 10, 1946, ibid.; William Mitch to Foreman, December 10, 1946, ibid.; Foreman to Mason, December 11, 1946, ibid.; Mason had complained of Dombrowski's work as administrator, and as Foreman reminded her, "it seems to me that you have lost sight of this and also the various communications which you have given me from Mrs. Roosevelt and others." Foreman to Graham, December 11, 1946, ibid.

97. Rebecca Gershon to Dombrowski, December 8, 1946, folder 5, box 18, Braden Papers; Gershon to Clark Foreman, December 8, 1946, ibid. The largest amount of correspondence on the subject is located in folder 11, box 35, SCHW Papers, though a few letters are in the Braden Papers, especially those between Dombrowski and Mason.

98. Mason to Foreman, December 3, 1946, folder 11, box 35, SCHW Papers; Mason to Dombrowski, December 6, 1946, folder 5, box 18, Braden Papers; Mason to Foreman, December 8, 1946, folder 11, box 35, SCHW Papers; Lewis Jones to Dombrowski, December 5, 1946, folder 5, Braden Papers.

99. Margaret Fisher to Foreman, December 29, 1946, folder 11, box 35, SCHW Papers.

100. Lewis Jones to Foreman, December 11, 1946, folder 11, box 35, SCHW Papers; Mason to Dombrowski, December 19, 1946, folder 5, box 18, Braden Papers.

101. Dombrowski to Foreman, December 6, 1946, folder 11, box 35, SCHW Papers; Foreman to Dombrowski, December 9, 1946, ibid.; Dombrowski to Foreman, December 12, 1946, ibid.; Dombrowski to Aubrey Williams, December 28, 1946, ibid.; Aubrey Williams to Dombrowski, December 26, 1946, folder 5, box 18, Braden Papers; Palmer Weber to Dombrowski, December 1946, ibid.

102. Foreman to SCHW board members, December 23, 1946, folder 11, box 35, SCHW Papers; Foreman to Graham, January 8, 1946, ibid.

103. Minutes, board meetings SCHW/SCEF, January 5, 1947, Greensboro, N.C., folder 112, box 10, SCEF Papers; Foreman to Dombrowski, January 21, 1947, folder, 3, box 18, Braden Papers. At least 22 of about 35 members attended.

104. Minutes, board meetings SCHW/SCEF, January 5, 1947, folder 112, box 10, SCEF Papers.

105. Dombrowski to Frank Bancroft, January 9, 1947, folder 1, box 36, SCHW Papers; Foreman to Dombrowski, January 22, 1947, folder 3, box 18, Braden Papers; news release announcing Bancroft's and Grant's appointments, February 4, 1947, folder 42, box 2, SCEF Papers.

106. Palmer Weber interviewed by Linda Reed, July 19, 1985 (Charlottesville, Va., author's possession); Weber interviewed by Reed, November 13, 1983, Manuscript Collection, Alderman Library (Charlottesville, Va.); Virginia Durr interviewed by Linda Reed, December 29, 1982, Lilly Library (Bloomington, Ind.).

107. Foreman to Dombrowski, January 24, 1947, folder 3, box 18, Braden Papers; Foreman to Freda Kirchway of the *Nation*, January 24, 1947, ibid.; Foreman to Frank Bancroft, March 3, 1947, ibid. All re: concern over a possible article appearing in the *Nation* over differences within SCHW/SCEF's administration.

108. Foreman to Dombrowski, April 9, 1947, folder 3, box 18, Braden Papers; Dombrowski to Foreman, April 11, 1947, ibid. The greater part of Foreman's incoming correspondence is at Atlanta, and Dombrowski's is at Madison.

109. Dombrowski to Virginia Durr, June 4, 1947, folder 8, box 31, SCHW Papers.

110. V. Durr to Dombrowski, June 1947, folder 2, box 17, Braden Papers.

111. Ethel Clyde of New York to Dombrowski, September 20, 1947, ibid.

112. Dombrowski to Jennings Perry, December 6, 1946, folder 11, box 35, notifying the NCAPT that SCHW cannot pay its staff's salaries; memo, Dombrowski to state committee chairpersons indicating that their salaries were paid to date even though the funds were borrowed to do so. The New York committee held a dinner for Joe Louis where it raised about $10,000, and "got a great deal of excellent publicity." (See Foreman and Lewis pictured at the dinner on page 42.) Dombrowski did not attend but sent a telegram. See Foreman to Dombrowski, December 18, 1946, ibid.

113. Minutes, meeting of SCEF board, Richmond, July 13, 1947, folder 2, box 22, Braden Papers.

114. Memo, Foreman to SCEF board, January 23, 1947, folder 2, box 22, Braden Papers; Foreman to Myles Horton, February 12, 1947, folder 3, box 18, ibid.; Jack McMichael to Foreman, February 15, 1947, ibid.; Dombrowski to Bethune, March 31, 1947, folder 2, box 17, ibid.; minutes, executive board, SCEF, Birmingham, April 20, 1947, folder 2, box 22, ibid. SCEF offered Josephine Wilkins, Jack McMichael, and Don West the job.

115. Minutes, SCEF board meeting, July 13, 1947, folder 2, box 22, Braden Papers.

116. Clark Foreman to Aubrey Williams, April 24, 1947, folder 3, box 18, Braden Papers.

117. Memo, Mason to SCHW board, April 19, 1947, folder 6, box 18, Braden Papers; memo, Dombrowski to SCHW board, January 5, 1947, folder 8, box 35, SCHW Papers. Although Dombrowski was more concerned with administrative policies, his and Mason's analyses are basically the same. Memo, Edmonia W. Grant, acting administrator, to SCHW board, January 23, 1948, folder 103, box 9, SCEF Papers. This memo, titled "The Crisis within SCHW," summed up the major reasons for SCHW's end.

118. Committee on Un-American Activities, House, 80th Cong., 1st sess., *Report on Southern Conference for Human Welfare* (Washington, D.C.: U.S. Government Printing Office, 1947); memo, Edmonia Grant to SCHW board, January 23, 1948, folder 103, box 9, SCEF Papers, on Wallace tour.

119. Walter Gellhorn, "Report on a Report of the House Committee on Un-American Activities," *Harvard Law Review*, 60 (October 1947), 1193–1234. Krueger, *And Promises to Keep*, 167–73.

120. Dunbar, *Against the Grain*, 217, where Dunbar makes this claim.

121. Minutes, SCHW board meeting, July 12, 1947, folder 5, box 18, Braden Papers; minutes, SCHW board meeting, October 16, 1947, folder 112, box 10, SCEF Papers; memo, Grant to SCHW board, January 23, 1948, ibid.

122. Foreman to boards of SCHW and SCEF, May 17, 1948, folder 3, box 18, Braden Papers; Krueger, *And Promises to Keep*, 185–89; Durr interviewed by Reed, December 29, 1982. Henry Wallace's presidential campaign is an important milestone in the history of the American left, and an excellently detailed account of it is Patricia Ann Sullivan, "Gideon's Southern Soldiers: New Deal Politics and Civil Rights, 1933–1948" (Ph.D. dissertation, Emory University, 1983), 296–357.

123. *Southern Patriot*, 7 (January 1949), 4; Foreman to Dombrowski, December 21, 1948, folder 3, box 18, Braden Papers; Dombrowski to Foreman, December 28, 1948, ibid.; Foreman to Dombrowski, June 15, 1949, folder 6, ibid.; Weber interviewed by Reed, November 13, 1983.

7. The Perpetuation of an SCHW Legacy

1. Paler Weber interviewed by Linda Reed, November 13, 1983, Manuscript Collection (Alderman Library, Charlottesville, Va.). The Southern Conference for

Human Welfare will be referred to as the Southern Conference, the Conference, and SCHW, while the Southern Conference Educational Fund will be called the Educational Fund, the Fund, and SCEF.

2. Minutes, SCEF board meeting, Atlanta, May 22, 1948, folder 2, box 22, Carl and Anne Braden Papers (State Historical Society, Madison, Wis.); Dombrowski to Albert Barnett, December 21, 1957, microfilm 306, reel 4, ibid.; Jerold Simmons, "The Origins of the Campaign to Abolish HUAC, 1956–1961, the California Connection," *Southern California Quarterly*, 64 (Summer 1982), 145.

3. John Salmond, *A Southern Rebel: The Life and Times of Aubrey Willis Williams, 1890–1965* (Chapel Hill: University of North Carolina Press, 1983), 232; Virginia Durr interviewed by Linda Reed, December 29, 1982 (Lilly Library, Indiana University).

4. *Southern Patriot*, 7 (April 1949), 4; ibid., (May 1949), 3: Salmond, *A Southern Rebel*, 223; Warren Ashby, *Frank Porter Graham: A Southern Liberal* (Winston-Salem, N.C.: John F. Blair, 1980), 243–47.

5. Minutes, SCEF board meeting, June 26, 1949, folder 2, box 22, Braden Papers; Ashby, *Frank Porter Graham*, 257–82, 288, 302, 309. Having been defeated in the senatorial election of 1950, Graham accepted an appointment the next year, one initially set for three months but which he kept for nineteen years, as United Nations Representative for India and Pakistan.

6. Ashby, *Frank Porter Graham*, 274.

7. Minutes, SCEF board meeting, Jan. 30, 1948, folder 2, box 22, Braden Papers. Those present at the meeting included: Foreman, Alva Taylor, O. B. Taylor, Louis Burnham, Virginia Durr, Modjeska M. Simkins, S. J. Rodman, Myles Horton, Charles Weber, and Dombrowski, barely a quorum with ten people.

8. William Mitch to Dombrowski, March 31, 1948, folder 9, box 21, Braden Papers; William H. Harris, *The Harder We Run: Black Workers since the Civil War* (New York: Oxford University Press, 1982), 124.

9. Dombrowski to Bethune, July 13, 1950, microfilm 306, reel 4, Braden Papers.

10. Bethune to Dombrowski, June 14, 1951, July 9, 1951, microfilm 306, reel 4, ibid.

11. *Southern Patriot*, 13 (March 1955), 4.

12. Minutes, SCEF board meeting, November 21, 1948, folder 2, box 22, Braden Papers.

13. Dombrowski to Bethune, January 14, 1950, microfilm 306, reel 4, ibid.; *Southern Patriot*, 11 (June 1953), 3; Salmond, *A Southern Rebel*, 226–27. See chapter 2 for more on SCEF's finances.

14. Minutes, SCEF board meeting, Atlanta, May 22, 1948, folder 2, box 22, Braden Papers; "Proposed By-Laws," with 1949 material, ibid. As late as 1981 confusion lingered about the difference between SCHW and SCEF. Clayborne Carson, *In Struggle: SNCC and the Black Awakening of the 1960s* (Cambridge, Mass.: Harvard University Press, 1981), 51. Carson says that SCEF, not SCHW, was founded in the 1930s.

15. *Southern Patriot*, 5 (August 1947), 3; memo, Dombrowski to SCEF board of directors, August 5, 1948, folder 2, box 22, Braden Papers; Salmond, *Southern Rebel*, 220.

16. *Southern Patriot*, 12 (May 1954) and ibid., 13 (February 1955).

17. Group II, Series A, "Board of Directors, Benjamin E. Mays, 1950–55" folder, box A130, National Association for the Advancement of Colored People (NAACP) Papers (Library of Congress).

18. Minutes, SCEF board meeting, July 13, 1947, folder 2, box 22, Braden Papers; "Statement of Revenues and Expenses 1948," ibid.; contributions and subscriptions, SCEF, year ended December 31, 1951, ibid.; SCEF, Inc., Financial Statement as of Dec. 31, 1951, in *Southern Patriot*, 10 (February 1952); Salmond, *A Southern Rebel*, 205–18.

19. Salmond, *Southern Rebel*, especially 38–39, 48, 171, 223.

20. Thomas A. Krueger, *And Promises to Keep: The Southern Conference for Human Welfare, 1938–1948* (Nashville: Vanderbilt University Press, 1967), 194.

21. Benjamin E. Mays, "Improving the Morale of Negro Children and Youth," *Journal of Negro Education*, 19 (Winter 1950), 421; Harris, *The Harder We Run*, 125.

22. Truman's interest in civil rights was sincere and genuine, contrary to Berman's assessment of the president's motive as largely political. Truman, even Berman himself admits, said that he was "dead earnest" about civil rights and that he would be in favor of civil rights legislation for the rest of his life. William C. Berman, *The Politics of Civil Rights in the Truman Administration* (Columbus: Ohio State University Press, 1970), especially 77–78, 231–32, 240.

23. Al-Tony Gilmore, "The Black Southerner's Response to the Southern System of Race Relations: 1900 to Post-World War II," in *The Age of Segregation: Race Relations in the South, 1890–1945*, ed. Robert Haws (Jackson: University Press of Mississippi, 1978), 86–88; Carl M. Brauer, *John F. Kennedy and the Second Reconstruction* (New York: Columbia University Press, 1977); Steven F. Lawson, "Preserving the Second Reconstruction: Enforcement of the Voting Rights Act, 1965–1975," *Southern Studies*, 22 (Spring 1983). These last studies point out that the late 1950s and the 1960s warrant the term Second Reconstruction.

24. President's Committee on Civil Rights, *To Secure These Rights* (New York: Simon and Schuster, 1947), especially 157, 160–61, 166, 167, 169, 173.

25. Peter J. Kellog, "Civil Rights Consciousness in the 1940s," *Historian*, 42 (November 1979), esp. 19, 22–23, 25–29, 31.

26. Memo, Dombrowski to SCEF board members, October or November 1947, folder 2, box 22, Braden Papers; *New York Times*, October 30, 1947, pp. 1, 14, 15, October 31, 1947, p. 22; *To Secure These Rights*, 166–67; Ashby, *Frank Porter Graham*, 206–23, 224–25. Graham was a United States representative with the United Nations Committee of Good Offices, which was negotiating matters concerning Indonesia independence.

27. James A. Dombrowski to Goodrich C. White, President, Emory University, December 17, 1947, folder 2, box 17, Braden Papers.

28. Anne Gambriel Braden to "Dear Mother and Daddy," 1954, folder 10, box 21, Braden Papers.

29. *To Secure These Rights*, 173; Berman, *Politics of Civil Rights*, 174–76.

30. "A Digest of Public Affairs" by the Committee for Alabama SCHW, folder 39, box 2, Southern Conference Educational Fund (SCEF) Papers (Hollis Burke Frissell Library, Tuskegee, Ala.); Foreman to Frank P. Graham, January 8, 1947, folder 11, box 35, Southern Conference for Human Welfare (SCHW) Papers (Robert W. Woodruff Library, Atlanta University Center); Anne Braden interviewed by Linda Reed, October 10, 1983, transcript in author's possession.

31. Minutes, SCEF board meeting, April 1947, folder 2, box 22, Braden Papers.

32. Ibid.

33. Ibid. Some of the outstanding southern editors who SCEF trusted included: Josephus and Jonathan Daniels, *Raleigh* (N.C.) *News and Observer*; Jennings Perry, *Nashville Tennessean*; Hodding Carter, *Delta Democrat-Times* (Greenville, Miss.); Percy Greene, *Jackson Advocate*; Nelson Poynter, *St. Petersburg Times*; Mark Ethridge, *Louisville Courier Journal*; P. B. Young, *Norfolk Journal and Guide*; Virginius Dabney, *Richmond Times-Dispatch*; and Roscoe Dunjee, *Oklahoma Dispatch*. Ethridge could sometimes be labeled a moderate, and recent studies reveal that Jonathan Daniels and Dabney, at best, were moderates. See Charles Eagles, *Jonathan Daniels and Race Relations: The Evolution of a Southern Liberal* (Knoxville: University of Tennessee Press, 1982); John T. Kneebone, *Southern Liberal Journalists and the Issue of Race, 1920–1944* (Chapel Hill: University of North Carolina Press, 1985). An anonymous reviewer for Indiana University Press brought to my attention that Greene accepted support from the White Citizens Council in the 1950s.

34. Minutes, SCEF board meeting, April 1947, folder 2, box 22, Braden Papers.
35. Salmond, *A Southern Rebel*, 199–206, 208–11.
36. Ibid., 38–39, 209–11.
37. Dombrowski to Ann Whitman of the Adele R. Levy Fund, Inc., of New York City, October 9, 1947, folder 3, box 18, Braden Papers; Dombrowski to Foreman, October 20, 1947, ibid.

8. SCEF and the Challenge of Desegregation

1. Memo, James Dombrowski to SCEF board members, October 23, 1947, folder 2, box 22, Carl and Anne Braden Papers (State Historical Society, Madison Wis.); Dombrowski to Foreman, November 6, 1947, folder 3, box 18, ibid.; *Southern Patriot*, 5 (October 1947), 1, 2.
2. Freeman Drake, Sr., to Dombrowski, December 21, 1948, "Segregation in Education, Alabama" folder, box 8, Southern Conference Educational Fund (SCEF) Papers (Hollis Burke Frissell Library, Tuskegee, Ala.).
3. *Southern Patriot*, 5 (October 1947), 3.
4. Ibid., 8; Benjamin E. Mays, "Improving the Morale of Negro Children and Youth," *Journal of Negro Education*, 19 (Winter 1950), 420, 423.
5. *Southern Patriot*, 5 (October 1947), 8; minutes, SCEF board meeting, January 30, 1948, May 22, 1948, folder 2, box 22, Braden Papers.
6. Charles H. Thompson, "Some Progress in the Elimination of Discrimination in Higher Education in the United States," *Journal of Negro Education*, 19 (Winter 1950), 4–6; Richard Kluger, *Simple Justice: The History of Brown v. Board of Education and Black America's Struggle for Equality* (New York: Knopf, 1975), 189–94.
7. *Southern Patriot*, 6 (May 1948); Kluger, *Simple Justice*, 258–60.
8. Ida Harper Simpson, *Fifty Years of Southern Sociological Society: Change and Continuity in a Professional Society* (Athens: University of Georgia Press, 1988), 12, 18, 29, 204–51. Formed in 1935 in Knoxville, Tennessee, the Southern Sociological Society was racially integrated from the start, unlike other southern regional societies, and the noted sociologist Charles S. Johnson served as its president in 1946.
The postmark on envelopes provided state identification information of respondents.
9. *Southern Patriot*, 6 (May 1948), 1, 2; Thompson, "Some Progress in the Elimination of Discrimination in Higher Education in the United States"; Ashby, *Frank Porter Graham*, 226–29.
10. *Southern Patriot*, 6 (November 1948), 1, 2. A recent study on North Carolina race relations dispels the myth of that state being more liberal on the race issue. See John Haley, *Charles N. Hunter and Race Relations in North Carolina* (Chapel Hill: University of North Carolina Press, 1987).
11. *Southern Patriot*, 7 (November 1949), 1; James A. Dombrowski, "Attitudes of Southern University Professors Toward the Elimination of Segregation in Graduate and Professional Schools in the South," *Journal of Negro Education*, 19 (Winter 1950), 118–33.
12. *Southern Patriot*, 6 (April 1948), 1, 2; ibid., (May 1948), 3, 4; *New York Times*, May 2, 1948, p. 1.
13. *Southern Patriot*, 6 (April 1948), 1, 2; ibid., (May 1948), 3, 4; *New York Times*, May 2, 1948, pp. 1, 37, May 3, 1948, pp. 1, 12, May 5, 1948, p. 2, May 8, 1948, p. 7; *Washington Post*, May 2, 1948, p. 1, May 3, 1948, p. 11, May 4, 1948, p. 4, May 5, 1948, p. 1; *Birmingham News*, June 12, 1948; Cicero Alvin Hughes, "Toward a Black United Front: The National Negro Congress Movement" (Ph.D. dissertation, Ohio University, 1982), 184–85.

14. Dombrowski on the Birmingham Story, May/June 1948, folder 6, box 17, Braden Papers.

15. Memo, Dombrowski to SCEF board members, October or November 1947, folder 2, box 22, ibid.; *Southern Patriot*, 6 (May 1948); ibid., Nov. 1948; Dombrowski, "Attitudes of Southern University Professors Toward the Elimination of Segregation in Graduate and Professional Schools in the South."

16. Memo, Dombrowski to SCEF board of directors, August 5, 1948, folder 2, box 22, Braden Papers.

17. *New York Times*, November 21, 1948.

18. For accounts of the November 20, 1948 gathering see: *Charlottesville Daily Progress*, November 20, 1948; *Richmond Times-Dispatch*, November 21, 1948; *New York Times*, November 21, 1948.

19. Proposed By-Laws," with 1949 material, folder 2, box 22, Braden Papers; *Southern Patriot*, 8 (January 1950), 3.

20. *Southern Patriot*, 8 (January 1950), 1; ibid. (June 1950), 1, 2; minutes, SCEF board meeting, April 7, 1950, folder 2, box 22, Braden Papers; Kluger, *Simple Justice*, 260–84.

21. *Southern Patriot*, 12 (March 1954), 2.

22. *New York Times*, July 18, 1952, p. 8, July 24, 1952, pp. 1, 16, 17; ibid. June 3, 1956, p. 67; *Southern Patriot*, 10 (September 1952), 1; Salmond, *A Southern Rebel*, 216.

23. *Southern Patriot*, 8 (June 1950), 3; ibid., 10 (June 1952), 4; ibid., 11 (December 1953), 4; ibid., 12 (March 1954), 2.

24. U. S. Congress, Senate, *Labor Practices in Laurens County, Ga.: Hearing before the Special Subcommittee on Labor and Labor-Management Relations of the Committee on Labor and Public Welfare*, 82 Cong., 1 sess., August 13, 1951, especially pp. 79–90, 94; *Southern Patriot*, 9 (October 1951), 1.

25. *New York Times*, September 10, 1953, p. 50, May 15, 1954, p. 16, December 17, 1954, p. 55; *Southern Patriot*, 11 (Oct. 1953), 1–2, 3; Pete Daniel, *The Shadow of Slavery: Peonage in the South, 1901–1969* (Urbana: University of Illinois Press, 1972), 188–92.

26. *Southern Patriot*, 9 (March 1951), 1; ibid., 12 (January 1954), 4.

27. Frank Adams and Myles Horton, *Unearthing Seeds of Fire: The Idea of Highlander* (Winston-Salem, N.C.: John F. Blair, 1975), 194–200.

28. For a full account of the hearings, Salmond, *Southern Rebel*, 228–46, is an excellent source. See also Irwin Klibaner, "The Southern Conference Educational Fund: A History" (Ph.D. dissertation, University of Wisconsin, 1971), 142–59.

29. Anne Braden, *House Un-American Activities Committee: Bulwark of Segregation* (Los Angeles: National Committee to Abolish the House Un-Activities Committee, 1964); Anthony P. Dunbar, *Against the Grain: Southern Radicals and Prophets, 1929–1959* (Charlottesville: University Press of Virginia, 1981), 252–53; John M. Glen, *Highlander: No Ordinary School, 1932–1962* (Lexington: University Press of Kentucky, 1988), especially 173–209; Adams and Horton, *Unearthing Seeds of Fire*, 200; Salmond, *A Southern Rebel*, 228–46. President Benjamin E. Mays of Morehouse College had resigned as SCEF vice-president in 1952 to take on a less demanding role as board member, but he even resigned as board member in 1954, citing his disagreement with SCEF leaders who pled the Fifth Amendment for their protection. Mays believed that strategy left the public suspicious that SCEF had something to hide. See minutes, SCEF board meeting, October 25, 1952, folder 3, box 22, Braden Papers on Mays's first resignation; Benjamin E. Mays to Aubrey Williams, February 11, 1954, folder 3, box 22, ibid.

30. William H. Harris, *The Harder We Run: Black Workers since the Civil War* (New York: Oxford University Press, 1982), 142, 146.

31. Virginia Durr interviewed by William D. Barnard, Columbia University's Oral History Collection, 1974, 265–94; Durr interviewed by Linda Reed, December

29, 1982, Lilly Library (Bloomington, Ind.); Martin Luther King, Jr., *Stride Toward Freedom: The Montgomery Story* (New York: Harper & Row, 1958), 40–45; Adams and Horton, *Unearthing Seeds of Fire*, 122. See also *The Montgomery Bus Boycott and the Women Who Started It: The Memoir of Jo Ann Gibson Robinson*, ed. by David J. Garrow (Knoxville: University of Tennessee Press, 1987; David J. Garrow, *Bearing the Cross: Martin Luther King, Jr., and the Southern Christian Leadership Conference* (New York: William Morrow, 1986), 11–82.

32. Anne Braden, *The Wall Between* (New York: Monthly Review Press, 1958) includes an in depth discussion of the reason for the purchase of the home for the Wades and subsequent actions.

33. SCEF raised $600 for the Bradens in 1956. "Highlights of 1956," folder 4, box 22, Braden Papers; Williams to Morgan Johnson, May 27, 1957, folder 5, box 17, ibid.

34. See Anne Braden interviewed by Linda Reed, October 10, 1983, in author's possession.

35. *Southern Patriot*, 10 (January 1952), 1; SCEF board meeting, June 3, 1956, folder 3, box 22, Braden Papers.

36. Subscriptions for the *Southern Patriot* had dropped from the once high 29,000 in 1943 to about 2,200 in 1957, with the monthly publication reaching major university libraries including Indiana University, the University of Virginia, and the University of North Carolina. See James Dombrowski to "Kit" (Katherine Shryver), November 16, 1943, folder 125, box 11, SCEF Papers; SCEF's Treasurer's Report, December 31, 1957, folder 4, box 22, Braden Papers. SCEF sometimes distributed vast quantities of special issues, as it did with the 1947 special issue, "Segregation in Education."

9. White Southern Backlash and the High Price for a Just Cause

1. Gilbert Osofsky, *The Burden of Race: A Documentary History of Negro-White Relations in America* (New York: Harper & Row, 1967), 479–80, 491–94.

2. Roscoe Dunjee to Roy Wilkins, December 2, 1955, group II, series A, "Board of Directors, Roscoe Dunjee, 1941–55" folder, box A126, National Association for the Advancement of Colored People (NAACP) Papers (Library of Congress, Washington, D.C.).

3. Wilkins to Dunjee, December 7, 1955, ibid.

4. News release information, February 3, 1956, folder 103, box 9, Southern Conference Educational Fund (SCEF) Papers (Hollis Burke Frissell Library, Tuskegee Institute, Ala.); Ramon Eduardo Ruiz, "La Cuestion Racial: El Enigma de los Estados Unidos," *Cuadernos Americanos* (marzo-abril de 1958), 25–33; Osofsky lists between January 1, 1955, and January 1, 1959, for Alabama alone over fifty-five acts of violence whites committed against blacks, over half of which occurred in Birmingham. In 1956 segregationists bombed Martin Luther King, Jr.'s home in Montgomery. The bomb blew out windows and damaged the front porch, but King's wife, Coretta, their daughter, and a visitor escaped injuries.

5. Osofsky, *Burden of Race*, 495–98.

6. Fred S. Shuttlesworth interviewed by Linda Reed, July 2, 1983, transcript at Lilly Library (Indiana University, Bloomington); Osofsky, *Burden of Race*, 500, 501, 505, 509. Cole, only stunned, suffered no injuries. Police later learned that 100 to 150 white men had planned to meet at the auditorium to disrupt Cole's performance and force him to leave, but the rest of the mob had failed to appear.

7. The advertisement appeared in August, and by September all but six of the fifty-four named persons asked that their names be withdrawn from the petition.

8. News release information, February 3, 1956, SCEF Papers.

9. Daisy Bates, *The Long Shadow of Little Rock* (New York: McKay, 1962), gives an account of how the black community clamored for school integration in Little Rock and united in this major effort for the nine youths involved in 1957 and 1958. Two whites give other perspectives in Virgil T. Blossom, *It Has Happened Here* (New York: Harper & Row, 1959) and Elizabeth Huckaby, *Crisis at Central High: Little Rock, 1957–58* (Baton-Rouge: Louisiana State University Press, 1980).

10. Daisy Bates to James Dombrowski, December 8, 1959, microfilm 306, reel 4, Anne and Carl Braden Papers (State Historical Society, Madison, Wis.); Bates, *Long Shadow of Little Rock*, 33, 159, 169, 170–78. Stress and strain from the Little Rock affair immediately brought Daisy Bates health problems. She had to be hospitalized, and the doctor advised her to take it easy for at least two months upon her release.

11. Dombrowski to L. C. and Daisy Bates, December 29, 1958, microfilm 306, reel 4, Braden Papers; L. C. and Daisy Bates to Dombrowski, January 2, 1959, ibid.

12. Dombrowski to L. C. and Daisy Bates, November 23, 1959, ibid. The letter contained a copy of the resolution.

13. Daisy Bates to Dombrowski, December 8, 1959, ibid.

14. Dombrowski to Dollars for Daisy Bates Trust Fund, Inc., February 29, 1960, ibid. The amount of money raised in this effort is not revealed.

15. Aubrey Williams to Morgan Johnson, May 27, 1957, folder 5, box 17, Braden Papers; Williams to Dombrowski, October 24, 1957, ibid.

16. Rayford W. Logan, ed., *What the Negro Wants* (Chapel Hill: University of North Carolina Press, 1944); Henry Lewis Suggs, "P. B. Young and the *Norfolk Journal and Guide*, 1910–1954" (Ph.D. dissertation, University of Virginia, 1976), 342; Clayborne Carson, *In Struggle: SNCC and the Black Awakening of the 1960s* (Cambridge, Mass.: Harvard University Press, 1981). 82, 94–96, 103–05, 141–44, 152, 227, 300–03.

17. Anne Braden, *The Wall Between* (New York: Monthly Review Press, 1958), 92–93.

18. Ibid., 213–14.

19. Alfred Maund, "Battle of New Orleans: Eastland Meets His Match," *Nation*, April 3, 1954, p. 282; Virginia Durr to Eleanor Roosevelt, March 31, 1954, "Family and Political Correspondence, 1950–1959" folder, unnumbered box, Virginia Foster Durr Papers (State Department of Archives and History, Manuscript Division, Montgomery, Ala.); Roosevelt to Durr, April 9, 1954, ibid.; Irving Brant to Senator William Langer, chairman of the Senate Judiciary Committee, May 25, 1954, ibid.

20. Brant to Langer, May 25, 1954, Durr Papers.

21. American Legion *Firing Line*, 4 (July 1, 1955) accuses nine black and white SCEF members of being Communist and cites the 1954 hearing as evidence in all cases. Copy of *Firing Line* in folder 14, box 21, Braden Papers; Aubrey Williams Press Statement, undated, folder 5, box 17, ibid.; Anne Braden, *House Un-American Activities Committee: Bulwark of Segregation* (New Orleans: Southern Conference Educational Fund, 1964).

22. Albert Barnett to Dombrowski, March 4, 1957, microfilm 306, reel 4, Braden Papers; Samuel Newman to Dombrowski, May 2, 1960, ibid.; Dombrowski to Newman, May 5, 1960, ibid. Dombrowski initially believed that when SCEF became the target of so many attacks that if the organization attempted to refute each one it would expend unnecessary time and effort that otherwise could be exerted on desegregation and ending discrimination.

23. Williams to Alan Barth of the *Washington Post*, May 28, 1958, folder 5, box 17, Braden Papers.

24. Dombrowski to Williams, May 28, 1958, ibid. The FBI even collected newspaper clippings of individuals who supported SCEF in editorials. SCHW and

SCEF FBI Files, nos. 248,237 and 248,238 (photocopies of Freedom of Information Act releases in author's possession).

25. Dombrowski to Williams, May 29, 1958, folder 5, box 17, Braden Papers.

26. Williams to Dombrowski, May 21, 1958, ibid.; Williams to Barth, May 28, 1958, ibid.

27. Notes, SCEF board meeting, New Orleans, October 18, 1956, folder 3, box 22, ibid.; Williams to Dombrowski, May 27, 1958, folder 5, box 17, ibid.; Williams to Barth, May 28, 1958, ibid. Although the Justice Department has made some material available for my use, I am still unable to describe specific FBI activities in regard to specific SCEF officers. Anne Braden and Fred Shuttlesworth, whom I have interviewed, are convinced that the FBI tried to disrupt the Civil Rights Movement by dividing blacks and whites.

28. SCEF Press Release, June 14, 1957, group III, series B, "Southern Conf. Educ. Fund, 1956–57" folder, box B204, NAACP Papers; Frank Wilkinson to Williams, November 23, 1959, folder 9, box 21, Braden Papers; Irwin Klibaner, "The Southern Conference Educational Fund: A History" (Ph.D. dissertation, University of Wisconsin, 1971), 258–63, 271–72, 279–80, 343–44, 350; Jerold Simmons, "The Origins of the Campaign to Abolish HUAC, 1956–1961, the California Connection," *Southern California Quarterly*, 64 (Summer 1982), 141–57.

29. Braden, *House Un-American Activities Committee*.

30. "Summary of minutes—Meeting on Civil Rights Legislation," December 23, 1946, folder 11, box 35, Southern Conference for Human Welfare Papers (Robert W. Woodruff Library, Atlanta University Center, Atlanta, Ga.).

31. See especially letters from Aubrey Williams to various congressmen, 1961, folder 7, box 21, Braden Papers; Durr to Alabama Senator John Sparkman, March 14, March 20, March 22, April 18, 1961, "Personal and Political Correspondence, 1960–1969" unnumbered box, Durr Papers; Braden, *House Un-American Activities Committee*; Simmons, "The Origins of the Campaign to Abolish HUAC, 1956–1961," 152–54.

32. Williams and Rev. Fred Shuttlesworth to "Friend of SCEF," October 10, 1963, folder 15, box 24, Braden Papers; Fact Sheet on the Raid and Arrests, October 10, 1963, folder 15, box 24, ibid.; Arthur Kinoy, memo on SCEF litigation, December 24, 1963, folder 7, box 24, ibid.; The Joint Legislative Committee on Un-American Activities, State of Louisiana, *"Activities of the Southern Conference Educational Fund, Inc. in Louisiana"* (Baton Rouge, November 19, 1963), Report No. 4; ibid., (April 13, 1964), Report No. 5; ibid., (January 19, 1965), Report No. 6 (copies of reports in folder 11, box 24, Braden Papers); untitled document, January 25, 1965, folder 5, box 24, ibid.; copy of the Supreme Court ruling in *Dombrowski* v. *Pfister* in folder 5, box 24, ibid.; *New Orleans Times-Picayune*, January 26, 1965, p. 5. SCEF files contain hundreds of letters and telegrams (even copies of letters of protest mailed to the U.S. Attorney General and other national and Louisiana officials and agencies) from the public from as far away as Mexico, Canada, and England. Several compared the episode to apartheid in South Africa. See folder 15, box 24, Braden Papers. SCEF, the NAACP, and the ACLU filed *amicus curiae* briefs on Dombrowski's behalf. The best secondary source for details on the 1963 raid is Klibaner's "The Southern Conference Educational Fund," 386–403.

33. James Roosevelt, "Voting Restrictions: A Report from the South," *Congressional Record*, 85th Cong., 2nd Sess., May 20, 1958, copy in folder 13, box 55, Braden Papers; James R. Forman (executive secretary of SNCC) to Dombrowski, June 16, 1962, folder 1, box 21, ibid.; John Robert Zellner and Forman to Dombrowski, April 18, 1963, folder 1, box 21, ibid.; SCEF news release, September 25, 1963, folder 3, box 21, ibid.; Klibaner, "The Southern Conference Educational Fund," 244–53.

34. Barnett to Ed Blair, September 27, 1955, microfilm 306, reel 4, Braden Papers; Barnett to Dombrowski, February 4, 1957, ibid.; memo, Dombrowski to

"Friends of the SCEF in non-Southern states," re: *Washington Post* ad on civil rights, July 27, 1957, group III, series B, "Southern Conference Educational Fund, 1956–57" folder, box B204, NAACP Papers. SCEF received broad radio coverage in Georgia where one of its members, Albert E. Barnett, commented, "it is the best break we have had over an Atlanta Broadcast."

35. *New York Times*, June 30, 1958, p. 14; unidentified newspaper clipping, Dec. 12, 1958, microfilm 306, reel 5, Braden Papers; Stephen B. Oates, *Let the Trumpet Sound: The Life of Martin Luther King, Jr.* (New York: Harper & Row, 1982), 108–9, 209–13. Aldon D. Morris, *The Origins of the Civil Rights Movement: Black Communities Organizing for Change* (New York: Free Press, 1984), is very important for its coverage of the role of the black church in the struggle for racial justice.

36. Newspaper clippings re: Shuttlesworth's speeches on microfilm 306, reel 5, Braden Papers; Anne Braden to Fred Shuttlesworth, April 30, 1959, ibid.; Shuttlesworth to Dombrowski, June 10, 1959, ibid.; Dombrowski to Shuttlesworth, June 12, 1959, ibid.

37. *New York Times*, April 3, 1960; Anne Braden to Shuttlesworth, April 2, 1960, microfilm 306, reel 5, Braden Papers; telegram, Ethel Clyde and northern liberals to mayor of Birmingham in protest of Shuttlesworth's arrest, April 3, 1960, ibid.; Williams to Dombrowski, April 18, 1960, folder 5, box 17, ibid.; SCEF news release, Sept. 1, 1960, microfilm 306, reel 5, ibid.; Williams to Dombrowski, Jan. 24, 1963, folder 7, box 21, ibid.; Williams to Dombrowski, Feb. 13, 1963, ibid.; SCEF news release, February 19, 1963, microfilm 306, reel 5, ibid.; SCEF news release, June 7, 1963, ibid., reel 4, ibid. Williams agreed with King's participation in the March on Washington and urged the civil rights leader to go forward with it. See Williams to Martin Luther King, Jr., July 1963, folder 7, box 21, ibid. Dombrowski welcomed the protest that the March represented, indicating other SCEF supporters and his plan to attend. Dombrowski to Bayard Rustin (deputy director for March on Washington for Jobs and Freedom), August 14, 1963, folder 15, box 48, ibid.

The notes by the detectives Connor sent to spy on Shuttlesworth are interesting to read. They understood little about African-American culture, often wondering why black preachers repeated themselves or why songs were sung differently from what they knew. See Birmingham Police Department Interoffice Communications between 1961 and 1963, folders 9.24, 12.17, and 12.18, Eugene "Bull" Connor Papers (Birmingham Public Library Archives, Ala.).

38. Julia Yenni Hikes to "My Dear Mr. and Mrs. Winters," July 18, 1960, Durr Papers.

39. Braden, *Wall Between*, 35.

40. Anne Braden interviewed by Linda Reed, October 10, 1983, transcript in author's possession. Anne Braden compares Eleanor Roosevelt's action in 1938 to sit-ins of the 1960s.

41. See Elizabeth Jacoway and David Colburn, eds., *Southern Businessmen and Desegregation* (Baton Rouge: Louisiana State University Press, 1982).

42. For instance, whites lynched Hansberry's uncle, prominent physician Lewis H. Johnston, in the infamous Elaine, Arkansas, "riot" of 1919, and the uncle's daughter (Hansberry's cousin) frequently attended Hansberry during the latter's childhood.

43. Robert Nemiroff, "From these Roots: Lorraine Hansberry and the South," *Southern Exposure*, 12 (September/October 1984), 33–35.

44. Williams to Simeon Booker (editor of *Jet*, a black weekly magazine), May 18, 1958, folder 4, box 22, Braden Papers; Williams to C. G. Gomillion, December 4, 1958, folder 5, box 17, ibid.; Louis Redding to Dombrowski, February 18, 1963, microfilm 306, reel 5, ibid.; Williams to P. D. East, August 22, 1963, folder 7, box 21, ibid.; Durr to Hugo Black, November 26, 1963, Durr Papers; Durr to "Robins,"

January 20, 1964, ibid. On Williams's enthusiasm for Robert Zellner's work, see Williams to Anne Braden, May 14, 1961, folder 3, box 62, Braden Papers; "Report by John Robert Zellner on White Southern Student Project (School Year of 1961–62)," May 19, 1962, folder 3, box 62, ibid.

45. Williams to Clark Foreman, November 26, 1960, microfilm 306, reel 5, Braden Papers.

46. Merton L. Dillon, "The Abolitionists as a Dissenting Minority," In *Dissent: Explorations in the History of American Radicalism*, ed. Alfred F. Young (Dekalb: Northern Illinois University Press, 1968), 84, 104; Martin Duberman, "Black Power and the American Radical Tradition," in ibid., 302–17. SCEF leaders did not compare themselves with the Abolitionists, but Williams did see a likeness of the struggle in the 1950s to the 1850s. In reference to the South's resistance for change, he said, "If I may say so, I fail to see what is anti-South in warning against present day firebrands like Griffin, Eastland, Thurmond, etc. They are the modern counterparts of Yancy, Toombs, etc., who led the South into the ruinous war of the "60s." Williams to Ralph McGill (editor, *Atlanta Constitution*), December 30, 1957, folder 5, box 17, Braden Papers.

Conclusion

1. Frances Fox Piven and Richard A. Cloward, *Poor People's Movements: Why They Succeed, How They Fail* (New York: Pantheon Books, 1977), 22.

2. Nell Irvin Painter, *The Narrative of Hosea Hudson: His Life as a Negro Communist in the South* (Cambridge, Mass.: Harvard University Press, 1979); Robin Davis Gibran Kelley, "Hammer n' hoe: Black Radicalism and the Communist Party in Alabama, 1929–1941" (Ph.D. dissertation, University of California, Los Angeles, 1987); William H. Harris, *The Harder We Run: Black Workers since the Civil War* (New York: Oxford University Press, 1982).

3. Jessie P. Guzman, "The Southern Race Problem in Retrospect: South Unable Psychologically to Solve Its Problem Alone," Feb. 10, 1959, microfilm, 306, reel 4, Carl and Anne Braden Papers (State Historical Society, Madison, Wis.). See Tinsley Yarbrough, *A Passion for Justice: J. Waties and Civil Rights* (New York: Oxford University Press, 1987), a recent biography of Judge Waties. Tracy K'Meyer, a graduate student at the University of North Carolina, Chapel Hill, is currently working on a much-needed study of Koinonia Farm.

4. Jean Wiley, "Organizing for Power," *Essence*, 16 (May 1985), 113.

5. Anne Braden to James Dombrowski, March 24, 1964, folder 1, box 21, Braden Papers.

INDEX

LINDA REED is Assistant Professor of History at the University of Houston.